A READER

SOUTH AFRICAN
landscape architecture

About the editors

Dr Hennie Stoffberg

Department of Architecture, University of Pretoria, South Africa

Hennie was a senior lecturer in landscape architecture and sustainability at the University of Pretoria until 2010. His academic qualifications and interests include sustainable design, green architecture, climate change commerce, the Clean Development Mechanism (CDM), corporate citizenship, environmental education, phyto carbon sequestration, phyto carbon footprints, urban ecology and landscape architecture. He also consults in the field of carbon commerce. During 2008, he held the position as the Programme Manager for the Exxaro Chair in Business and Climate Change at the Centre for Corporate Citizenship of the University of South Africa. Hennie publishes and conducts research in diverse fields and often reads papers internationally and locally. He co-authored a book entitled *Climate Change: A Guide for Corporates* (Unisa Press) in 2009.

Mr Clinton Hindes

School of Architecture, Planning and Geomatics, University of Cape Town, South Africa

Clinton Hindes is the Convenor of the two-year Master of Landscape Architecture programme. His teaching focus is primarily design studio and the history and theory of landscape architecture. He graduated with a Bachelor of Landscape Architecture and a Master of Landscape Architecture (by research) from the University of Pretoria. His Masters degree focused on teaching in landscape architecture. Clinton taught landscape architecture and architecture at the University of Pretoria where he ran the second year combined design studio for a number of years before taking up his current position. His research interests lie in developing the theoretical foundations of the discipline of landscape architecture. He is currently working on his PhD, entitled 'The application of an organisational framework to the body of theory in landscape architecture for improved critical engagement'.

Ms Liana Müller

School of Architecture, Planning and Geomatics, University of Cape Town, South Africa

Liana Müller is a practising professional landscape architect with a Masters Degree in Anthropology. After lecturing in the Department of Architecture at the University of Pretoria, she took up a position as lecturer in the Masters of Landscape Architecture Programme at the School of Architecture, Planning and Geomatics of the University of Cape Town. Liana is actively involved in the landscape architecture and heritage field, completing heritage audits, management plans and designs for cultural landscapes across Southern Africa and internationally. She also completed numerous Visual Impact Assessments for national-scale projects. Her academic research and publications revolve around the representation of cultural landscapes, specifically focusing on people's present and past connection with the environment and landscape acting as anchoring point for memory and meaning.

A READER

SOUTH AFRICAN
landscape architecture

Edited by
Hennie Stoffberg, Clinton Hindes & Liana Müller

Unisa Press

Pretoria

First edition, first impression
Reader: ISBN 978-1-86888-662-3
Set: ISBN 978-1-86888-687-6

Published by Unisa Press
University of South Africa
P O Box 392, 0003 UNISA

Book designer: Doris Hyman
Editor: Lynne Southey
Project editor: Arnika Ejsmund-Osrin
Typesetting: Thea Venter
Indexer: Hannalie Knoetze
Printer: Lebone Litho

Contents

Acknowledgements

The editors and authors of this reader gratefully acknowledge the following people and institutions for their most valuable support and contributions to this manuscript:

- Mr Stuart Glen, President of ILASA, 2009–2011
- Mr David Gibbs, President of ILASA, 2007–2009
- Dr Hennie Stoffberg is also especially grateful to Prof Karel Bakker, Head of Department Architecture, University of Pretoria, for his support in obtaining funding and providing time and infrastructure for the birth and creation of the early parts of the manuscript
- The editors and in particular Dr Hennie Stoffberg would like to thank Prof Roelf Sandenbergh, Dean, EBIT, University of Pretoria for financial support during the early stages of the preparation of the manuscript. Funding was in part provided from the RDP grant. Prof Sandenbergh's encouragement through research proposal iterations and approvals is thankfully acknowledged
- Prof Vanessa Watson, Acting Director (2009–2010): School of Architecture, Planning and Geomatics, University of Cape Town
- Prof Alta Steenkamp, Director (2011–): School of Architecture, Planning and Geomatics, University of Cape Town
- Mitha Theron for the extensive text and image manipulation during the preparation of the manuscript
- Leon Pienaar is gratefully acknowledge for IT support
- Excellent Library (AIS) support was provided by Katrien Malan, Hettie Groenewald and Elna Randal
- The editors would like to thank our colleagues, families and friends for their support and encouragement during the creation of this book
- We thank each author for their submissions and the permission for publication
- We would like to thank Unisa Press as academic publisher for the independent double blind peer review process and the reviewers for their valuable contributions that we could incorporate into the finalised book.

Foreword by Ian Thompson

The New Kid on the Block

It is a great but daunting honour to be asked to write the preface for this book. It is great because I can see, even at the distance of some 6 000 miles, that this is a milestone in the development of the discipline of landscape architecture in Africa. It is daunting because my direct acquaintance with Africa is limited to a three-week visit to Kitwe in Zambia, back in 1994 when I was only two years into my academic career at Newcastle University. It was the rainy season and I remember giving a lecture in the middle of a thunderstorm while a noisy student protest about the late payment of grants took place outside the lecture theatre. I doubt that I said much that was of relevance to the lives and aspirations of those students and here I want to quote Finzi Saidi, one of the contributors to this volume, who was once a student of mine in the United Kingdom. This is his trenchant observation about the usual landscape architecture curriculum:

The perception of the built environment by students in landscape architecture given curriculum content is one that is dominated by a Eurocentric culture that largely excludes other cultures (African) in history and participation in the creation of the urban form.

He is right, of course. Landscape architecture grew out of the European tradition of landscape gardening. The first person to use the term 'landscape architect' was Frederick Law Olmsted, an American who had visited Joseph Paxton's Birkenhead Park on a trip to England and thought that New York needed something similar. The result was Central Park, and Olmsted and his collaborator Calvert Vaux launched a whole profession when they called themselves 'landscape architects' on their successful design competition entry. That was in 1857. The American Society of Landscape Architects was formed in 1899 and the (British) Institute of Landscape Architects in 1929. The Institute of Landscape Architects in South Africa, however, was not founded until 1962, so African influence upon the values, principles and priorities has been absent for most of the profession's history. As I write this, two phrases are sitting on my shoulder, nagging to be included. The first is 'new kid on the block' which sounds a bit pejorative until one realises that a new kid is always an object of fascination and sometimes a bringer of novelty. The second is 'coming of age' which is in danger of sounding patronising, but somehow seems appropriate for a country which has emerged from a turbulent formative period to astonish the world. But as I write this, I reflect upon the fact that, to quote Gwen Breedlove, 'South Africa has a history of human occupation as long as the time of humankind itself'.

There is a wealth of interesting research in this volume and it really does declare the burgeoning confidence of South Africa's landscape research community. In its breadth it embraces topics that range from the value of Jacaranda trees in carbon sequestration to the importance of listening to the songs, stories and legends of the country's many cultural groups; from the role of oral history to the treatment of mineral tailings; and from the value of botanical gardens to the need for a more active engagement with landscape theory. This is well-informed, well-conducted research produced in Africa, not imported from Europe or the United States, and so, I would hope, it should be of direct interest not just to the sort of students who milled around my lecture back in the nineties, but to the whole population of southern Africa, who stand to benefit from the efforts of landscape architects to improve general living conditions. But the readership of these papers will not be confined to Africans; this book is going to be widely read by the landscape research community worldwide.

I may not know South Africa first-hand, but it has long been on my mental horizon. On the TV news of my youth, images of the violence of apartheid were interlaced with similarly disturbing scenes of the 'troubles' in Northern Ireland. Both seemed intractable. Later, after university, I got friendly with a card-carrying communist who told me that he'd smuggled packages into South Africa to help the ANC. I have no way of knowing whether he told the truth, but he also gave his opinion, true to his creed, that there wouldn't be any progress in South Africa without a bloody revolution. Thankfully he was wrong and, though it took a very long time, the pessimists were proved wrong in Northern Ireland too. Now the world looks to both Ireland and Africa for examples of conflict resolution and reconciliation, though not without a lingering concern that the progress, if not sustained, could begin to unravel.

Issues of land, ownership, democracy, belonging and justice were involved in both of these struggles. So when Saidi writes, as he does, about the irrelevance to landscape architecture education in South Africa of 'originality, symbolism, form experimentation and peer group approval' (and, he could perhaps have said, to the practice of landscape architecture too), he makes a powerful point. The really important issues are about who controls land, who shapes it and to what end. The shaping in question is sometimes a matter of planning or design, but very often it is about cultural practices which, in benign form, can indicate a sense of belonging and harmony with the land, but in malevolent form can be territorial markers serving the interests of exclusion. Landscape architects have much to learn from cultural geographers such as Steven Daniels, Kenneth Olwig, and W.J.T. Mitchell who have revealed that landscapes are implements of cultural power and tools which can, for good or ill, shape the creation of national and social identities. Landscape, whether we like it or not, is political.

Landscape is also, whether we like it or not, a matter of ethics, indeed the ethical and the political ought to go hand-in-hand. Landscape architecture is not just a matter of pleasing drawings or fashionable schemes which make it into the design magazines. Happily, the moral aspect of landscape architecture comes through in many of the papers in this collection, particularly those which examine the role of the landscape profession in addressing issues of disadvantage and unequal life chances, but also those, which may appear technical or scientific, but are premised on the need to ameliorate or rectify unhealthy or unliveable environmental and climatic conditions. Landscape architecture's obligation to promote justice among existing societal groups (intra-generational justice) is, in these times of anxiety about global warming, climate change and food security, matched by another powerful obligation to promote justice for future generations (inter-generational justice). We ought to hand on to our successors a world which is better, or at least no worse, that the world we have enjoyed. The research collected in this volume is a contribution to that end.

Ian Thompson
Reader in Landscape Architecture
School of Architecture, Planning and Landscape
Newcastle University

Foreword by Jo Watkins

Now as I was young and easy under the apple boughs

'Fern Hill' by Dylan Thomas

We all emerge from landscapes. City landscapes, rural landscapes or from somewhere in-between. Childhood places are engrained upon us through scent, sight and sound, linking us to far-off notions of family, friendships, joy and tragedy. Landscape is far too important to be abandoned to whim. It is core to our very soul, wherever and whoever we are.

But for the minor inconvenience of the outbreak of the Second World War, I may well have been South African. My father was about to begin training as an architect at, I think, Stellenbosch University when war was declared and he was despatched home to Swansea in Wales – a far more dangerous place, I imagine. To my good fortune he survived, settled in that glorious place and eventually, indeed, became an architect, which I suppose in some way led me to becoming a landscape architect, and I say that with no sense of irony intended at all.

As it is I find myself writing this, a little disappointingly it has to be said, as an outsider. To this outsider, the most satisfying of all the political events of the last 25 years has been the birth of the new South Africa. It has given us such hope for the future. The emergence of a new country has been thrilling to watch from afar. In this new world, the growth in confidence of a fledgling landscape profession is good to see. There is much work to do and without question the skills of landscape architects will be needed.

This book is overdue. The richness of the writing and breadth of content seems to me to be a metaphor for all that is good about the landscape of South Africa, a landscape which is so engrained upon the psyche of the nation. We Celts understand this. We will need to learn from our mistakes and there are many, both in South Africa and here in the UK where we find ourselves sometimes encumbered by the weight of history. South Africa has the chance to seize the moment and start afresh, throwing off the shackles and creating new landscapes which truly reflect the needs of its citizens.

Landscapes need to be carefully designed. It is no longer acceptable to create vast swathes of nothingness at an enormous expense when some children don't have enough to eat. So we need to think carefully and work with people and environments in a truly sustainable way to deliver what they need and where they need it. Good landscape design doesn't need to cost the earth, it just needs a bit of thought, care and creativity. We will need to prepare for climate change, population growth and food shortages, and landscape architecture will become the necessity. We cannot pretend to do without it. It is not a luxury – it is integral to all our futures, for how else will we survive unless we are able to marry human habitation with our ever more fragile environments.

South Africa has taken its place, embarking on a journey of incalculable opportunity, and how it conserves and manages its extraordinary landscapes will go much of the way to future well-being and towards creating the prosperity it so richly deserves.

Jo Watkins
Blackheath
President of the Landscape Institute, United Kingdom

Foreword by Karel Bakker

Humanity has come to a critical juncture in terms of conceptualising and actualising a sustainable form of life that is shared with other living systems.

In writing a foreword for this publication, I found it heartening to realise that South African landscape architects have been in the vanguard of those who propagate an ecosystemic epistemology. The early work on ecosystemic epistemology by Ludwig von Bertalanffy, followed by Gregory Bateson and others, the understanding of reflexive feedback and living systems by Humberto Maturana, as well as the nature of stochastic process by Ervin Lazlo, acted as foundational knowledge for the formation of what can broadly be termed the environmental movement. In landscape architecture, this movement was most clearly expressed through the living systems landscape architecture movement that emerged and flourished under Ian McHarg.

The fledgling Chair of Landscape Architecture at the University of Pretoria, established through an Oppenheimer endowment in 1971, allied itself closely to these early beginnings of an ecosystemic epistemology, and as such this movement became seminal in directing research, as well as the teaching and practice of landscape architecture in South Africa. In 2002, as part of the celebration of 30 years of tertiary education in landscape architecture in South Africa, a series of open lectures on 'landscape', delivered at the Department of Architecture at the University of Pretoria, were published as a Festschrift that clearly indicated that the discipline's early emphasis on living systems had broadened to include culture, forms of cultural expression and the subjective experience of and reflection on landscape. Now, at the marking of 40 years of landscape architecture since the local planting of the discipline, the initiative has been taken to compile a *South African Landscape Architecture: A Reader* that assembles a collection of research and theory reflecting a state of thinking about the discipline in 2011. The footprint of the discipline has since grown as a result of the formation of a new postgraduate school of landscape architecture in Cape Town, and the *Reader* thus initiates what is intended to be an on-going academic dialogue with, and across, the South African landscape.

This *Reader* elicits current critical realisations of this dialogue. Firstly, it introduces the concept of cultural landscapes and identifies intangible content of landscape, either as intangible heritage, knowledge systems, associations or transient aspects of urban life, and stresses the critical role of memory landscapes to reimplace and disseminate memory where it resides so, as to build ties between people and landscape, as well as between individuals and societies. We are brought to realise that the conceptualisation of space involves both the visible, the phenomenological, but also that which is imagined, the story, and that in reading the landscape, the intangible can become accessible through empathy to the intangible values that derive from a biophylic relationship to landscape. Secondly, the focus of the discipline has turned to the development of theory and methodologies for the assessment of landscape character, qualities, conservation of embodied energy, carbon sequestration and the mitigation of negative impacts from human interventions in the landscape. Lastly, critical reflection on a body of seminal South Africans landscape designs shows that design activity is not separated from, but relies on and is recursively bound to the research that is discussed in the first two sections of this publication.

May these critical dialogues in service of humanity and the shared biosphere, continue well into the future.

Prof Karel Anthonie Bakker (PhD)
Head of the Department of Architecture, University of Pretoria
Programmes in Landscape Architecture, Interior Design and Architecture

Introduction

**An emerging body of documented academic
South African landscape architecture theory
and its expression in the discipline's built work**

The discipline of landscape architecture in South Africa has been extensively covered in the popular printed media in the form of trade-related journals and magazines. This *Reader* is, however, the first collection of papers written by academics actively involved with original landscape architecture research. The *Reader* serves as a platform for current South African landscape architecture research and theory to be locally and internationally distributed, making it widely accessible to peers involved with research. Unisa Press (the largest local academic publishing house) was for these reasons the appropriate publisher to use.

All the papers have undergone editorial review in order to maintain academic rigour. Every paper was also double blind peer reviewed (a process independently facilitated by Unisa Press). The editors are grateful to the reviewers for their comments which added value through the amendments that were made. All contributors (with one exception) have Masters or Doctorate degrees in landscape architecture or a related field, and are directly or indirectly involved in original research pertaining to certain aspects and developments in landscape architecture. The academics are all current or recent staff of either the University of Pretoria or the University of Cape Town. This book provides an accessible vehicle for the dissemination of this research.

The editors requested that the various authors contribute a research paper comprehensively covering an aspect of landscape architecture, as well as shorter papers gleaning lessons from the investigation of particular projects through the lens of a particular position. These papers thus represent scholarly inquiry into contemporary developments in the discipline. The content and writing styles of the authors are diverse, and the approach to and content of their papers display the wide variety of aspects involved in the planning and design of the landscape. In order to maintain the uniqueness of each paper no attempt was made by the editors to harmonise the various writing styles.

The longer papers in the *Reader* tend to be more theoretical, while the project descriptions focus on the application of theory to design projects. These shorter papers are usually more comprehensively illustrated. The value of these project investigations lies in establishing closer relationships between academia and practice, allowing the research of practice to be juxtaposed and related to that of academia in a mutually beneficial relationship. Many of the authors are also involved in practice and supplement their research with results from inquiry undertaken through practice – design as research. These project descriptions add tremendous value to the discipline as they contribute to the integration of academia and the profession.

The editors trust that this *Reader* will influence contemporary landscape architecture academia through the collection of a body of contemporary theory from South African authors. We look forward to the response to this publication and trust that it will significantly add to discussions and debates on the developing discourse of South African landscape architecture, thus further enhancing the reciprocal dynamic between praxis and academia. Please contact the editors at the following email addresses:

Hennie Stoffberg: hennie.stoffberg@gmail.com
Clinton Hindes: clinton.hindes@uct.ac.za
Liana Müller: mulliana@gmail.com

The organisation of the papers

Any collection of papers forming a reader should be categorised and packaged in some way to facilitate the gleaning of lessons and the identification of patterns or trends. All systems of categorisation possess a degree of generalisation, particularly when a wide variety of topics is covered in diverse contributions. Reflecting on the content of the papers collected for the *Reader*, three categories emerged into which most papers were very comfortably arranged, Culture and heritage, Science and strategy, and Design.

The first two categories originate from two distinct decision-making domains driving action within the discipline. These domains represent different ways of understanding knowledge (epistemology), and form the intellectual context (values, methods and principles) for the justification of particular design action. The pitfall of then having a section called 'Design', standing separately from 'culture' or 'science', is that it creates the impression that science and/or culture are somehow separate from design. The rationale however for the decision to include a section entitled 'Design' is that it collects papers directly discussing particular landscape architectural design projects, and not necessarily design influences in a more generic way.

Culture and heritage, Science and strategy

The essays in these two categories focus primarily on the particular decision-making utilised in a specific kind of landscape architectural intervention, but do not necessarily focus on the resultant landscape architectural design expression or product (this is the focus of the 'Design' category). These categories are defined on epistemological grounds (relating to the way knowledge is constructed). Culture and heritage recognise the subjective construction of knowledge through the eyes of society, whereby science advocates the objective construction of knowledge.

Design

This category collects papers which more aggressively focus on the discussion of a particular designed landscape/s, and tangibly addresses the factors affecting their physical configuration. The article 'Structuring thinking' is included in this category as it focuses on aspects directly affecting decision-making regarding the actual configuration of the designed landscape from various epistemologies. It is the first paper in the section as familiarisation with its content will assist readers in positioning the various discussions that follow within the spectrum of the body of landscape architectural knowledge from objective to subjective ways of knowing.

part ONE

Culture and Heritage

This section collects the papers which address bodies of knowledge relating to cultural and heritage aspects of relevance to landscape architectural planning and design.

The papers in this section can broadly be divided into two distinct themes. The first addresses the cultural landscape, meaning, memory and the intangible landscape, while the second addresses social aspects of landscape design, all within the context of some of South Africa's previously disadvantaged areas. The final paper is the most practical of this section and addresses a much under-emphasised aspect of landscape heritage, namely botanical heritage.

The paper 'Landscapes of Memory: Interpreting and Presenting Places and Pasts' focuses directly on the workings of memory in landscape and introduces 'intangible landscapes', an increasingly popular conception referring to the metaphysical cultural meanings associated with landscape. Extensive theory is quoted and the paper goes a long way in consolidating an informed framework for decisions in a realm of theory often approached in an overly subjective manner. The case study application at the end of the paper applies the concepts to quintessentially South African places and clearly illustrates the shortcomings of neglecting the intangible aspects of landscape.

'De-picturing the Landscape: Notes on the Value of Text for the Conception and Experience of Landscape' exposes in tremendous detail the notion of landscapes being as much metaphysical as they are physical. The nature of inquiry is similar to that of the first paper; however, this one addresses the metaphysical quality of landscape through the experience of beauty, and how through different historical paradigms the relationship between the visible and the invisible have changed. The paper's investigation stretches far back in history and illustrates the cultural richness of 'landscape', and is a reminder of the importance of the study of history as prerequisite for unlocking concepts associated with truly understanding the complexity of the contemporary landscape. The paper concludes with a discussion of the use of text as a non-graphic tool to enhance the design of the visible and the invisible landscape.

The understanding of context is always strongly emphasised in landscape architecture. The role of a thorough understanding of the functioning of the natural systems associated with a place has always been believed to be paramount to the success of design intervention. 'The Transient Aspects of City Life: Their Understanding and Interpretation for Design Purposes', however, succinctly illustrates how necessary it is to understand the specific social aspects related to people's perceptions of place when designing living environments. The underlying assumption behind the previous papers, that landscapes are interpreted differently between individuals and cultural groups, is explained in terms of its applicability to the creation of urban places. The paper extensively explores residents' perceptions of the specific environment in which they live, and demonstrates how preconceived, or narrowly defined social understandings superimposed onto a place by designers can often be completely inappropriate.

The two papers 'Rethinking the Role of Landscape Architecture in Urban Cape Town' and 'Community Factors in the Planning and Design of Parks in South Africa: Thokoza Park, Soweto and Three Parks in Atteridgeville, Tshwane', both directly address one of the most important aspects landscape architects were involved with post-1994, namely the design of public open space in previously disadvantaged areas.

The role of landscape architects and how they frame and define the value systems that ultimately drive the nature of their design and practice methodologies and approaches is the subject of the first paper. Landscape architecture, having a very influential and substantial American and European history, can find itself sitting uncomfortably in the uniqueness of African informality. 'Rethinking the Role of Landscape Architecture in Urban Cape Town' comprehensively describes how landscape architecture practice and curricula need to adopt social aspects as one of the primary domains through which to understand the South African urban environment, and through which to develop appropriate planning and design interventions.

The second paper directly addressing the social aspects of previously disadvantaged areas, 'Community Factors in the Planning and Design of Parks in South Africa: Thokoza Park, Soweto and Three Parks in Atteridgeville, Tshwane', illustrates in practical terms how social aspects form tangible design generators for appropriate design response. The paper illustrates how important it is to understand the social and cultural history of a place before successful and appropriate design can happen. The specific lesson of how a community attaches value and meaning to public open space is learnt from the specific social and cultural history of parks in townships. This (a community valuing parks as their asset) is then set as a fundamental pre-condition for the successful design, implementation and sustainability of parks in previously disadvantaged areas.

'An Extension of the Fields into the Intangible for the Reading of the South African Cultural Landscape' gives a comprehensive overview of one of the most prominent aspects of contemporary landscape architecture, namely the cultural landscape. The paper adopts a very broad approach in unpacking the notion of the cultural landscape in that it draws on a wide variety of very well-known landscape architectural theory, not necessarily traditionally associated with the 'cultural landscape'. Its reference list is a 'who's who' of the theoretical world of landscape architecture and thus functions as an extremely useful resource. The paper also serves as a reminder of how 'landscape' and its many facets, including cognition, identity, meaning, interpretation and symbolism are all 'value laden', and how this value is culturally determined and interpreted.

'Historic Schools as an Intangible Landscape: The Role of Oral Histories in Development' is a well structured example of how the theoretical aspects of the previous papers concerning the intangible landscape are practically applied in landscape interpretation. The study of historic schools is used to particularly illustrate the value of oral histories in understanding landscapes. Various collections of cultural landscape legislation and guidelines are discussed with relation to the intangible landscape, and then discussed with reference to heritage analysis. The paper makes a significant contribution to the understanding of how subjective and intangible aspects relating to landscape can be framed within a defendable theoretical structure.

The final paper in this section, 'The Botanical Garden at the University of Pretoria: A Unique Heritage and Valuable Academic Training Facility' serves as a motivation to landscape architects in South Africa to develop sincere interest in South African landscape architectural and botanical heritage. The value of the comprehensive documentation of completed landscape architecture projects is tremendously underestimated. The paper acts as a model for documenting projects in that it demonstrates rigour in the research undertaken regarding the extensive scope of people involved in the development of this particular botanical garden and also in the scientific rigour of the description of the garden's 'special features'.

chapter 1

Landscapes of Memory:
Interpreting and Presenting Places and Pasts

Liana Müller

Department of Architecture

University of Pretoria

Pretoria

South Africa

I had a farm in Africa.

Or rather, I grew up on a farm in Africa.

A dairy farm just outside Bloemfontein, to be exact.

My grandparents have since sold the farm – the landscape of my youth was transacted to provide security for old-age. A neat, solid full-stop to a life well lived.

I often reminisce about our farm. Every time I drive to the Cape my neck cranes to catch a glimpse of my koppie and the stone reservoir my grandmother quarried and built with her bare hands. I briefly see the tops of the tall cypress trees and in a moment I am transported back to my childhood of lions in the tall grass, the secret world of gullies and the owl-tree of dreams. I turn the radio to RSG and their distinctive sound evokes mornings in the kitchen, aniseed rusks, brewed rooibos tea and readings from *Uit die Beek*.

The landscape of our farm in the Free State had a profound impact on my life. It provided me with the basis of my identity: it provided me with an inner landscape of places and memories, locating me as an individual within a larger context. It provided me with a landscape of anchoring points to remember the key events in my life, and with places to invoke memories and narrate my story from.

True understanding of individuals and communities and their relationship to place is only achieved through emotional resonance from one person to another. Usually, the medium for this resonance is a story – text, written or verbal, narrating the inner landscape and ushering the intangible into the realm of the perceived.

Landscape, tangible or intangible, provides the setting for narration, whether it's the story of the self, the story of a place or the story of a people. However, in order to narrate a story, you need to remember the details. You need anchoring points to guide you through the landscape of the story, anchoring points to bring to mind the memory of the story.

South Africa is a country of heart-wrenching beauty. It is a country with diverse landscapes that have the capacity to narrate the inner landscapes of individuals and even communities and cultural groups. It is the contrast between the beauty of the physical landscape and the tragedy of the story it has to tell which contributes to its significance. These stories are, however, often buried deep inside the rich soil or hidden between the rocks, with the people, whose footsteps helped shape the landscape, holding the only key to unlock its meaning.

Post-apartheid South Africa is experiencing a near obsession with the 'identification, celebration, evaluation, reassessment and, not least, commodification of "heritage"' (Marschall 2005:103). This is being expressed in a plethora of new heritage sites, museums, monuments and statues. Most of these sites attempt to address previously or recently misrepresented history as well as non-represented or suppressed history. The main theme is that of needing to forge a nation with conditions better and different from the pre-1994 one, and of adding to the body of representation of the memories, values and heroes of the Struggle that led to the new. The production of cultural identity in post-apartheid South Africa is directed by two major forces: firstly, heritage commemoration is being embraced by the State as a main driver of nation building. Secondly, the realisation of the importance of heritage as a mode of wealth production and development has lead to wholesale commodification of heritage and an emphasis on cultural tourism.

Within this context, it has transpired that there is a lack of guidance in the South African heritage legislation on the nature of intangible heritage – intangible heritage being inadequately defined as being those intangible aspects of 'living heritage' (*NHRA 1999* Act 25: Clause 2 (xxi)). Legislation also does not address aspects of landscape, place, associations and memory (as argued in Bakker (2003); Müller (2009)). This results in an emphasis on the implementation and design of static monuments, direct and simplistic use of symbolism, ignorance of the cultural dimensions of landscape, a lack of interpretation of place, event and oral history and subsequent deficiencies in presentation and meaning (Bakker & Müller 2009:2).

In a series of articles addressing the concept of the 'Memorial Landscape', Judith Wasserman (1998:42) states that: 'Landscape architects are uniquely poised to influence the design of memorial landscapes. In doing so, they can transform space into a place of significance, a place of storytelling, a place of lessons.' This places a huge responsibility on the profession in not only South Africa, but indeed worldwide. The first step in achieving this would be to address the lack of understanding of the very nature and definition of 'landscape' and the role, impact, action and character of memory within the landscape. The perceived reason for this is that there is currently an incongruity between the inherent variableness of landscapes and memories and conventional formal strategies of commemoration (Ware 2005:62).

In the first section of this chapter I will focus on the intangible dimension of memory. I will investigate recent and ancient theories, debates and studies on the concept of memory, its manifestation in societies and individuals, and its impact on identity creation. I will explore the process of memory, elaborate on its fluid nature and determine those aspects that influence memory creation. The section will investigate how memory works to locate individuals within a familiar 'place' and how it creates and establishes identity and notions of belonging. I will then shift my focus to the concept of landscape, discussing contemporary definitions of the term and elaborate on different approaches to the relationship between the intangible dimension of memory and landscape. I will look at how landscape, through memory, roots individuals to a particular place by informing the notions of self, community and, ultimately, heritage. I will also investigate the influence of change in the perceptions and role of landscape.

Whereas tangible aspects are thoroughly defined and understood in the development field, I believe methods of gaining insight into the intangible aspects should be further explored. Greater integration of the intangible dimension into the design (architectural, landscape and urban design fields) and development (governmental, provincial and non-governmental) process could lead to a more satisfactory solution. As a result of subsequent training in the field of anthropology, I now understand that it is possible to access the intangible aspects related to the landscape by applying qualitative anthropological fieldwork methods (participant observation, individual and focus group interviews, accompanying individuals or groups to places of interest). These intangible values of meaning, memory, lived experience and attachment, in relation to people's connection to locality and landscape, can then be traced back to the tangible fabric of place as previously documented. The nature and methodology of anthropological investigation illuminate our understanding of the tangible and intangible aspects of landscape.

Hodgkin and Radstone (2003:13) noted that memory work is often done in 'liminal spaces', that is, spaces between disciplines or at the threshold of the senses. Anthropologists, usually doing fieldwork in sociocultural contexts different from their own, are characteristically in liminal spaces. The core character of anthropology allows practitioners and researchers to establish the role of contexts and connections, and to convey their resultant meanings to individuals or groups (Climo & Cattell 2002:2). As a result, there are no set boundaries defining where the scope of anthropology starts and where it ends: it overlaps regularly with history and sociology and in this case, landscape architecture. What makes anthropological fieldwork methods even more relevant in establishing and understanding the meanings and connections certain cultures have with landscape is the fact that in recent anthropological discourses, the sociocultural background

and current position of the researcher is revealed together with those of the researched. The resultant conclusions are therefore more involved, introspective, interpretive and, therefore, multivocal (Cattell & Climo 2002:9).

The effects of the poor identification, interpretation and representation of intangible heritage (memory) in the recent commemoration of the neglected layers of history will subsequently be discussed in a case study located within Soweto. However, for the reasons stated in the paragraphs above, the second section of this chapter will feature predominantly my own opinions, experiences and ideas within the theoretical context provided. Subsequently, the two sections will appear as somewhat schizophrenic in nature with the writing style changing from 'detached academic' to 'involved personal'.

I consider the theory, thoughts and conclusion a work in progress as I am still actively engaging with the subject (at present I have 14 books on landscape, memory and cultural identity on my desk). However, while I'm still reading, discovering, perceiving and noticing new dimensions to this subject, this is what I know thus far.

Memory

We all experience memory: we are acquainted with its process, the emotions that remembering evokes and the impact of memories in our lives. Memory is not merely a storage place for information to be retrieved later, but rather a process whereby the past is continuously constructed, based on certain social and mental conditions (Holtorf 2000–2007). The notion of memory being a simple process of recall should thus be broadened to encompass the idea that it is an intricate, continuous and complicated process of selection and negotiation over the details of what is remembered and what is forgotten. Memory surfaces hesitatingly, it needs to be called up, called upon, and addressed like the Greek goddess Mnemosyne, mother of the Muses (Haverkamp 1996). This process of recall involves changing perceptions of the past in light of present needs and situations. Societies and individuals, therefore, continuously construct, reconstruct and, consequently, reinterpret the past based on the present and the future (Teski & Climo 2005; Natzmer 2002:164; Nesper 2002:191).

Maurice Halbwachs (1939; 1980), a sociologist, applied the term 'collective memory' to define the process whereby social groups construct their own perceptions of the past based on consented versions of previous events. This occurs through communication between individuals, based in the sphere of language. Individual remembrance only forms part of the process. Collective or social memories are therefore defined and shaped by 'social, economic or political circumstances; by beliefs and values; by opposition and resistance. They involve cultural norms and issues of authenticity, identity and power. They are implicated in ideologies...they create interpretive frameworks that help make experience comprehensible' (Cattell & Climo 2002:4).

The concept of collective memory was adopted into archaeological disciplines by the archaeologist Jan Assmann (1992, in Holtorf 2000–2007). He discussed the concept of cultural memory, which he defined as the process whereby a society preserves its collective knowledge between generations through cultural mnemonics. Cultural memory in this context, therefore, may be seen as the collective constructions of the past to aid future generations in establishing and maintaining their cultural identity (Holtorf 2000–2007). This definition is in line with Halbwach's (1980) use of the term 'collective memory' and may be used interchangeably. For the purposes of this discussion, I will use the term 'collective memory'.

An individual's memories are never detached; memory involves a dynamic relationship with generations of the present and past (Climo 2002:119). Memories of an individual and society are inextricably intertwined, that is, rooted in the concept that memory is an organic process (Cattell & Climo 2002:12). The process of memory shapes and perpetuates the sense of self, that is, the personal awareness by which we define ourselves as individuals and the collective awareness by which societies identify themselves (Cattell & Climo 2002:12; Holtorf 2000–2007).

Furthermore, shared memory or collective memory not only aids in establishing an individual's self-identity[1] in juxtaposition to the identities of others, but also creates crucial relationships and social ties between people: families, friends, neighbours and communities. Collective memories therefore develop and sustain relationships, develop understanding and trust between other people, and help us to define ourselves as individuals. It should be stressed, however, that exclusive or contradictory memories can create mistrust and result in separation from groups or societies (Archibald 2002:78).

Gillis (1994:3) explains as follows:

The notion of identity depends on the idea of memory, and vice versa. The core meaning of any individual or group identity, namely, a sense of sameness over time and space, is sustained by remembering; and what is remembered is defined by the assumed identity. We need to be reminded that memories and identities are not fixed things, but representations or constructions of reality, subjective rather than objective phenomena. We are constantly revising our memories to suit our current identities. (Gillis (1994:3)

The process whereby collective identity is transmitted from one generation to the next was defined by Jacob Climo (2002:119) as vicarious memory. Vicarious memory is memory that an individual values and is emotionally committed to. The individual, however, never experienced this memory personally; rather, it was constructed from the related experiences of direct relatives, elders or teachers. Vicarious memory can thus be ascribed to a 'pattern of remembering' or a 'memory repertoire' characteristic of a particular group which, according to Climo, are 'essential components in the persistence of both individual and collective identity' (Climo 2002:19).

Memory, whether individual or collective, is constructed and reconstructed by the dialectics of remembering and forgetting, shaped by semantic and interpretative frames, and subject to a panoply of distortions...Just as social memory is marked by dialectic between stability or historical continuity and innovations and changes, individual memory is characterised by continuity and change. (Cattell & Climo 2002:1, 15)

It is clear that collective and individual memories very seldom remain constant; they are also not always true representations of events. Rather, memories are interpretations of experiences. As stated previously, an individual's sense of identity is integrally connected to the constructed narratives and memories which interweave the past, present and future. Memories, therefore, have the potential to be distorted and influenced by the emotions of the individual experiencing the event. Distortions can also occur through various other factors, such as the structuring of an individual's memories by social or cultural norms and practices, socially ordered recall-patterns, details of the retrieval environment and prior knowledge of the recalled event (Lowenthal 1985:193–210; Cattell & Climo 2002:13). When considering intergenerational memory or vicarious memory, the form, content and symbols of collective identity may change over time, but the concept of collective identity persists from one generation to the next (Holtorf 2000–2007; Climo 2002:121).

Memory culture is the way a society ensures cultural continuity by preserving, with the help of cultural mnemonics, its collective knowledge from one generation to the next, rendering it possible for later generations to reconstruct their cultural identity. References to the past, on the other hand, reassure the members of a society of their collective identity and supply them with an awareness of their unity and singularity in time and space – an historical consciousness – by creating a shared past (Assmann 1992:30–34, in Holtorf 2000–2007).

Landscape

The term 'landscape' has been debated over the past ten years. Many authors have proposed different meanings or roots for it. In the assimilation of different definitions, it may be stated that the term may refer to both an environment shaped by human action and to a representation (particularly a painting or artwork) which signifies its meanings (Ucko & Layton 1999:1). The term 'landscape' is therefore not tantamount to the countryside or nature, but rather a generic term for the expression of particular ways of perceiving the environment (Darvill 1999:105; Duncan & Ley 1993:262). In addition, this polysemic term amalgamates a number of different disciplines and approaches, ranging from classical geography, history, socioeconomics and even design professions (Scazzosi 2004:337; Bender 1993).

Landscape is the spatial manifestation of the relations between humans and the environment, the visual signature of a territory – a vista – that both forms and is formed by the people who inhabit it (Crumley 2002:41).

Landscape is seated in perception and does not exist as a material object *per se* (Ucko & Layton 1999:1, 7). We should thus view landscapes primarily as social phenomena. The term 'landscape' implies human beings as its key element: human ideas and concepts about a certain landscape differentiate it from the environment and usher in the cultural. Physical features and relationships in the landscape are socially mapped through cultural or cognitive factors, and meanings or values are attributed to them (Allison 1999:276). We consequently perceive, understand and create the landscape around us through social and cultural filters, as well as through specific time, place, material and historical conditions (Schama 1995:12). In most cases, therefore, the term 'landscape' may have different significant[2] meanings and interpretations for different cultural groups or individuals (Todeschini 2003; Mbangela 2003:1; Cooney 1999:46). Occasionally, the cultural significance of such landscapes is understandable to outsiders, but typically, even in those cases, concealed meanings and levels of significance (the intangible dimension) are attainable to only a few. The response to landscape is therefore not necessarily universal (Green 1996:31).

Ermischer (2004:380) further developed the concept of landscape as a mental construct and looked at the role of the image or perception in change. He premised that the image of a landscape, that is, that which is determined by the cultural or social background of the viewer, determines the way it is perceived, observed or treated. People's ideas and concepts are therefore part of landscape change and the change of perception. Landscape is therefore a 'living canvas' and will inevitably change.

Stewart and Strathern (2004:4) linked the term 'landscape' with the concepts of place and community:

While we see the concepts of place, community and landscape as intersecting or overlapping, we do not regard them as synonymous...In our view landscape refers to the perceived settings that frame people's senses of place and community. A place is a socially meaningful and identifiable space to which a historical dimension is attributed. Community refers to sets of people who may identify themselves with a place in terms of notions of commonality, shared values or solidarity in particular contexts. (Stewart & Strathern 2004:4)

Landscape is thus seen as a perception determined and influenced by cultural constructs. It is subject to change and will invariably be either misunderstood or not understood at all by those that are not from the landscape. On various levels this is reminiscent of the description of memory in the previous section.

Landscape and memory

Memory of place implaces us and thus empowers us: it gives us space to be precisely because we have been in so many memorable places (Casey 2000:215).

The philosopher Edward Casey (2000) argued that the concepts of place and site (physical environment) comprise two entirely incongruent concepts. He defined a site as a space that acts to define and exclude, whereas a place entails the inclusion and overlap of a set of co-inherent spaces (Casey 2000:202). He included Aristotle's argument that place is 'the innermost motionless boundary of what contains' and concluded that the principal function of place is that of containing. Place maintains or retains, therefore, whereas site divides or disperses (Casey 2000:186).

He continued to include the concept of landscape in the basic definition of place. 'When we are in a landscape setting…we are very much in the presence of place in its most encompassing and exfoliated format, a format in which we are sensuously attuned to its intrinsic spatial properties rather than imposing on our own site-specific proclivities' (Casey 2000:198). Landscape can thus be seen as the full spectrum of body sensing in conjunction with perception (Casey 2000:197).

Supporting the premises of Steward and Strathern (2004), Lowenthal (1985; 2007), Holtorf (2000–2007) and Halbwachs (1939; 1990) discussed previously, Casey continues to establish that place and landscape serve to 'situate one's memorial life, to give it a name and a local habitation' (Casey 2000:183–184).

His previous definitions of place as a container of experiences leads to the idea that place (landscape) and memory are intrinsically connected: 'An alert and alive memory connects spontaneously with place, finding in its features that favour and parallel its own activities. We might say that memory is naturally place-oriented or at least place-supported' (Casey 2000:186–187).

Steward and Strathern (2004:8) support this view by stating as follows:

The inner landscape merges the perceived experience of the place with the imagined symbolic meaning of the place to the individual. Landscape, in a meaningful sense thus encompasses environment plus relationships that emerge from or exist in a place.

It is clear that landscape and memory are inextricably intertwined, as discussed by Guo (2004:193):

we find that landscape is a key component of how people perceive, memorise and represent history (i.e. their historicity), and how they configure the sense of themselves.

Landscape therefore leads to the construction of a social group or population's collective memory, which is one of the sources of identity (Halbwachs 1980; Holtorf 2000–2007; Lowenthal 1985:41–46). 'The landscape becomes a physical manifestation of a culture's knowledge and understanding of its past and future' (Kuchler 1993:85, Spiegel 2004:8–9). Places, landscapes and other references to the past can therefore support and enhance the cultural identities of groups and the social identities of people within a society (Holtorf 2000–2007; Lowenthal 1985:41–46).

Intangible landscapes

It is in providing outward display for things and pathways as they exist within the horizons of landscape that places enable memories to become inwardly inscribed and possessed: made one with the memory itself. The visibility without becomes part of the invisibility within (Casey 2000:213).

From the previous two sections, it is clear that landscapes are seated in the perceptions of individuals and societies, and that this is part of a continuous process which leads to ever changing character. We have also established that the perception of landscape helps us to maintain our identity through the process of memory. It is therefore clear that landscapes comprise intangible and tangible aspects: tangible in terms of the biophysical aspects that define place, and intangible in terms of the process of memory in place. Recent academic discourses argue that there is an inseparable relationship between the tangible and the intangible. The intangible is materialised by the tangible and the intangible plays a vital role in the establishment of the tangible (Ito 2003). The concept and perception of landscape can therefore be used to help build a crucial link between the tangible fabric of places and the meanings, memories, cultural traditions and social practices that form part of its associated intangible values. This connection or critical link is clearly explained by Clarke and Johnston (2003):

The notion of landscape encompasses connections – routes, links, events, stories, traditions – that cross the 'boundary' between intangible and tangible heritage, and offers opportunities for a more holistic understanding. Landscape also has the potential to be the medium that helps in understanding the commonalities and differences in the way that indigenous and non-indigenous communities perceive cultural heritage. (Clarke & Johnston 2003)

Reading or perceiving the landscape as an expression of meanings and memories seated in past or present cultures (i.e. its intangible dimension) will depend on 'identifying a community's reference to external features that we can also perceive' (Ucko & Layton 1999:11).

In the perception of landscape, however, we find a dichotomy. Within a typically Western society, there is a predominantly visual perception and experience of landscape. It is thus an individualist and predominantly pictorial landscape (Bender 1993:1). Kuchler (1993:85) argues that the 'Western' view, which developed from landscape art during the Renaissance, 'treats landscape as an inscribed surface, as an *aide memoir* of cultural knowledge and

understanding of its past and future'. In less complex societies, however, landscapes are experienced through multiple senses: oral recollections, storytelling, touch, olfactory exploration and social experience (Franklin 2002:186). In this case, the visual may not be the most significant aspect. For these societies, landscape is not the inscription of memory or encoding of memories, but rather the 'process of remembering' (Kuchler 1993:85).

The western conceptualisation – 'landscape of memory' – sees landscape as a fixed, objectifiable and measurable description of a surface, while the indigenous conceptualisation – 'landscape as memory' – sees landscape as something that is affected by the project of its representation and remembrance, as part of the process of remembering (Guo 2004:200).

Pierre Nora edited a monumental work about the places of memory of France, entitled *Les lieux de mémoire* (1984–1992), which is a clear example of the 'landscape of memory' concept. *A lieu de mémoire* is any significant entity, whether material or non-material in nature, which by dint of human will or the work of time has become a symbolic element of the memorial heritage of any community (Nora 1996:xvii). What is interesting, however, is that Nora claims that sites of memory are a phenomenon of this modern era, which leads to the fact that the 'living' memories of the past (based in oral traditions) are replaced by these sites of memory.

Scazzosi (2004:335) introduced the idea of landscape as a document or palimpsest[3] also leading from the perspective of landscape of memory. He states, however, that landscapes should be viewed as archives or living documents, where the history of the place and traces of eras are combined with the activities of the present. Landscape is thus a 'reading of the world in its complexity; a means to contemplate our own history and to build our future, being fully aware of the past' (Scazzosi 2004:339). It is a multi-layered document with elements of the past merged with the tangible present.

The alternative to landscape as defined as an inscribed surface and *aide memoir* of culture is the perspective of landscape as a key component in the process of memory. This perspective of landscape as memory, rather than as an inscription of memory, follows from the above discussion on the dichotomy between Western and traditional views of landscape (Kuchler 1993:103). Spiegel (2004:8) subsequently argues that landscape is an agent of memory inscription and that it exists in a dialectical relationship with memory.

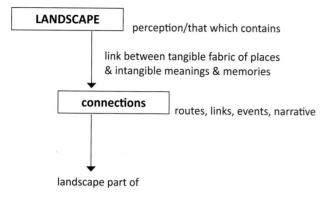

LANDSCAPE — perception/that which contains

link between tangible fabric of places & intangible meanings & memories

connections — routes, links, events, narrative

landscape part of

process of remembering

Memories and stories are significant parts of the living heritage of a community or an individual, and include the social and cultural connections between people. Spiegel proposed the premise, however, that the only way landscape can make memory (landscape as memory) is through intellectual or cognitive processes. It is therefore necessary for memory to cognitively reinterpret and (re)compose the landscape through the intellectual processes in order to recollect earlier experiences (Spiegel 2004:3, 7).

An essential part of any discussion of landscape and memory is the efficacy of mnemotechnics. It had its inception during the Greek and later Roman times, and was primarily a sub-discipline of speech making, that is, the 'art of memory' (Parker 1997:147). Place analogies were used extensively by classical orators as an aid in memorising arguments or speeches. 'Study of mnemonic theory – including constructs of modern art theory, philosophy and cognitive psychology, along with ideas developed by classical orators – suggests that mental organisation structures itself in a fundamentally spatial manner' (Parker 1997:147). This concept was originally explored by Jan Vansina, the Belgium anthropologist who worked in Central Africa (1985:45). He advocated that memory often needs mnemotechnic devices (mnemonic = designed to aid the memory) to be efficiently activated. These can be objects, landscapes or forms of music. Van Vuuren (1993:59) describes some of these memory-activating objects as defined by Vansina (1985:44–45):

stones on a heap (such as the Zulu *isivivane* stone heaps on which stones are added by passers-by for a prosperous journey). The leopard skin worn by local African rulers, the staff carried by an *imbongi* and the ox tail (*umsila*) used by a *ngaka* or *isangoma* act as mnemotechnic devices to prove the origin of incumbency, and traditional legitimacy in terms of skills and practice. There are a great number of examples of landscapes which serve as mnemotechnic devices, including the well-known battlefields, graves and ruins of settlement sites.

In line with the concept of mnemotechnics where landscape elements can serve as devices to trigger memory (Vansina 1985), Casey (2000) discussed the role of the body in the process of memory 'as psycho-physical in status, the lived-body puts us in touch with the psychical aspects of remembering and the physical features of place' (Casey 2000:189). He described the function of living bodies as giving direction, level and distance to landscapes and places, which, in turn, serve as anchoring points in remembering. Continuing the idea of the 'art of memory'[4] described previously, remembering is thus not merely a form of recollection, but rather a process of 're-implacing and re-experiencing' past places (Casey 2000:210). One gains access to the past, as described by Archibald (2002:68), through emotional resonance, where landscapes, places and objects stimulate memory. These places support the continuity of memory. This concept is summarised by Spiegel (2004:8) as follows:

Landscape 'out there' does have autonomy when it is inscribed in memory in ways, and through parts of the body, whereby cognitive processes (the intellect) appear to be bypassed in the recollection process...The very ways in which landscape occurs 'on the ground' – the lay of the land – can determine the extent to which its inscription as bodily memory enables or hinders recollection. And by doing that, it demonstrates again that the landscape 'out there' does have an autonomous existence, an inscriptive capacity, and the power to affect, even to determine, the intellectual process of representation that is memory construction. (Spiegel 2004:8)

Going back to the discussion on 'landscape of/as memory', we have established that both these concepts can be seen as processes involving individuals or societies, where the past is re-interpreted or re-composed through cognitive processes (Spiegel 2004:3, 7), and where past places are re-implaced and re-experienced through psycho-physical processes (Casey 2000:210). One might therefore understand landscape and the perception thereof as a result of the process of memory, that is, from a cultural process of remembering to a personal and measurable capacity (Kuchler 1993:103). The practices that perpetuate memory are inscribed on the landscape and inscribe the landscape itself into memory (Spiegel 2004:8).

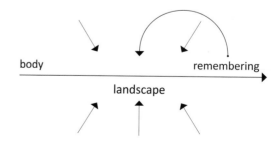

body — remembering

landscape

Memory is never constant and always prone to distortions or changes based on either individual or collective factors. Landscape is inextricably part of the intangible dimensions of memory and culture. The perception of the landscape therefore changes as it is essentially embedded in the intangible dimension of culture (Franklin 2002:37, 38):

natures (i)s cultural specific and embedded and prone to change in relation to shifting economic, ethical and moral conditions...nature is socially embedded in the vectors of space and time, while at once a physical reality, amenable to the senses and discursively ordered.

This is supported by Morphy (1993:205) who states as follows:

(t)oday's landscape is inevitably processual and transforming, integral to processes of objectification and the sedimentation of history, subjected to poetic and hermeneutic interpretation and a place where value and emotion coincide. (Morphy 1993:205)

Continuity of intangible cultural values therefore requires a tangible materialisation. Memories are based on referents, which are places, landscapes, structures or other elements of representation (mnemotechnic anchoring points). These may be places where the relationship between the fabric of the place and the intangible associations (meanings and memories) with that place to a specific culture or group, have continued through time. In the event of the continuity of the relationship of intangible value and place being disrupted, however, often due to external or material changes, the intangible connection to that place is at risk of breaking (Archibald 2002:73; Truscott 2003). If referents are altered or changed beyond recognition, a change in the perception of reality could occur, ultimately resulting in altered perceptions of the past and future and a restructuring of the existing memory narrative (Archibald 2002:73; Natzmer 2002:166, 178).

As stated in the introduction, South Africa plays host to a number of sites of commemoration. These have been dealt with in various levels of success, either ignoring the role of the landscape in memorial design or divorcing the design from its context – the community and place it's seated in. The next section will provide a brief description of a case study whereafter the efficacy of the design of memorial spaces will be reflected upon.

Kliptown and the Walter Sisulu Square of Dedication

After commenting to a colleague that I intended to write about the Walter Sisulu Square of Dedication, she exclaimed: 'Oh, not that again – it is such a favourite with academics.'[5] It is true. Numerous articles have appeared in journals and magazines, thesis documents and Internet sites. My interest in the square, however, stems from previous exposure to Kliptown in 2003. While researching the cultural landscape[6], interviewing residents and documenting places of social and historical significance, I was awed by the vibrancy and cohesiveness of the community, the robust nature of the fabric of the township itself and how even younger generations basked in the legacy of what it meant to live in Kliptown.

Kliptown used to be characterised by a multi-racial society consisting of Malawian, Somalian, Angolan, Sotho, Tswana, Chinese, Indian, Muslim, Xhosa and Zulu residents. Its origin lies in a number of unfortunate events that occurred in the early 1900s. After the pneumonic plague broke out in the Coolie Location of Johannesburg, the residents were forcefully relocated to a site on the Klipspruit River. This site was located outside the city's municipal boundary and remained as such for over 60 years. This 'left-over space' attracted people from the fringes of society, individuals and families that did not fit in. Kliptown became one of the few places where 'non-Europeans' could own a business. 'Kliptown was a place where people experimented, through undisciplined, hybridised, and frequently illegal encounters, with change, exchange and fusion' (Bremner 2008:339). The place had immense significance emanating from its residents. Community cohesiveness and a scale that supported an integration of cultures, traditions and lifestyles represented its strength. The following quotation from my research (Müller 2003) provides a synopsis of its social significance:

Colour didn't matter to us because we had friends whose fathers were white and whose mothers were black and they were coloureds. In Kliptown there were lots of white people. They actually lived there right along the railway line. They were friends of mine. (Anonymous, pers. comm. in Müller 2003)

In 2003, a number of older residents accompanied me on a walking tour to help locate important spatial localities in the context of the Freedom Charter. The first stop was the large open, dusty field where around 3 000 delegates and 7 000 spectators from all over the country gathered for the signing of the Charter in 1955. The masses congregated on the north-western corner of the square. Interestingly enough, the negotiations of the charter occurred in the WW Brown Memorial Baptists Church a few hundred metres from the square. The following quotation from Bremner (2008:337) offers an apt description of the field in 2003:

Today, Freedom Square is an open, windswept tract of land, lying between a shack settlement, a railway line, and a taxi rank and bounded by the back façades of warehouses and wholesale stores. The trees that once lined its edges, providing shade

Photograph by **Drum** *photographer © Baileys Archive[8] (left)*

Original traders (Müller 2003) (right)

for local traders and commuters have long since died, and the farm that once cultivated the land around it has long been abandoned.

After documenting the oral histories of the event, I poured over archival photographs, fascinated by the jubilant, but resigned atmosphere that seems to have reigned during the day. I caught glimpses of the original square, but it was the descriptions of residents and current hawkers at the new square that confirmed my perceptions.

The outer fringes of the square were originally utilised by a large group of hawkers capitulating on the main pedestrian route from Kliptown suburbs, through the commercial centre to the station and eventual taxi rank. The main concentration of hawkers was located at the south-eastern corner of the square. They had an informal, but strict organisational system determining the location of shelters and tables in specific locations. But other than that they were free to promote and sell their goods in any which way they chose. According to oral recollections, this place was always vibrant and was considered the informal commercial centre of Kliptown (pers. comm. Angelina Mahalelo December 2009).

It was not only the square that caught my attention. The entire township reads like a history book, with numerous houses and other structures depicting the passing or perpetuation of different eras. Significant buildings include remnants of the original farm buildings, the house where Nelson Mandela hid before he was captured, the tragically beautiful San Souci movie house, the music precinct 'Angola' or 'Twist lane', which still houses prominent marabi musicians from the bygone Sophiatown-Jazz era, the Tree of Justice and Peace and the Tree of Accountability, to name only a few. The children accompanied me to the Vlei, a popular swimming hole under the bridge to the north-east of the township. They showed me the tree under which hundreds of young boys courted girls over the years. They reminisced about Kliptown's main thoroughfare, Union Street, which used to be lined with bluegum trees, while Main Street boasted a row of oak trees.

Even though the residents live in ramshackle houses and shacks with only the basic or no services, it is the spaces between the houses that activate and support the community. Kliptown residents live outside, with open spaces within the town, but especially the streets, supporting innumerable social practices (Bremner 2008:336). Due to the fact that Kliptown was located outside any municipal area until the 1980s, a spatial

Photograph by **Drum** *photographer*
© Baileys Archive[7]

The music precinct 'Angola' or 'Twist lane' (Müller 2003) (left)

Tree of Accountability (Müller 2003) (centre)

San Souci Theatre (Müller 2003) (right)

configuration emanated which was largely determined by the residents themselves. This significantly distinguished Kliptown from other townships such as Orlando, where spatial configuration was essentially a result of apartheid planning schemes. This was truly a unique place, with the stories of the potpourri of people living there merging to create a truly unified community in contrast with the racially charged status quo of that era. The following collection of quotations from personal interviews with residents (Müller 2003) highlights several aspects integral to the rich intangible, but also tangible legacy of this vibrant 'town':

The landlords of that time just rented their houses out to anybody. There would be lots of people in one house. **Shanties** sprung up. The Shanties were made of **mud bricks**.

We miss the **church bells**. The bells were our main source of sending social **messages**. We structured our lives around the ringing of the church bells.

The vlei taught me how **to swim**, how to **socialise** with my friends and gave me a **sense of responsibility**.

There are 22 **cultural groups** in Kliptown. They would perform for free if they just had a place to do it.

Two **bioscopes** served our community for many years. New Year's Day people would come from all over Johannesburg to come picnic along the river. I learned to swim in that river.

Our struggle is also a struggle of memory against forgetting.

There were several doctors' rooms. One of these doctors was the first black female doctor in Kliptown, known only as **Dr Mary**.

The people would not go to the **Square**, they would say that it is not for them and that they would rather stay where they belong. It would be too foreign, big cars, flashy lights, it would not be a place for us... The **people of the old houses** are disappearing.

It would make no sense at all to plant flowers! The roads would be DEAD! It is **the people that are important**. Any development that takes the people into consideration would bring life. It would bring the people together.

Beacon Street is the real **heart of Kliptown**, not the square. (personal interviews with residents (Müller 2003))

After previous unsuccessful attempts at commemorating the signing of the Freedom Charter, a design was procured through a competition process run by the Johannesburg Development Agency. The original winning design by StudioMAS is a grandiose urban vision of a series of axially linked squares that included Freedom Square as well as a new South African Parliament complex (Noble 2008: 23). The design is a geometrically abstract concept laden with overt, but shallow symbols and metaphors. It focuses on the freedom to vote, the winding voting queues of the first democratic election and the act of voting, the putting a cross on a ballot paper (Bakker & Müller 2009). The landscape architects' contribution seems to have been contained to the internal squares, where the ballot-cross theme is repeated in the form of low benches/tables under rows of indigenous trees.

When I returned to Kliptown roughly seven years later, I was shocked by the change. Where my original perception of the place was that of a small-scale, poor but albeit cohesive community town, my attention was now grabbed by the gross disparity in scale between the new Walter Sisulu Square of Dedication and the original town. The overbearing, self-obsessed structure towers over the existing historical structures, ridiculing them by contrast. Was this structure aimed at paying homage to the significant role this place played? Surely the development team understood the value of this place in the larger context of Kliptown, the community and the narrative of democracy? Even though a number of historic buildings were demolished to make way for

Difference in scale between new structure and existing commercial infrastructure immediately adjacent to it (Müller 2009)

this grand statement, surely the remaining referents to the past had to be honoured in some way?

The opinion of Richard Malunga, one of the original traders of Kliptown, is quite telling:

There are only two historic buildings left after the rest was demolished. This new building is not welcoming. The people were never consulted when it was built. The people who were here when things were still right were never consulted. When we are in the square, it's a different world from Kliptown. Our expectations of a better standard of living were never met. The history of the place is lost. We cannot read the information boards, they are too big and the words too many. Nobody reads these boards; you have to stand in the sun for a long time if you want to read it. There is not enough respect towards the heritage. We need a proper facility or a living museum where we can tell our story. (Richard Malunga, pers. comm. in December 2009, Müller)

The most unfortunate aspect of the design is the fact that it is essentially focusing inward, turning its back to Kliptown. It refuses to engage with the community at large, refuses to contribute anything to community life. It features a four star hotel, an ATM (which the community fears to use due to numerous cases of theft), expensive clothing stores and an underground parking area: 'A parkade? Why? People don't even have homes to stay in. And this fancy hotel? It's not going to benefit us; it's just for 2010' (pers. comm. Samantha, December 2009). A case in point is that, at the time of publication, all the restaurants in the square have closed down due to little or no clientele.

The tourist centre is located on the periphery of the square. In an interview with one of the members of the administration staff it became clear that they never venture into the square and never interact with the community, 'There are not that many tourists that come here. It does not work, it is too unsafe.'[9] The design culminates in a contrived conical memorial to democracy. The people that use the space surrounding the memorial become part of a spectacle, where numerous 'Soweto Tours' sweep tourists into the space, ushering them to the memorial, and evacuating the group before any real contact between either group could be achieved. The significance and meaning of the structure is lost to the community and is rarely if ever visited by Kliptown residents.

A key flaw in the design of the square is that the designers did not understand the mode of commerce employed and understood by the community. In an interview with original trader, Angelina Mahalelo, aspects pertaining to the original trading space on the square were illuminated:

It used to be a large open field. There were many footpaths crossing through the field and many people walked along these footpaths to the transport every day. We were many traders who erected stalls along these footpaths. We had our own shade structures and tables, we could do what we want. Some people even slept at their stalls. It was very safe, because everyone knew each other. Not like now. There are too many strangers now. You have to lock everything. This place changed everything. In the past everyone knew that this was the place where the Freedom Charter was signed. I was even there. We told the story to our children. But now, we don't know this place. We don't understand it. And it is not looking after us. I am old and there is no place for me to sell my goods. (Angelina Mahalelo, pers. comm. in December 2009, Müller)

Informal trading formed the foundation of commerce in Kliptown. Due to the nature of this mode of trading, each stall presented different requirements with goods ranging from fresh produce to CDs and tapes to clothes or herbal medicine. The design, however, treats everyone the same, providing small, inadequate lockers and waist-high tables in the main covered trading space. In the square, the idealistic crosses are being rented out as additional trading space with no shade or any other amenities. The public toilets have proven to be grossly inadequate for the number of people they cater for and have been monopolised by a group of gangsters.

The rent is very expensive. We are not getting what we were promised, which was lockable trading spaces, shade and proper stands. What do the trees help? What happens when it rains? The paving is uneven rocks, making it difficult to walk. Nobody wants to walk here. The drinking fountains never worked and do not fit. Why do we need drinking fountains? And the shade structure under the large three-storey structure: why do we need two roofs? Is one not enough? (pers. comm. Amin Amin, December 2009, Müller)

Impromptu trade on the crosses, being rented out to traders (Müller 2009)

Large containers for storage of goods (at additional cost) with waist-high surfaces for trade (Müller 2009) (left)
Inadequate storage facilities resulting in makeshift covered heaps clogging entrance areas (Müller 2009) (centre)
Traders forced to resort to boxes to solve issues not addressed in design (Müller 2009) (right)

The introduction of a number of art interventions within the area at first seemed like a positive, healthy contribution to the cultural landscape. At closer inspection, unsafe spaces, corners for vagrants to build homes and pockets for the collection of rubbish provide another layer to these grand and idealistic structures. Furthermore, the symbolism of the tall columns with sculptures [10] seems to be lost to most community members. Most people I interviewed, young and old, had no idea that the sculptures represented the ten clauses of the Freedom Charter. Furthermore, the large open space adjacent to the columns and sculptures at the entrance to the square is used for periodic events. During these events, the original traders are banned from the square for the entire day, not being allowed to trade in the space they've rented. The statement of Sam (pers. comm. December 2009), a herbalist and healer with a market stall, sums up the situation:

The architecture is a blunder. We cannot walk freely and it is difficult to get access to the place. The police take your goods if you have it on the street, so you have to rent a place here. But now business is less, there are no people here. When it rains, you have to quickly remove everything and half get spoilt because there is no cover. (Sam, pers. comm. December 2009, Müller)

Apart from the disintegration of a community, secondary impacts of the intervention have been identified. On 3 September 2007, more than twenty community activists were arrested in community protests organised by the Anti Privatisation Forum against the slow or non-delivery of services in Soweto. After more than twenty appearances and almost two years, five were found guilty of 'public violence'[11]. The Kliptown Concerned Residents (KCR), however, continue to actively protest against the conditions in the township, where basic services such as a clinic, library or a recreational facility have been promised, but never delivered. Another increasing problem cited is the deterioration of the existing historic dwellings of Kliptown. An article in *The Citizen* (Mokati 2010) highlighted the views of residents fearing for their lives in crumbling structures and sagging foundations.

Furthermore, an illuminating document on crime statistics[12] in Kliptown indicates that, while certain incidences of crime have declined over a five-year period, there has been a prevalent increase of commercial, organised and drug-related crimes. From interviews it became clear that, after the unveiling of the WSSD and related housing schemes, the number of foreigners living within the township increased. According to the community, the increase in crime is directly related to the fact that residents from the community could not afford to purchase property in the housing schemes, which then attracted wealthy foreigners who are responsible for managing organised crime within the area and beyond. The previously safe and cohesive township became a playing field for people preying on the weak.

A study on Land Use Management in Johannesburg by Wits and PlanAct (Himlin, Engel & Mathoho 2008:30–33) drew attention to the gross disparity between the dire living conditions of the residents in Kliptown and the development of the WSSD. The original aims of the project were to, apart from commemorating the Freedom Charter, create economic opportunities for the residents. From the outset, however, the project negated this aim on various levels. Despite the laudable initial intentions to provide capacity building for improving the skills of local builders and employing them in the construction process, none of it was realised. No training was provided nor were any residents employed. Furthermore, the business opportunities within the development – retail, hotel and museum – have not been designed or structured for any level of community appropriation in the future.

It would seem as if the development intentionally aimed at providing the infrastructure for attracting residents with a higher income to the area, ignoring the needs of the current community. For this reason, many of the residents view the 'heritage development' with increasing scepticism and resentment (Himlin, Engel & Mathoho 2008:30–33).

The most tragic aspect of this design is the fact that it does not narrate the impact of the Freedom Charter in South Africa. There is no emotional resonance, either from tourists or the community and the profound significance of the charter is negated by sheer architectural egotism. The community has become more aware of their poverty as they are daily confronted by the foreign imposing design. The designers were responsible for understanding the historical, but also social significance of the site and larger context. Through an unsympathetic design solution they've managed to

Entrance with columns and sculptures (Müller 2009)

Large uninviting open space with memorial structure to the back (Müller 2009)

alienate the people integral to the place. The community has been displaced yet again, having to fend for themselves from the fringes of this grand statement of supposed urban affluence and progress. When taking all the primary and secondary effects of the introduction of the Walter Sisulu Square of Dedication into consideration, one can conclude that the design achieved, in essence, the direct opposite of what the Freedom Charter stood for.

Conclusion

Whose stories should be remembered?

Democracy calls for an ongoing process of commemorating shared memories and considering what others have to tell. We learn from the past in the present, and we learn about ourselves from the way we remember the past.

The stories people tell about the past contribute to an understanding of who we are – of the identity of individuals and a nation – in the present.

(Quote on plaque at Hector Pietersen Memorial, Soweto)

Landscape is intangible. It forms an intricate part of the people whose stories give meaning to an environment. Landscape can change, just as the perception of a landscape can change according to the fluctuating nature of communities and even individual hearts and minds. The stories of individuals and communities are located in memory. Landscape serves as the container for these memories, whether in a tangible or intangible form. However, both container and contained are subject to our fleeting nature and our tendency to narrate the past based on our present needs.

With this in mind, it is useful to consider the above quote: Whose stories should be remembered? In a country like South Africa, where a myriad of different races, cultures, clans, tongues and tribes are vying to survive, this question is indeed quite valid. Whose stories should be remembered? Better still, should these stories be remembered?[13] And if so, how should these stories be remembered? And by whom?

The current 'culture of commemoration' within South Africa reiterates the crucial role of the designer in designing spaces of memory. However, judging from the collection of commemorative and memorial projects throughout the country, it would seem as if this role has been largely misunderstood. The preoccupation with space creation and infusing it with meaning has divorced the designer from the core of design – its user – the people reading the story being narrated by the design.

If a designer does not understand the original story and the people narrating the story, how can he/she translate that story into design? And if the designer failed to understand the people narrating the original story, how will the subsequent readers – people with no prior knowledge of the story – be able to perceive it?

The practice of anthropology, immersing oneself in a culture [or story in this instance], presents successful techniques for accessing the intangible dimension of a landscape in order to understand its underlying stories. Practices such as interviews[14] or participant observation could be employed to understand the human dimension in site assessment. A designer cannot underestimate the value of personal connection with the context. Understanding the people should be considered the first step in any design process.

Most importantly, as deduced from the theoretical section of this chapter, landscapes of memory play a crucial role in the formation and perpetuation of individual and collective identity. If the designer understands the context of a particular site of commemoration, the design resolution will ultimately contain those intangible values acting as the life-fibres of identity within a landscape. These fibres are alive and constantly in flux, and by embracing and trying to understand them, one can weave them into a design proposal.

Memory and landscape are considered crucial ingredients in the building of relationships between individuals in societies and the formation of social ties between people. The story of our planet is comprised of people actualising themselves, rising above or over one another based on their perception of who they are. Whatever we design has the potential to influence people in the most profound way.

The Walter Sisulu Square of Dedication and the larger Kliptown development project is a case in point. With the introduction of a largely inward-looking design intervention with no or little response to context or the community interacting with it on a daily basis, the identity of the people of Kliptown has been slowly eroded. The introduction of a foreign-scaled intervention, narrated with an urban-tongue without any reference to the markers and anchor points within the communities' text of the past, deteriorated not only the tangible fabric of the place, but also the intangible bonds that kept the memory of being free alive.

Kliptown has so many stories to tell. It is a landscape of layers, like the pages of a book, with people and places providing pause points and illustrations for illuminating aspects of memory of a community. The identity of its residents were anchored in these layers of landscape and provided the opportunity for the perpetuation of vicarious memories to be transferred from one generation to the next. It is unfortunate that the development team failed to recognise this aspect as the most crucial design generator. Instead, the designers subjected themselves to the developer's aspirations and produced a structure that attempted to 'heal' the narrowly perceived 'township as a not-yet-urban, incoherent and dependent periphery' (Bremner 2008:345). They only saw the landscape of lack marked by poverty and devoid of easily distinguishable form and structure. As a result, they failed to access the significant and intangibles hidden beneath the surface. They failed to identify those mnemotechnic anchoring points that re-implace memory into the landscape and provide the opportunities to disseminate the narrative of Kliptown. The result is a design intervention which ultimately destroyed those narratives and any possibility for the perpetuation of the values that formed the core of the communities' identity.

Bibliography

Allison, J. 1999. Self-determination in cultural resource management: indigenous peoples' interpretation of history and of places and landscapes, in *The archaeology and anthropology of landscape: shaping your landscape*, P.J. Ucko & R. Layton (eds). Routledge: London.

Archibald, R.R. 2002. A personal history of memory, in *Social memory and history: anthropological perspectives*, J.J. Climo & M.G. Cattell (eds). Walnut Creek: AltaMira Press.

Assmann, J. 1992. *Das kulturelle Gedächtnis. Schrift, Erinnerung und politische Identität in frühen Hochkulturen.* München: Beck.

Bakker, K.A. 2003. Preserving intangible heritage resources: examples from South Africa, in ICOMOS International Scientific Symposium entitled 'Place, memory, meaning: preserving intangible values in monuments and sites'. Online: http://www.international.icomos.org/victoria-falls2003/papers.htm (Accessed 18 June 2007).

Bakker, K.A. & Müller, L. 2009. Intangible heritage and community identity in Post-Apartheid South Africa. Unpublished paper presented to Thematic Plenary Session – Communities: from Conflict to Consensus, at the Heritage in Conflict and Consensus: New Approaches to the Social, Political, and Religious Impact of Public Heritage in the 21st Century, New York: UMass Amherst Center for Heritage and Society, November 9–13, 2009.

Bender, B. (ed). 1993. *Landscape politics and perspectives.* Oxford: Berg.

Bremner, L. 2008. Reframing township space: the Kliptown Project, in *Johannesburg: The Elusive Metropolis,* S. Nuttall & J.A. Mbembe (eds). Durham: Duke University Press.

Casey, E. 2000. *Remembering: a phenomenological study.* 2nd edition. USA: Indiana University Press.

Cattell, M.G. & Climo, J.J. 2002. Meaning in social memory and history: anthropological perspectives, in *Social memory and history: anthropological perspectives*, J.J. Climo & M.G. Cattell (eds). Walnut Creek: AltaMira Press.

Clarke, A. & Johnston, C. 2003. Time, memory, place and land: social meaning and heritage conservation in Australia, in ICOMOS International Scientific Symposium entitled 'Place, memory, meaning: preserving intangible values in monuments and sites'. Online:' http://www.international.icomos.org/victoriafalls2003/papers.htm (Accessed 8 April 2005).

Climo, J.J. 2002. Memories of the American Jewish Aliyah: connecting individual and collective experience, in *Social memory and history: anthropological perspectives*, J.J. Climo & M.G. Cattell (eds). Walnut Creek: AltaMira Press.

Climo, J.J. & Cattell, M.G. 2002. *Social memory and history: anthropological perspectives*. Walnut Creek: AltaMira Press.

Cooney, G. 1999. Social landscapes in Irish prehistory, in *The archaeology and anthropology of landscape: shaping your landscape*, P.J. Ucko & R. Layton (eds). Routledge: London.

Crumley, C.L. 2002. Exploring venues of social memory, in *Social memory and history: anthropological* perspectives, J.J. Climo & M.G. Cattell. Walnut Creek: AltaMira Press.

Darvill, T. 1999. The historic environment, historic landscapes, and space-time-action models in landscape archaeology, in *The archaeology and anthropology of landscape: shaping your landscape*, P.J. Ucko & R. Layton (eds). Routledge: London.

Davie, L. 2009. *Sculptures added to Kliptown square*. Official Website of The City of Johannesburg. http://www.joburg.org.za/content/view/3620/203/

Duncan, J. & Ley, D. 1993. *Place/culture/representation*. London: Routledge.

Ermischer, G. 2004. Mental landscape: landscape as idea and concept. *Landscape Research* 29(4):371–383.

Franklin, A. 2002. *Nature and social theory*. London: Sage.

Gillis, J.R. 1994. Introduction: memory and identity: the history of a relationship, in *Commemorations: the politics of national identity*, J.R. Gillis (ed). Princeton, NJ: Princeton University Press.

Gillis, J.R. (ed). 1994. *Commemorations: the politics of national identity*. Princeton, NJ: Princeton University Press.

Green, N. 1996. Looking at the landscape: class formation and the visual, in *The anthropology of landscape: perspectives on place and* space, E. Hirsch & M. O'Hanlon (eds). Oxford: Oxford University Press.

Guo, P. 2004. Island builders: landscape and historicity among the Langalanga, Solomon Islands, in *Landscape, memory and history*, P. Stewart & A. Strathern. London: Pluto.

Halbwachs, M. 1939. Individual consciousness and collective mind. *The American Journal of Sociology* 44(6):812–822.

Halbwachs, M. 1980. *The collective memory*. New York: Harper & Row.

Himlin R., Engel H. & Mathoho, M. 2008. *Land Use Management and Democratic Governance in the City Of Johannesburg – Case Study: Kliptown & Diepsloot*. Study funded by Ford Foundation & Urban LandMark, coordinated by PlanAct and Wits Centre for Urban and Built Environment Studies.

Hodgkin, K. & Radstone, S. 2003. *Contested pasts: the politics of memory*. London: Routledge.

Holtorf, C. 2000–2007. *Monumental past: the life-histories of megalithic monuments in Mecklenburg-Vorpommern (Germany)*. Electronic monograph, University of Toronto: Centre for Instructional Technology Development, Toronto: Online: http://hdl.handle.net/1807/245 (Accessed 8 July 2008).

Ito, N. 2003. Intangible cultural heritage involved in tangible cultural heritage, in ICOMOS International Scientific Symposium entitled 'Place, memory, meaning: preserving intangible values in monuments and sites'. Online: http://www.international.icomos.org:80/xian2005/papers/3-38.pdf (Accessed 21 June 2006).

Kuchler, S. 1993. Landscape as memory: the mapping of process and its representation in a Melanesian society, in *Landscape politics and perspectives*, B. Bender (ed). Oxford: Berg.

Lowenthal, D. 1985. *The past is a foreign country*. Cambridge: Cambridge University Press.

Lowenthal, D. 2007. Living with and looking at landscape. *Landscape research* 32(5):635–656.

Marschall. S. 2005. Making money with memories: the fusion of heritage, tourism and identity formation in South Africa, in *Historia,* 50, 1, pp.103–122.

Marschall, S. 2008. Pointing to the dead: victims, martyrs and public memory in South Africa. *South African Historical Journal*, 60:103.

Mbangela, E.N. 2003. Processes of identification and documentation, in ICOMOS International Scientific Symposium entitled 'Place, memory, meaning: preserving intangible values in monuments and sites'. Online: http://www.international.icomos.org:80/xian2005/papers/3-38.pdf (Accessed 8 April 2005).

Mokati, N. 2010. Kliptown residents living in fear. *The Citizen*. Accessed online http://www.citizen.co.za/index/article.aspx?pDesc=114707,1,22

Morphy, H. 1993. Colonialism, history and the construction of place: the politics of landscape in Northern Australia, in *Landscape politics and* perspectives, B. Bender (ed). Oxford: Berg.

Müller, L. 2003. Greater Kliptown Development Project – Landscaping in Kliptown, Soweto. Landscape Architect Proposal: Johannesburg Development Agency.

Müller, L. 2009. Memory, landscape and heritage at Ngqusa Hill – An anthropological study. Unpublished MA (Anthropology), University of South Africa.

Natzmer, C. 2002. Remembering and forgetting: creative expression and reconciliation in post-Pinochet Chile, in *Social memory and history: anthropological perspectives*, J.J. Climo & M.G. Cattell (eds). Walnut Creek: AltaMira Press.

Nesper, L. 2002. The Meshingomesia Indian village schoolhouse in memory and history, in *Social memory and history: anthropological perspectives*, J.J. Climo & M.G. Cattell. Walnut Creek: Alta Mira Press.

Noble, N. 2008. Memorialising the Freedom Charter: contested imaginations for the development of Freedom Square at Kliptown, 1991–2006. *South African Journal of Art History*, Vol.23 No.1: 13–32.

Nora, P. (ed). 1984–1992. *Les lieux de mémoire* (seven volumes). Paris: Edition Gallimard.

Nora, P. 1996. *From lieux de mémoire to realms of memory*. In: P. Nora & L.D. Kritzman 1996: XV–XXIV.

Nora, P. & Kritzman L.D. (eds). 1996. *Realms of memory: Rethinking the French past. Vol. 1: Conflicts and divisions.* New York: Columbia University Press.

Nuttall, S. & Mbembé J.A. 2008. *Johannesburg: The elusive metropolis.* Durham: Duke University Press.

Parker, R.D. 1997. The architectonics of memory: on built form and built thought. *Leonardo* 30(2):147–152.

SAPS. 2009. Crime in the Kliptown (GP) Police Precinct from April to March: 2003/2004 –2008/2009. Crime Information Management – South African Police Service. Online: www.saps.gov.za/statistics/reports/crimestats/2009/.../kliptown.pdf (Accessed 28 February 2010).

Scazzosi, L. 2004. Reading and assessing the landscape as cultural and historical heritage. *Landscape Research* 29(4):335–355.

Schama, S. 1995. *Landscape and memory.* London: HarperCollins.

Spiegel, A.D. 2004. Walking memories and growing amnesia in the land claims process: Lake St Lucia, South Africa, *Anthropology South Africa* 27(1&2):3–10.

Stewart, P. & Strathern, A. (eds). 2004. *Landscape, memory and history.* London: Pluto Press.

Teski, M.C. and Climo, J.J. (eds.). 1995. *The Labyrinth of Memory: Ethnographic Journeys.* Westport, CT: Bergin & Garvey.

Todeschini, F. 2003. Some reflections on place, tangible and intangible heritage and on identity construction, in ICOMOS international Scientific Symposium entitled 'Monuments and sites in their setting: conserving cultural heritage in changing townscapes and landscapes'. Online: http://www.international.icomos.org:80/xian2005/papers/1-25.pdf (Accessed 21 June 2006).

Truscott, M. 2003. Tradition or invention: remembering and reviving meaning of places, in ICOMOS international scientific symposium entitled 'Monuments and sites in their setting: conserving cultural heritage in changing townscapes and landscapes'. Online: http://www.international.icomos.org:80/xian2005/papers/1-25.pdf (Accessed 21 June 2006).

Ucko, P.J. & Layton, R. 1999. *The archaeology and anthropology of landscape: shaping your landscape.* London: Routledge.

Van Vuuren, C.J. 1993. People, Space and Displacement: The transformation of settlement pattern in South Africa, unpublished paper presented at The making of place in rural Africa conference.

Vansina, J. 1961. *Oral tradition: a study in historical methodology.* London: Aldine & Routledge.

Vansina, J. 1985. *Oral tradition as history.* London: James Curry.

Ware, S. 2005. Anti-memorials and the art of forgetting: Critical reflections on a memorial design practice. *Public History Review*, No 1 (2008): 61–76.

1   The concept of identity has become a substantial discourse in the humanities. According to Arnesen (1998:49), the 'disembeddedness' of 'modern society man' is explained by Giddens (1991), where the perception of the self and identity is not developed in a confined space as is implied in many recent theories documenting the relationship between people and landscape. Handler (1994:30) furthermore argues that Western perceptions of collectivity, which form the basis of our concept of identity, are grounded in a Western concept of personal identity which is different or even altogether absent in other cultural contexts. This is summarised by his statement that '... if other cultures imagine personhood and human activity in terms other than those that we use, we should not expect them to rely on Western individualistic assumptions in describing social collectivities' (Handler 1994:33).

2   Social significance encompasses 'people's attachment to place, the meanings and associations built through history, direct experience and cultural memory, often across generations' (Clarke & Johnson 2003).

3   The term 'palimpsest' is referred to here in its etymological sense (from the Greek pali`n 'newly' and psa`n 'to scratch out', when parchment manuscripts were newly written on, on top of the old writing scratched out) to signal the existence, in the present state of places, of numerous physical traces left over time by the work of man and nature, each time adding to or changing or erasing or overlapping one another and not necessarily being re-interpreted or re-used (Scazzosi 2004:350).

4   Within the modern art world, many projects are focused on this 'art of memory'. In Australia, the exhibition 'Mnemotech: sense + scape + time + memory', asked artists to consider memory in relation to place. Its title refers to mnemotechnics, the technique of using physical elements of architectural space and landscape to trigger memory. Another group, Memoryscapes, based in South Africa, also utilises the technique of mnemotechnics in their works of art, being an 'artistic manifestation of a shared memory' (Raub 2007 & Flynn 2007).

5   Individual chose to remain anonymous.

6   Müller, L. 2003. Greater Kliptown Development Project – Landscaping in Kliptown, Soweto. Landscape Architect Proposal: Johannesburg Development Agency.

7   http://www.sahistory.org.za/pages/governence-projects/freedom-charter/gallery/BAHA-Freedom-Charter-01-195.htm

8   http://www.sahistory.org.za/pages/governence-projects/freedom-charter/gallery/BAHA-Freedom-Charter-07-195.htm

9   Individual chose to remain anonymous.

10 There are 10 clauses in the Freedom Charter and each figure represents a clause. http://www.joburg.org.za/content/view/3620/203/#ixzz0gIHT6qJb

11 KCR 2010 Five Kliptown activists convicted after 18 month 'trial' http://apf.org.za/spip.php?article342

12 Crime in the Kliptown (GP) Police Precinct from April to March: 2003/2004-2008/2009. Crime Information Management – South African Police Service. www.saps.gov.za/statistics/reports/crimestats/2009/.../kliptown.pdf

13 Especially considering our violent past.

14 Structured or unstructured, individual or focus group interviews or image-assisted interviews, with necessary consent as per Ethic Statement.

chapter 2

De-picturing the Landscape:
Notes on the Value of Text for the Conception and Experience of Landscape

Johan N. Prinsloo
Department of Architecture
University of Pretoria
Pretoria
South Africa

This is a Western story.

Prologue

For me, I pray first of all to the kind Muses,

whose votary I am, inspired with passionate love,

that they may welcome me, show me the paths of the skies,

the sun's various failures, the travails of the moon:

how the earth trembles, by what force the deep seas swell,

bursting their barriers, and then return to themselves again;

why the suns in winter hasten to plunge themselves

in the ocean, and what clogs the slowly passing nights.

Yet if I cannot reach these distant realms of nature

because of some cold spiritless blood around my heart,

then let me love the country, the rivers running through valleys,

the streams and woodlands – happy, though unknown. Give me

broad fields and sweeping rivers, lofty mountain ranges

in distant lands, cold precipitous valleys, where I

may lie beneath the enormous darkness of the branches!

Landscape is visible and invisible

Virgil (*Georgics* 2 475–489) harvested here the perennial duality of the cognitive ('show me...how...by what...why') versus the phenomenological ('let me...give me...where I may') experience of landscape; 'the inherent contradictions between sensation and cognition, visibility and ideality' (Weiss 1998:9). This characteristic of the experience of landscape is reflected in the creation of landscapes, and designers of outside spaces from Antiquity to the present have oscillated their attentions in varying degrees between the invisible (experienced through the imagination, intellect and reason) and the visible (experienced through the senses) landscape; between its virtual and material existence. The virtual and the material, of course, form a bi-unity [duality] – the presence of both being the very conditions for an environment to be valued as a *landscape*: without the virtual we have merely surroundings, without the material we have merely dreams.

I must interrupt with a definition to avoid the probable chance that 'virtual landscape' will be understood as or associated with a digital landscape found in computer games, films or other non-material contemporary realms; virtual realities. I do not use it here to signify another type of reality, nor oppose the term with 'reality', rather posit it as that which accounts for the total experience of landscape that cannot be held entirely by the spatial-material world: 'Among its [landscape's] least analysed paradoxes is precisely its "virtual reality" – this combination of a felt experience of both organic and inorganic materials with a deliberate creation of fictive worlds into whose inventions, systems and mythological or metaphorical languages we allow ourselves to be drawn' (Hunt 2004:37–38). In physics 'virtual processes, entities, etc., are not actual, but their existence is postulated to explain certain effects' (Ross 1998:176). In the Middle Ages, certain concepts were developed to 'save appearances': the inaudibility of the ever present music ringing through the universe, was 'saved' by the idea that perpetual music cannot be differentiated with a state of no music and will thus seem silent; so there is something 'behind the sensuous curtain' (borrowed from Lewis 1935:152) of the garden that explains a rare moment of joy not accounted for by the water, grass and wind. Unlike the application in physics, I also do not imply that these 'virtual landscapes' are not 'actual' in the sense that they are not real; I only certainly mean that they are not material. I have therefore strayed from using 'fictive landscapes' which I find a term poetically more suited for the subject, but would imply that they are mere figments of the imagination.

I have also used the term 'designer' and not 'landscape architect' which might be expected for this publication. This simply because the latter term is such a recent one and one can hardly call Petrarch a 'landscape architect' and exclude his words of design wisdom because he wore not the title. I include all here concerned with outside space 'that has been created and shaped and therefore can be represented' (Vroom 2006:177–180); all concerned with the making of landscape, from landscape architects to dead poets.

To avoid writing an article of definitions, I will only briefly mention that with 'visible' landscape I include those unseen phenomena that are sensed, i.e. smells and sounds since they are, for those able, unavoidably experienced as part of matter, unlike the experience of the 'invisible'. I also include an abstract concept such as 'ecology,' which cannot be 'seen' but consists of a web of material (organic and otherwise) parts; an abstracted network of the visible.

Beauty is seeing the invisible in the visible

When we reflect on moments of experiencing Beauty in the landscape, we might find this duality inherent and agree with Joseph Addison who wrote in his essays *On the Pleasures of the Imagination* in 1711–1712: 'Our Imagination loves to be filled with an object, or to graspe at any thing that is too big for its Capacity. We are flung into a pleasing Astonishment at such unbounded Views, and feel a delightful Stillness and Amazement in the Soul at the Apprehension of them' (in Ross 1998:164). It is those precious moments (that we often do not find when we look for them) – that are akin to revelation, when understanding is *sensed* – when the virtual radiates from the material in a single moment; when we 'see the invisible in the visible' (Milbank 2003:2); when myth becomes fact. I have argued elsewhere (Prinsloo 2009:157–169) that the longing for these moments is what is desired when we look for Beauty in landscape and we never quite *arrive* in its fullest sense; we continually search for the virtual in the material and vice versa, yet the twine seldom meet.

Yet, in our graphic-based design world our expectation of Beauty is formed by pictures. Whether it be looking at a painting of a sublime landscape and then setting off in search of that *view*, or whether it is seeing the latest realistic rendering in a landscape architecture magazine, and waiting for the project's completion to see the image realised, we go in search to see the visible (the graphic) in the visible (the place). The distinction between the visible and the invisible landscape has imploded, in that the former has been dissolved into the latter through a (non-linear degressive) historic process; landscape was not always experienced as 'Views', which is a habit cultivated in modernity – this story begins long before the Romantic movement.

Bringing beauty to the surface: A short story of how the landscape became a (perspective) picture

A different perspective from the Middle Ages to the Renaissance

In an article 'I'm not there: on the ex situ experience of landscapes in texts' (2009) I reflected on two texts that represent a fundamental change in the conception, perception and representation of landscapes from the Medieval to the Modern world: from the world of *Roman de la Rose* [RR] by Jean de Meun (ca. 1230) and Guillaume de Lorris (ca. 1275), to that of the *Hypnerotomachia poliphili* [HP], possibly by Francesco Colonna (1499).

The first mentioned is an allegory of love set partly in a walled garden [*hortus conclusus*] and affirms that the material qualities of designed landscapes in the Middle Ages were similar to that of Antiquity – an expected continuity for the Medieval mind who had a great veneration for the old books and seldom wished to stray far from the wisdoms they contained: the Roman wall painting 'View of a garden' (ca. 20 BC) in the villa of Livia, wife of Augustus at Primaporte, could have been an illustration of the garden described in RR with 'so little in it that seems specific, tactile, visual' (Fleming in MacDougall 1985:201). Also expected of the age is the encyclopaedic nature of the text filled with pagan mythologies and Christian morals – contradictions in unity. (The world had not to wait for the Renaissance for the God of Love [Venus] to wake from her slumber on Cythera after the invasion of the barbarians.) It is important to note that the 'design ideas' (guidelines governing the visible landscape) were transmitted from Antiquity through texts, not images which had merely a representational value in the form of manuscript illuminations and paintings as the one mentioned; the makers of gardens imitated not drawings but followed the guides as interpreted by Albert the Great, Creschenzi *et al.* The virtual landscape (in this case wholly 'actual' and not merely fictive), however, reflected the Christianised world and the garden is represented as a shadow of the eternal garden: the text can be seen as a mediator between the material and the virtual to form a trinity of garden-text-heaven [empyrean]. It is in this unity that the 'aesthetic' can be found, not in the mere appearance of trees, flowers and fountains:

In the High Middle Ages, the possibility and experience of seeing the invisible in the visible, or of seeing the invisible **as** invisible (this is the necessary other aspect), was generally assumed and pervaded life, art and understanding. Therefore, there was no specific discipline of 'aesthetics', which only arose in the eighteenth century. Beauty took care of herself. (Milbank 2003:2)

In juxtaposition to the archetypal garden of the RR, the landscape, or rather artifacts, of the HP are lavishly detailed and 'is offered in place of a building' (Harbison 2000:76), i.e. the verbal descriptions of the series of landscapes through which Poliphilo strives after his love Polia in a dream, are very graphic: a reader with a thorough vocabulary of Classic architecture and symbolism can formulate a clear vision of what the places would **look** like – the woodcut illustrations bear witness to this, although in some cases the graphics differ slightly where, for example, mathematical errors crept into the text. The places described, which read more as surfaces, are no imitations of Classic architectural elements, but a fusion of these into original creations; the text of the HP provides not just a depository of architectural memories, but a method for reusing memories creatively – a genetic method...' (Lefaivre 2005:46).

For the sake of clarity and in a spirit of historic generalisation, we can view the HP as the beginning of an aestheticised attitude towards the design of landscape (Lefaivre 2005:3) – it was conceived with words, but set birth to a thousand images; a thousand pictures translated to objects in space; endless *views*. The Renaissance obsession with artifice leads to the desire to translate Ideas to form; to not see the invisible *as* invisible:

For the task of the artist, precisely like that of Eros, is always to join things that are separate and opposed. He seeks the 'invisible' in the 'visible', and the 'intelligible' in the 'sensible'. Although his intuition and his art are determined by his vision of pure form, he only truly *possesses* this pure form if he succeeds in realising it in matter. (Ernst Cassirer in his *The Individual and the Cosmos in Renaissance Philosophy* in Weiss 1998:24)

It was the dawn of modernity and the dawn of the perspective drawing: for the first time in history, drawing became the principal tool for the generation of design (Forty 2005:29); the slow, verbal transmission of ideas were supplanted by the conjuring of forms (strange, novel, awesome, bewildering, fantastic, wow, new) through images. I have speculated before (Prinsloo 2009:164) that the desire for materialising Idea was perhaps a result of 'the emptiness felt in the growing symbolic vacuity which rendered the planting of mere lilies [symbols of Mary] too **thin,** and paved the way for statues of Venus...as the study of nature moved beyond an inquiry of the purely symbolic into the structure of things **in themselves.**'

The third nature of the Renaissance thus became emblematic, i.e. idea and form (text and object) imploded, unlike the Medieval garden of which the material and virtual realities were distinct, both as mentioned, transmitted through texts: the former through practical guidelines, the latter through poetry. Another important shift occurred, this concerning first nature: poets regained *wylder nesse* as beautiful; Dante emerged from the 'gloomy wood' and gazed upwards to a mountain peak washed with the early morning sun (Dante *Inferno, Divine Comedy* ca. 1314, Canto I, 13–17):

> But when a mountain's foot I reach'd, where closed
>
> The valley that had pierced my heart with dread,
>
> I look'd aloft, and saw his shoulders broad
>
> Already vested with that planet's beam,
>
> Who leads all wanderers safe through every way.

'In *The Civilization of the Renaissance in Italy,* Jakob Burckhardt describes this paradigm shift in the perception of the external world, the moment in which the distant view, the "landscape" proper, was first valorised' (in Weiss 1998:9). 'This appreciation of natural beauty, couched in the poetry of the sublime, was further instantiated in the work of Francesco Petrarch (1304–1374)' (Weiss 1998:19) who ascended Mont Ventoux simply 'to see what so great an elevation had to offer' (in Weiss 1998:11) – the virtual landscape was found inside the observer.

It was, however, the perspective drawing that forever captured first nature as landscape that henceforth became a deified symbol of the pure and unspoilt. However, for the designers of landscapes in the Renaissance and ensuing Baroque period, it was the emblematic garden which held their interest with the exhalted natural landscape as background. Through a gradual process of boredom with symbols, the latter was brought to the fore.

The Romantic view

We have caught up with Joseph Addison whose love for landscapes with 'unbounded Views' prompted our brief story of how the landscape became a picture. Whereas the Renaissance picture of the natural landscape was not the ideal strived towards by designers, the Romantic spirit grew tired of emblematic gardenry and Mr. Addison in *The Spectator,* 'railed against the lack of sensitivity within the formal gardens in England, with their carefully clipped hedges trimmed to form "cones, globes, and pyramids"… [that] seemed out of step with the new naturalism' (Pregill & Volkman 1999:244–245). This sentiment was shared by many, including Antoine Joseph Dézallier d'Argenville who wrote in *La Théorie et la Pratique du Jardinage* (1709) 'there is nothing more pleasurable and agreeable in a garden than a good view of a fine landscape' and Toman (2007:231) notes that 'it may even be supposed that Dézallier d'Argenville's emphasis on the landscape factor and his commitment to nature provided some of the initial impetus for the adoption of the English landscape garden'. The orginal Promethean fire and orginality with which the symbols were forged from the old texts as artifacts in spaces, faded into imitation and perhaps, as the link to the texts was forgotten (graphics imitated graphics not texts, unlike the woodcut illustrations of the HP), they became, as with post-modernism, mere symbols of symbols. Stephanie Ross (1998:163), drawing from John Dixon Hunt, gives a good summary of this change in the taste for landscape:

Rather than the hard work of puzzling out the fixed meanings of such gardens, viewers desired landscapes that would mirror their feelings and moods … The answer to our question, then, about tiring of a garden seems to be this: we are most likely to tire of a garden's cognitive component, the meaning conveyed by its iconographic component … But the aspect of a garden which Hunt, Whately before him, focus on – the garden's ability to answer our changing feelings and moods – derives not from sensory appreciation or intellectual analysis but from imaginative play.

It seems that a desire to see the invisible *as* invisible (although in this context, unlike during the Middle Ages, not 'actual') recurred during the eighteenth and nineteenth centuries. As we know from the well-known Stourhead follies, these expressive (to use Hunt's term) landscapes were not wholly void of coded artefacts, but there only to unlock the sublime:

Gradually eighteenth-century aestheticians refined their theories to include the possibility that landscape also had the potential to elicit the sense of the sublime, if it contained sufficient historical references to elevate scene beyond mere natural effect. (Pregill & Volkman 1999:244)

With the experience of the sublime the invisible is acknowledged, yet always remains **unknown** (not 'actual') and before it we can **stand** in awe, but not understand – that of course was the Romantic view of Beauty: not senses alone, not understanding, but through spiritual illumination:

> The awful shadow of some unseen Power
>
> Floats though unseen among us – visiting
>
> This various world with as inconstant wing
>
> As summer winds that creep from flower to flower –
>
> Like moonbeams that behind some piny mountain shower,
>
> It visits with inconstant glance
>
> Each human heart and countenance;
>
> Like hues and harmonies of evening –
>
> Like clouds in starlight widely spread –
>
> Like memory of music fled –
>
> Like aught that is for its grace may be
>
> Dear, and yet dearer for its mystery.

Shelley (*Hymn to intellectual Beauty,* 1816:1–12) expressed that feeling of Beauty (in nature) as something Other and mysterious, a power of its own, unknown to Medieval man (for whom the distant skies above – which render us into a nihilistic feeling of smallness – were ordered, knowable and in perfect harmony), reminiscent of Classic writers (as in our opening lines of Virgil), glimpsed in Dante coming out of the wood and realised by Petrarch.

Nature thus (*wylder nesse* left behind in the Middle Ages, beautified in the Renaissance) became an exalted image of the primitive, the pure, the superior force, the unbounded from archaic laws, a *picture* – lost Eden:

> Immortal amarant, a flow'r which once
>
> In Paradise fast by the Tree of Life
>
> Began to bloom but soon for Man's offence
>
> To Heav'n removed where first it grew, there grows
>
> And flow'rs aloft, shading the Fount of Life
>
> And where the river of bliss through midst of Heav'n
>
> Rolls o'er Elysian flow'rs her amber stream.
>
> (Milton, *Paradise Lost,* III, 354–360)

The Romantic view was thus not superficial and the virtual landscape as virtual was to some extent regained by not fully translating it to objects, although the invisible became less defined than in the Middle Ages, yet its effect was of reducing landscape to image – again it was (and is) the imitation of the picturesque image of rolling hills and woodland that survived and countless unsustainable sprawling suburbs and golf courses are a-natural imitations of those sublime visions of nature. Nature was brought from its background status in the Renaissance to the foreground, as a façade.

The birth of the profession of landscape architecture, modernism and postmodernism and the lost text

Emerging from the end of the nineteenth century, the landscape architectural profession held the Romantic view. Taking this view to the complexities of the city, the pioneers such as Olmstead with his Emerald Necklace Park in Boston, managed to understand landscape as an ecological and even infrastructural system, and not merely as a picture. As with all great minds they were few, their works imitated with little thought and the landscape picture was taken to the suburbs, the parks in cities of smoke.

The landscape park was, however, not the only style (the stale reduction) for outside spaces, since the emblematic garden did not decay completely (as many Neoclassicist gardens testify) as have hereto been convenient for the story. Modernist landscape architects such as Dan Kiley and Garrett Eckbo sought, as the *zeitgeist* dictated, to create *Landscapes for Living* (also the title of an Eckbo publication of 1950) – words like 'form,' 'space' and 'function' were the necessary antidotes to a staled landscape tradition of dead symbolism and flat pattern-making; as railway stations looked like cathedrals, parks and gardens looked like the palace gardens of kings.

The ecologist movement that originated in the 1960s (though similar sentiments of the deification of nature and the *Myth of the Eternal Return* can be found throughout history) following Ian McHarg's (also necessary) ideas as presented in *Design with Nature* (1966), also purposefully negated the invisible landscape; Nature is pure, culture is harmful. [Both 'movements' fought the alienating and destructive landscapes created by industrialised urbanisation.] It should not come as a surprise that this movement started in a country with, from its colonial origins, a primitivist exaltation of nature unspoilt by the complexities of cultural tradition:

America...

you're not disturbed within your inmost

being

Right up till today's daily life

By useless remembering

And unrewarding strife. (Goethe 1821)

Meaning was missed and during the 1970s and 80s young landscape architects such as Martha Schwartz embraced the postmodern project's attack of the anti-symbolic attitude of the modernists and the anti-aesthetic attitude of the ecologists. Marc Treib (in Swaffield 2002:92–101) classified these attempts as expressions of various types of ideas such as genus of place and vernacular landscapes; attempts to make the **visible** visible. He has, however, criticised much of the work as being mere grapplings towards old symbols – meanings forced onto the land. This confirms the monistic tendency of postmodernity (Goosen 2007:176): a self referring system in which symbols only signify other symbols and communion between the visible and invisible is left unbridged:

Within a logo centric [not logocentric] economy, signs do not refer to a more basic, fundamental or essential reality but are signs of signs, figures of figures, images of images. Since everything appears to be image, nothing appears but appearance. (Taylor 1992: 188)

By having thus imploded the invisible into the visible, I suspect modernity has reduced landscape to surroundings and pruned Beauty to prettiness: the Webster dictionary defines landscape as 1) those portions of land which the eye can comprehend in a single view, and 2) representations of such land. Any person dabbling with the subject of landscape knows that it is a far more vague and complex construct and this definition inadequate, yet it reflects on a possibly serious degeneration of the Occident's Idea of landscape.

The ecology movement and the lost picture and the lost text

I have briefly mentioned above the ecological movement in landscape design, but need to digress on this movement's important role in de-picturing the landscape. The invisible associated with nature was no longer the symbolic, but the 'natural', the processes and laws, the forces which make 'the deep seas swell'. The invisible was thus not the invisible anymore, but the un**known**, which, through study, will eventually become known and visible – as the scientists (and phsycologists, anthropologists, marketing researchers *et al*) dig deeper into the world, less and less becomes unseen until the very landscape is left void of the virtual, thus of meaning and thus of Beauty.

But, the ecological movement importantly understood that landscape is more than *view* and through its focus on systems (not pictures) and processes paved the way for us to depicture landscape. It must, however, be noted that applications of 'ecological thinking' have rendered a new picture: the layer upon layer of diagrams which instil in the onlooker a positivistic calm that science is in control and a fine landscape shall be begotten from this thorough analysis. Scientism is not always un-Romantic, but it is almost always unliterary – within this mode of rational planning there is little room for the virtual landscape of texts.

The re-writing of the invisible landscape and the crafting of the visible

It would thus seem that throughout landscape design history, and I am speculating profusely, whenever a weariness for artifice was developed and Beauty was sought to be experienced in the imagination and not in the intellectual decoding of objects, a greater emphasis was placed on the virtual landscape to carry meaning, often existent in texts. Come the twentieth and twenty-first centuries though, and we find this to be less true: generally, we can say that the modernists were against the making of 'coded' landscapes and for the creation of spaces driven by concerns such as function and movement patterns. The ecological movement was (and is) similarly sceptical of landscapes filled with, what they might call 'artificial', symbolism and in favour of landscapes which are the result of natural processes, aided by scientifically sound (based on rigorous analysis) interventions of which the formal (and thus spatial) aspects thereof are of less importance and even unknown: 'McHarg's method insinuated that if the process were correct, the form would be good, almost as if an aesthetic automatically resulted from the objective study.' (Treib in Swaffield 2002:91.) Meaning will come from within, as to an onlooker of an abstract painting.

Yet, unlike the Romantic Movement, there was no thought of the virtual landscape; no texts to invite our imaginations to see the invisible in the visible, no texts to make the invisible. Not that these paradigms had no imaginative underpinnings: for some (perhaps unconsciously), modernism evoked a Wagnerian sense of that cold and vast **northerness**[1] and ecological thinking a primitivist longing for untouched Nature, present in culture long before the scientists discovered our impending, self-inflicted doom:

> One impulse from a vernal wood
>
> May teach you more of man,
>
> Of moral evil and of good,
>
> Than all the sages can

From *'The tables turned'* (William Wordsworth 1798)

The modernist and ecologist virtual landscapes can be said to be crafted and held in the seminal texts associated with these movements (such as Le Corbusier's *Towards a new architecture* and Carson's *Silent spring* respectively), but as works of literature not written intentionally for the imagination, they only manage to dimly make themselves present *in situ*.

It is perhaps for this reason (as with the 'symbolic vacuity' in the wake of the Middle Ages) that the emblematic landscape resurged with postmodernism. But the signs mediate not between the visible and the invisible, but between the visible and the visible – they are like branding logos, not like texts.

In the twentieth century, we do thus not find the text-like landscapes of the Renaissance, but we also do not find the landscapes-in-texts of the Middle Ages and Romantic era; an experience of the invisible has been reduced to subjective feelings.

In attempting to understand the processes of landscape and create more than landscapes for living, but living landscapes, the ecologists made an important step to de-picture the landscape, yet the reactionary postmodernism's symbolism reminds us of the perpetual need for men to engage with the earth on a level deeper than management for posterity. Standing at the end of the first decade of the twenty-first century, the theoretical field of landscape urbanism, tired as others have been before of the emblematic (in this case, postmodernism) and re-valuing the scientific approach of the ecologists, is thus at danger to repeat the latter's inability to acknowledge and cultivate the invisible landscape. Concerning the visible landscape, landscape urbanism's scepticism of 'spatial order' and focus on 'irrigation of territories with potential' (Koolhaas & Mau 1995:969) is at danger to negate spatial qualities; much time is spent on overlaying data with GIS packages and producing vague collages (since the final outcome of 'staged'[2] landscapes are not known), little time is (rather intentionally) spent on exploring details, proportions, space and other aspects which enjoyed the modernist's full attentions. The profusion of collages (typically of people jogging, cycling and listening to iPods) that have been created for landscape urbanist project proposals, importantly shows a commitment to keep the balance of nature-culture-technology – it is the invisible which is still eluded, the visible ill crafted. If twenty-first century landscape architecture does not wake the virtual landscape from its hundred year slumber, and if it does not produce landscapes which are richly sensed on foot, it will perpetuate a **thin**, albeit sustainable, world.

In the design process, the type of notation system plays an important role in the type of landscape produced as for example the perspective drawing established landscape as view, from the clean line drawing emerged spatially centred places void of symbolism, from the collage comes the eclectic logo, from the map overlays and diagrams grows the return-to-nature; by designing and communicating with pictures, landscapes are reduced to surfaces and by designing with abstract notations, landscapes are reduced to nature. In the following section, I have summarised and expounded some thoughts (which ori inated in my professional Master's degree dissertation, entitled *stadskrif* (2006)) on the uses of text as a non-graphic design tool in an introductory attempt to move beyond the scientific diagram and the seducing collage. These are categorised as follows, but note that the order and some of the descriptions have been altered for clarity from Prinsloo 2006 and 2009. Text as:

I. as a graphic *in situ*

II. a mediator between form and phenomenological experience

III. a way to thicken landscape as signifier

IV. a way to alter landscape perceptions

V. a way to thicken *in situ* and *ex situ* landscape experiences

I to III are directly associated with the act of design, whereas IV and V are more closely related to the experience of landscape, before and/or after the design process and landscape installation.

I: An application of text as a design tool (or rather element) that has not been lost in contemporary landscape architecture, is the physical placement of words in spaces – either presented purely as information on signage boards (from 'don't walk on the grass' to descriptions of site-related historic events) to texts that are designed to be formal elements in themselves. When applied in the latter manner, unlike the other applications of text discussed below, verbal language *in situ* gains a material presence thus contributing to the visible landscape in addition to the cognitive experience it induces, thus facilitating the seeing of the invisible landscape. These texts can refer the occupant of the space to external worlds (e.g. words from a poem or names of dead soldiers) or relate purely to the immediate context (e.g. create a tension between the content of the word and the content of the space through irony or paradox). Designers who have successfully used text (both for its physical and thought-provoking qualities) to create memorable places are Ian Hamilton Finlay, Maya Lin, Willem Boshoff and Dieter Kienast. First-mentioned inserted Latin inscriptions in landscapes such as Little Sparta and Stockwood Park to create anachronistic moments in a world where serious references to Antiquity (not pastiche Neo-Classicism) are branded as highbrow conservative and intellectual with its negative association of being exclusive, priggish and 'out of touch'. The texts engraved in stone, not being understood by most, 'jar on our secularism' (Finlay) as a 'counterattack against modern culture' (Claude Gintz on Finlay's Stonypath garden in Ross 2001:101). For those visitors of these places not affronted by the act of thinking or opening a dictionary, the words tap into that eternal sunwashed virtual landscape born in Antiquity – accessed through the gates of gardens in the Middle Ages, Renaissance and Romantic era until, when landscape architecture became a profession at the end of the nineteenth century, no more gates were built; texts *in situ* can mediate between the visible and invisible – they do not create or enhance virtual landscapes, they grant access.

As with many good ideas, it has become a stale practice through unthoughtful imitation and repetition: as text-covered walls in coffee shop and deli interiors with words such as 'eat', 'pure', 'indulge' have become a common sight, so lines of text in outdoor spaces can be found wherever there is a desire for meaning simply because words, by their very nature, *appear* to say something. Where the words lose their mediative role and become *things in themselves* they are reduced to artifacts, as words in concrete poetry are often reduced to pictures. Reflecting on her 'Reading a garden' project at the Cleveland Public Library (1996–98), Maya Lin expressed caution against this:

I have often combined text with sculptural forms, but I have always wanted the integration between sculpture and text to be less a surface-applied event than one in which the words and the meaning correspond to the space and one's movement through it (Lin 2000:6:36)

Although the words are not merely 'surface-applied' they are more sculptural than textual, quite intentionally as the collaborative poet Tan Lin has said of the work: 'I have tried to create poems in which the words themselves are central and can be seen as objects in themselves' (Tan Lin in Lin 2000:6:38).

II: As mentioned, *landscape* exists both visibly and invisibly, and is experienced empirically and cognitively; through the senses and in the mind. For a designer, an attention to the phenomenology (Heidegger's 'a return to things' (in Safranski 2002:75)) of place should thus be an intrinsic part of his creative process – a landscape is 'nothing if it does not insist on its own tangible existence' (Hunt 2004:37–38). The commonly used graphic tools that are used to generate designs are, however, not appropriate for the full exploration of place as it would be sensed *in situ*. As the illustrations of a story book can only tell part of the tale (the beautiful illustration by Doré of Virgil and Dante standing at the gate of hell, can alone not say 'All hope abandon, ye who enter here'), so design graphics cannot completely represent places, especially '... everything that they [architects] find difficult, or choose not to be precise about – nuances, moods, atmosphere...' (Forty 2005:38).

That the Science of Cartography is Limited

and not simply by the fact that this shading of

forest cannot show the fragrance of balsam

(Eavan Boland 1994)

The graphic-centred design process of contemporary landscape architecture should then come as a surprise and its shortcomings obvious; perspective drawings should be labelled 'This is not a landscape'.

In the book *Writing worlds: discourse, text, and metaphor in the representation of landscape*, the editors Barnes and Duncan (1992:xii) 'examining what it is that we do as geographers when we represent landscapes, real or imagined, through our writings' state that 'the one thing we believe geographical writing is not is a faithful duplication of an external reality. Much more is going on than mechanical reproduction'. With the popular use of realistic computer rendered imagery (representations), as landscape architects we have perhaps forgotten they do not create a 'faithful duplication of an external reality'[3] and fool ourselves in believing that if a pretty perspective has been made, a good landscape will follow. We are outside drawings, we *view* them, yet we are *in* landscapes, we experience them. To more fully explore the latter, we must speak or write:

More particularly, both projections [orthogonal and perspective], like all drawings, presuppose that one is outside the object...its exteriority to us requires us to suppose that perception, as well as the thing perceived lies outside the mind. Language places no such demands on us: the words themselves carry no illusions, but act directly upon the mind; language allows perception to happen where it belongs, within the mind. (Forty 2005:41)

Much richness of the materiality (phenomenology) of a landscape cannot be represented or crafted (generated) through graphics; a smell cannot be as well drawn as it can be described in words, nor the intended value of a place:

(m)ake a place in the house, perhaps only a few feet square, which is kept locked and secret; a place which is virtually impossible to discover – until you have been shown where it is; a place where the archives of a house, or other more potent secrets, might be kept (Alexander 1977:931).

Psychologists like Goldstein and Scheerer have gone as far as to state that thoughts bound with images limit the intellect to one fixed on the appearances of things (in Lym 1980:22–23). Therein, according to Bruner (ibid.), goes lost an understanding of the world as being more than surfaces and produces, as I have named it elsewhere (Prinsloo 2009), a **thin** world – worryingly, by the way, contemporary teaching methods support image-based learning. Since, as mentioned before, one easily tires of surface (of pictures) this leads to the never-ending production of new aesthetics, of new appearances for landscapes and a tradition of constantly breaking tradition. The obsession with object is warranted by the graphic centred design process: 'Where spoken and written language, as a matter of course, appeals constantly to the metalanguage, allowing it to be both ambiguous and precise, architectural drawings generally aim to stick to the "object language" and to restrict "additional, shifted meanings"' (Forty 2005:39).

Generating design using text thus forces the creator to describe the quality of **phenomenon** in addition to their mere appearances before form is generated graphically. This was experimented, for example, by Archizoom in the 1960s:

Listen, I really think it's going to be something quite extraordinary. Very spacious, bright, really well arranged, with no hidden corners, you know. There will be fine lighting, really brilliant, that will clearly show up all those disordered objects.

The fact is, everything will be simple, with no mysteries and nothing soul-disturbing, you know. Wonderful! Really very brilliant – very beautiful – very beautiful, and very large. Quite extraordinary! It will be cool in there too, with an immense silence.

My God, how can I describe to you the wonderful colours! You see many things are quite hard to describe, especially because they'll be used in such a new way...You see, there'll be a lot of marvellous things, and yet it will look almost empty, it will be so big and so beautiful...How fine it will be...just spending the whole day doing nothing, without working or anything...You know, just great ... (Ambasz in Forty 2005:34)

The text describes the essential character of the design (that which is to be sensed) without delineating form – this allows for a multitude of design translations, all differing in *appearance*, but not in **sense**. This was one of the original motivations for Christopher Alexander's *Pattern language*, which attempted not to prescribe the surfaces of objects, but the principles of good place-making which, if not applied as one would a recipe, would result in the making of positive place:

We have tried to write each solution in a way which imposes nothing on you. It contains only those essentials which cannot be avoided if you really want to solve the problem. In this sense, we have tried, in each solution, to capture the invariant property common to all places which succeed in solving a problem. (Alexander 1977:xiii–xiv)

This aspect of text is fortuitous for the landscape urbanist spirit of staging rather than fixing spaces. In being bent on achieving a drawn 'view', natural and cultural processes are often frozen or bulldozed artificially; in keeping **qualities**, one can work with a much lighter hand and be open for the unknown outcome of a staged approach in which interventions only catalyse and guide the evolution of a landscape.

In achieving the 'view', clients often point to pictures (which they are sometimes given by the designer) to say 'that's what I want' and the **idea** of the picture is lost. Relevant to South Africa is the want of a 'Tuscan' or 'Provincial' garden, or house for that matter. Since the client is not educated in the language of the design, he cannot translate, nor understand the picture – what is it therein that he finds to be pleasing and worthy of imitation? If the principles of the picture are to be spoken (or written) it might become apparent that it was not the statue of Cupid (the Client is most often unaware of the mythical identity and importance of the figure) that is sought, but the presence of symbolism (often lacking in the precedents brought forth by the designer who has since the misunderstood Loos regarded all literal symbolism as folly); not the hedge of lavender, but the presence of fragrance and soft texture; not the terracotta tiles and 'rusticated' plaster, but texture of surface and acceptance of decay; not the made-to-look-old shutter windows (of fixed position), but devices for passive climate control. The client must be asked to de*scribe* – to script – the desired space for that will force him to consider the phenomenology and not fall into the empty confusion of pictures; the story is written, the designer gives it form as a director translates a script into a film.

As part of an explorative design process in *stadskrif* (Prinsloo 2006), I wrote a series of texts that describe the sought phenomenological qualities of left-over spaces in the inner city of Pretoria, **before** the designs for these sites were generated graphically. The descriptions were written from the perspective of an onlooker as if the places have already been transformed through interventions that react to the physical realities of the sites as studied through site analysis. One such site is on the corner of Vermeulen and Palace Streets:

The trees' evergreen foliage provides shade. The sound of running water softens the street noise – a well with deep, clear water is taken by hands to wash faces that sweat. Old men sit with their backs against a wall and gaze at children that splash each other wet. They sail boats carved from the branches of the *Acacia karoo* trees in Vermeulen Street. Around the well the dappled light glistens the wet patterns of pavement pebbles (Prinsloo 2006:74. Translated from the Afrikaans by the author).

These descriptions captured the essence of the visible qualities that the designs needed to capture and ensured that the design was not merely the result of pictures. It must be confessed that the final design for the given example contained neither a water feature nor patterned pebbles! This was due to a flaw in the verbal description that negated the problem of maintenance associated with urban water elements. As usual to any design process, it is circular and reiterative by nature. Philip Webb (in *Forty* 2005:34) will conclude this section for us: 'The ability to make picturesque sketches was a fatal gift to the architect.

III: Whereas the above discussion was concerned with text as a medium to explore the visible landscape, we now shift our attention to the invisible. As mentioned, the graphic driven design process which is inherently occupied with the visible, the surface, provides us with little to make places that are more than themselves and therefore bereave us of Beauty.

We have talked about the virtual landscape and how it faded from experience in the twentieth century, but how do we re-access a place that is not there: the virtual landscape of Cythera, the winds of Zephyrus, the avenging seas of Juno, and the beach of a shipwrecked Aeneas exist, but not in the minds of visitors to contemporary outside spaces. That is why the statues of Venus have become dead symbols, for they no longer mediate between two real worlds: the material and the virtual. A Coca-Cola logo means more. The virtual exists, but the texts are not accessed. New virtual landscapes need be created in new texts for new landscapes of meaning to grow.

Perhaps another reason for the death of the virtual landscape is the multi-cultural milieu in which most designers work ensuring a hesitance to grapple with meaning for the sake of political correctness – to please everyone in the public realm, form is generated within the lowest common frame of reference. The result is a diluted shade of grey. And this is expected, for we should ask: even if virtual landscapes are created in texts and translated into material places as suggested, whose meanings do we infuse in the text, whose values, whose ideas, myths, ideals:

Is there a history common to all in a society or is there no shared past? Whose history should be remembered and celebrated in public places? Is art separate from the everyday, or rooted in the normal processes of living? Is art the province of the expert, or can, and does, everyone participate? Should places exert power over people or empower them? The opposing answers to such opposing questions lead to opposing natures, histories, arts, powers... (Spirn 1998:244)

In South Africa this 'problem of meaning' is evident in projects such as Freedom Park where designers (mostly grounded in a Western design tradition) had to grapple with the translation of ideas foreign to their own backgrounds.

Texts can successfully be used to act as depositories of complex and conflicting ideas. As argued in the discussion on Medieval landscapes, texts can carry some of the content of a landscape without the need to translate, as is often the desire, every idea associated with the landscape into form – seeing the invisible as invisible. By thus linking a design and a created text, the two stand together in a reciprocal relationship: the landscape signifies the ideas captured in the text and the former is thereby not cluttered with content, yet not void of meaning. This, significantly, allows for multiple texts to be associated with a single material landscape; various virtual landscapes that 'save appearances' differently for different people. This is what we typically find in 'natural' landscapes with strong cultural meanings: one landscape is the front of many (sometimes colliding) narratives.

Writers, wake from your inward looking nihilism and write again of landscapes – join our struggle!

IV: Perceptions of landscapes, influenced by the metaphors associated therewith (Spirn 1998:24), greatly affect the way that they are experienced – physically or virtually. We now thus move our attentions away from the making of place to being in place, *in situ* or *ex situ*.

For example, the following are extracts from William Burchell's exploration of the nineteenth-century Cape Colony to assess South Africa's potential for British settlers:

There was a small garden fenced round with a dry hedge, and irrigated by a trench which conducted water from a spring not far off; and in it were cultivated chiefly tobacco, maize, pumpkins and dakka. The lowing of the oxen, the milking of the cows, and the playfulness of the goats butting against each other, or familiarly browsing close to the huts, or mingling with the dogs and cattle, gave a truly pastoral character to the spot; while the abundance of trees rendered the scene rich and harmonious to the eye, and solicited the attempts of my pencil...in this romantic valley...(Burchell 1824:7)

The **delightful scenery** of the Gariep had lost nothing of its power of pleasing, by having been admired so often before; but as I had not until now beheld the willows in their sober **autumnal colors**, they possessed for me, a new charm. In Africa we look in vain for those mellow beautiful tints with which the sun of autumn dyes the forests of England. Examples of this change of color meet the eye so rarely in these arid deserts, that whenever they do perchance occur, they will forcibly, and by a natural association of ideas, remind the European traveller [sic] of his native land... (Burchell 1824:10)

He praises, with the delight of one lost in a desert on the sight of an oasis, those views which resemble the Romantic landscape paintings of his native England. The Karoo was one of the landscapes which was not to Burchell's taste and described as 'wild, desolate and singular'. It took those who grew up in that vast landscape (N.P. van Wyk Louw and Eve Palmer come to mind) to see her Beauty and transform the landscape for others into a place of rich phenomenology. The virtual landscape of nineteenth century Karoo, that landscape which – by not conforming to the criteria of picturesque Beauty – explained Burchell's experience thereof, was altered. Thus, the same landscape is changed by altering its virtual existence in words. In Europe we look in vain for the Karoo copper light of dawn that washes the dying afternoon's clouds of cream. In describing the unique characteristics of a landscape, texts are powerful means to unlock beauty and alter our perceptions of landscapes – often a requirement before there is a felt need to transform a place through design.

It need of course not be doubted that graphics too can profoundly (positively or negatively) alter perceptions of landscapes and thus the relationship of men therewith. We need only think of the photographs of the overgrown tracks in New York that partly inspired the creation of The Highline park or any image of natural disaster that stirs feelings of environmental responsibility. Again, it is only on an aesthetic level (as with moving journalistic photographs that often, being void of contextual or background information, evoke unjustified feelings, be it of sentimental pity, misplaced anger or stirring passions of revolt) and thus the complete character of a landscape – not merely its appearance – can be transformed with the exaltation of its inherent (oft unseen) qualities.

In a residential project proposal with the architect Elmo Swart, I attempted to persuade the clients not to demolish the existing house on the site (as was their request), but to transform the house into a garden. This drastic proposal (which was admittedly not accepted) required a change of perception – decay can be a design agent – which was introduced by a text:

More than a house

What makes a house a dwelling? Is it the walls, roof and windows; the beds, bath and kitchen cabinets; the linen drawers, bookshelves and stairs? Or should we rather ask, what makes dwelling possible, rather than **a** dwelling? The Middle English meaning of 'dwelling' is related to 'tarry', i.e. to stay longer than intended; to delay leaving a place. If our idea of dwelling is expanded beyond those activities associated with a normal suburban house, to that of simply **being** or even **lingering**, we can also expand our idea of what a house can be, or more importantly for our discussion, can **become**.

The sublime ruin

The origin of the word 'ruin' is related to the verb 'to fall'. As with ruin, we usually associate falling with something negative, but therein lies a special paradox to be discovered: falling presupposes rising, organic decay presupposes plant growth, death presupposes life and ruin presupposes the sublime.

Synthesis: To dwell in ruin

To achieve dwelling in a house, we can deconstruct the house. We can search for a different way for it to fulfil its purpose. We can bring the house to **ruin** and create hidden gardens. The house is deconstructed from something that keeps the outside outside to something that brings the outside inside. One enters out. The **ruined** house becomes a place to **linger**. The house **becomes** a dwelling.

The necessary beauty of the South African landscape is impeded by perceptions: farms, highways, high-speed railways, power plants are functional, talk not of aesthetics; inner cities are dangerous, stay in the suburbs; walls are walls, garden on the ground; veld grasses are home to snakes, plant lawn; landscaping is a frivolous luxury item, cut the budget – pave the surface; pave this land – it is cheaper and easier to maintain. A culture of appreciating landscape is restricted to the bountiful natural areas of national pride (as views of first nature), and a positive perception towards third nature lacks – what benefit a literary project of altering landscape perceptions holds, I am unsure, and how to go about it I am completely uncertain, but I suspect that such a task is necessary to de-picture the flower bed.

Altering perceptions can thus benefit our efforts before the making of a place – to instigate interest – or afterwards to translate the value of a place where previously it was thought uncomely and support the vitalisation of the landscape urbanist Alan Berger's 'drosscapes'.

V: For all the reading and writing on landscapes we do, we spend little time **in** landscapes. Many who are well acquainted with gardens from the Baroque Versailles to the deconstructed La Villette, Turrel's desertscapes, inaccessible roof gardens, heroic modernist plazas and any other outside spaces that deserve attention, have never been there. More accurately, have never been to the material, the visible, landscapes, but have certainly dwelt in the virtual. Text (comfortably accompanied by graphics) is an excellent medium through which to experience the virtual component of landscapes: when we **read** a landscape we are drawn into the world of its meaning and mytho-romantic resonance which oft evokes a feeling akin to *sehnsucht* (Prinsloo 2009:166) – however, when we arrive at the place longed for, our experience is shifted to the material landscape and it is the senses that form our impression of the place: the radial layout of Versailles representing the power of Louis XIV so admired in the lecture hall, so eagerly sought to see, vanishes softly behind a **sense** of grandeur; is the sound of water here different from elsewhere; is the sitting in the shade not the same as at home; does the gaze at statues not tire us quickly, and has the long walk not made us seek rest as the everyday walk to work? And days after the visit, on recollecting the experience *ex situ*, suddenly the virtual and material seem to make out one place and 'we once again long for **there**' (Prinsloo 2009:166).

Texts thus commonly enhance our experience of landscape through the reading of articles, magazines, books (these act as *ekprases* (Prinsloo 2009:165)), but seldom do designers make use of this fact in the making of place. The visual poem by Tan Lin (that visitors take with them) for Maya Lin's library garden is a contemporary exception.

The *in situ* experience of eighteenth century Romantic landscapes, however, was and still is greatly enriched by a knowledge of the Greek elegies which partly informed the landscapes' content – scenes from the Ancient texts, embodied in statues and structures, unfold to the beholder as one moves through the landscape, reminiscent of Tschumi's *Cinégramme Folie* (Prinsloo 2006:30). The reverse is also true: one often finds an *ex situ* experience of a landscape, when transported there through a text, to be more enriching than when being there (Prinsloo 2009).

The Portuguese architect Pancho Guedes (who practised in Mozambique and South Africa) talked of drawings, paintings and sculptures being part of buildings – not mere representations or means to material ends. This fact is to an extent acknowledged and designers go to great pains to create beautiful imagery that becomes part of the place, yet words are left to others.

Two types of text: A suggestion

In an attempt to synthesise these 'applications' of text in the design process, I suggested (Prinsloo 2006) that two types of text can be written for the two spheres of landscape: to write the visible, a **phenomenological text** and to write the invisible, a **story**. Both texts are written as mediums for the formal and ideal conception of landscapes and, by being made accessible to users, to enhance the experience of the visible and invisible landscape by mediating between these realms. The first mentioned text draws much from site analysis; from the more quantitive aspects of landscape. The second draws from the qualitative realm: the designer's background, the history of the site, the *genus loci et cetera*, from whence the virtual landscape starts taking form.

Conclusion

Preceding the above discussion on the value of verbal language (I have focused on texts) for the design and experience of landscape, I argued that contemporary landscape architecture (with landscape urbanism being a potential leader of thought and practice) must not, with its focus on process, neglect the phenomenological landscape (the visible) nor leave the virtual landscape (the invisible) unmediated. This plead and dim guide to verbalise the landscape is at risk to abstract the landscape, which will only perpetuate the 'disenchantment of the world' (Max Weber in Graham 2007:45) for, while making this appeal to re-value the non-visual, I am confronted with a paradox: the design of landscapes is not visual enough! In any given landscape project, the amount of time spent on written communication via e-mails and faxes, the endless verbal battles in meetings, the pages and pages of magazine articles, the booming Internet blogs, the environmental reports, reports, reports, project descriptions for competition entries...often outweigh the process of drawing and we can still wonder with Garret Eckbo (1969:ix–x) whether it is possible for us 'to imagine a world in which visual experience would be as important as verbal'. The West has become increasingly abstract, increasingly verbal and now increasingly virtual (here I mean it in the digital sense), while the physical landscapes outside our windows are increasingly ugly. May landscape-texts guide us from this winter of disenchantment, not shut the windows.

Epilogue[4]

Between the water pond

and the nymph

is a myth;

between the midnight grotto

and the sex

is a text.

Between the ice forest

and the battle drum

is a song;

between the desert sky

and the Nothing

is the longing.

Between the lilac fields

and Elysium

is a dream;

between the lit street trees

and the longing

is nothing. (finding)

Between the mountain peak

and a soul pristine

is St Augustine;

between the pictorial scene

and heaven's glory

is a story.

For the kingdom is around the bend

Bibliography

Alexander, C. 1977. *A Pattern Language: Towns, Buildings, Construction.* New York: Oxford University Press.

Barnes, T.J. & Duncan, J.S. (eds). 1992. *Writing worlds: Discourse, text, and metaphor in the representation of landscape.* New York: Routledge.

Barzun, J. 1961. *The house of intellect.* London: Secker and Warburg.

Brayer, M. (ed). 2004. *Archilab's urban experiments: Radical architecture, art and the city.* London: Thames and Hudson.

Burchell, W.J. Esq. 1824. *Travels in the Interior of Southern Africa: Volume II.* London: Longman, Hurst, Rees, Orme, Brown and Green, Paternoster-Row.

Eckbo, G. 1969. *The landscape we see.* Michigan: McGraw-Hill.

Forty, A. 2000. *Words and buildings: A vocabulary of modern architecture.* New York: Thames & Hudson.

Goosen, D. 2007. *Die Nihilisme.* Dainfern: Uitgewery Praag.

Graham, G. 2007. *The re-enchantment of the world: Art versus Religion.* Oxford: Oxford University Press.

Hunt, J. D. 2004. *The afterlife of gardens.* Philadelphia: University of Philadelphia Press.

Koolhaas, R. & Mau, B. 1995. *S, M, L, XL.* New York: Monicelli Press.

Lefaivre, L. 2005. *Leon Battista Alberti's Hypnerotomachia poliphili : Recognizing the Architectural Body in the early Italian Renaissance.* Cambridge, Massachusetts: MIT Press.

Lewis, C.S. 1935. *The Allegory of Love: A Study in Medieval Tradition.* London: Oxford University Press.

Lewis, C.S. 1955. *Surprised by Joy.* New York: Harcourt Brace Jovanovich.

Lin, M. 2000. *Boundaries.* New York: Simon & Schuster.

Lym, G.R. 1980. *A psychology of building: How we shape and experience our structured spaces.* New Jersey: Prentice Hall.

MacDougal, E. 1985. *Dumbarton Oaks Colloquium on the History of Landscape Architecture IX: Medieval Gardens.* Meriden-Stinehour Press.

Milbank, J. 2003. *Theological perspectives on God and beauty.* New York: Trinity Press International.

Milton, J. 1952. *The poetical works of Milton.* London: Oxford University Press.

Pregill, P. & Volkman, N. 1999. *Landscapes in history design and planning in the Eastern and Western traditions.* New York: John Wiley & Sons.

Prinsloo, J.N. 2006. *stadskrif.* Pretoria: University of Pretoria. (ML (Prof) thesis).

Prinsloo, J.N. 2009. I'm not there: On the ex situ experience of landscape architecture in texts. *South African Journal of Art History 24* (1), pp.157–169.

Ross, S. 1998. *What gardens mean.* Chicago: University of Chicago Press.

Safranski, R. 2002. *Martin Heidegger: between good and evil.* Cambridge, MA.: Harvard University Press.

Spirn, A. W. 1998. *The language of landscape.* London: Yale University Press.

Swaffield, S. 2002. *Theory in Landscape Architecture: A reader.* University of Pennsylvania Press: Philadelphia.

Taylor, M. 1992. *Disfiguring.* Chicago: University of Chicago Press.

Toman, R. 2007. *European garden design: From classical antiquity to the present day.* Tandem Verlag GmbH.

Treib, M. (ed). 2008. *Representing landscape architecture.* New York: Taylor and Francis.

Vroom, M. J. 2006. *Lexicon of garden and landscape architecture.* Basel: Birkhäuser.

Waldheim, C. (ed). 2006. *The Landscape Urbanism Reader.* New York: Princeton Architectural Press.

Weiss, A.S. 1998. *Unnatural horizons: Paradox and contradiction in landscape architecture.* New York: Princeton Architectural Press.

---

1   As was used by C.S. Lewis to describe a 'cold, spacious, severe, pale and remote' (1955:17) place that is perpetually longed for, evoked, for example, by Norse mythology.

2   The term 'staging of surfaces' is used by James Corner in an essay *Terra Fluxus* in *The Landscape Urbanism Reader* (Waldheim 2006:28) as one of the themes of landscape urbanism, echoing Koolhaas' 'staging of uncertainty' in S, M, L, XL (1995) to denote a less object-driven design approach.

3   Marc Treib has also expressed a concern with the prevailing mode of graphic representation: 'the advent of software programs such as Photoshop has granted an enormous power to designers in terms of realism and accuracy, but these may be achieved at the expense of a sense of life and a confusion of detail for idea' (Treib 2008:xix) and there is 'a call for representation to be linked to thinking rather than to the mere creation of special effects that capture the eye without necessarily effectively engaging the brain'.

4   This poem was inspired by T.S. Eliot's *The Hollow Men,* written in 1925.

chapter 3

The Transient Aspects of City Life: Their Understanding and Interpretation for Design Purposes

Ida Breed

Departamento de Estudios Urbanos

Universidad Autónoma Metropolitana

México D.F.

Department of Architecture

University of Pretoria

Pretoria

South Africa

Introduction

The constant debate in the public realm about the design and construction of the built environment and its accompanying urban space influences the way in which cities are perceived, created and transformed over time. Neglected aspects of urban space and city life need to be identified and revealed for more encompassing considerations in the future of these cities. As designers of urban environments, living in these environments does not naturally give us the ability to acknowledge the forgotten or neglected. Even those who occupy themselves with social phenomena find this a difficult task due to the density and corresponding anonymity of the post-industrial city. As pointed out by Berger and Luckmann (1968:53):

I am constantly surrounded by objects that 'proclaim' the subjective intentions of my fellow man [sic], although at times it is hard to know with certainty what a particular object 'proclaims', especially if it has been produced by people that I have not been able to get to know well or in totality, in face-to-face situations... (Berger & Luckmann 1968:53)

The complexity of the urban environment seen from a humanist perspective confronts us with the convolutions of human nature: subjectivity, meaning and experience.

In South Africa since the nineties the socio-political environment has encouraged a greater degree of public consultation and dialogue in government planning, precisely due to the discrimination in the past. This concept of people-centred development aims to incorporate the 'multifaceted differentiated experiences of people in space (geographically specific localities) punctuated by particular historical phenomena (archived, indexed and narrated in distinct memory forms)' (Williams, 2000:168). There has been a preoccupation with social justice, equity and efficiency in studies of urban space, a tendency to view South African cities purely as a product of the apartheid system. Included in these discussions are also the flaws of spatial restructuring, i.e. polarisation of our cities, restricted spaces and exclusive suburban enclosures. The argument is held that the apartheid city is extended and re-produced since the utopian visions for the future of cities are controlled by the way in which current problems of these cities and therewith their potential solutions are de-fined. It would be advantageous to situate South African cities in relation to the urban verve that underscores the unique and unusual aspects of our city life and city forms (Mbembe & Nuttall 2007).

Globally there has been a marked critique and a follow-on attempt to move away from anonymous standardisation in the design of the built environment (urban form) (Goh, 2001:1597). Despite the economic and psychological advantages of homogenisation and mass production in a globalised world, it is through this abstraction of society that the unique and unusual aspects of the lived experience are lost. 'In our own daily prac-tice, we deal more and more with abstract representations and codifications of society which are wrenched out of the lived experience of both ourselves and others' (Merri-field 2000:181). Consequently variety, diversity and individuality hold more weight than before (Simon, 2004). This has increased the motive for the understanding of differ-ence with impartiality and at an urban design level has encouraged a search for more fitting design solutions in urban public spaces for present-day society that counteracts homogeny.

People-centred development in South Africa has revived the interest in the concrete realities of everyday life that deals with the functional, social and personal needs of specific users and also deals with this concern for difference. In design, these concrete, active and changing aspects of the urban environment are not easy to quantify. As cities and the cultures and lifestyles within them are continuously changing a socio-spatial dialectic transpires where we shape the city and the city shapes us (Lefebvre 1991). As a consequence these concrete realities of the urban environment are not only hard to capture but often regarded as transitory and therefore inconsequential (Kallus, 2001).

According to Kallus (2001) the common dilemma is that 'although the city is examined and designed on the implicit premise of human experience, this experience is never discussed or considered specifically enough to make a difference' (Kallus 2001:130). In design narrative, the complexity and continuity of the urban space is examined and understood as related to the physical form of the built environment. It is this abstrac-tion of urban space and its functions that enables a spatial dialogue that is often used to inform the design of physical form. This dialogue views the city as a physical spatial structure and is more preoccupied with the nature of space than with its uses. 'Con-centrating on the abstract concept of the spatial experience rather than on concrete day-to-day life has ignored the users and their functional, social and emotional needs' (Kallus 2001:130).

The physical and tangible form of the city often takes precedence in design narrative and its role in the social realm of the city is therefore dwelled on and has been criticised in New Urbanism assumptions (Talen 1999). Dyckman (in Talen, 1999) points out that physical form has varied significance and is subject to the homogenous or diverse na-ture of urban communities:

Where a population is socially, culturally, and economically very homogenous, and of uniform family condition, physical proximity and physical arrangements may strongly influence interpersonal pattern affiliated behaviour. But where social, cultural, economic and familial differences are great, these will outweigh physical spatial factors in affiliative behaviour (Talen 1999:1373).

Therefore, even if physical form can influence and even restrict social interactions and activities, it is seldom enough to motivate new social conduct or a sense of community by itself in a multicultural society. Hence awareness has been raised for those factors that are not part of the physical urban environment that play an indispensable role in social and communal conduct. This draws attention to the importance of non-environmental considerations in view of spatial analysis and design (Talen 1999). These non-environmental considerations that can be portrayed as the physiology of the city, comprise the system that is temporal, moving and changing (Kallus 2001).

In order to design cities one needs to understand them, how they operate and what they mean to people. This requires people-derived, specific and substantive information. This type of information often derived from social science methodology, rarely convinces urban designers; it is often too specific, referring to particular urban situations, or to distinct urban places. It tends to treat the urban environment as made up of intermittent and incremental phenomena, focusing on urban details in a way that does not fit the urban designer's perception of the urban spatial system's complexity and continuity (Kallus 2001:132).

The ideal is that the complexity and continuity of the urban space as related to physical form is considered in conjunction with the social activities, ideas and mental perceptions that compose the social and symbolic space of the urban environment. Socio-cultural perception of form (and space) is related to institutions, ideas (including values and world view) and conventional activities that substantiate their considerations in the design process (see Gyuse in Breed, 2008; Lefebvre in Merrifield 2000). The goal of incorporating concrete realities of daily life into design is the creation of heterogeneous and plural urban environments that accommodate and celebrate local identity. The physical environment can become an element of emancipation if it corresponds to the actual behaviour and activities of existent people (Foucault in Leach 1999).

In design practice public consultation is one way to interact with these concrete social realities of the environment. Because the South African government supports people-centred development, participation is employed more frequently in planning and design projects. Globally community participation has taken two main forms in the design process: it is used to gain a local under-standing to inform professional recommendations or it is seen as an empowering process where locals are given the opportunity to act for themselves and change conditions to their advantage (Juarez & Brown 2008). With remaining prevalent social economic and class disparities worldwide participation in empowerment has become a central argument for community engagement in design (Hamdi 2004).

Public participation is not an uncomplicated matter even for experts. The difficulties faced in community participation are well-known. It can be used as a means to conciliate rather than to truly recognise the needs of the community; the process often goes hand-in-hand with a lack of ability and the right support structures while in the community itself many contradictory and conflicting ideas may surface (Van Huysteen, Schoonraad, Boden in Lodi 2000). The main challenge remains to assess the effectiveness of participatory processes for enabling community residents to articulate problems and needs (Juarez & Brown 2008:191).

The aim of the paper is to emphasise the importance of local and contextual understanding and interpretation for design purposes. The paper specifically focuses on the concrete aspects of the living and changing urban social system. Community participation is demonstrated to be a method of engagement with the concrete dynamics of urban space as shaped by the built environment. A case study is used to show how qualitative methods of data collection effectively deal with the phenomenon of fleeting and changing identities. It is precisely in qualitative research that the role of the physical form of the built environment can be distinguished from the non-environmental factors that also play a part in the perception and use of urban space. The continuing importance of the transient aspects of city life as design informant is argued through this example.

Brief contextual background

Mamelodi is a black township area that was founded (1945) during the apartheid years in the city of Pretoria, South Africa. The history of Pretoria and Mamelodi was strongly influenced by the politics of apartheid. Figure 1 explains the basic logic behind the layout of the apartheid city that will serve as a reference for the discussion that follows. The townships were residential areas created between 1905 and 1960 for non-white citizens on the periphery of the city and were separated from white residential areas by industrial buffer zones (Van der Waal 1995).

Three acts supported and brought about spatial segregation in South Africa. (1) The *Natives Land Act* of 1913 was the first that served as a basis for the later development of the townships. Blacks were allocated corresponding ethnic 'homelands' or reserves to live in and any purchase or lease of land by blacks

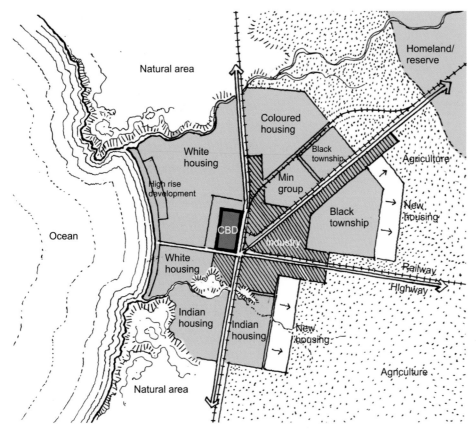

Figure 1: Diagram of the apartheid city (Image by D. Schoulund, 2010 – adapted from Beavon 1992:233 in Bremner 2007:20). Note the racial segregation of residential areas by means of main routes, railway lines and industrial areas; the prime location of white neighbourhoods close to the CBD (central business district) and natural resources and beauty; black townships were located farthest from the CBD and buffered from it by means of industrial zones. Access from township areas to the city was mainly given by means of the rail system

outside these homelands was prohibited. (2) The *Population Registration Act* of 1950 classified every South African by race: whites (from European descent, blacks (from African descent), coloureds (persons of mixed race) and Indians (South Asians). (3) The *Group Areas Act* established in the same year (1950) and reinforced in 1966, established residential and business sections in urban areas for each race; members from other races could not live, operate a business or own land in these areas. Thousands of non-white citizens were removed from the city core to the city outskirts (Malan 1996). A resident of Mamelodi recalls the influence of the *Group Areas Act* on life in Mamelodi Township where people were moved to ethnic-based neighbourhoods that are still evident today (see also Figures 2 and 3):

When Mamelodi was designed it was also designed along ethnic lines. A section called Malani is predominantly Tsonga and Venda speaking, they are usually mixed like that. Go to Section 17 – the same thing, if you go to B3, B1, B2 they are the same. Go to S&S it's predominantly Nguni speaking and Zulu, Ndebele, and Swazi. Go to Section 14 it's predominantly Pedi speaking and 16 is a bit of Pedi and Zulu and Ndebele (Interview with Ben, 50 years old, government spokesperson).

According to Malan (1996), while public services were controlled by the white population, private business and families depended on the labour of non-whites. The black population in the cities located outside the homelands was viewed by the government as temporary and acknowledged only in terms of the city's labour needs (Malan 1996). 'In 1952 the Ministry of Native Affairs declared that each city had to have one corresponding African township. They had to be separated from 'white areas' by industries; they had to have transport to the city, preferably by train and not by national

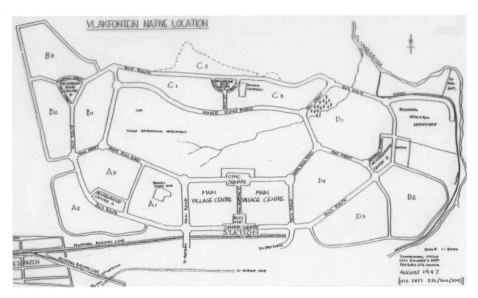

Figure 2: The farm Vlakfontein in 1947 was developed and renamed as Mamelodi Township. Note the prime position of the railway station next to the village centre that would allow people to go to and from work every day (Map from Van der Waal 1991. Van der Waal Collection, University of Pretoria, Merensky Library)

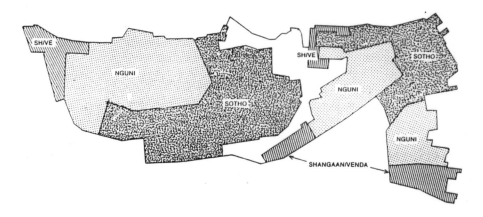

Figure 3: Mamelodi divided into ethnic neighbourhoods, 1960. In township areas, after the 1950s Group Areas Act, residential areas were divided according to ethnic origins (Map from Van der Waal 1991. Van der Waal Collection, University of Pretoria, Merensky Library)

roads; they had to be big and located in an exact position with vacant space surrounding them (see Figure 1), permitting growth without encroaching on areas set aside for other racial groups' (*Cape Times*, 14 July 1949 in Williams 2000:167). Existing areas that were incorrectly situated had to be relocated. These relocations of so-called 'black spots' from the central business district (CBD) area made space available for the growth of the city's business core and provided privileged access for white citizens, while allowing the required labour to live on the city outskirts. Several forced evictions occurred. Figure 4 indicates the removal of 'black spots' from the central area of Pretoria to Mamelodi and Atteridgeville. These evictions caused a community that lived in cohesion to be completely uprooted and dislocated as recalled by an interviewee:

Well, let me say in Lady Selbourne [inner city area relocated to Mamelodi, see Figure 4] we were free even if there were all that loss but we were used to the area and we could get anything very cheap … but, then from there to Mamelodi things started changing. That was the feeling that we had, that life was not as it used to be in Lady Selbourne. There were more expenses in Mamelodi than in Lady Selbourne and then of course in Lady Selbourne it was a mixed society: Chinese, Indians, some Whites nearby Blacks, all in the same vicinity. Now coming here to Mamelodi it was only blacks (Interview with Ben, 50 years old, government spokesperson).

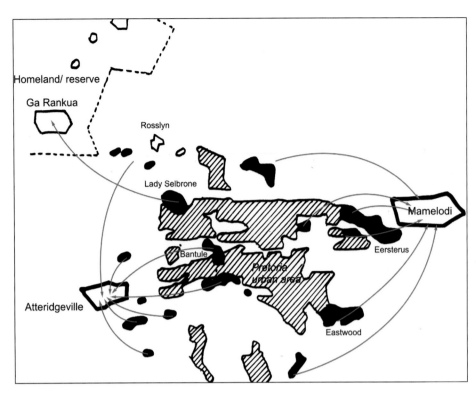

Figure 4: Removal of black spots from the inner city of Pretoria (1953–1967) to Mamelodi (north-east), Atteridgeville (south-west), the two black townships developed for Pretoria and Garankuwa (north-west) the closest homeland/reserve (Image by D. Schoulund 2010 – adapted from Van der Waal 1991)

Figure 5: The four-roomed brick houses constructed by government in Mamelodi in 1956. Local authorities have been responsible for housing since the 1920s, although control over black housing reverted to central government in 1971 (Photo from Van der Waal 1991. Van der Waal Collection, University of Pretoria, Merensky Library)

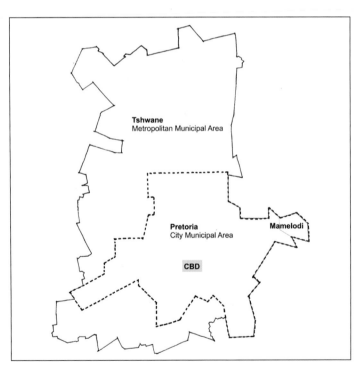

Figure 6: The position of Mamelodi in the context of the city of Pretoria and the Tshwane Metropolitan Municipality which was formed in the late 1990s (Image by D. Schoulund 2010 – adapted from IDP 1999)

Figures 7 and 8: Photographs of Mamelodi township (Breed 2002). Left: The Magaliesberg Mountains in the distance prevent the township from spreading further north and east. Right: basic infrastructure has been provided while the development in the area remains informal

The conditions in the townships were exceptionally meagre and sub-standard, causing the inhabitants many problems. The number of non-white inhabitants in cities was controlled to assure that they did not threaten the superior position of the white population in the urban economy. In spite of the measures of control, the African population continued growing, since the men brought their families to live with them in the city. This made the situation of the townships worse since there was no planning that included sufficient space and services for these people. Moreover, the change to the cities was financially difficult as people were largely illiterate and had to join in the unskilled labour section of the economy (Malan 1996).

In 1968 development in Mamelodi was halted due to the influx of non-white people from the countryside. People were newly forced to move to Bophuthatswana as a homeland/reserve, forty kilometres from Pretoria. (This area was earmarked as residence for the labour force of Pretoria by the *Group Areas Act* 1966.) It was an attempt to control and demotivate further emigration to urban areas and resulted in a scarcity of resources and amenities shared by many (Van der Waal 1995; Malan 1996). Development was only resumed again in the 1980s. The situation is recalled by an interviewee:

There were houses in Mamelodi but most of the people were not able to get a house, because they were from the farms or from other places. So they did not qualify to get houses in Mamelodi, that was the problem, and the reason why they were hiring backyard shacks from other people (Interview with Magda, aged 58, pensioner, who has lived in Mamelodi all her life).

The Tshwane Metropolitan Municipality was formed around the turn of the century and encapsulated Pretoria and its surrounds (see Figure 6). The intention was to facilitate urban and social administration and integration, while at the same time the undeveloped peripheral areas could gain access to the municipal budget and upgrade their sparse infrastructure (Williams 2000). Mamelodi is situated north-east of the Pretoria municipality (see Figure 6). It is approximately 20 kilometres from the old city centre (CBD) at the foot of the Magalies Mountains and lies within a valley with its central axis in an east-west direction. The Integrated Development Plan of 1999 for the City of Tshwane Metropolitan Municipality indicated a population of 270 000 people that represents approximately 25% of the total population of Pretoria who live in 6% of the land surface of the municipality. It is one of the poorest areas in Pretoria. The average income in this municipal zone is R150 (approx $15 in 2002) per person per year and only 45% of the population is economically active. The residents are predominantly 'African'.

Question: And, are you happy to live in Mamelodi, do you like living here?

> *Respondent's answer:* Yeah, I am happy, I don't think of going anywhere. My church is here; I am near schools, and transport and shops. I think everything is easy for me, that's why I like it (Sophia, aged 43, Show House sewing project).

Mamelodi East started to form in 1961 (Van der Waal 1991), but the Far-East (where the research was done) was only established in the late 1980s during the transition period from the apartheid government to the democratic government 1986–1994 (Malan 1996). It is therefore a relatively recently inhabited area that comprises diverse people, of whom a percentage arrived from rural areas that now share a living space.

The research regarding urban open space was undertaken by the author in Mamelodi East in 2002 (see Figures 7 and 8). Comprehensive research that can be found in Breed (2003) was done on historical conditions, statistical demographics and past, existing and future planning for Mamelodi. The research area includes various housing and planning schemes created on behalf of the local government and it is valuable to study the relation between the different projects and the expressed preferences and needs of the people who reside there. This paper is based on urban ethnographic research and concentrates on the use and perception of open space in Mamelodi East. In the following section the motivation is given for qualitative research, with a brief explanation of the fieldwork methods and their effectiveness. The focus of the findings was specific to the methodological approach that is also clarified.

Qualitative fieldwork motivation and methodology

The effects of the global market that include multiculturalism and international design offices that have led to changing built environments and user groups have complicated design for shared identity. According to Simon (2004:64) 'while individual identity may hold a relatively privileged status in the (post) modern world, collective identity as such tends to be highly context dependent and variable, with each specific instantiation of collective identity being rather transitory and fragile'. As has been mentioned before, the non-lasting aspects of city life are often regarded as unimportant by designers precisely due to their being hard to pin down (Kallus 2001). Another reality is that the contextual collective identity between designers and the community they design for commonly does not match in South Africa due to the historical spatial divide between cultures and races. For this reason design projects for public space and buildings allocated through national or local authorities enforce community participation as a means to reach a shared understanding. As explained by Mead (1972), the individual as reflection of the social process is still our only means to a collective understanding. 'The unit and structure of the complete person reflects the unity and structure of the social process as a whole and each elemental person of which the complete person is made up reflects the unit and structure of one of the various aspects of this process in which the individual is involved' (Mead 1972:175). Public participation is a way of engaging with individuals who are representative of the social process that is situated in history and is fragmented by geography.

Foucault (in Philo 2000) acknowledged the fact that events, processes and the structure of history are always fragmented by geography, by the complicated reality of situations that have different solutions in different locations. He explains that the *a priori* imposition of total history over determined phenomena and events in a defined spatial-temporal area is doubtful because it introduces an order that is not acquainted with the details and the differences of history in specific times and places. As an alternative to total history, Foucault suggests the concept of general history (in Philo 2000). In this methodology the theoretical material should be linked to the empiric details of a situation, event or object. This method has been applied to anthropology by Geertz, who states 'The aim is to draw large conclusions from small, but very densely textured facts; to support broad assertions about the role of culture in the construction of collective life by engaging them exactly with complex specifics' (Geertz in Philo 2000:233). This is a way to reinstall the human scale in social thinking that can be called post-hierarchical but also post-structural. In the same fashion, the important theoretical confirmations of a specific study should not come first, but rather have to manifest gradually as the study reaches more depth (Philo 2000). Although this methodology aims to avoid giving structure and order to empirical details and theory, Philo (2000:212) reminds: 'The very practice of researching and writing inevitably brings a semblance of order – whether unacknowledged or unwanted – to the empirical stockpile.'

The research methodology for this case study was drawn from this *Foucauldian geography* (as discussed by Philo 2000). As a consequence, qualitative research was selected for the case study since it is a search for the detailed and specific which is the key to identifying a type of empiricism, that without separating itself from generalisation and the construction of abstract categories, insists on a humanist approach to the social reality that reestablishes the leading role of the individual subject (Esquivel 1999; Pujados 1992). Qualitative research has the function of understanding the social world from the perspective of the social actor, i.e. a resident or user of the study area taking part in social acts and activities that relate to the place of study or to other residents or users.

The investigator has to involve him- or herself personally with the subjects of the investigation, since the data intend to discover the user's vocabulary, ways of 'seeing' things, sense of what is of value and what is not (Schwartz in Esquivel 1999). The importance of the individual as a key to the collective identity and the meaning attached to place is reiterated: 'Meanings may be attributed to places in different ways by different people, and thus they are individually, as opposed to environmentally, constructed.' (Talen 1999:1372). This approach is also concerned with gaining knowledge of the context to scrutinise the complexity of behaviour of people and can hence assimilate itself more easily within the system of meaning applied by a particular community of the society that is being studied.

In this line of thought, Esquivel (1999) insists that the application of a qualitative perspective is not only a question of technique but it personifies the adoption of an alternative epistemological paradigm.

Qualitative investigation is an indispensable approach to understand certain dimensions of reality such as human subjectivity, identities, gender relations, social interactions and shared systems of meaning among others. It seems to be a necessary approach when the point of view of the actors is the perspective of reality that is longed to be known, i.e. interpretation of a lived experience (Esquivel 1999:65).

Due to this intimate involvement in the investigation, there have been concerns from positivism for objectivity and reliability of data. The argument for the authenticity of data is that in qualitative fieldwork the observer is thoroughly implicated in his/her research.

In the field of his subject of investigation, knowledge does not have the 'other' as its object; on the contrary, it is about the inextricable integration and reciprocal existence between observer and the observed. It is about mutually shared understanding, based on the inter-subjectivity of the interaction. The more the knowledge is integrated and intimately subjective, the more its depth and objectivity becomes (Ferrarotti in Pujados 1992:10).

The actor always has a feeling of 'motive-for' his action. The task of the interpreter or investigator, i.e. the person interpreting the action of the actor, is to analyse the language and behaviour of the other. The motive for an action is imaginatively projected as if it were our own; later it is used as a scheme that allows us to interpret the experience of the actor. Each act or sign has a double meaning: an objective meaning – the meaning as such – and the subjective meaning – the aura or sphere that perpetuates from the subjective context in the mind of the person who uses the sign. Any sign implies reference to a specific audience; in the same way subjective interpretation implies reference to a specific person. In the process of interpretation we are always guided by the acknowledgement of both, not denying that what is known from the perspective of the other is still limited (Schütz 1993).The implication of this in terms of the fieldwork process and methodology was that the author had to reside in the area of study (for a period of two months) to become fully acquainted with the area and actors of study and enable a subjective reading of signs used by the actors.

The mental (abstract) and physical (concrete) realities that are portrayed differently by different urban actors and parts of the social system can be recorded as a concrete experience and converted to understanding through the use of qualitative methods. It was, however, necessary to select methods relating to an encompassing understanding of urban space. The dimensions that the social urbanite, Lefebvre, uses for discourse on urban space (interpreted as physical, social and symbolic) were used as they are deemed capable of reconciling traditional concepts of space and place (see Merrifield 1993). This methodology will duly attempt to bring together the traditional spatial analyst's concern for space (abstracted), the Marxist concern with social relations and structural factors (as also seen in Foucault), and the humanists' appeal for subjectivity, place meaning and place experience (as seen in phenomenology and qualitative research) (Merrifield 1993:516). Lefebvre's theories on space:

render intelligible qualities of space which are at once perceptible and imperceptible to the senses. It is a task that necessitates both empirical and theoretical research … it journeys between the concrete and the abstract, between the local and the global, between self and society. (Merrifield 2000:173)

The key elements that have been taken and reworked from each of Lefebvre's dimensions are spatial practices, i.e. the way space is organised and used **socially**; the representation of **physical space** conceived primarily by architects and other designers and relating to the physical matter; and representational space or **symbolic space**, i.e. the image and meaning of the environment associated with the mental perception of the user (Lefebvre in Merrifield 2000:174). United under the terms **mindscape**, **matterscape** and **powerscape**, the relation of these dimensions is demonstrated in Figure 9.

Qualitative methods according to Lefebvre's dimensions that would be appropriate in capturing and exploring each dimension of the urban environment (see Figure 9) were selected by the author at the time of the research. To discover the symbolic **mindscape**, mental maps (as explored by Lynch 1960; Silva 1992; Wildner 1998) and photo-interviews (Vila 1997) were employed. To explore the physical **matterscape** the methods of systematic observation (Berger & Luckmann 1968) and participant observation (Atkinson 1994) were used. The social **powerscape** that explains social hierarchies and structures in society was investigated through periodical analysis (Aguilar 1998) and in-depth interviews, while participant observation also shed light on the latter theme.

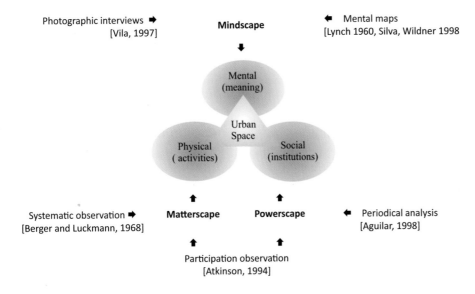

Figure 9: An interpretation and schematic representation of Lefebvre's dimensions of space. Corresponding qualitative methods for data gathering and analysis were selected and are indicated (Breed 2009)

The case study discussed in the following pages encompasses all the methods stated above. The aim is to capture the abstract and the concrete realities that influence the formation of the urban environment and decode the mental perceptions to distinguish between factors of influence that are determined by the physical environment (environmental factors) and those influences that are not related to the physical environment (non-environmental factors). Faithful to Foucault's theories (as discussed by Philo 2000), the disparities and irregularities were used to get to the core of urban issues (see findings in item 4 for further clarification).

Furthermore the views, understanding and perceptions of different social actors (interest groups) were considered for Mamelodi East as identified by the Integrated Development Framework for Zone 5, 1999. Eleven interest groups were identified for Mamelodi East: (1) Resident community, labourers, actual and future users – nine interviewees fell into this category (2) Wards and committees for zones 3, 4 and 5 – four councillors were interviewed (3) Land owners, property developers with contracts or agreements in the area, business, etc. – none were interviewed (4) Specific companies and individuals – a medical doctor and a school master were interviewed (5) Interest groups – two lecturers from the University of Pretoria were interviewed (6) Special interest groups such as sports clubs and churches – two missionaries, two women from the Show House sewing project and one woman from the cooking project were interviewed (7) Individuals – an urban planner and landscape architect student that grew up in Mamelodi were interviewed (8) Tshwane Metropolitan Municipality officials – three officials were interviewed (9) Municipal officials for Mamelodi – three officials were interviewed (10) Officials of the planning zone and the directive commission of the zone – one was interviewed (11) Other consultants for the revision of the IDP – the author of the IDP 1997 and the Guide Plan 1980 were both interviewed. Thirty-two interviews were conducted amounting to more than 40 hours of interview time.

The different field work methods were each chosen to deliver empirical data that reveal specific aspects of urban space. The field work methods selected (as indicated in Figure 9) are briefly discussed in the following section, indicating their specific application and value for this study.

Fieldwork methods

A condensed explanation of the qualitative research methods that were utilised in this investigation is given to clarify the perceived difficulty of going beyond criticism of the rationalist impulse of structuralism. The theoretical argument has to be taken beyond the scholarly into something that is physical and useful and therefore only intellectual by abstraction.

Systematic observation

Systematic or descriptive observation is used when the researcher observes a social space and tries to record or remember everything as far as possible. It is to approach space without any preconceived questions or judgments in mind; the researcher simply asks: 'What is taking place here?' Or 'What are these actions and place all about?' These questions can be very useful as a first approach to the object of study, while the researcher is adapting to the specific space and the residents get used to seeing the researcher in their space. Moreover, through observation we analyse how people construct, adapt and use space and the socio-spatial relations can be better understood. To make sure that nothing is taken for granted and nothing escapes the attention of the observer, it is necessary to monitor systematically what is seen: the space, actors and activities, but more than this the physical objects, singular actions executed by individuals as well as related activities executed in a group. Other factors are the sequence of events in time, objectives that people are trying to meet, as well as feelings and emotions felt and expressed by the observed or by the observer self (Spradley 1980:78). Jotting down these details in sequence of time and days is quite essential; the list can be used to search for reoccurrences, contradictions and to make comparisons or hypotheses that can be tested in the data.

During the two month period that the author resided in Mamelodi East, systematic observation was used on a daily basis to steer away from preconceived ideas and perceptions and to be preoccupied with the actual reality and dynamics of the urban open space – the **matterscape**: that what is there. Although observation is habitually employed by designers, it can become a casual verification of preconceived ideas and perceptions. Time constraints on projects and distances from study areas do not always allow for the verification of sequences of events over time, including weekends and evenings. Once-off observations are therefore used as validation for design decisions. Furthermore, where designers sometimes are over-familiar with areas of study, a de-familiarisation process seems to be required, where one is made aware again of the well-known phenomena of the everyday environment that one has grown to ignore due to their familiarity.

Participant observation

In participant observation there are two objectives – one is to get involved in activities and the other to observe these activities, the people and the physical aspects of the situation. Additionally, there are guidelines that should be adhered to: the observer needs a high awareness or intuitive capacity to observe the details that are often lost in daily life; it is also important to observe each

Figures 10, 11 and 12: A few of the photographs that were used in the photo-interviews (Breed 2002). A variety of housing typologies with different material use, context and ethnic character was used to elicit responses from interviewees. (To witness the complete collection of photographs used, see Breed 2009)

situation in retrospect and include all necessary information that conceivably played a part in it; the experience of being included and excluded in each situation should be understood. This 'game' should always be real in the mind of the researcher to allow him/her to feel the emotions and feelings of the ordinary participants but also to see the situation for what it is and to have the ability to analyse it objectively. This takes us to the next point of introspection, an effective tool to comprehend new situations and to get accustomed to following the socio-cultural rules that each situation calls for. Finally it is necessary for researchers to keep a record of their objective observations and subjective feelings to discriminate between the two (Spradley 1980:78).

The participant observer can gain a more subjective understanding but also a more realistic and objective view of the object of study. It allows an understanding of the direct relations between the physical space and the social activities, but also the symbolic or mental aspects attached to both. This type of investigation depicts the urban environment not only in a descriptive and analytical way but also lived and witnessed, interpreting not only the merely urban condition but also the human one (Morse 1985). Popularised by Walter Benjamin (see De Certeau 1984) is the concept of the *flaneur*; the two described techniques of urban observation are quite renowned in social studies and urban design but less so in landscape architecture.

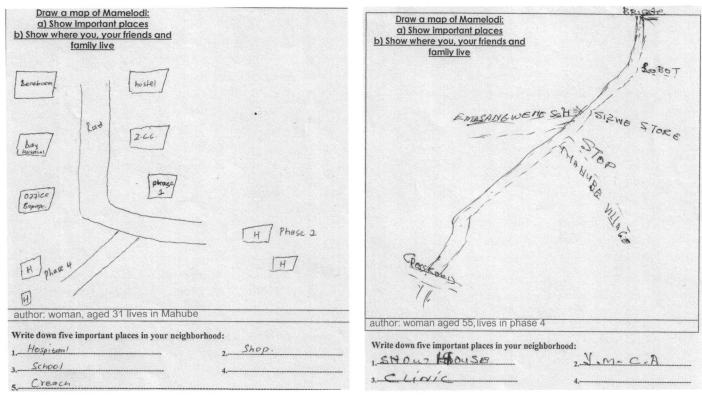

Figures 13 and 14: Mental maps that were drawn by interviewees indicating their spatial understanding of Mamelodi. The instruction was to draw a map of Mamelodi and indicate important places as well as where the interviewee lived, friends and family (private collection, Breed 2002). Note the use of signals, area and street names (left) while building phases and uses are utilised for orientation and reference (right)

In-depth and photo interviews

The explanation of qualitative fieldwork in the previous section explains in detail the complexities and consequent considerations involved with in-depth interviews. Most importantly, for phenomenologist approaches the avoidance of *a priori* judgements and perceptions is fundamental for the quality of research outcomes. Questions that were thus employed in interviews were extremely broad; rather than asking interviewees about their present conditions, interviews would be started off by inquiries into the past and then used as a comparative analysis of the present.

In-depth interviews were conducted with twenty-five community members, eight of which were done with the help of photographs. Five of these community members can be considered experts, and five additional non-residential experts were consulted. (The term 'expert' is used here to refer to someone whose vocation is related to planning and administration within the area of study.) The technique of including photographs in an interview and the outcomes for this case study has been discussed in detail in Breed (2009). Interviewees were asked to arrange the photographs of houses (that had been prepared by the researcher) in order of preference. The most preferred and least preferred options were then used as a point of departure for an in-depth interview. The value judgements reflected by the selections could thus be tested in terms of cultural identity, technology, spatial and material preferences, etc. The photographs were used as a frame of reference for a discussion throughout the interview.

A photograph is a useful tool in an interview to uncover attached meaning which is linked to the identity of the speaker. According to Vila (1997:131) each individual reads the reality that appears in a photograph through a specific gaze that is linked to his or her peculiar understanding of the surrounding reality. This again is linked to one's narrative identity, which one constructs to make one aware of one's identity and that of 'others'. 'In reality we see only what we want to see and in the way we want to perceive it.' In other words, we select aspects of reality that surround us in accordance with the specific identity that we want to construct. 'The photographs, per definition, always require the interviewee to project his/her specific narrative identity in the demonstrated scene, so much so that the scene only acquires meaning inside the narrative of the interviewee' (Vila 1997:136). In this way much very meaningful contextual knowledge is shared with the researcher.

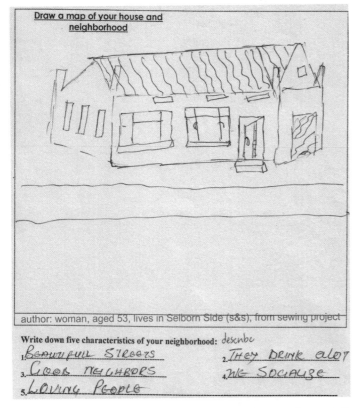

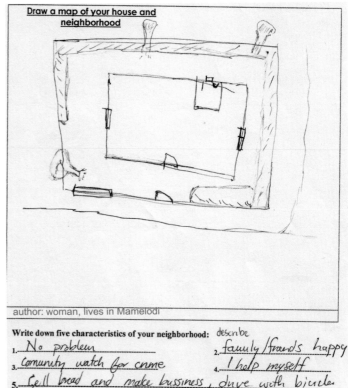

author: woman, aged 53, lives in Selborn Side (s&s), from sewing project

author: woman, lives in Mamelodi

Write down five characteristics of your neighborhood: *describe*

1. BEAUTIFULL STREETS
2. THEY DRINK ALOT
3. GOOD NEIGHBORS
4. WE SOCIALIZE
5. LOVING PEOPLE

Write down five characteristics of your neighborhood: *describe*

1. No problem
2. family/friends happy
3. Comunity watch for crime
4. I help myself
5. Sell bread and make bussiness, drive with bicicle

Figures 15 and 16: Mental maps that were drawn by interviewees indicating the spatial understanding and preferences on an individual and private scale in Mamelodi. The instructions were to draw a map of the interviewee's house and neighbourhood (Breed 2002)

Including photographs in interviews has the following advantages in qualitative research: the photographs stimulate the memory of the interviewee; the description and interpretation of images open different perspectives about something that might not be familiar to the researcher; the photographs give a dynamic nature to the discourse; they provoke more emotional reactions and they allow a narrative addition by the viewer that reflects an interpretation of the real and the imaginary, i.e. physical and symbolic aspects (Wildner 1998:163).

Mental maps

Probably the most renowned user of mental maps is Kevin Lynch (1960), although few urbanites would be able to elaborate on the technique or its application. A total of 25 mental maps were collected throughout the research period. With this method the informants draw their image of the researched space as they organise it through attached meaning as retained in their memory. In a first evaluation the maps can be organised by looking at similarities and differences, repetitive symbols and names; repetitive characteristics are also searched for. In the second phase they are combined with information and the interpretation of the researchers. The result is a catalogue of repetitive elements and of the way in which the actors perceive, interpret and represent the concrete urban environment or urban space.

The maps are more objective than photographs since they are constructed by the interviewee according to his/her memory and preference on a blank piece of paper. However, these are often harder to obtain because of the inhibitions, lack of confidence or lack of drawing ability. For interpretation it is sometimes more useful to ask the interviewee

Figures 17 and 18: Images from the Mamelodi Record *indicating real social activities and public cultural events in Mamelodi. Left: Mamelodi traditional dancers showcased Swazi dancing in the State Theatre in Pretoria CBD. Nominated as the best group in Tshwane they went on to represent their city in Newtown, Johannesburg,* Mamelodi Record *9 (23), cover page. Right: Women participating in a sewing project to empower themselves. Image indicating graduates in knitting, manufacturing of school wear and curtain making in Mamelodi West Community Hall,* Mamelodi Record *9 (23), p.4 (Oct. 2002)*

for a short explanation of his/her drawing or to use it to initiate an interview. This technique was used during the research.

Two kinds of maps were requested from interviewees: one that explains the spatial layout of Mamelodi (see Figures 13 and 14), the other that shows the spatial layout of the resident's house and neighbourhood (see Figures 15 and 16). The aim was to become aware of the social spatial arrangement and potential boundaries and edges at different scales (private and public) within the study area.

Periodical analysis

For Aguilar (1998) when the press writes about the city a double process is revealed: Collective forms are recuperated and exhibited by giving value, themes and hierarchies to the urban context (or space) – it can be in politics, housing or development where something is lacking, e.g. facilities or amenities, or something is going to happen, such as new proposals by government or consultation between different parties involved. At the same time, these values are recuperated in a convenient form (which can be an informative note, a report or the advice given) that orientates, models and gives representation of social recognition to a previous social discourse.

Aguilar makes use of periodicals and newspapers that appear at regular intervals; similarly flyers or websites and blogs that have been identified as important means of interaction between the media and the specific study area can be collected or studied (over a decided period or intervals of time). Some basic criteria to select information are to analyse newspapers that refer to the

Figures 19 and 20: Images from the Mamelodi Record *indicating real conflicting situations and acts that occur in Mamelodi. Top: Public demonstration in Ext. 22 against being placed in temporary stands to wait for government housing development,* Mamelodi Record *9 (23), p.3. Bottom: Teachers struggling with overfull classrooms but good news is that 10 new classrooms will be added to this school,* Mamelodi Record *4 (30), cover page (Oct. 2002)*

metropolitan zone of the city or neighbourhood and broadly discuss a defined urban theme that is related to life in the city or neighbourhood.

The formal structuring of the newspaper, its orientation or political representation, the value given to different topics, the use of photography and images, the type of publicity or propaganda and the type of consumers should be analysed. Other aspects that are important to consider are the leaders, the editor or head of information, director and owner, the cost, the language of publication and the way of distribution.

In the case of Mamelodi, the *Mamelodi Record* that is freely distributed on Fridays was used. The weekly newspaper is delivered across the whole of Mamelodi (East and West) and is written in English but contains some Afrikaans advertisements. It is the biggest local newspaper for Mamelodi. In January 2002, 20 000 copies were distributed per week. The eight exemplars with 16 pages each that were delivered during the period of residence of the researcher/author in Mamelodi East were analysed. Figures 17 to 20 indicate typical news that is celebrated by the *Mamelodi Record*. Social interests, activities, needs and conflicts were identified in this way and the social power relations and discourse revealed.

Discussion of findings: Terms of spatial organisation and spatial perceptions

Remaining within the post-structuralist thinking of social theorists such as Lefebvre, Derrida and Foucault, sense-making activity now has to be taken into something that is bodily and practical. The data gathered through the various fieldwork methods were scrutinised for indications of terms used by those speaking about Mamelodi East. These terms do not have any identity in themselves; the capturing of identity is made possible through the detection of differential relations between the terms. The presence of these terms can be analysed according to Derrida's renowned discourse on difference (see Derrida 1982:21–22). Derrida sees the presence of difference as a prerequisite to comprehension of terms. A term exists in relation to space and time. In time it needs to be distinguished from past and future moments. In space its presence needs to be isolated and identified through differentiation in both a temporal and a spatial sense, then this presence arises out of difference. Accordingly each term has been identified by distinguishing it from other terms used by the interviewees (space); the terms have also been analysed in relation to past and future projections (time).

Furthermore, the idea of difference as explored by Foucault was also employed, but in its more traditional sense, i.e. as opposed

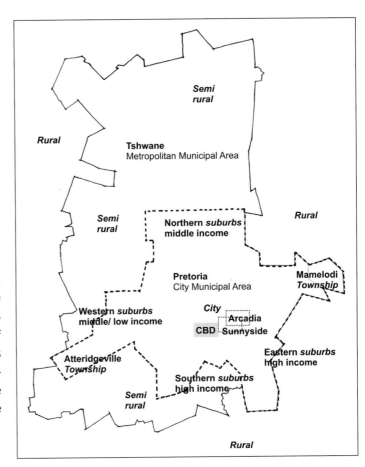

Figure 21: Map of Pretoria indicating the physical locations of rural, township, city and suburban areas. Compare also to Figure 1 (Adapted from IDP 1999)

to preference. Foucault suggests that the study will reveal a region of difference and a discernable order or system will be created through these differences. By looking at the exceptions and contradictions the norm is also uncovered and understood. This order that can be identified has the function of recuperating local, renewable rules that in a simplistic arrangement relate to many objects of study and give structure to collective life (Philo 2000). As argued by Lefebvre (in Merrifield 2000:173):

Theory must somehow trace out the actual dynamic and complex interplay of space itself – of buildings, monuments, neighbourhoods, whole cities, the world – exposing and decoding those multitudinous imperceptible processes involved in production.

What follows is a summary of terms, physical entities and concepts that have been found to be present in time and space in the vocabulary of those speaking about Mamelodi East. The local renewable rules identified by these that can be useful in terms of design thinking are considered.

Terms of spatial organisation

More about Mamelodi East can be understood if it is analysed in terms of its comparative contrasts and contradictions. Ideas of difference in terms of spatiality (place identifications and definitions) and temporality (change before and after) that have surfaced from the accumulated data were used to get to an understanding of the complexities of the social-cultural context and identity in Mamelodi East. The main intention (as suggested by Foucault in Philo 2000) is to oppose the tendencies of a priori ordering that totalise historical cross-examinations. The aim is therefore not to homogenise the components, nor to put them in a single container, but rather to preserve and even accentuate the details and the differences. It is thus important to maintain a human scale in all reflections and to draw attention to differences. Thereafter to find the order of a system (observable relationships) in these differences that point to local, renewable rules that relate to social practices and the urban space (or form) in which they are practised (Philo 2000). These terms or themes were mainly uncovered through the in-depth interviews with different social actors. They are discussed in order to reveal the spatial and then temporal proximity, moving in small steps between terms that gain identity and presence due to the accentuation of their differential relations.

Rural versus urban

During the interviews and conversations four spatial references were identified that were repeatedly used by the residents to define their idea of values and world view attached to Mamelodi East (articulated as 'township'). These references reveal information about the socio-spatial dialectic, i.e. the social practices in relation to the urban space in which they are practised (see Lefebvre 1991).

First of all the nature of the township is discussed in terms of its level of urbanisation. This implies infrastructure, amenities and access to work, goods, etc. The terms 'rural', 'township', 'city' and 'suburbs' are used as general terms of reference in this section. The terms indicate existing physical and social realities but also the perception (physical, social and symbolic) of the interviewees. The term 'city' in this section mainly refers to the historical central business district (CBD) in Pretoria and the surrounding high density residential areas (Arcadia and Sunnyside), while the term 'suburb' refers to former whites-only residential areas that comparatively had better service provision, infrastructure and amenities than township areas. Figure 21 indicates the spatial location of the above-mentioned terms. See also Figure 1 and the accompanying explanation of the apartheid city as reference to the historical background on these physical realities.

Rural areas: Accepted implication – that which is away from cities and industrial areas associated with agricultural life style. In South Africa in physical terms this includes fewer amenities, infrastructure, technology and transport systems and subsequently less access to opportunities and choice in terms of work, education and goods.

From the interviews it appeared that many residents originated from rural areas and had positive associations with the traditions and lifestyles associated with them. Other residents have lived in semi-urbanised areas all their lives and associate rural areas with drawbacks and poverty. It was evident that rural areas are strongly connected to ethnicity, culture and tradition and not necessarily in a negative way.

The difference is Mpumalanga (rural area) – how can I put it – it's a place that has traditional things. Especially respect, yes, you can respect the old person but here they don't always; another thing is the crime rate. But Mpumalanga is better, the next door neighbour can help you, and here sometimes they can too, but if you don't socialise with them they don't (Gertrude, aged 53, Sewing Project, Stanza Bopape Community Centre).

There are very few places where you can find houses decorated by Ndebele tribes, very few in Mamelodi, but in Mpumalanga (province), yeah you could find that (Alex, in his thirties, liaison officer).

In comparison to the townships, rural areas are seen to be more isolated, without transport and with little infrastructure. There is no social space and the dwellings do not often belong to the residents; they are more dangerous and there are shortcomings that may include infrastructure, amenities and activities. There are also a greater prominence of traditions and fewer problems.

Implications for design vision: Mamelodi East is a place of activity; it is connected and has amenities. The houses belong to the people and there is dedicated social public space, activities, amenities and infrastructure. Tradition is not prominent in Mamelodi East and this might currently be leading to different ways of doing things, which creates conflict.

Townships: The townships were residential areas created for non-white citizens on the periphery of the city and were separated by industrial buffer zones from white residential areas. In general this implied far poorer service provision, infrastructure and access compared to the white suburbs.

The townships are seen to be more like the city (referring to the denser residential areas around the CBD) than the rural areas. Although the level of infrastructure varies much, townships have a rapid lifestyle and better access to services and commodities.

The culture of the townships is often contrasted with city culture. Reference to race, i.e. 'black' and 'white' is often employed when explaining lifestyle differences.

In terms of the issue of taking with me my township culture to the city [referring to CBD and surrounds] – I think a lot of it has to do with the involvement in the physical space that has been created by whoever else to a different space in the past. In such a way that, if Jacob decides to move to Hatfield, and Jacob is black and Jacob's neighbour is white, the other neighbour is white and three other neighbours are white... if he tries to be a little bit noisy, stand outside and so on (laugh) the neighbours will tell him: 'Stop doing that'...but in a township no one will be bothered. I mean in a street there's five or six people, you chat with them, you drink your beer or whatever, it's not a big deal, but then it's like you enter into a new world or a new society, with different values (Jacob, aged 26, urban planner, researcher, government official, lived in Mamelodi).

In the townships the houses are all the same, there is less access to products and information, less work, there is public transport but less access to it and life in general is more difficult. The townships are also special: they have a different culture, the people are African and practise their culture; there is more life in the streets and more social interaction.

Implications for design vision: Mamelodi East is different; it is a place of African culture that implies life in the streets and social interaction. It is part of the rapid lifestyle of the greater city and has equal access to services and commodities.

The city: The term 'city' in this section is used to refer to the CBD specifically but also the former white suburban areas with greater levels of access to goods, services, etc.

The city is associated with access and information, with government, the municipality, big commercial centres and so on. From older interviewees the political changes that occurred in terms of freedom of access to the city [non-township area] for Africans are specifically noted. Some see the city [CBD] as being more dangerous and others as a safer place. It is associated with progress, better schools and better infrastructure but also seen as eurocentric, unsafe and problem ridden.

In the city I would say many things are different to here, it's very difficult to get things here. There the library is just a stone throw away, and I would say here it is very difficult to get information. There everything is convenient, maybe if I want to get food, fresh fruits I can always get them, they are just a stone throw away, many things are right there, and in one place, because it's in town [referring to CBD] (Sipelele, aged 27, communication engineer and resident).

Implications for design vision: Mamelodi East is not the central business district of the city, it is not dominated by eurocentric symbols and planning; yet it lends access to information, government and commercial centres while being safe.

The suburbs: In general the former white neighbourhoods have far better service provision, infrastructure, amenities and access to the city centre (CBD) when compared to the townships. The physical reality is that of comparatively large erven with big houses and gardens in tree-lined, paved streets.

The suburbs are associated with whites and wealth and a lack of community interaction. Some interviewees felt they did not want to live in the suburbs, while others confessed that they would like to, especially referring to large erven and big gardens. The suburbs are criticised for not having life in the streets and it is said that people are individualist and forget their culture there. In contrast Mamelodi has more life, more activities and interaction with people.

The difference between Mamelodi and the white suburbs is that you know in Mamelodi there's life! (laughs) [T]here's life in Mamelodi. You go to town in the suburb you know in the street there's nobody in the street, you may see one person that is going to the shops and returns to his yard, then you won't see him again, you might see him tomorrow, when he goes again. But in Mamelodi you mix with people, you talk with people, you interact with people all day for 24 hours, if you are awake in 24 hours, there's life, more life in Mamelodi, in the townships than in the white areas. I don't know why it is so different, maybe the people in the suburbs think only of themselves, each family think only of themselves, they do not think about the other people, the neighbours around them; but here in Mamelodi any time if I think of visiting you I go there...(Richard, aged 55, councillor).

Implications for design vision: Mamelodi East is a place of life, interactions and activity. The streets serve as activity nodes and a communal culture predominates.

Love-hate relationship with townships

From the previous section a positive design vision could be formulated for the current and future identity of Mamelodi East. According to various interviewees the 'culture' (i.e. lifestyle) of Mamelodi is a reason for living there. There is life in the streets, interaction with neighbours and familiarity among residents; there is the possibility of getting help from a neighbour or of buying on credit from the corner store. Nevertheless many people leave at the first opportunity. Obvious reasons are distance to work, lack of services and infrastructure of a good quality, but also the possibility of greater access to information and goods (this access implies greater comfort) and the idea of making social and financial progress in society.

Figures 22, 23 and 24: Photographs indicating real social activities and physical spaces that serve as evidence of ethnic and popular culture in Mamelodi. Left: A wedding in Mamelodi in attire with ethnic references; the 'white wedding' was held and then attire was changed as per the image. Centre: 'Rasta's Kitchen', an auto-constructed vendor stall that reminds of patterns used by Ndebele people. Right: A group of high school girls performing a song that was popular on radio at the time (Breed 2002)

Sunnyside [a suburb with high density housing close to the CBD] had a lot of white people before, a lot of white people stayed there. But now if you are walking in Sunnyside it's like all black people from everywhere you can ever imagine, and mostly maybe students that come in to study or something. What I want to mention is, in one block of flats maybe 75% of the people staying there are black, but we still get out and meet each other on the corridor and we won't talk to each other. I am thinking, this guy where he's from he's probably greeting everybody there, but because he's in town [the city, i.e. CBD and former white suburbs] he's behaving otherwise. I think, that's our culture, we greet everybody. You go to Venda and sit outside under a tree, one guy passes you going to the shop: 'hi', he comes back 'hi' (laughs). So I think that is the culture that we are losing us black people because of town influence. Or maybe we think we're in town and should behave differently. I don't know maybe people do not trust each other anymore:[...] I think we are living in fear of each other. I know for sure that's not how black people are, we greet each other, we smile, you know that type of stuff, that is lost there (Simon, aged 23, student, resident).

Implications for design vision: Mamelodi East is a place of trust and sharing where people greet each other and speak to each other on the streets. This implies physical space that is aimed at encouraging communal interaction and activities as opposed to individual privacy (which is the predominant consideration in former white residential areas). A well-connected transport system with better services and infrastructure that improves physical comfort will put Mamelodi East at the same level as the rest of the city. Upmarket housing areas that speak of financial progress and success are also required to encourage people to stay.

Identity versus ethnicity

Words that are used to distinguish between self and others are **black** and **white** as well as references to language that distinguish ethnicity. However, there is also a specific Mamelodian identity that reaches beyond ethnic boundaries that is also associated with language and ethnic groups and specifically encompasses those that are historically predominant in the area.

Question: These different languages, which sometimes connect to different cultures, doesn't that separate the people from each other?

Reply: No it generally doesn't; I think if you've been to other places, you'll also notice that there's a special Mamelodi lingo that we usually use. It's not entirely Northern Sotho, or Tswana or South Sotho, it's a mixture of all these, there's a little bit of Zulu and a bit of Afrikaans. Ehhm and I must say, Mamelodi is predominantly Sotho speaking...But during the past 36 years, people have learned to identify around one lingo, which is the mixture of what I just said. If you go to Jo'burg they identify it very quickly that we are from Pretoria, because we always speak typically;...even when it comes to general meetings we speak this very same language, you know the mixture. It hasn't in anyway impacted how we grew up and get along with people (Ben, in his fifties, government spokesperson, live in Mamelodi).

Implications for design vision: Mamelodi East is a place with a specific cultural identity that is captured in the way people speak and the words and language they use. Catch-phrases from this lingo can become slogans that capture and represent the identity of place. Furthermore, words and appropriate naming of public places, parks and streets can also become significant when well chosen.

Tradition versus culture

Tradition: handing down from generation to generation of customs or practice, beliefs and thought, i.e. a custom or practice of long standing.

Culture: the total of the inherited ideas, beliefs, values, and knowledge which constitute the shared basis of social action, i.e. the total range of activities and ideas of a people.

Although these terms are used differently by different interviewees, it appears that tradition is used to refer to ethnic attire, ethnic housing styles and old customs that make use of earlier technologies. A tradition is a specific practice that one family has retained and for them remains symbolic of their belief and identity.

Culture is related to common ways of doing things, ways of living and interacting; thus culture is more encompassing and applies to all, while traditional customs or practices might not be practices by all. Mamelodi has a hybrid culture which consists of a mixture of ideas and ways of doing; nevertheless it has merged to form a single identity and point of reference.

Question: What do you see as the culture of Mamelodi and of the people here?

Reply: Usually people who are going to live in suburbs they forget about their culture, I need that, I don't want to forget that. We still speak our own language, and still live in our old life. I think it's very important also, that we must know where we are from, Ehhm, our tradition, basically, our culture you mustn't forget it' (Sophia, aged 43, Show House sewing project).

Implications for design vision: Mamelodi East is a place with a singular identity, yet this encompasses a multitude of practices that are different for different people. Ethnic traditions are not similar for all people and the practice of these might also be inconsistent. Therefore cues should rather be taken from public collective behaviour, such as greeting and speaking, which is representative of former values and belief systems and embodies the collective identity of Mamelodi East. The connection between practices and space also becomes important, especially where taboos can be avoided or positive connotations can be guaranteed.

Past versus present

Interviews were often started by asking people where they were born, thereafter following their lives up to the present moment. Subsequently they were asked to make comparisons between circumstances. The recent change in political dispensation and implications for everyday life inevitably formed part of these conversations.

Past: The past usually refers to the apartheid government and the restrictions it implied to Africans; there is also a reference to forced removals and the hardship it brought about; for these reasons the present is referred to as being better. It seems as if youngsters are quite unaware of the difficulties and struggles of the past.

Of the past you know people were not very free, the *pass laws* [laws that restricted the location of permanent or temporal residence of non whites, i.e. thorough motivation was needed if people were found residing or travelling outside their place of birth], people were not free to go from one area to another, you must apply, you cannot stay in town until late at night, things like that. Now everybody does what they feel like...some lives were affected, let me say my own life was affected, of course. As I said, that forceful removal from Lady Selbourne to Mamelodi, and then from here on to say where I want my children to be, you know, I wanted to make sure that my children do not suffer as I did, and that's why I have participated in all these social structures (Richard, aged 55, councillor).

Implications for design vision: Mamelodi East certainly has negative connotations with the past; nevertheless group identity is strongly encouraged by hardship (Talen 1999). These memories are important connections to the collective identity and can be employed to motivate and strengthen future action when used in a positive light.

Present: The present is almost always seen in relation to the past. Speculating whether conditions have improved or not – mostly with reference to politics but also comparing development and infrastructure.

Yeah, now I think it's very different, there are a lot of changes; because before people didn't have places to stay, now it's open for everyone to get his own place, you used to find something like 40 people staying in one four-roomed house, so now everyone is free to get his own; and there are also shops or markets next to our places, and there's a lot of transport, we have taxis, before we were only using buses and the train. Yeah, there were only spazas (shops) far from our site, so now it is very easy (Sophia, aged 43, Show House sewing project).

Implications for design vision: Mamelodi East has come a far way and a celebration of the present might be required to emphasise this fact.

Change: Some interviewees felt that there has been great change in the country since democracy while others felt that nothing has changed.

Yeah, I think that it has changed in terms of migration, if you can call it that, in the townships first of all; and for the houses that government funded; and other things are poverty and crime, which I think have escalated; and I think people in townships now have a say, people for the first time can really say: 'You know I don't like this government'…Or the fact that you could live in Mamelodi for instance, I mean it's something that I'm sure would never have happened in the past (Jacob, aged 26, town planner, researcher, lived in Mamelodi, works for Provincial Government).

New Government, I think it's just the same. My life didn't change that much. What happened is that we got this place here, of which even in the old government we were going to get it, because it was promised to the people from phase one I think 1992 or 1993 somewhere (Abram, aged 19, scholar, resident).

Implications for design vision: Change in Mamelodi East has been a reality but due to expectation it is often soon forgotten. The marked reference of change by means of commemorative plaques or perseverance of historical symbols, even when negative in connotation might be a way of celebrating change in public space.

Future: The future vision of Mamelodi is very positive from the perspective of the experts working for the government while the residents could not really respond to this question. Academics see it as complex and hard to predict.

I think, the ten years that I've been there I have seen a lot of change and actually physical change for the better, you know it's actually starting to develop, people are investing there. I see it developing into a very special place, really, really special place that are integrated with the rest of it. Ehhm maybe I don't, maybe that's my dream… maybe that's not what will happen, because it is very difficult to get people from outside to move into the townships (Frida, late thirties, lecturer and researcher).

Implications for design vision: There is not currently a strong vision that drives future development in township areas. It is crucial not to re-invent the past; without a clear plan and vision the city does not make true progress.

Spatial perceptions

In Mamelodi East the spatial perceptions of the residents were revealed mainly through the photographic interviews and the mental map interviews. It is, however, fundamental to the nature of this research to point out that the quest was not for universal answers in terms of housing and open space design in townships or even Mamelodi East *per se*. The danger would be to end up with a recipe that represents the exact *a priori* judgment that this study aims to expose and avoid. The answer to spatial perceptions and preferences should remain context specific, i.e. to place, people and most importantly to time as explained so well by Hamdi (2004:131):

But what does a house equal? The opportunities are immense in terms of both process and product, and are more qualitative: wellbeing, dignity, status, self-respect, security, entitlements, skills, employment, enterprise, privacy and so on. When we add the variable **here** and then **for you**, when we contextualise the question, it gives us a chance to ensure the answer is tailor-made to the specifics of place and people. The answer in other words will be different every time – it is open and even less certain. The same holds true for all other development initiatives.

The dwelling

This research on housing conducted through photographic interviews, its methods and findings have been published in greater detail in Breed (2009). The photographic interviews assisted more than any other qualitative field work method used in the case of Mamelodi to open up intimate discussions on preferences based on or motivated by social identity. Several themes that would have been either difficult to bring into the conversation or tricky

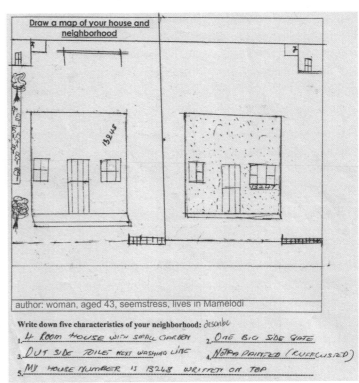

Draw a map of your house and neighborhood

author: woman, aged 43, seemstress, lives in Mamelodi

Write down five characteristics of your neighborhood: *describe*

1. 4 ROOM HOUSE WITH SMALL GARDEN
2. ONE BIG SIDE GATE
3. OUT SIDE TOILET NEXT WASHING LINE
4. NOT PA PAINTED (RUFFCUSTED)
5. MY HOUSE NUMBER IS 13248 WRITTEN ON TOP

Figures 25 and 26: Left: Photograph of resident at her house (Breed 2002). Right: Mental map of house by interviewee (From collection: Breed 2002). The interviewee was asked to draw a map of his house and neighbourhood. Note the stand number that is used to identify the house. A fence, gate and vegetation are also indicated on the left-hand stand to distinguish it from the neighbour's stand. The houses seem to be identical but are distinguished by colour/texture

to communicate were easily and spontaneously introduced. The researcher did not want to steer conversations into predetermined topics of interest or preconceived ideas. The photographs allowed for memory and association to be stimulated that generated responses based on the interviewees' spontaneous reaction to the image and less so on the guidance of the interviewer. The complexity of social preference, social economic realities, matters related to group identity and practical considerations regarding form and space were all easily revealed and led to a concrete understanding of socio-spatial reality.

From the interviews the following findings were made: The interviewees have in common a preference for large houses with several bedrooms. The size is related to privacy and to large family sizes. Varying opinions were expressed about preferred size – what is considered big and what is small. The house's potential to be enlarged was seen as a very important aspect. The safety of houses was also an important theme – more often than not interviewees referred to environmental safety against the elements rather than criminal activity. Materials are important in terms of environmental security but also to provide an agreeable climate inside the house. For this reason large windows are favoured to provide sufficient air and light.

Some interviewees prefer a neat/simplistic house while others prefer decorations that can include cultural and traditional aspects. Cultural diversity, especially relating to

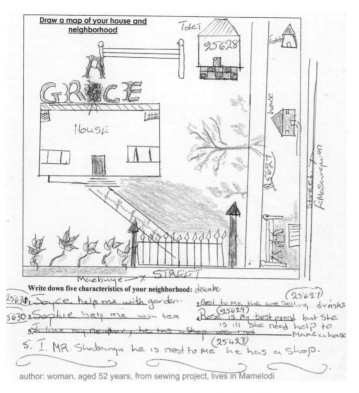

Figures 27 and 28: Left: Mental map of yard by interviewee. Note the toilet that is separate from the main house; clothing lines and vegetation are indicated, as well as a decorative gate. The stand number of each stand is shown and the street names for orientation. Right: A man showing his vegetable garden in an informal housing area, Mamelodi East, Ext. 11 (Photographs from private collection Breed 2002)

immigrants, seems to be a contentious issue that leads to the desire for homogeneity. There were also contradictions regarding aesthetics; in most cases the idea of something made the houses attractive not as much as the physical reality. For example, some people like decorations or materials because these reminded them of tradition, ethnic associations, culture, nature, etc. Others, however, noticed the physical reality without symbolic connotation, complaining that decorations mean additional work in terms of cleaning and organising. There are also those who prefer a simplistic house that does not reveal any ethnic identity.

Rural areas enjoyed preference in some cases while the proximity of the city was also an important consideration. The space around the house is important because it permits enlargement of the house in future. In the exterior of the house it is important to have a patio or a garden to rest in, or a garage or other entrances to the house. The additional entrances also refer to a social-economic reality of additional dwellers on the premises that might need to use ablution facilities, etc.

There does seem to be a negative connotation to repetition and homogeneity, houses constructed in the same layout and a similar size and quantity. Similar colours and forms are not favoured, as if this would rob the identity of the families. The negative connotations towards these include that they are primitive, old, poor, unorganised and similar to shacks, which is possibly more a mental perception than a spatial reality. This reaction is potentially due to its association with the political discrimination of the past.

Money as a necessity to obtain or finish the house is another important theme. The availability of basic services or high quality services is also deemed important. Interviewees referred to the houses shown as **acceptable** and not as **good** choices, which indicates high aspirations.

The following table summarises the important considerations concerning housing preferences according to the conducted interviews that could be used at the time of the research as guidelines for housing in Mamelodi East. As can be seen from the above discussion many aspects would have had to include flexibility in design and allowed for individual adaptations and appropriations.

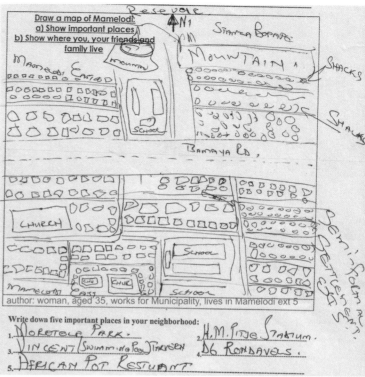

Table 1: Summary of recurring themes and their substantiation when discussing housing in photo and map interviews

Figures 29 and 30: Left: Photograph of two children playing in the street in Mamelodi East, Ext. 17 (Breed 2002). Right: Mental map of street by interviewee. The main street, Tsamaya Road, is indicated as well as the Magaliesberg Mountains. A school and a church are distinguished from the repetitive 'shacks' (from collection, Breed 2002)

Present considerations for housing	Justifications and elaboration
Importance of size	Of house and lot for privacy
Cost	Access to capital
Maintenance	Implied cost and access to capital
Privacy	Position of entrance, position of house on the erf
Aesthetics	Culture, nature and tradition motivates preferences
Climatic comfort	Presence of windows, choice of materials and door position
Material preference	Provide security, have climatic implications
Windows	To regulate the climate and provide air and light
Lot	Considerations include size to allow for garden, garage and activities. The position of house on the erf is also important for privacy and maximum use of surface in terms of expansion and additional units
Contextual considerations	The location of the house is important; access to services and goods

The yard

In terms of the yard around the private dwelling a number of considerations came out of interviews and mental maps. First of all it was noticed that fencing of yards was an important consideration to improve privacy by avoiding jay walkers from taking shortcuts through private stands. Secondly, the yard was seen as a means of additional income and therefore the position of the house on the yard had to allow for tenant quarters to be erected. The position of a toilet inside or outside the house was related to whether tenant quarters were available and had to share the toilet. Again a question of privacy

Figures 31 and 32: Photographs showing the nature of physical space in Mamelodi informal areas: Left: A woman with some children and a vendor stall at the back that sells vegetables, Mamelodi East, RDP zone. Right: An agricultural project at the community centre of Ext. 5 (Breed 2002)

where tenants would have to enter the main dwelling in case only an interior toilet was available. Ownership of the yard and house was important in terms of financial security.

As far as aesthetics were concerned a garden, fence and decorations (or the lack of the latter) were important considerations. The word garden referred to and included flowers, vegetables, beauty, relaxation, establishment/permanency, ownership, pride and environmental quality.

Common activities that were to be considered and positioned in the yard included sitting outside, cooking, relaxing, vegetable garden and fruit cultivation, a *spaza* shop that sells common household goods, space for collective events. Objects that had to be positioned within the yard included: a washing line, a toilet, the fence, a veranda, the garage, external rooms, a spaza shop, collective event space, a house number for orientation and identification and plants.

The above indicates recurring themes when discussing the yard in photo and map interviews. These elements and considerations would be crucial when considering a programme for design interventions at the time of the research. The information is also useful in considering the transition area between public and semi-private space. Again flexibility and individual adaptations would need to be incorporated in these designs.

The street

The streets in Mamelodi East have often been referred to in interviews as the current place of interaction and communal activities. The following actors and activities were positively associated with streets by the interviewees and can be considered in the design of streets and public spaces: children playing, neighbours, vendors, transport and movement, street life and culture, reciprocity and communication. Negative associations included: unemployment, vagabonds and crime. The fact that the mentioned activities improve security was also noted.

Figures 33 and 34: Photographs showing the nature of amenities in Mamelodi East: Top: Stanza Bopape memorial erected for a fighter against the apartheid regime who was born in Mamelodi; there is a clinic in the background. Bottom: The ward councillor's rather informal office in Mamelodi East, Ext. 11 (Breed 2002)

When discussing the streets in photo and map interviews the following hierarchy was unravelled in terms of access and land marks, in order of importance: National road (N1), main road (Tsamaya Road); taxi routes, bus stops, traffic lights and stops in streets. These indicators are important for planning and layout in terms of public space location and activity nodes. Surface material and lighting were mentioned considerations in terms of road quality, as many people walk considerable distances and arrive and leave home before and after dark.

In terms of orientation the following important landmarks and activity nodes were key: the street name, the street size and quality (surface material and lighting), taxi routes, number of the house (address in the street), location of shops, schools, nurseries, recreational spaces, the church, houses of friends and family. Framework and neighbourhood planning should consider these activities and amenities and their proximity to residential areas.

Activities in Mamelodi East

Activity-wise the following existing activities were recorded during the research in Mamelodi: music festivals, specifically jazz festivals, traditional dances and performing arts, sport, church activities, community centres that house sewing projects and communal vegetable gardens, weddings, funerals and social clubs (where people collaborate funds and celebrate birthdays and other happenings in small groups). These common activities would have to be considered in the overall planning and spatial provision in the area at the time of the research.

Needs that were expressed in terms of shortage of activities and amenities included installations for public events, entertainment and activities for the young, garbage removal, housing and education. Although these needs are mainly government service provision, it can be considered and promoted in terms of development in and around public space as part of spatial frameworks by designers.

Two reoccurring challenges that were mentioned were crime and HIV/Aids. Crime is a constant challenge in South African open space and although it cannot be solved through open space it can be addressed. Important considerations in open space concerning crime include attention to good access; formal and informal surveillance promoted through activities and numbers; good visibility through clear sightlines and good lighting; considerations regarding proximity between traffic and pedestrians and good maintenance of open space that discourages vandalism, littering and neglect.

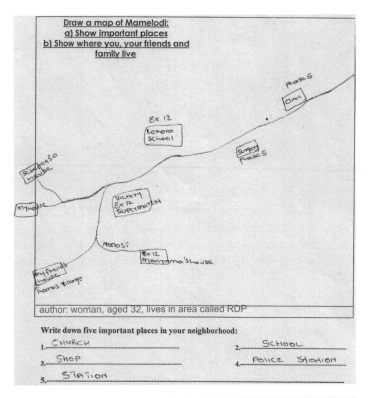

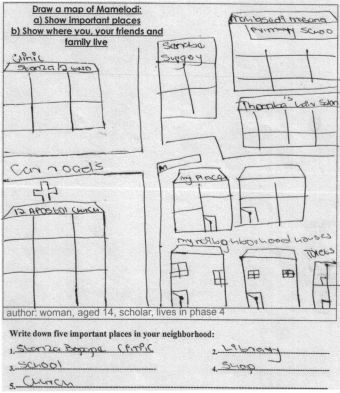

Figures 35 and 36: Mental maps drawn by interviewee indicating Mamelodi. Top: The neighbourhood. Bottom: Houses in the interviewee's neighbourhood; note the term 'car roads', 'my place', 'my neighbourhood houses'. The school and the church are again indicated, and also the clinic (From private collection, Breed 2002)

Spatial reference for Mamelodi East

The mental maps and map-interviews revealed the spatial orientation at regional and local level through the eyes of the residents. They help the designer understand the spatial references of the residents that might include names, landmarks, activities, amenities and traffic signs. The following recurring themes and terms were encountered when discussing mental maps in interviews that can be informative for open space design and development.

Destinations and activities that were recognised as important landmarks included: commerce, education, health, religion, residences, services, transport, community/social activities, open space, residential community, employment, sport activities and facilities, security and crime spots, names of streets, natural elements, children (in terms of activities), and a sense of belonging (in terms of own identity).

In terms of orientation important routes served as main spatial reference, place names, types of housing, housing zones (in terms of time of development), and services were also used for orientation. The role of memory in past and present occurrences played a definite role in this orientation system. Recurring names used include the East, the Far-East, Stanza Bopape, Mandela Village, Extension x/Phase x (referring to government housing developments), Mamelodi Gardens, Mahube Village and Cullinan as existing place names.

The regional and local spatial understanding of the designer can greatly and swiftly be improved through the use of the maps and map-interviews. This can be of great help in becoming familiar with the study area, its movement routes and destinations. The maps can be used by the designer for initial orientation purposes of the **landing** in the designer process, i.e. when the designer prepares to initiate research and discovery, a first contact with the site, a highly intuitive occurrence provoked by the sensory experience of an unknown area (as described by Girot, 1999).

Conclusion

The abstraction of space and user needs by designers to facilitate understanding and dialogue on urban space is an antecedent to homogeneous urban built form. In contrast with this the subjective reading of space by means of the concrete realities of the urban environment argues for the expansion of pluralistic public space that is accommodating to its users and allows for appropriation and increases diversity (Kallus, 2001). The predicament with design that rests on objective reading alone is the reality that

'what is ostensibly good for all is in fact good for no one' (Kallus 2001:147).

The challenge is to identify and consider the local vocabulary in the design of the urban environment. In this way local spatial expression can be fostered through an understanding of the spatial preferences and differences of the different users. The cultural dialogue becomes comprehensible when seen in the greater picture of the differential relations that give identity to terms and is brought about through the comparisons and contrasts that occur within the local vocabulary. The study of these exact, complex specifics of a collective identity can reveal the renewable rules of collective life when the researcher identifies and recognises the observable relationship between the various objects under study. This data can be obtained through qualitative research methods that engage the researcher to a personal subjective level with specific individuals that in their thoughts and interpretations reveal the structure of the social process. Of real meaning is that these methods also reveal the non-environmental factors that influence the preferences of the users (Talen 1999).

The satisfaction of the basic necessities, appropriated aesthetics, the maintenance of family structure, intimacy and territoriality and the adequate continuation of social interaction are all important spatial consideration that are socio-culturally defined yet specific in terms of time and space (Gyuse 1993:160).

The terms and themes revealed by the data of the qualitative research done in Mamelodi East provide a framework of differential relations that can inform a design vision. The spatial considerations and orientation can provide spatial parameters to guide decisions on design of urban form and space. When considered for design, these can lead to a greater morphological inclusiveness and richness (Kallus 2001:130). However, these spatial considerations are not usable when devoid of the cultural dialogue that validates them or the contextual appropriateness in terms of time and space.

A compatible interaction between the organisation of space, its practices, its values, and the discourse in itself is required to foster social change (Foucault 1993). In South Africa, as in the past, these factors can play a crucial role in the future of our cities and country. As designers of urban space the organisation of this space and the discourse attached to it are within our reach and with it an immense opportunity. As confirmed by Lefebvre: 'To change life is to change space. To change space is to change life' (in Merrifield 2000:173).

Bibliography

Aguilar Díaz, M. 1998. Espacio público prensa urbana. En N. García Canclini (coord.) *Cultura y comunicación en la ciudad de México. La ciudad y los ciudadanos imaginados por los medios.* (Segunda parte). UAM-I/Grijalbo, México.

Atkinson, P. & Hammersley, M. 1994. Ethnography and participant observation. In N.K. Denzin and Y. S. Lincoln, (eds) *Handbook of qualitative research.* London: Thousand Oaks, CA: Sage.

Beavon, K.S. 1992. The post-apartheid city: hopes, possibilities and harsh realities, in D. Smith (ed) *The apartheid city and beyond.* London: Routledge.

Berger, P. & Luckmann, T. 1968. *La construcción social de la realidad.* Buenos Aires: Amorrotu Editores.

Breed, C.A. 2003. El Proyecto Urbano. Un acercamiento cualitativo para el diseño de la ciudad. El caso de Mamelodi-Este, en Pretoria, Sudáfrica. Disertación de Maestría en Diseño. Mexico: Universidad Autónoma Metropolitana. No publicada.

Breed, C.A. 2008. The dimensions of space in the urban environment: three methodological approaches for designers that encompass the dynamics of urban space. *South African Journal of Art History.* 23 (1) pp.214–224.

Breed, C.A. 2009. Mindscape: exploring living space in the urban environment by means of photographic interviews. *South African Journal of Art History.* 24 (1) pp.89–105.

Bremner, L. 2007. Making life public in contemporary Johannesburg. In T. Casartelli (ed) *Johannesburg: emerging/diverging metropolis.* Mendrisio: Mendrisio Academy Press.

De Certeau, M. 1984. Walking the city. In M. de Certeau. *The practices of everyday life.* Berkeley: University of California Press.

Derrida, J. 1982, Difference. In Derrida, J. (ed) *Margins of philosophy.* Hemel Hempstead: Herts: Harvester Press.

Esquivel Hernandez, M.T. 1999. Familia, espacio habitacional y vida cotidiana: los programas públicos de vivienda en la Ciudad de México. Disertación de doctorado en Diseño: UAM – Azcapotzalco. No publicada.

Foucault, M. 1993. Space, power and knowledge. In S. During, (ed). *The cultural studies reader.* 2nd ed. London: Routledge.

Girot, C. 1999. Four trace concepts in Landscape Architecture. In J. Corner (ed) *Recovering Landscape, Essays in Contemporary Landscape Architecture.* New York: Princeton Architectural Press.

Goh, R.B.H. 2001. Ideologies of upgrading in Singapore public housing: Postmodern style, globalisation and class construction in the built environment. *Urban Studies,* 38 (9), pp. 589–1604.

Gyuse, T.T. 1993. Socio-cultural dimensions of public housing. In R.W. Taylor, (ed). *Urban development in Nigeria – Planning, housing and land policy.* Brookfield: Avebury.

Hamdi, N. 2004. *Small change: The art of practice and the limits of planning in cities.* London: Earthscan.

Integrated Development Plan. 1999. *Revision Planning zone 4 & 5.* Tshwane District Municipality: Cadre Plan.

Juarez, J.A. & Brown, K.D. 2008. Extracting or empowering: A critique of participatory methods for marginalized populations. *Landscape Journal,* 27 (2), pp.191–204.

Kallus, R. 2001. From abstract to concrete: Subjective reading of urban space. *Journal of Urban Design,* 6 (2), pp.129–150.

Leach, N. 1999. Architecture or revolution? In N. Leach, (ed). *Architecture and revolution: Contemporary perspectives on central and eastern Europe.* London: Routledge.

Lefebvre, H. 1974/1991. *The production of space.* Oxford: Basil Blackwell.

Lodi, J.D. 2000. Township lifestyles and their impacts on the utilization of the built environment and spatial planning with specific reference to an informal settlement in Mamelodi East. Bachelor's mini-thesis. University of Pretoria. Unpublished.

Lynch, K. 1960. *The image of the city.* Cambridge: MIT Press.

Malan, M. 1996. *The Black Community of Pretoria 1923–1938.* Pretoria: University of Pretoria. Masters dissertation in History. Unpublished.

Mbembe, A. & Nuttall, S. 2007. The elusive city. Writing the world from an African metropolis. In T. Casartelli, (ed). *Johannesburg: Emerging/diverging metropolis.* Mendrisio: Mendrisio Academy Press.

Mead, G. 1934/1972. La persona. En *Espíritu, Persona y Sociedad.* 3ª edición. Buenos Aires: Piados.

Merrifield, A. 1993. Place and space: A Lefebvrian reconciliation. *Transactions of the Institute of British Geographers,* New Series, 18 (4), pp.516–531.

Merrifield, A. 2000. Henri Lefebvre: A socialist in space. In M. Crang & N. Thrift (eds) *Thinking space.* London: Routledge.

Morse, R. 1985. Ciudades 'periféricas' como arenas culturales (Rusia, Austria, América Latina). En R. Morse y J.E. Hardoy, (comps.) *Cultura Urbana Latinoamericana.* Buenos Aires: CLASCO.

Philo, C. 2000. Foucault's geography . In M. Crang, & N Thrift. (eds). *Thinking space.* London: Routledge.

Pujados Muñoz, J.J. 1992. *El Método Biográfico: El Uso de las historias de vida en ciencias sociales.* Madrid: Centro de Investigaciones Sociológicas.

Schütz, A. 1993. Fundamentos de una teoría de la comprensión ínter subjetiva. En A. Shütz, (ed) *La construcción significativa del mundo social. Introducción a la sociología comprensiva.* Barcelona: Paidos.

Silva, A. 1992. *Imaginarios Urbanos. Bogotá – Sao Paulo: cultura y comunicación urbana en América Latina.* Bogotá: Tercer Mundo Editores.

Simon, B. 2004. *Identity in modern society: A social psychological perspective.* Oxford: Blackwell Publishing.

Spradley, J. 1980. *Participant observation.* New York: Holt, Rinehart & Winston.

Talen, E. 1999. Sense of community and neighbourhood form: An assessment of the social doctrine of new urbanism. *Urban Studies,* 38 (8), pp.1361–1379.

Van der Waal, G. 1995. Clashing cultures: Planning in Mamelodi. Unpublished. Van der Waal Collection. University of Pretoria Merensky Library.

Vila, P. 1997. Hacia una reconsideración de la antropología visual como metodología de investigación social. *Estudios Sobre las Culturas Contemporáneas,* 3 (6), pp.125–167.

Walker, J. & Van der Waal, G. 1991. A working history of Mamelodi. Unpublished. Van der Waal Collection. Special collections. University of Pretoria Merensky Library.

Walker, J. & Van der Waal, G. 1993. The story of Mamelodi. Unpublished. Van der Waal Collection. Special collections. University of Pretoria Merensky Library.

Wildner, K. 1998. El Zócalo de la ciudad de México. Un acercamiento metodológico a la etnografía de una plaza. En *Anuario de Espacios Urbanos 1998.* México D.F.: UAM – Azcapotzalco.

Williams, J.J. 2000. South Africa: Urban Transformation. *Cities.* 17 (3), pp.167–183.

chapter 4

Community Factors in the Planning and Design of Parks in South Africa: Thokoza Park, Soweto and Three Parks in Atteridgeville, Tshwane

Graham Young
Department of Architecture
University of Pretoria
Pretoria
South Africa

It's hard to design a space that will not attract people. What is remarkable is how often this has been accomplished.
William Whyte[1]

Urban parks did not enjoy a high profile in South African townships during the apartheid era. In fact at times the attitude towards them seemed downright hostile. In townships, the few parks that were developed by the authorities fell prey to the wrath of youths during the 'struggle' and were broken down as a means of protest. Ironically, 'People's Parks' evolved in their place but mostly as a form of protest and to keep youths off the streets and out of the way of the apartheid police. The parks would literally spring up overnight and would often contain some form of political statement, only to be demolished by the police as soon as they realised the actual intent of the park. The creation of the parks allowed youths to meet and to discuss political protest action as it was illegal for large groups to gather or to engage in any form of political protest. So these parks were an ingenious way to get around the authoritarian apartheid police – at least for a few days!

The parks started as a small but quickly spreading movement in the black townships during widespread violence and unrest in 1985. They were most prominent in the township of Mamelodi, near Pretoria. With no funding, it was up to the creators to draw on their own imagination and inventiveness in making these small pockets of life-giving force work. The equivalent 'conventional' situation is known as a neighbourhood park. Artists, gardeners, community workers and children joined in to heal the torn environment. Mamelodi residents explained that the parks, in addition to their obvious political statement, had three distinct

purposes. The first was to transform the harsh environment into something beautiful and imaginative. The second, to keep the youths occupied by giving them something constructive to do, keeping them out of the apartheid police's way and thirdly, to bridge the gap between adults and youths by means of group involvement. The parks therefore represented the diverse concerns prevalent in the townships with comrades building monuments to those who died in the struggle using different ideological and cultural symbols. However, these parks were not to last, they were only a transitory symbol of hope. Their loss was primarily the result of police personnel destroying them, especially those parks with the most overtly political symbols. For a while, youths tried to protect them but within a year of their appearance they were all gone.

Other than this specific movement, the urban park prior to the emergence of the 'new' South Africa was a relatively unknown entity in the townships. Social engagement and recreation mostly took place in the streets and dusty, over-used soccer pitches. Park space was not a phenomenon that most township dwellers had a chance or the 'luxury' to appreciate and people had few points of reference as to what makes a park 'good'.

Moving into the new political dispensation in the late 1990s, the challenge for designers and public entities concerned with the provision of parks was to aggressively promote the important role that parks could play in uplifting communities. The very real perception that they were places of fear, crime and vandalism[2] would have to change and evolve into a vision of parks being catalysts for community development and enhancement; parks could become an essential component in transforming and enriching life in the townships (Figure 1).

With this residual negative perception of parks, it is helpful for landscape architects, as designers concerned about the development of urban parks, to make reference to the objectives of the People's Park movement and to remember that what people don't understand they will not value. And what they do not value, they will not embrace! It is within this thought that the People's Park movement again has relevance; that when

Figure 1: Moroka school children on a visit to the park with their teacher (top)

Figure 2: Public workshop explaining the vision for the park (bottom)

Figure 3: Sketch plan conceptualised by 4th year landscape architecture students and members of the community (right)

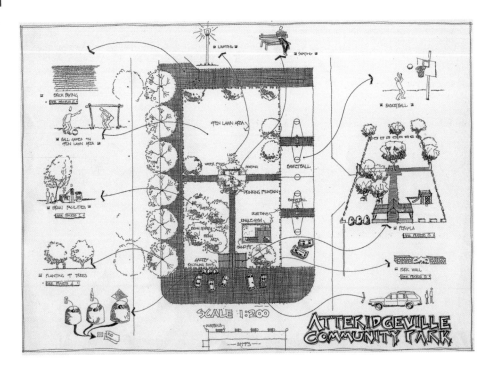

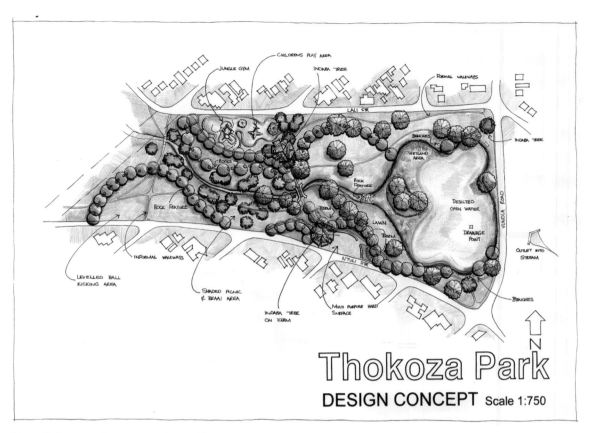

Figure 6: Concept plan presented at public meeting which illustrates the community's vision for the park

the community is passionate about their environment, is actively engaged in the process of its betterment (Figure 2), and by doing away with single-minded outside designers, something of meaning and relevance can be created.

In an article I wrote in 1993, 'Towards a model for urban parks in South Africa', I suggested a flexible design approach that brings social and ecological principles together with security, economics and productivity[3]. None of the principles[4] stands alone but they all stand together really well and remain relevant today. The focus of three of the principles is on social and community issues and I have come to realise that it is in these areas of concern that the essential ingredient that separates most success stories from failures lies. Where failures occur, they mostly relate to poor maintenance combined with the lack of ongoing community involvement, resulting in 'rejection' or confusion of ownership of the park[5].

To illustrate how some of the ideas were put into action two successful case studies are discussed.

Community parks, Atteridgeville

In 1994 the Atteridgeville and Saulsville Environmental Forum (ASEF) approached the Department of Landscape Architecture at the University of Pretoria for help with the design of three parks in the township. These projects formed part of the ASEF programme which had a mandate to educate the community about littering and waste, as well as the environment and the important role its protection and nurturing must play in community affairs.

Figure 4: 'Att-Park', a neighbourhood park currently maintained by members of the community

Figure 5: Students hanging out at the community park that they helped conceptualise

Figure 7: Moroka Dam with its associated wetlands and bridge crossing (left)

Figure 8: Play area at edge of park and near the local crèche (centre)

Figure 9: Existing bridge restored to connect pathways and communities across the park (right)

The objectives of the project were to create an amenity which:

◆ contributes to the recreational needs of the community
◆ makes a positive contribution to environmental health
◆ alleviates the litter problem at the park sites.

The project formed part of the department's fourth year students' design studio which included the design of park spaces based on urban ecology principles and community involvement in the planning process. Its purpose was also to introduce students to environmental and cultural/community issues relevant to the planning and design of urban areas.

Led by Lucky Ngale[6], the community was actively involved in the three park projects. Students met with community leaders and people living in residences surrounding the parks to establish their needs and conceptualise the plan. The concept plans (Figure 3) were presented to the community who ultimately endorsed them with refinements. The students were then tasked with documenting the process and compiling a report that the community used to convince the authorities to budget for and install the parks.

In each instance the park was built, although not necessarily exactly as was designed. However, the important issue was that they were built! During installation, community members were actively engaged with the construction process. Today the parks remain in reasonably good shape and are being maintained by council officials along with locals living in the immediate area (Figures 4 and 5).

Moroka Dam and Thokoza Park, Soweto

At the beginning of the planning process in 2001, the landscape architect together with the local ward councillor set up a working group who would guide the project. The group included the City Council of Johannesburg, Johannesburg City Parks, Department of Agriculture, Conservation, Environment and Land Affairs (DACEL), Working for Water, Department of Environment and Tourism (DEAT), Department of Water Affairs and Forestry, DANCED[7], politicians, the ward councillor and members of the local community.

A series of public meetings between the community and landscape architect led to a vision for the park (Figure 6) that focused on the rehabilitation of the Moroka Dam, its

Figure 10: Women from Moroka being trained in the art of mosaic (left)

Figure 11: A mosaic thanking the children from the nearby orphanage. The children contributed drawings which were turned into mosaics by the trained ladies (bottom left)

associated wetlands and the land that was derelict and strewn with garbage. The community had fond memories of a clear, open dam in the 1970s. The vision was to create a beautiful and safe place for the people of Moroka. The area around the dam (Figure 7) was designed to function primarily as a 'neighbourhood park' with facilities that encourage socialising and a play area (Figure 8). The park is easy to access and well connected to the surrounding community. It is visible from the street and the surrounding residences and people can see right across it (Figure 9). This is important from a safety

Figure 12: The park was a showcase project for the World Summit on Sustainable Development held in 2002

point of view because many people use the park as a short cut between neighbourhoods.

Employment of local labourers was an issue raised at community meetings that resulted in approximately 300 local residents being employed during the construction phase. The landscape architects, supported by the community, felt it necessary that the park gain 'added community value'. An arts training programme to run concurrent with the implementation process was introduced. The programme allowed individuals to add personal touches to their environment through the creation of mosaics. The works were installed in strategic locations throughout the park. Arts in Action

was employed to undertake the project[8]. In total 14 women and local artists were trained and the mosaics (Figure 10), reflecting neighbourhood and park activities as well as political and social issues associated, were installed about the park (Figure 11). The programme has been a huge success. It has added a unique aesthetic to the park, trained people in the art of mosaic and contributed to the community's sense of pride and ownership.

The park was profiled as a Showcase Project at the World Summit on Sustainable Development held in Johannesburg in August 2002 and has won a number of local and international industry awards (Figure 12).

1 Project for Public Spaces (2000), Eleven Principles for Transforming Public Spaces into Great Community Places, project for Public Spaces Inc., New York.

2 Oryx Environmental & Newtown Landscape Architects (August 2000), An open space framework for the Klipspruit River corridor, its tributaries and the adjacent open land, Unpublished Report, Johannesburg.

3 Young, G.A., Towards a model for an urban park in South Africa, *Ekistics*, Vol 60, No 360/361, May/June – July/August 1993.

4 Young, G.A. Towards a model for an urban park in South Africa, *Ekistics*, Vol 60, No 360/361, May/June – July/August 1993. pp. 218–219.

5 This statement is based on the author's observations of installed projects in Soweto, Ekurhuleni and the Cape Flats.

6 Mr Lucky Ngale who was chairman of the ASEF at the time, played a vital role in the success of the project. He brought enthusiasm and a keen sense of the community's needs and perceptions to the debate around the provision of facilities for each of the parks. One year, at the final social function in Atteridgeville, when traditional township food was laid on, he even brought his band to provide music for the dancing that carried on late into the night. It was a great scene to see young students and elder members of the community 'jiving' the night away!

7 DANCED is a Danish aid organisation that contributed funding to the development of the park.

8 Arts in Action is a group of artists working on collaborative interactive public arts, participatory community projects and developmental programmes concerned with social transformation and change. Projects include temporary and permanent artworks, community outreach, educational workshops, as well as entrepreneurial projects. In addition the group promotes public knowledge and awareness of the community arts and 'new genre public art'.

chapter 5

Rethinking the Role of Landscape Architecture in Urban Cape Town

Finzi Saidi

Faculty of Art, Design and Architecture

University of Johannesburg

Johannesburg

South Africa

Introduction

Landscape architects have always thought of themselves as providing for open space needs of society, be they aesthetic, functional, spiritual or ecological. Some have carried out a social agenda by attempting to provide open space that can be enjoyed by the masses with varied successes.

Equitable provision of quality open space has been identified as one of the major challenges in the City of Cape Town. Inequitable distribution of space is illustrated by the estimation that 20% of Cape Town's affluent communities occupy over 40% of the total land in the Cape Town Metropolitan area.

In Cape Town where there is a clear and disturbing separation between the formal and the informal city, articulating the role of landscape architecture in the latter can be a complex process that questions the value systems underpinning the practice of landscape architecture. Training for landscape architects is understood and can be said to be designed for intervention in the formal city. But increasingly landscape architects find themselves working in the informal sector of the city as part of the government's and city authorities' need to address equity in terms of provision of basic services to the public that includes open space.

This paper examines two participatory projects in which landscape architects have been involved located in a less affluent township part of Cape Town. Further the paper uses two students' dissertations to explore and illustrate how a 'transitional' landscape architectural curriculum can be developed in order to address the varying needs for open space of Cape Town's diverse population. An alternative approach for teaching urban landscape architecture and design in developing contexts is suggested. An analysis of all projects suggests that the roles of landscape architects, in a resource-stressed society, are as listeners, innovators and facilitators rather than professionals with ready-made solutions to problems. The paper identifies principles that can be incorporated in landscape architecture curricula in order to facilitate change in the formal and informal urban context of Cape Town as well as in other developing contexts.

The African experience in the physical urban landscape

Man cannot live by "Drudge" alone. (Joane Pim, 1971)

Writing in 1971, Joane Pim, who is recognised as the first South African landscape architect, described the environmental and social plight of the pioneer Africans as ... 'living in drudge'. These 'new' urban Africans had ventured to the unknown urban areas, forcibly or not, in search of work, from their village environment that had shaped their character and moulded their culture into formidable frames of reference. What the new environment had on offer for the African migrants is captured in Figure 1 below, bland nondescript, treeless settlements with regimented matchbox houses. Perhaps more important was Pim's realisation and concern for future descendants of these Africans who would have had to live in such urban environments without the benefits of knowing the forefathers' countryside and the culture of appeasing legends and anecdotes of nature. In the urban context there was normally nothing to replace that which was lost in the move from the village to the township.

In driving the point about spatial hostility of the urban townships Pim argues that:

hardly a tree in the street, so-called parks, dreary wastes, although there are notable exceptions, but even worse, virtually nowhere where they can go even by bus, should funds be available, for a day in the country. 'Man cannot live by Bread alone' – I should like to substitute 'drudge' for 'bread' – 'Man cannot live by "Drudge" alone'. How that describes the average dweller of Soweto's existence I leave to the reader to decide. Pim (1971:38)

How very poignant to note that even though the above quote may have been describing the African urban experience in the 1960s and 1970s, it is more or less the same experience by many impoverished urban dwellers who have moved to the city since the end of apartheid in South Africa. This experience is worse if one considers the dehumanising conditions in which shack dwellers in informal settlements currently live. Whether in formal or informal housing, the bland urban landscape experience is very characteristic for most contemporary African city dwellers. Acknowledging that this experience of the poor urban African is real brings into question, therefore, the content and methods of teaching new landscape architects. How can teaching of landscape architects be fine-tuned to respond to these unique demands of the culturally changing developing context in Cape Town?

Changes in cultural context and education for landscape architects

What kind of culture does a deprived urban landscape described by Pim above engender for its dwellers? The black population constitutes the biggest group of people in South Africa. It is also the group that has seen the most change in their social setup, i.e. from the traditional through to the colonial and apartheid periods to the post-apartheid era. In this period, forces that originate

Figure 1: An African urban township (Pim 1971:39)

from beyond the tribal life have eroded their beliefs and ways that are grounded in spiritual forces of the tribes. While black peoples' beliefs have been eroded, the colonial and apartheid forces have not allowed for the evolution of new beliefs that address the needs for safety, security, belonging, esteem and self-actualisation (Motloch 1991:171). The result has been a young black population that has not been acculturated into an urban lifestyle that expresses their real needs. Motloch (1991) argues that the native South African still lives in an alienated environment because the meaning of the urban environment is determined by regulations, standards and design concepts that originate from Western ideas of what is good.

While the devices that prevented black people from attaining equal social and economic status were removed in 1991, it still remains to be seen whether this black alienation in the urban environment is true thirteen years after democratic elections.

Others argue that while interest in cultural heritage continues to grow, the young generation in the developed context is unsure of what values they ought to adopt in their lives. They are caught in the rift between indigenous customs and Western values, and for most, the latter choice becomes obvious because it is thought to represent 'being developed' (Habraken, 1983:7).

But the problems of the South African society cannot be simply reduced to the accommodation of the real needs of the black African population – which are recognisably important. The new South Africa is not a homogenous culture and answers to its built environment problems will be found if landscape architectural design, practice and education reflect on its multicultural context.

This casts uncertainty on the suitability of the objectives of the landscape architectural profession and education. What and how should the students be taught? What values should landscape architects uphold if their designs have to work? Originality, symbolism, form experimentation and peer group approval – the yardstick of traditional professionalism – are hardly the criteria on which to base landscape architectural education in South Africa.

The perception of the built environment by students in landscape architecture given curriculum content is one that is dominated by a Eurocentric culture that largely excludes other cultures (African) in history and participation in the creation of the urban form. Naturally students want to relate to designs by landscape architects of the same cultural background as theirs so that they can gain a better understanding of the cultural aesthetics that influence design. Where there are neither critical bodies of practising landscape architects nor a critical mass of students from the 'minority' races in the practice of landscape architecture, it is imperative that a method of addressing environmental and urban demands

is developed to enable students to develop a new sense of their own values and research initiatives rather than simply being receivers of traditionally established methods.

Some authorities contend that landscape architects can't solve all the problems of mankind in the urban environment (Benson & Roe: 1999). Others are bolder in their criticism of the landscape architecture profession and argue that there is no scope for landscape architecture in the South African urban context. It is not uncommon to hear other professionals cynically questioning what role the landscape architects will play in a typical urban project apart from planting trees. These are only a few of the prejudices that landscape architects face in the South African context in their daily practice. Though some of the above utterances may hold some truth, it is also true to argue that there is a role for landscape architects in the South African context and that there are indeed some genuinely creative efforts by landscape architects to solve the problems of the urban poor.

The suggestion supported by this paper is that students of landscape architecture should be encouraged to work in contexts other than their own and one that aims to further the human values of providing an equitable and healthy environment for all South Africans.

The following discussion examines landscape projects that were implemented in the late 1990s, as part of the urban renewal movement of Cape Town in Khayelitsha townships which were designed to create vibrant open spaces. Their performance is examined with a view to understanding the utilisation and subsequent problems of these spaces. The second part discusses two students' thesis proposals for open space making in informal settlements of Khayelitsha.

Cape Town context

Cape Town is the oldest city in South Africa and known over the world for its natural beauty and its tourist sites: Table Mountain, Cape Point, Robben Island and the picturesque wine farms. Cape Town's proximity to other areas of natural beauty such as the natural botanical wonders of Namaqualand flora sites, the scenic Garden Route and whale spotting sites makes it an attractive destination for tourists.

It is therefore not surprising that the initial landscape architecture practice that evolved is one that served the interests of a society that placed a high value on conserving, preserving and developing sites that would enhance the perceived beauty of Cape Town. Evidence of this focus can be seen by the many landscape architecture projects on wine farms, tourist spots, centres and resorts, many of which have won prestigious design awards.

The south-eastern low lying areas of Cape Town which include Khayelitsha and Mitchells Plain have, historically been marginalised in terms of development of quality living environments despite having a population of over 600 000 residents between them. According to MCA Planners (2006) Khayelitsha and Mitchells Plain have been neglected, particularly in terms of access to higher order facilities and amenities. Khayelitsha, where more than half the area's (Khayelitsha and Mitchells Plain) population resides, is severely under-serviced in terms of residents' access to regional facilities and amenities. MCA Planners (2006) add that:

The fact (neglect) is evident when reflecting on the fact that [Khayelitsha Mitchells Plain] has been marginalised in terms of access to high quality environments such as regional parks. High order amenities such as Kirstenbosch, the Company Gardens and developed coastal spaces such as the Promenade in Sea Point are all closer to historically better off city residents. Despite the proximity of the coast and major areas of MOSS, opportunities for the creation of quality environments in the form of regional amenities have not been fully realised. (MCA Planners 2006)

However, since the demise of apartheid policies in 1994, Cape Town has been characterised by wider social problems as is typical of many other developing African cities. In the main most of the problems are the result of in-migration of people, especially poor Africans in search of better life, who previously were denied access to settle in the city of Cape Town. A 200 000 housing backlog continues to stimulate informal housing, whose inhabitants are largely poor. The number of informal dwellers continues to increase (Davidson 2007).

Unemployment had quadrupled since the 1980s with 120 000 unemployed and more than 165 000 people working in the informal sector (Dewar & Uytenbogaardt 1999:68). Unemployment has grown from 13% in 1997 to 23% in 2004, with a drop in 2005 to 21%. Between 25% (1996) and 38% (2005) households are living below or marginally above the household poverty line. People living in informal settlements increased from 23 000 families in 1993 to 115 000 families in 2006. HIV prevalence also continued to rise in line with national trends from 3% in 1996 to 15.7% in 2005 (Davidson 2007).

Understanding of these human problems needs to be taken in the context of the redefined post-1994 South African social and physical context. The City of Cape Town, according to Dewar and Uytenbogaardt (1991) can be understood in terms of a number of settlement patterns identified in the following categories (see Figure 2):

- Integrated finer-scaled and older development – in the northern, southern and western spines of the city
- Sprawling private suburban areas
- Formal and informal highly planned townships on the Cape Flats and beyond – including Mitchells Plain , Khayelitsha, Blue Downs and Atlantis
- Pockets of squatter settlements – occupying areas that they don't own.

It can be argued that the first two categories of settlements are largely populated by people who are financially able or secure. It is here that traditionally the landscape architecture profession has practised and produced a highly valued landscape.

In contrast the last two categories consist of groups of people who are largely just breaking even or are under severe financial stress. Some large parts of the last two categories are featureless, less hospitable low-lying areas that are frequently exposed to high-velocity winds and prone to flooding due to the shallow water table. The harsh environmental conditions in these areas are well known and have been described as spatially inhospitable, offering no security and serving as dump sites for waste. The areas lack a sense of human scale and are devoid of all elements necessary for making positive urban spaces (Dewar 1992:244).

Dewar (1992:244) further argues that 'the heavy-handed planning control and planning approach in these settlements has resulted in sterile, monotonous and boring environments that are difficult to redeem through various 'design techniques' with convoluted configurations'.

Unemployment, environmental degradation and unequal distribution of income are the pressing social problems that the city has to address. Attempts to solve some of the housing problems are compounded by the fact that 20% of the population owns about 40% of the land in Cape Town.

In the last decade, government policy focused on delivering public infrastructure to the less affluent sections of society, which saw landscape architects produce designs for public open spaces in townships at important transit points under the direction of city planner urban designers.

Dewar (1992) has identified problems with the response and approach of government to addressing the needs of the poor in Cape Town. Generally government public investment in urban infrastructure consists of utility services, houses and essential social services and schools and health. It has treated everything else including the natural environment as luxury. But, as Dewar argues, treating nature as a luxury fails to recognise the immense potential it holds for meeting the needs of the urban poor, if managed well.

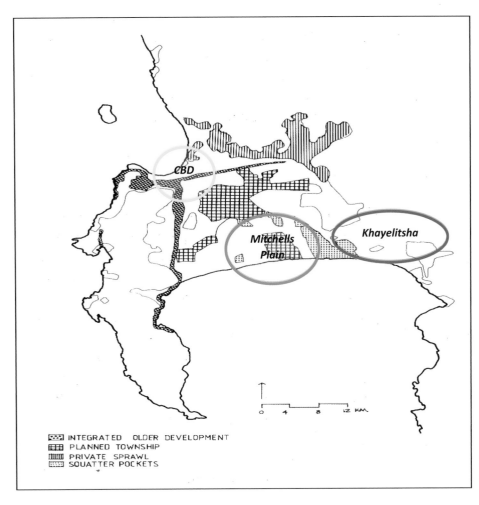

Legend:
- INTEGRATED OLDER DEVELOPMENT
- PLANNED TOWNSHIP
- PRIVATE SPRAWL
- SQUATTER POCKETS

Figure 2: Cape Town's urban structural sub-types (Dewar & Uytenbogaart 1991)

Four multifunctional ways have been identified in which urban natural resources can be utilised for the benefit of the urban poor (Dewar 1992). They are as follows:

- Small-scale urban agriculture
- Urban woodlots for environmental improvement
- Creation of water bodies for recreation and fish farming
- Improvement of public spaces where people will be able to experience the city and engage in its collective life.

Given the above assertions with regard to what the urban and landscape problems are in the Cape Town context, the next section discusses Khayelitsha's township environment and recent landscape projects.

Khayelitsha

At the city level Khayelitsha and Mitchells Plain have been planned as contained dormitory townships (see Figure 2). Land has been used as a means of containment and major areas of land (buffer areas) exist, notably the Swartklip Products site, fragmenting Khayelitsha and Mitchells Plain into distinct areas. This pattern of land utilisation forms a barrier effect and isolates rather than integrates the areas with each other and the rest of the City of Cape Town.

Figure 3: Northern mosaic entrance to Khayelitsha Wetlands Park (Saidi 2006) (left)
Figure 4: Khayelitsha Wetlands Park showing the water body with no functions for human use (Saidi 2006) (right)

The township open spaces in Khayelitsha and Mitchells Plain are locations where social experiences are played out and they become in the process, extensions of the individual dwelling unit which is in many instances very modest space. The richness and multifunctionality of such open spaces have the ability to create positive environments even where the quality of individual dwelling spaces are poor.

Dignified Projects Urban Renewal Programme was a pilot project where a series of specially selected sites were picked and developed as multifunctional landscapes that would stimulate the informal business sector of townships but they would further serve as open spaces for people to play out their lives in a dignified manner (Daniels, C.,pers. comm., March 2007). This involved the redesign of public space and socio-economic facilities such as markets, taxi ranks, bus stations, community parks, playgrounds, pedestrian walkways and open spaces. This approach was a top-down process that was led by local authorities. Success of this approach has been partial while social problems still persist, some with increased intensity. While some public spaces have been successful, others have failed miserably. In some cases the problems are obvious, such as lack of maintenance; while in others subtle problems that require political intervention have hampered progress.

Two of these initial projects were landscape schemes designed in the mid 1990s by landscape architects Robinson-Swift in Khayelitsha. The first is the Khayelitsha Wetlands Park (Figure 4) which includes a children's play park as the main function. The project included involving the local community in construction of the mosaic celebrated entrances. Teaching the community mosaic was a way of empowering the local women. It was envisaged that after the training these women would go into the mosaic business.

The other component was a recycled water feature with water spouts that children could play with in the summer time. The wetland was not designed to offer any other functions except as part of a storm-water system, due to shortage of funds. Though children use the park, its scale is too large for the park to function efficiently and with lack of maintenance it is falling into disrepair. The park's size fails to integrate with dwellings in its vicinity making self-policing by the local population very difficult. The local

Figure 5: Lookout Hill timber staircase going down to ecotourism centre (Saidi 2006) (left)
Figure 6: Children 'sand dune' sledging on a stabilised sand dune (Saidi 2006) (right)

authorities are now thinking of how to revitalise the park by creating work through training of young people to make street furniture and establish nurseries on the site as a way of encouraging maintenance of the environment by the locals in Khayelitsha.

The second project is the Lookout Hill, an ecotourism node that includes conference facilities and an art gallery. Lookout Hill (Figure 5) is the highest point in Khayelitsha with view to the sea in the south and Cape Peninsular mountain range in the west and in the east is another mountain range. The Lookout Hill was designed as a viewing deck on a remnant sand dune by Robinson-Swift (personal communication, May 2006) and is a popular site for tourists and local children who go to play all kinds of games. The design included rehabilitation of the sensitive sand dune ecosystems, but there is conflict between the children's need for recreation and maintaining the ecological integrity of the site. While the landscape architect tries to retain and preserve the remaining small patch of indigenous dune vegetation, children used the hill for sand games, one of which is 'sledging', which are detrimental to the retention of the vegetation. Interestingly the buildings which were designed for art exhibitions and tourist functions serve very well as congregation venues for numerous religious communities on weekends for many in Khayelitsha – a function for which they were never designed.

These two projects perhaps reflect what Dewar (1992) calls the 'heavy handedness' of the local authorities who prescribed the solution to open space design by their restrictive briefs. The result has been vast open spaces which are of such a scale that it is difficult for the inhabitants to relate to or engage with them in terms of monitoring the activities or maintaining them. They have largely remained 'white elephants' with only a small percentage

of the inhabitants using them. In a few cases the township dwellers have found their own use for the parks which are at odds with local authorities. Figure 6 illustrates unauthorised uses that people make of the designed open spaces.

The above discussion has highlighted the problem of formally designed open spaces in Khayelitsha in which landscape architects were involved but perhaps either didn't have the mandate to modify the briefs or perhaps lacked the skills to observe, present and argue for an alternative solution to city authorities in a different manner. Those new skills are what should be included in a new curriculum for landscape architects.

Landscape architecture and informal settlements

The historical response to informal settlements has been to relocate the 'squatters' to newly-built lower income housing. But since 2000, the South African Governments' 'Breaking New Ground' policy has shifted to upgrading of informal settlements where there are no environmental health risks such as annual flooding. This, coupled with an inability to deliver lower-cost housing quickly by the local council authorities has resulted in a mushrooming of informal settlements. Generally the characteristics of informal settlements are:

- ◆ Narrow streets often inaccessible to amenity vehicles
- ◆ Temporal structures made from every kind of material – mostly recycled materials
- ◆ Overcrowding
- ◆ Lack of services within unit – water and toilets
- ◆ Lack of open space.

In such a context one could ask what should be the role of landscape architects. What values should guide the practice of landscape architecture? The Millennium Development Goals provide the ideal starting point for landscape architecture practice in articulating their role in the urban environment especially in the informal settlements. Water scarcity and provision of open space, and environmental protection provide a guide to the process of formalising informal settlement into new urban landscapes.

Millennium Development Goal number 7 states the following:

- Integrate the principles of sustainable development into country policies and programmes; reverse loss of environmental resources
- Reduce by half the proportion of people without sustainable access to safe drinking water
- Achieve significant improvement in the lives of at least 100 million slum dwellers by 2020.

Before practical approaches to the upgrading process of informal settlement can be considered it is important to discuss the educational process of landscape architects. Most landscape architects have the initial training in design disciplines such as architecture. It is reasonable to assume that the kind of curriculum that students undergo has influence on the manner in which they would ultimately practise landscape architecture.

The Western influence in the theoretical content of courses is very evident. While there are courses that teach students an understanding of society's social ills, there are numerous difficulties in articulating the design studio to address these social ills. Understanding the social ills and what the solutions entail are issues which many landscape architects are not equipped to address. Coming from a profession that is perceived to value the aesthetic concerns above anything else, the problem of the open space in townships and informal settlements requires a different kind of engagement. A re-examination of what is taught in the landscape architecture programmes is required given the complex social, political and economic context of Cape Town.

In such a context knowing what knowledge content to include in a curriculum, and when and how to teach it, is an important process in ensuring that education is relevant and responsive to the context.

Two hypothetical projects carried out by students in the master of landscape architecture programme at the University of Cape Town provide direction with regard to making intervention in informal settlements and also on how landscape curricula can be adapted to give students knowledge of their wider context. Both projects are located in the informal parts of Khayelitsha, i.e. Victoria Mxenge and Nkanini informal settlements.

Figure 7: Victoria Mxenge informal settlement (Blignaut 2006)

Case Study 1: Victoria Mxenge informal settlement – MLA Thesis 2007

Victoria Mxenge informal settlement, situated in the North-Eastern section of Khayelitsha, is a high-density residential area with few facilities provided. Its proximity to Nonqubela Rail Station adds to the pressure for every available space to be used for housing – in the form of informal dwellings. Originally the central core of Victoria Mxenge was designated to remain as open space functioning as part of the storm-water system of Khayelitsha. However, because of the need for land for housing, the open space was taken over by informal dwellers which subsequently led to the problems of raising ground water that created wet, muddy living conditions every rainy season.

There is generally a lack of basic services within the informal dwellings in Victoria Mxenge informal settlement. Lack of essential services such as waste management, emergency fire services and ablution facilities combine to create a multitude of urban problems experienced by the informal settlement dwellers. Hygiene is highly compromised especially for children as they are

Figure 8: Victoria Mxenge informal settlement – Landscape framework proposal (Blignaut 2006)

exposed to dirty areas and dangers of waterborne diseases in these spaces.

The solution to such problems cannot be achieved by a single draconian approach such as removal of the informal settlement. Upgrading has been muted as an alternative approach to intervention on such areas and it is with such understanding that landscape architects can contribute to the creation of healthy livable environments. In this case study the student uses water through its transformation, celebration and harvesting in public open spaces to achieve multifunctional living spaces. In the crowded informal settlement, public open space is developed around public facilities such as water taps, toilets and, where it abuts, open school ground. This case study proposes that water is made visible by designing troughs through which it can be collected, purified and reused, i.e. for urban food or flower gardening.

Each open space may, apart from being multifunctional, have one dominant theme to serve various groups in the settlement. Thus one may find an open space being dominated by a particular function such as agriculture or recreation.

Case Study 2: Nkanini informal settlement

The second case study for a thesis exploration is an informal settlement called Nkanini informal settlement also in Khayelitsha. The settlement is situated on the southern periphery of Khayelitsha. To the north of the settlement are the standard township council housing units and to the south is a vast tract of natural undulating dunes reaching False Bay on the Atlantic Ocean. The Nkanini settlement was established in the late 1980s and has grown considerably in size over the years.

Residents of Nkanini can be classified as being generally below the poverty datum line and with a large percent of the population being unemployed. As with any other squatter settlement problems of crime, fire, lack of land tenure, poor services and facilities and pollution of the natural environment abound. Services are located outside the settlement and people have to walk long distances to access them.

The cheapest form of transportation is by rail, and is accessed through Khayelitsha Station which is a considerable distance and many times walking to the rail station is a dangerous affair

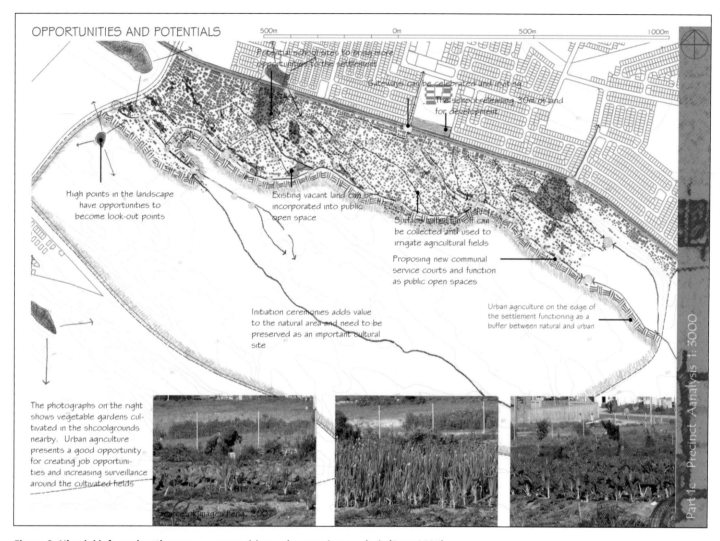

OPPORTUNITIES AND POTENTIALS

High points in the landscape
have opportunities to
become look-out points

Existing vacant land can be
incorporated into public
open space

Surface water run off can
be collected and used to
irrigate agricultural fields

Proposing new communal
service courts and function
as public open spaces

Initiation ceremonies adds value
to the natural area and need to be
preserved as an important cultural
site

Urban agriculture on the edge of
the settlement functioning as a
buffer between natural and urban

The photographs on the right
shows vegetable gardens cultivated in the shcoolgrounds
nearby. Urban agriculture
presents a good opportunity
for creating job opportunities and increasing surveillance
around the cultivated fields

Figure 9: Nkanini informal settlement – opportunities and constraints analysis (Feng 2007)

as gangsters stand on the corners of the pedestrian routes to rob passersby of their belongings.

This pedestrian route connecting the railway station to Nkanini settlement is part of an urban renewal scheme that addresses the issues of violence in society by using environmental upgrading. It proposes a multifunctional approach to reducing violence and improving the quality of life of the inhabitants of the area starting with the Harare Pedestrian Route. Along the safe route are a series of activity boxes serving as landmarks which function on a twenty-four hour basis as refuge points (Feng 2007).

But the intervention of the safe pedestrian route terminates at the entry point into Nkanini settlement. The proposal by the student was to extend these safe routes into Nkanini settlement by repeating the activity boxes to form a continuous safe route.

The dwellings are densely packed with shacks closest to each other along the length of Mew Way and gradually spreading out towards the dune area. The settlement configuration is very organic in nature but with strongly defined route systems throughout the settlement (Figure 9). Although the formation of the informal settlement appears to be haphazard, there is an underlying structure determined by the natural response to environmental conditions on site. Public open spaces are limited if not non-existent, as any piece of ground is seen as a potential area to house new inhabitants. Thus in a place where individual dwelling units cannot provide for all total living functions, open space is necessary, not only to allow people to carry out their functions but also to fulfil their need for socialisation and interaction. Feng (2007) adds 'the public open space is the only place where the inhabitants can gather and socialise'. By formalising open space in the informal settlement Feng (2007) hopes to achieve a sustainable livelihood for the informal inhabitants and maintain a balance between development and conserving the natural environment. In conceptualising the open space intervention in this informal settlement Feng (2007) proposed four main goals:

◆ Ensuring the future productivity of natural resources
◆ A baseline of economic health and maintaining it in the long term
◆ Reducing social exclusion and inequality
◆ Ensuring abilities of institutions to carry out their duties for the benefit of all actors in the long term.

The student sees the role of landscape architects in such a context as helping to create positive public spaces that give identity and dignity to the squatter dwellers. In creating these positive spaces, the concept of multi-functionality informs the design. Space is designed to enhance security, create business opportunities through urban gardens, and heal the environment through slowing down water runoff. Pedestrian safety is enhanced by the inclusion of activity boxes along the main access as shown in Figure 12.

Deprived as they may seem, the people in these informal settlement carry themselves with dignity as evidenced in the unique boundary edges which may either be planted sometimes with indigenous hedges or constructed of recycled materials, old planks, doors, car parts, etc (see Figure 11). Occasionally one finds immaculately mowed grass patches which can be interpreted as a transfer of ideas of beauty from the suburban areas where the informal dweller may be working as a garden attendant.

Conclusion

These open spaces of the two student case studies illustrate an achievement of a complex form of multi-functionality through spatial segregation, time segregation and spatial integration. The result can be said to be real sustainable open spaces because of the activities that are generated on the sites which in turn support their existence and continued use.

Such an approach begins to reveal the intrinsic beauty of informal settlements as can be seen by the inhabitants' use of elaborate and careful 'hedge' row property boundaries and ingenuity of

Figure 10: Nkanini informal settlement. Fence made of recycled timber (Feng 2007)

Figure 11: Nkanini informal settlement. Fence made of recycled tyres (Feng 2007)

using recycled materials. Although the thesis looks at maximising utilisation of open space within informal settlements, uses of open space adjacent to the settlement reveal other cultural uses such as collection of herbs for 'muti' medicine and also camps for initiation rites and religious ceremonies. These uses normally fall outside the realm of services that authorities provide but the fact that they happen suggests that landscape planning has to allow for them.

In contrast to the first case study of the Khayelitsha Wetlands Park the two dissertations address issues of scale in a more sensitive manner that is sympathetic to the scale of area and dwellings.

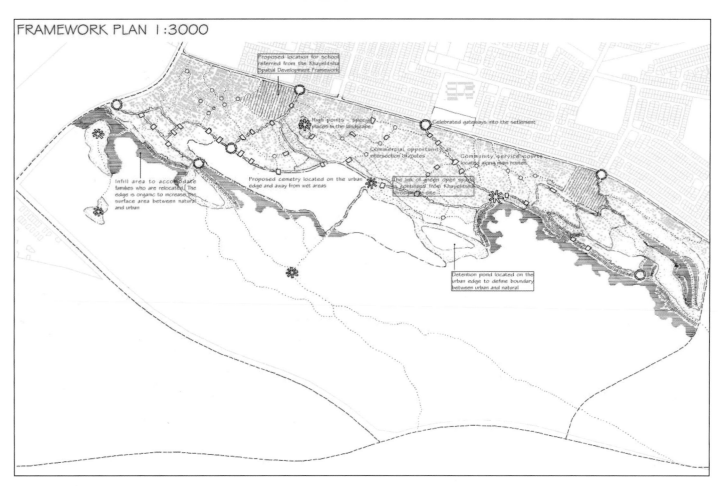

FRAMEWORK PLAN 1:3000

Proposed location for school referred from the Khayelitsha Spatial Development Framework

High points – special places in the landscape

Celebrated gateways into the settlement

Commercial opportunity at intersection of routes

Community service courts located along main routes

Infill area to accommodate families who are relocated. The edge is organic to increase the surface area between natural and urban

Proposed cemetry located on the urban edge and away from wet areas

The link of green open space continued from Khayelitsha towards the site

Detention pond located on the urban edge to define boundary between urban and natural

Figure 12: Proposed framework of communal spaces and activity boxes in Nkanini (Feng 2007)

Rethinking the landscape architecture curriculum and the student in the broader context

The work of the landscape students discussed above illustrates a kind of learning that is based on understanding and solving contemporary social problems affecting the City of Cape Town and numerous other African cities across the continent. It can be argued that the social problems approach appears to be relevant in such a context and that it should inform all (design) education.

The suggestion by this paper, given the discussion above, is that social problems should be the basis of designing a new landscape architecture curriculum. Normally such curricula, which integrate education with social responsibilities, would be organised based on themes such as environmental problems, and/or urban problems (Conrad 1978:32). The new programme is a deviation from the traditional curricula organisation that was based on discipline distinctions.

The main advantage of using social problems to develop a curriculum is that it provides a powerful motivational force for students to pursue their studies – that of making meaningful change in society through the landscape architecture knowledge. Such learning programmes for landscape architecture students are forward-looking, and introduce a positive outlook for the future as opposed to the traditional disciplinary approach to landscape architecture.

Such projects engage students critically and assertively with proposed changes in society especially for the urban poor, and begin to prepare landscape architects as agents for change, 'catalysts' as they are referred to by Hester (2005:74). They promote democracy by highlighting to the municipal authorities the spatial inequities of squatter dwellers but more importantly the design opportunities and initiative that exist within such communities.

Including projects such as those discussed above in landscape architecture curricula cultivates in students multiple kinds of knowledge and learning processes. Excellence in both learning and teaching is extended to include many aspects of society that traditionally may have been deemed to be outside the realms of landscape architecture in its traditional sense.

The process of engaging in landscape architecture with the informal settlement is important because it challenges students' and teachers' established knowledge systems. Through these processes students begin to question their long-held assumptions and value systems of society and design ideas. In that way students become co-creators of knowledge with the teachers.

This paper argues that for change in the practice of landscape architecture and in the curricula to be meaningful it is important to have a learning framework that provides learners with the intellectual, social and emotional capacity with which to critically examine the contemporary urban environment. In this respect this learning is accessed through engaging the problems and realities of township and informal settlements and their dwellers.

This approach to landscape architecture can be criticised as being 'value-laden' and perhaps too practical. But it is the contention of this paper that in the context of the City of Cape Town's extreme social discord and deprivation, curricula in general must be flexible to be relevant to its context and if it is to contribute positively to overall development. At this level of development of the City of Cape Town where poverty has to be dealt with in more ways than one, it is essential that landscape architecture students should be prepared for more than just one context in which to practise the profession.

Bibliography

Benson, J. and Roe, M.H. 2000. *Landscape and sustainability*. London, New York: Spon Press.

Blignaut, C. 2006. The value of water in informal settlements. Unpublished Masters Dissertation. University of Cape Town.

Conrad, F.C. 1978. *The undergraduate curriculum: A guide to innovation and reform*. Colorado: Westview Press.

Davidson, B. 2007. Housing issues in Cape Town now. Public lecture at University of Cape Town 22 August 2007.

Dewar, D. 1992. *Urbanization and the South African city: A manifesto for change in the apartheid city and beyond*. D. Smith (ed). Routledge: London.

Dewar, D. & Uytenbogaardt, R.S. 1991. *South African Cities: A manifesto for change*. Urban Problems Research Unit, University of Cape Town.

Dewar, D. & Uytenbogaardt, R.S. 1995. *Creating vibrant urban places to live: A primer*. Headstart Developments New Housing Company, University of Cape Town.

Feng, A. 2007. *In-situ* upgrading of informal settlement through securing public spaces. Unpublished Masters Dissertation. University of Cape Town.

Habraken, J.N. 1983. The general from the local. *Architectural Education* 2. p. 7–14. London: RIBA Magazines.

Hester, R. Whose politics do you style? *Landscape Architecture*. December 2005.

MCA Planners. January 2006. Urban Renewal Spatial Development Framework for Khayelitsha and Mitchells Plain. Final draft. Unpublished.

Motloch, J.L. 1991. PhD Thesis: Delivery models of urbanisation in emerging South Africa. University of Pretoria. pp. 171–180.

Pim, J. 1971. *Beauty is necessary*. Cape Town: Purnell and Sons SA Pty.

chapter 6

An Extension of the Fields into the Intangible for the Reading of the South African Cultural Landscape*

Gwen Breedlove
Department of Architecture
University of Pretoria
Pretoria
South Africa

* Extracted, edited and expanded by her study leader, Roger Fisher, from a thesis submitted in fulfilment of part of the requirements for the degree of Philosophiae Doctor in Landscape Architecture, in the Faculty of Engineering, Built Environment and Information Technology, University of Pretoria, Department of Architecture: Breedlove, Gwen. 2002. A systematics for the South African cultural landscapes with a view to implementation.

Reading the landscape

J.B. Jackson[1] in the founding of the journal *Landscape* (1951), a trade magazine dedicated to landscape interpretation, took as a guiding principle the notion that landscape is to be read and interpreted according to function rather than merely appraised visually. Mere seeing was deemed less important than understanding landscapes as lived-in places. Real comprehension grew from awareness of function in the identification of cultural, social, economic, and political contexts.

It is thus necessary to understand the interrelated components that constitute a particular landscape. The components of how people relate to the landscape can be divided into five broad categories, here in the main deduced from Smith[2], namely:

◆ People observing – thus visual perception
◆ People growing or breeding – thus agricultural crop production or animal husbandry
◆ People conquering or defending – thus protection or defence
◆ People living – thus human settlement, ancillary uses and recreation
◆ People digging or mining – thus extraction of resources and deposition of waste.

Krampten[3] observes that all languages are made of words and all words are signs, therefore, all things made up of signs are languages. Landscape, thus, has a language and can so be 'read'. Therefore the landscape is seen to represent a language, a 'to whom it may concern' message with its own syntax – the relationship of signs among themselves; semantic – the relationship of signs to object; and pragmatic – the relationship of signs to the user.

Anne Whiston Spirn[4], has focused her life's work on landscape as language. In her book *The Language of Landscape* she says that[5]:

The language of landscape is our native language. Landscape was the original dwelling; humans evolved among plants and animals, under the sky, upon the earth, near water.

She also states that landscape has all the features of language. It contains the equivalent of words and parts of speech – patterns of shape, structure, material, formation and function, meaning of landscape elements is only potential until context shapes them.

Her main concern is with our inability to manage the earth. In her search for a solution she studies the value of landscape for people. She says that[6] the power to read, tell and design landscape is one of the greatest human talents:

It enabled our ancestors to spread from warm savannahs to cool, shady forests and even to cold, open tundra. But the ability to transform landscape beyond the capacity to comprehend it, threatens human existence.

For authors, from Cicero to Marx, 'first nature' represents a nature unaltered by the human endeavour. Cicero[7] wrote:

We sow corn, we plant trees, we fertilise the soil by irrigation, we confine the rivers and straighten or divert their courses. In short by means of our hands we try to create a second nature within the natural world.

Hence labour yields the 'second nature'. The Latin words *natura*, *naturans* refer to the given – biophysically occurring material, forms and phenomena – and *natura/naturata* to those reworked by human hands.

This is the cultural landscape – the second 'nature'.

Cultural imposition on the landscape

Whiston Spirn[8] discusses stories, actions and other intangible qualities that shape human relationship with landscape, especially in terms of its cultural expression. She says that:

landscape stories have common themes across cultures, such as:

◆ struggle for survival
◆ the character of human society (the relations of individuals to

family, deities, state or corporation)
◆ the nature of nature and the place of humans within it
◆ where things come from and how specific places came to be (stories of origin and creation – of mountains and rivers, and flowers and humans).

She goes further to explain that process[9], as a deliberate act by a conscious being, is a means to an end. All human processes are cultural, deliberate means by which humans sustain themselves, adapt to their environment and relate to one another. Most basic are those processes essential for survival of individual and species:

◆ physical – moving – exchanging, sensing, reproducing, growing, and decaying
◆ social – identifying, communicating, making/building, trading, playing, learning, competing and fighting
◆ spiritual – dreaming and worship.

Human habitats satisfy these basic human processes.

Characteristics of culture

Whiston Spirn[10] discusses the relationship of people to the biophysical realm. She says that every nation has its 'native' nature, worked by physical and mental labour into landscapes, with which its people identify.

Others emphasise an even greater relationship between humankind and the land. Edward O. Wilson[11] calls this phenomenon 'biophilia', which he describes as the innate tendency to focus on life and lifelike processes. In culture the biophilic relationship to landscape is preserved through association and reverence, intangible aspects of culture. Tradition is the means by which such associations travel through time and it is these that are often unrecorded in any physical act of the modeling or changing of the landscape features. By way of example, the following: Makhonjwa, the name of the mountains separating South Africa from Swaziland, is in the process of being inscribed as a World Heritage Site:

Makhonjwa – 'It means "those pointed at/those to which are pointed". *Khomba* is "point at", *khonjwa* is "to be pointed at", and the *ma*– is a plural noun prefix. Now this is [if it is] Zulu. I have no Swazi reference to hand. I am not even sure if there is a Swazi dictionary yet. But I am pretty sure that this is [the same for] Swazi too, as the difference between Zulu and Swazi boils down to several predictable sound changes, none of which would take place in the word *khomba*. Pointing is considered rude. If one points at a chief one certainly gets into trouble, so I would assume that they look upon these mountains with the necessary respect. It could be an example of irony, and I certainly would not point at them if I were you.[12]

We see that embedded in the name of a natural feature are oblique references to cultural practices, even as to be so disguised as to take on an ironic tone.

In his book *On human nature*, Wilson[13] lists the characteristics as identified by George P. Murdock that he states have been recorded in the history and ethnography of every culture. These characteristics provide us with a clear understanding of the uniformity of cultures and at the same time these terms indicate the differences among them. Although these practices or customs are presented as being universal, their application is radically different from one culture to another. It is possible to either qualify or quantify each of these characteristics of a community and, therefore, it is possible to use these in a descriptive manner to establish the character of the cultural landscapes or culture of a community.

Table 1: Characteristics of culture as recorded by Murdock[14]

Age-grading	Ethics	Inheritance rules	Property rights
Athletics	Ethno-botany	Joking	Propitiation of super-
Bodily adornment	Etiquette	Kin groups	natural things
Calendar	Faith healing	Kinship nomenclature	Puberty customs
Cleanliness	Family feasting	Language	Religious ritual
Community organisa-	Folklore	Law	Residence rules
tion	Fire making	Luck superstitions	Sexual restrictions
Cosmology	Food taboos	Magic	Sports
Co-operative labour	Funeral rights	Marriage	Soul concepts
Courtship	Games	Mealtimes	Status differentiation
Dancing	Gestures	Medicine trade	Surgery
Decorative arts	Gift giving	Obstetrics	Training
Divination	Government	Penal sanctions	Tool making
Division of labour	Greetings	Personal names	Visiting
Dream interpretation	Hair styles	Population policy	Weaving
Education	Hospitality	Postnatal care	Weather control
Eschatology	Incest taboos	Pregnancy	

What should, however, be highlighted is that these are, for the most, tangible characteristics, although there are some intangible characteristics in the list. Other intangibles, such as singing, story-telling and trancing, are missing from the list. The explanation may be that these practices may not occur in all communities. The more likely explanation is that their form of expression in one community may not be recognised by another.

Contested landscapes

The idea of a homogeneous cultural landscape filled with universal values is questioned by those who, in the past, were marginalised and excluded from the frame of reference which sustained such a concept. The traditional and indigenous peoples of those landscapes today contest historical values and meaning of landscapes, which could be attributed to western conservation philosophies.

Drawing on both literary theory and cultural studies, many contemporary cultural and historical geographers have begun to examine the meanings assigned to the cultural landscape[15]. For the geographers, culture has come to be understood as

a way of life encompassing ideas, attitudes, languages, practices, institutions and structures of power and a whole range of cultural practices: artistic forms, texts, canons, architecture, mass-produced commodities and so forth.[16]

Whelan discusses the contemporary historical geography reflection of the theoretical shifts that have taken place in the humanities and social sciences. She states that much recent work reveals a preoccupation with questions of power and meaning. She[17] is of the opinion that a more interpretative approach to the study of the cultural landscape has emerged and the (urban) landscape has come to be approached through the guise of a range of metaphors such as landscape as text and the iconography of landscape. She states that[18]

while the (urban) landscape can be read as a complex, contested and symbolic power system it is important to recognise that some landscapes are more overtly symbolic than others, depending on the context in which they are shaped.

The Cultural Landscape Resource Unit[19] under the leadership of Prof. Helen Armstrong and in collaboration with others at Queensland University of Technology in Brisbane, Australia, has been studying the Queensland cultural landscape as contested terrain. They have realised that the significance of cultural landscapes cannot easily be defined. In a discussion document of the unit the following statement is found:

The concept of cultural landscape enables us to balance the traditional focus on discrete heritage elements with a broader concern with the diversity and dynamism of the wider human environment. The management of such places raises challenges for contemporary practice. Cultural landscapes are never 'complete' and unchanging: the process of landscape making continues with the everyday priorities and decisions of those who own, use, control, value and contest the land.

The unit lists four issues of particular concern regarding the Queensland natural landscapes[20]: These are:

◆ There are divergent values associated with Queensland's natural landscapes ranging from tropical rainforests to arid deserts; each of which has deep cultural significance for Aboriginal and Torres Strait Islander communities. These landscapes also have significance for the non-Aboriginal peoples of Australia.
◆ There are vast pastoral leases and forest reserves as well as areas of mineral extraction which contain historical relics of the nineteenth and early twentieth centuries. Current land uses are creating strongly contested values about these places, including Indigenous Land Titles.
◆ The cultural landscapes from the mid nineteenth century to the present time reflect the contributions of different voluntary migrants to Australia. There are also the involuntary migrants, the South Sea Islanders, who have made a particular contribution to the cultural landscapes of Queensland.
◆ There are conflicting approaches to the management of heritage landscapes including the strong push by natural heritage lobbies to restore landscapes to a former 'natural' state, thus removing evidence of human activities.

As stated by the Australian Environmental Defender's Office[21], heritage, or cultural landscapes, can be part of the natural or built environment. Heritage management involves conserving items and places that are culturally significant, that have aesthetic, historic, scientific or social value for present and future generations. Because heritage is an anthropocentric, or 'human centred' concept the cultural significance may be contested or defined by more than one stakeholder or group. Recognition of these differences in the management of the cultural landscapes is crucial.

It is, however, necessary to ensure that the fields for evaluation and reading of the landscape are as broad as possible. So as to be over-arching and all-encompassing of all those cultures that have either lived in biophilic harmony with or acculturated the landscape it is necessary to revisit Murdock's list of what can be seen as representative of tangible traditions. South African oral traditions, when recorded, particularly as contribution to the literary tradition, offer just such opportunity, both in adding to the tangible, but more significantly, the realm of the intangible.

South African literature

Different cultures occupying the same landscape at different times often embrace the same significant landscape features for purposes of their own cultural resonance. Because South Africa has a history of human occupation as long as the time of humankind itself, a single place may represent an overlay of many landscapes containing residual features of different pasts, which create a palimpsest of these. Hence the 'natural' veld or grassland, when fenced and given to game farming arborifies and becomes a low-density forest, the climax vegetation to which such landscapes tend. This alerts us to the fact that even the grasslands may be a relic landscape of human activity, where natural or human-made fires were allowed to burn to encourage the growth of grass and hence attract grazing herds.

The cultures of South Africa have a strong oral tradition. The people did not read and write until the colonists came to the Cape. Dancing, singing, talking and drawing were the major forms of communication in the southern part of Africa. Today these songs and stories are being recorded and these African myths, legends and stories (literature) provide a rich source and evidence of daily living.

It is of critical importance to recognise these intangible indigenous resources as part of the heritage of South Africa. Much of South African literature[22] represents tales of animals, birds, fish, reptiles and insects; places and events; rituals and death; rivers and waterfalls; sacred things and life's joys and sorrows. The list of terms below are distilled from readings of South African texts and here summarised to indicate identified topics:

Alphabet
Beliefs
Bio-physical features
Bio-physical threats
Bravery
Communications
Currency
Dates of discoveries
Drink
Elderly
Expansion
Furniture
Geographic location
Head coverings
History of place
Household
Hunting
Inspiration to others
Material use
Mining
Performance
Possible extinction
Products
Recording events
Rites of passage
Singing fabrics
Storage
Struggles
Suicides
Supernatural beings
Superstition
Technology
Travelling
Utensils
War
Waste
Water
Weaponry
Wildlife
Writing

Recapitulation

The landscape can be 'read'. In reading the landscape there are three domains that offer access for legibility. The first two are in the realm of the tangible of the biophysical and the cultural. In conjunction with these is the realm of the intangible, usually preserved in the oral traditions of cultures. It becomes imperative to be empathetic to the intangible values that derive from a biophilic relationship to landscape, even when such landscape has not been domesticated, merely appropriated. Only through empathetic familiarity with the oral traditions of culture can the biophilic associations be 'read'.

Bibliography

Armstrong, H. 2001. Myth and the landscape. Spectacle and tourism at the Faustian bargain: Sustaining the myths of landscape. Unpublished paper submitted to the journal *Spectator*. University of Southern California's Media Studies.

Australian Committee for IUCN 1999. Natural heritage places handbook. Applying the Australian Natural Heritage Charter to conserve places of natural significance. Canberra: Australian Heritage Commission.

Coetzee, P.H. & Roux, A.P.J. (eds). 1998. *Philosophy from Africa. A text and readings*. Durban: Thompson Publishing.

Environmental Defender's Office Ltd. Publication date: July 2000.

Gray, S. (ed). 1985. *The Penguin book of Southern African stories*. London: Penguin.

Gray, S. (ed). 2000. *African stories*. London: Picador.

Grossberg, L., Nelson, C. and Treichler, P. (eds.). *Cultural Studies*. New York: Routledge.

Hilton-Barber, B. 2001. *Weekend with legends*. Claremont: The Spearhead Press.http://www.edo.org.au/edonsw/publications/factsh/factsheet28.htm 5/19/01 2:26:31 PM.

Jakle, J.A. 1987. *The visual elements of landscape*. Amherst: University of Massachusetts Press.

Krampten, M. 1987. The meaning of the urban environment, in Jakle, J.A. *The Visual elements of landscape*. Amherst: University of Massachusetts Press.

Marsh, G.P. 1974 [1864]. *Man and Nature*. Cambridge: Harvard University Press.

Murdock, G.P. The common denominator of culture, in Wilson, E.O. 2000. *On Human Nature*. UK: Penguin Books.

Smith, A.B. 1992. *Pastoralism in Africa. Origins and development ecology*. London: Hurst & Company.

Whelan, Y. 1997. Monuments, power and contested space – the iconography of Sackville Street (O'Connell Street) before independence (1922). School of Environmental Studies, University of Ulster at Coleraine.

Whiston Spirn, A. 1998. *The language of landscape*. New Haven and London: Yale University Press.

Wilson, E.O. 1978. 1995, 2000. *On Human Nature*. Harvard University Press and Penguin.

---

1   Jakle. 1987.p.x
2   Smith. 1992
3   Krampten. 1987. p.14
4   Former Head of Department of Landscape Architecture, at the University of Pennsylvania
5   Whiston Spirn. 1998
6   Whiston Spirn. 1998. p.25
7   Whiston Spirn. 1998
8   Wilson. 1984 p.49
9   Whiston Spirn. 1998
10 Whiston Spirn. 1998 p.31
11 Wilson. 1984 p.1
12 E-mail from Beven Hoek [alias Hook] in Amsterdam, Netherlands Fri, 5 Mar 2010 16:03:49 +0100 [17:03:49 SAST])
13 Wilson. 1978, 1995, 2000
14 Murdock. 1978 p.12
15 Whelan. 1997
16 Grossberg,Nelson Treichler. 1992 p.1–16
17 Whelan. 1997 p.12
18 Whelan. 1997 p.12
19 http://www.dbe.bee.qut.edu.au/research/CLRU/ 5/01/02 2:01:04 PM
20 http://www.dbe.bee.qut.edu.au/research/CLRU/ 5/01/02 2:01:04 PM
21 Environmental Defender's Office Ltd 2000
22 Gray, 2000; Gray, 1985; Hilton-Barber, 2001; Coetzee & Roux, 1998

chapter 7

Historic Schools as an Intangible Landscape: The Role of Oral Histories in Development

Liana Müller

Department of Architecture

University of Pretoria

Pretoria

South Africa

Introduction

Landscapes are not synonymous with an environment or nature. Landscape is primarily seated in perception; it is a reflection of who we are and how we perceive the world. A cultural landscape is the vehicle for the perpetuation of collective identity and memory. Cultural landscapes are containers or vessels of meaning. It is often the intangible values – the stories, rituals or other meanings attached to a place – which contribute most significantly to its worth.

When presented with a project steeped in history, the conscientious landscape architect would endeavour to understand the numerous layers of meaning inherent to the place. Heritage practitioners operating in the development field are primarily mandated to express a statement of significance for a cultural landscape or historic buildings in order to guide proposed development. In the absence of a statement of significance, landscape architects are tasked to gain a thorough understanding of the historic context in order to produce design solutions that support the heritage significance of a site. This often takes the form of archival research comprising historic documents, maps and other pertinent information on the history of the site. Whereas tangible aspects are thoroughly defined and understood through these methods, techniques for gaining insight into the intangible aspects are generally lacking. It is easy to dismiss an open field, a copse of *Indica ferrea* trees or crumbling stone wall as insignificant. What role did they play in the story of the place? And why should they be included in future development proposals?

Most often, the answers lie with the people who were intimately connected to the site and not the dusty archives. It is thus necessary to access this living heritage – meaning memory, lived experience and attachment in relation to people's connection to locality and landscape. These intangible values can be traced back to the tangible fabric of place through means of quantitative and qualitative anthropological fieldwork methods. This includes oral history documentation which comprises participant observation, individual and focus group interviews and accompanying individuals or groups to places of interest as part of the research phase.

This methodology was applied in the compilation of Cultural Landscape Heritage Audits for a number of historically significant schools in South Africa. The Historic Schools Restoration Project, commissioned by Archbishop Ndungane and the Department of Arts and Culture, is a Section 21 company based in Cape Town, South Africa. The project's mandate is to revive historically significant and currently under-resourced South African secondary schools into centres of cultural and educational excellence (HSRP 2010)[1]. The decayed conditions of the various schools have been documented, with restoration and re-appropriation being proposed. The heritage analyses of the cultural landscape of Lemana, Healdtown and St Matthews were undertaken by Cultmatrix cc and Liana Müller under the guidance of Ms Laura Robinson of the HSRP Professional Task Team.

Historic schools

Lemana Campus, located on a hill outside the town of Elim in Limpopo Province, was, together with Healdtown Comprehensive School, part of a handful of institutions offering education to black inhabitants during pre-apartheid South Africa. Lemana has consistently provided for the educational and spiritual needs of the community with great success. The Swiss Missionaries' efforts at Lemana Training Institution (1906) and Elim Hospital (1899) not only attracted Xhosa, Zulu, Tswana, Swazi, Ndebele, Coloured, and Venda students, but also Shangaan students from South Africa and the neighbouring Mozambique (F. Maboko, *The Valdezia Bulletin*, Vol. V, No 57, September 1935:1 as quoted in Masumbe, B.M.C. & Coetzer, I.A. 2001:227). The Institution has produced many leaders in the academic and business world who have excelled within and beyond the borders of the country (Mabunda 1995:56). Alumni of the school are still highly respected and sought-after in the business and political spheres.

Figure 1: The Lemana Church building. Key informants remembered how this was the biggest building in the district and that the interior felt like being in heaven (Müller 2008) (top)

Figure 2: The path to the north-east of the Church with the row of Lagerstroemia indica *along the fence (Müller 2008) (bottom)*

Figure 3: The northern, main school building. Oral traditions indicate that the original school emblem and name used to be prominently displayed on the gable (Müller 2008) (left)

Figure 4: The Lemana Training Institution monument (Müller 2008) (right)

Figure 5: Original location of the orchard with expansive view towards Elim. Nothing remains of the orchard; key informants, however, all remembered its location (Müller 2008) (left)

Figure 6: The matron's house of the girls' hostel on the hill. The students gathered at the tree every morning before breakfast (Müller 2008) (right)

The school grounds have evidence of a cultural landscape that was developed over time by previous occupants. Now mature Eucalyptus and Jacaranda trees have been planted along pedestrian routes and boundaries. Outdoor spaces have been complemented by an assortment of indigenous and exotic species, creating a lush and beautiful setting that enhances the academic buildings, religious structures and dwellings. Historic stone terraces provide structure to the site. The academic campus and the classroom blocks are situated on a number of these terraces that continue down the hill towards the site boundary and communal land to the north of the school property. A monument commemorating the significance of the school is located near the entrance to the academic precinct.

Apart from the academic campus, the site also contains a number of students' hostels and dwellings for staff members. Most of these are in a state of disrepair. A noteworthy discovery of an expansive indigenous botanical garden by the wife of a long-term missionary at Lemana, Mrs Colette Junod, added another layer of significance to the site.

The Healdtown High School and Teachers Training College is located approximately 20 kilometres north-east of Fort Beaufort in the Eastern Cape Province of South Africa. It is a cultural landscape resulting from the Methodist Mission Society's beginnings in South Africa and most successfully reflects their integrated approach to religion, education and health, as it manifested in the Eastern Cape region. As an educational institution with a strong missionary Christian basis, it played a major role in the training of African teachers in South Africa. As with the Lemana School, it produced a large number of alumni who have made a significant mark in South African society, including Nelson Mandela. Furthermore, the evolution of the Healdtown cultural landscape is indicative of major epochs in the socio-political evolution of South African society as it pertains to race relations and the approach to the education and cultural progress of the African segment of society (Cultmatrix & Müller 2009:85). The mission was founded in 1853 by the Rev. John Ayliff for the Mfengu (or Fingo) people. Ayliff established the mission on the site of the earlier station of the London Missionary Society, founded in 1844 by the Rev. Henry Calderwood and named Birklands. In 1855, Governor Sir George Grey visited Healdtown and granted money to build the majority of the school complex (from Ayliff's writings, in Jubilee 1906:9). The subsequent erection of the Industrial Institution building (for training of blacksmiths, carpenters, wagon builders and shoemakers and the first pupil teachers) was supervised by Rev. Ayliff and completed on May 26 1857. From 1885 to 1940, continuous further construction work and renovations were conducted on the site.

The Healdtown campus features an extraordinary landscape quality, both in terms of its setting on a promontory in the rolling landscape of the Eastern Cape, and the architectural quality of the historic buildings. The early founders of the school were extremely sensitive to the environment in which they established the mission settlements and school. They situated built interventions carefully, with respect for features such as water courses,

natural access routes, vistas and visual axes. This sensitivity to the natural landscape formed the basis of the exceptional qualities that are experienced when visiting the site. The mandate of the Heritage analysis was to respect and enhance this sense of place by understanding the various elements with respect to the campus as a whole, in order to guide future interventions to enhance the existing characteristics of the site.

Before expounding on the basic methodology employed in the compilation of the heritage analyses for both schools, it is necessary to understand the legislative context in which the study was conducted.

Cultural landscape legislation

The concepts of intangible landscapes and memory and their role in cultural landscapes and heritage are anchored in an elaborate legislative framework comprising of various international conventions, acts and organisations instrumental in guiding cultural landscape conservation. The lengthy process to define the function and significance of cultural landscapes, and the subsequent conventions and other legislative documentation supporting its importance spans more than a century. UNESCO and ICOMOS paved the way for new approaches to understanding, protecting and managing cultural landscapes. During the late 1990s, tangible and intangible aspects in culture were becoming more prominent in multi-disciplinary discussions. There is currently a global academic, institutional and governmental move towards a unified vision of landscape, which focuses on the integration of culture and nature, and which incorporates the conservation of the identities of people and places (Scazzosi 2004:336). The recent *Xi'an* Declaration on the Conservation of the Setting of Heritage Structures, Sites and Areas and the *Teemaneng* Declaration on the Intangible Heritage of Cultural Spaces have paved the way for landscape to be viewed as an integral part of cultural heritage.

The following table presents a summary of most charters, declarations and guiding documents relating to the conservation and management of cultural and intangible landscapes:

Figure 7: A View of Healdtown taken in 1906 (Healdtown Centenary 1955 Booklet, p.21) (top)

Figure 8: The view towards Healdtown campus from the road leading up the escarpment (Müller 2008) (top centre)

Figure 9: The girls' hostel, front view (Healdtown Centenary 1955 Booklet, p.33) (bottom centre)

Figure 10: Girls' hostel with garden and original wall (Müller 2008) (bottom)

Table 1: Cultural and intangible landscape documents

ICOMOS

1964	The Venice Charter: International Charter for the Conservation and Restoration of Monuments and Sites
1982	The Florence Charter (Historic Gardens)
1983	Appleton Charter for the Protection and Enhancement of the Built Environment
1987	The Washington Charter
1990	Charter for the Protection and Management of the Archaeological Heritage
1994	The Nara Document on Authenticity (1994)
1996	ICOMOS New Zealand - Charter for the Conservation of Places of Cultural Heritage Value
1999	The Built Vernacular Heritage Charter
1999	International Charter on Cultural Tourism (Managing Tourism at Places of Heritage Significance)
1999	The Australia ICOMOS Charter for the Conservation of Places of Cultural Significance (The Burra Charter, 1999)
2005	Xi'an Declaration on the Conservation of the Setting of Heritage Structures, Sites and Areas
2007	The Teemaneng Declaration on the Intangible Heritage of Cultural Spaces
2007	The Ename Charter for the Interpretation and Presentation of Cultural Heritage Sites
2007	World Heritage Cultural Landscape
2009	The Zacatecas Charter – Cities and their heritage engagement with integral planning
2010	The Valletta Principles for the Safeguarding and Management of Historical Cities, Towns and Urban Areas

ICOMOS – IFLA

2001	The Buenos Aires Memorandum on Cultural Landscapes and Historic Gardens (2001)

UNESCO

1962	Recommendations Concerning the Safeguarding of Beauty and Character of Landscapes and Sites, 11 December 1962
1972	Recommendation Concerning the Protection, at National Level, of the Cultural and Natural Heritage, 16 November 1972
1972	Convention for the Protection of the World Cultural and Natural Heritage, Paris, 16 November 1972
1997	Proclamation of Masterpieces of the Oral and Intangible Heritage of Humanity
2003	Convention for the Safeguarding of the Intangible Cultural Heritage
2004	Yamato Declaration on Integrated Approaches for Safeguarding Tangible and Intangible Cultural Heritage (2004)
2005	Vienna Memorandum on World Heritage and Contemporary Architecture – Managing the Historic Urban Landscape

COUNCIL OF EUROPE

2004	European Landscape Convention

Figure 11: Jubilee Buildings – back view (Healdtown Jubilee 1906 Booklet, p.26)

According to Frank Proschan, ex-president of the UNESCO Intangible Cultural Heritage Section (2008:9), the Convention for the Safeguarding of the Intangible Cultural Heritage (2003) considers intangible heritage to be a 'phenomenon perpetually created and recreated, transmitted from one generation to the next or shared from one community to another'. He continues to quote the convention by stating that intangible heritage 'is constantly recreated by communities and groups in response to their environment, their interaction with nature and their history' (Proschan 2008:9). Intangible heritage, as defined by the convention, must therefore always be living heritage: 'It must continue to be actively produced, maintained, re-created and safeguarded by the communities, groups or individuals concerned, or it simply ceases to be heritage' (Proschan 2008:9). As living heritage, the intangible is based in the past and may often evoke it, but it is manifested in the present and future and lives on in the minds and bodies of human beings, that is, the communities and individuals who are its bearers, stewards and guardians (Proschan 2008:9).

It is clear that landscapes form part of cultural heritage. With oral traditions, rituals, cultural practices and knowledge integrally connected to the landscape, its intangible dimension becomes apparent. This relationship should be recognised and conserved in order to provide holistic and sustainable management of cultural heritage. To date, 132 countries, or State Parties, have ratified, accepted, approved or accessed the Convention for the Safeguarding of the Intangible Cultural Heritage (2003), which points towards an international move towards increasing awareness and significance of intangible heritage.

Within the South African development industry, the realities of preserving intangible heritage are still misunderstood or ignored. Most South African development projects show little or no regard for the role of memory and the meaning of place either in the present or for future conservation policies (Bakker 2003). While current legislation provides broad guidelines on how cultural heritage should be interpreted, the field of intangible landscapes remains vague.

South Africa, with its rich and diverse cultural heritage and numerous examples of highly significant intangible heritage, is still in the process of becoming part of this global movement by ratifying the Convention for the Safeguarding of the Intangible Cultural Heritage (2003). South Africa is a State Party to the Convention Concerning the Protection of the World Cultural and Natural Heritage (1972), and legislation concerning the protection and conservation of cultural heritage has developed significantly over the past few years. The following section is a brief synopsis of heritage legislation in South Africa.

A brief synopsis of heritage legislation in South Africa

Pre-1994, the following South African Acts served to protect and conserve cultural heritage resources: the *Bushmen Relics Protection Act* (Act 22 of 1911), the *National and Historical Monuments Act* (Act 6 of 1923), the *Natural and Historical Monuments, Relics and Antiques Act* (Act 4 of 1934) and the *National Monuments Act* (Act 28 of 1969). South Africa's new dispensation encouraged the need to enact legislation to protect South Africa's cultural heritage. The subsequent White Paper on Arts, Culture and Heritage (1996) provided the grounding for the *National Heritage Resources Act* (Act 25 of 1999) (hereafter referred to as the NHRA) which was promulgated during 1999 and became operative in 2000. The main aims of the NHRA (Act 25 of 1999) are to create an integrated framework for the management and protection of cultural heritage, and to encourage and promote participation in and access to heritage resources (Kotze & Jansen van Rensburg 2002). Presently in South Africa, the White Paper on Arts, Culture and Heritage (1996), the Policy on Indigenous Knowledge Systems, the *National Heritage Resources Act* (Act 25 of 1999) and the *National Heritage Council Act* (Act 11 of 1999) constitute the major policy and legislative frameworks which attempt to define intangible heritage and the protection thereof.

The guidelines contained in the White Paper were further expounded by the *National Heritage Resources Act* (Act 25 of 1999). The term 'national estate' is described in the NHRA as consisting of heritage resources of cultural significance for present and future generations. It also comprises places to which oral traditions are attached or which are associated with, among others, living heritage. According to the NHRA (Act 25 of 1999), a number of conservation categories fall under the Act, specifically clause (2):

(2)(b) places to which oral traditions are attached or which are associated with living heritage

(d) landscapes and natural features of cultural significance

(e) geological sites of scientific or cultural importance.

Furthermore, according to clause (3), a 'place' is considered to be culturally significant due to

(3)(a) its importance in the community, or pattern of South Africa's history

(b) its possession of uncommon, rare or endangered aspects of South Africa's natural or cultural heritage

(c) its potential to yield information that will contribute to an understanding of South Africa's natural or cultural heritage

(e) its importance in exhibiting particular aesthetic characteristics valued by a community or cultural group

Figure 12: The practising school with a section of the cloistered garden (Müller 2008)

Figure 13: One of the key informants' childhood home (Anne Webster – parents were both teachers at the school) (Müller 2008)

Figure 14: Remnants of the once verdant garden of Anne's childhood, and boundary wall (Müller 2008)

(g) its strong or special association with a particular community or cultural group for social, cultural or spiritual reasons.

All of the above categories underpin the importance of the intangible dimension of heritage, especially the biophysical environment. They emphasise the fact that non-physical heritage can be defined in association with tangible heritage, as it adds value and meaning to the material dimension of heritage.

Heritage analysis and assessment of the historic schools cultural landscape

Heritage analyses were procured as the first phase of the restoration and development of Lemana High School Campus and Healdtown Comprehensive School. The analyses aimed at providing a comprehensive picture of both sites, to offer sufficient guidance to the Historic Schools Restoration Project (HSRP) and its advisors to inform all future development, rehabilitation, restoration or alteration of buildings and services, hard and soft landscaping, services infrastructure, access, security and any other planning requirements.

The studies for both schools included a photographic record of plant material, spaces and buildings, identification and assessment of building ensembles, architectural typology, heritage value and development guidelines. The documents further included a historic narrative and a definition for understanding the cultural landscape. This encompassed interrelated tangible and intangible aspects, and included components such as historic vistas and view corridors to and from the campuses. Development guidelines were proposed in conjunction with mapped areas of sensitivity and an Issues Report that included significant socio-cultural and socio-economical aspects. The documents provided relevant material to enable a workshop to develop a Statement of Significance (SoS) with the local community, the identification of responsibilities as well as identification and mapping of development opportunities by means of a Spatial Development Framework. The information assisted in the formulation of development guidelines suitable for inclusion in a Heritage Management Policy and Plan, in terms of which the

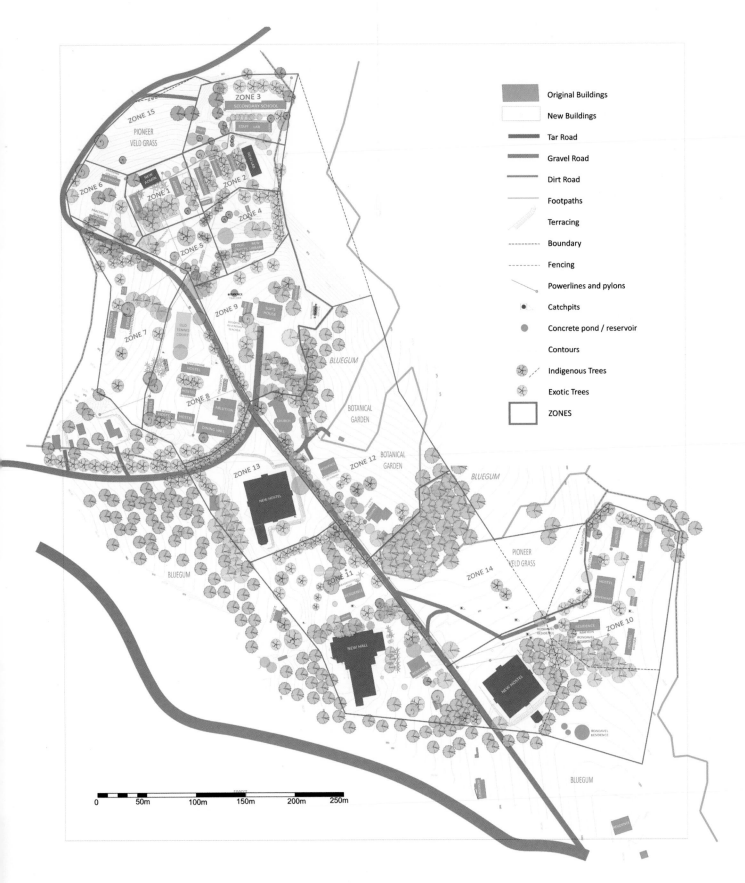

Figure 15: Cultural Landscape Zone map of Lemana School (Cultmatrix cc & Müller 2009a)

Figure 17: Mr Makhuba reminiscing about the Lemana woodwork centre and tuck shop (Müller 2008) (left)

Figure 18: Respondents at Lemana School Monument (Müller 2008) (centre left)

Figure 19: Mrs Colette Junod, wife of an early missionary at Lemana, showing off her impressive botanical garden (Müller 2008) (centre right)

Figure 20: Mrs Anne Webster in front of her now-overgrown childhood garden (Müller 2008) (right)

impact of any new developments must be evaluated. Furthermore, the above heritage component was presented in a format as required by the South African Heritage Resource Agency (SAHRA) when considering the nomination of the schools for national heritage site status.

The description and analysis of the cultural landscape was structured according to a number of zones comprising the entire site for each school. These zones are illustrated in Figures 15 and 16 and the respective numbering follows the chronological order of the site visit and the documentation of oral traditions. A short discussion on landscape elements of value and the general significance, plus a few general management objectives were included for all of the respective zones. These statements were combined to form the basis of the Statement of Significance for the entire site.

The zone-by-zone descriptions were anchored by two detailed studies: the vegetation analysis and the oral history research. The vegetation analysis is an informative record of the landscape and horticultural aspects of both campuses, with specific attention to the identification of trees species. Avenues, copses, hedges, orchards, gardens, lawns and ornamental plantings are all important features in the historic development of the schools. This description of the cultural landscape was supplemented by a commentary on the historic legacy, past performance and future suitability of the species contained within each site.

Oral history

To fully understand the significance of each school site, it was necessary to investigate the intangible dimensions together with the tangible fabric of the place. Who were the people who populated the spaces? Where did the children play, dream, learn? How did the teachers and missionaries experience life in isolation from larger cities? What has changed, what has stayed the same, what has disappeared? What are the stories that weave a narrative that holds the decaying pieces of the schools together?

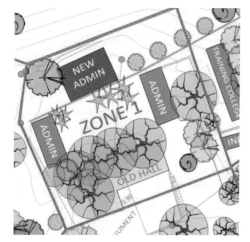
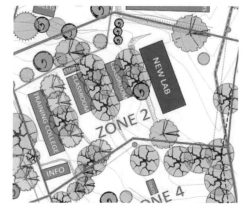

Figure 16: Vegetation analysis of Lemana School with significant trees, terraces and avenues (Cultmatrix cc & Müller 2009a)

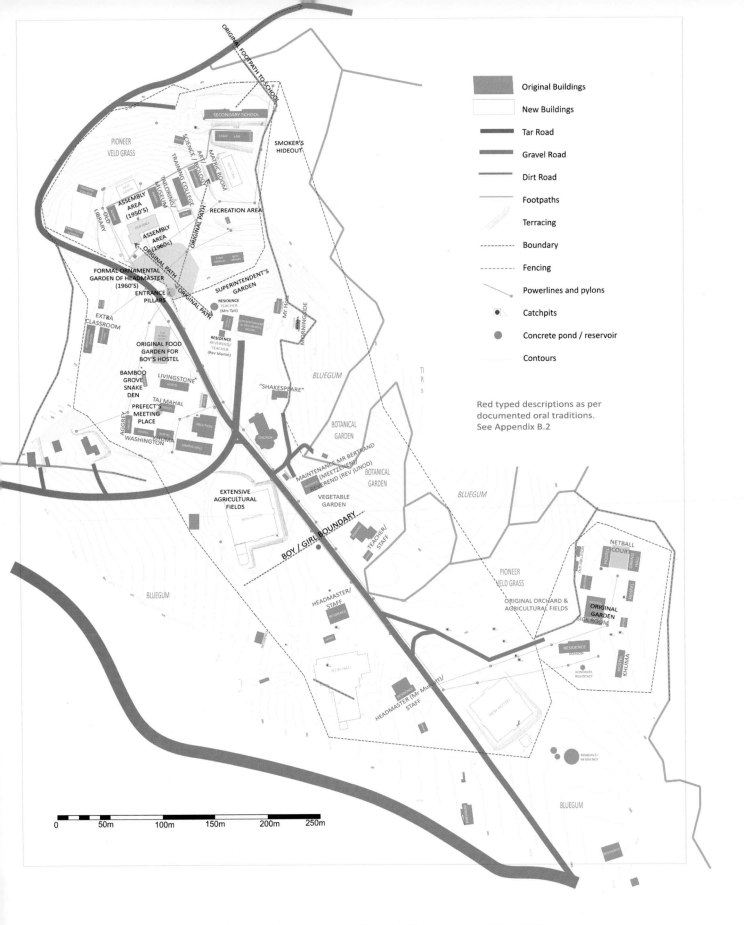

Figure 21: Detail of Lemana School spatial mapping of oral histories (Cultmatrix cc & Müller 2009a)

Research into the oral traditions inherent to the Lemana and Healdtown School was conducted using a two-pronged method. The first stage of the research included a desk-top survey of available literature. Relevant quotations pertaining to the school were documented and related to specific locations of the site where possible. The second stage of the documentation process included the documentation of the oral traditions connected to the sites. This was performed by employing quantitative and qualitative anthropological research methodology in compliance with Bernard's strategy for fieldwork (1988:110). The methodology was furthermore roughly based on the guidelines in Spradley (1979) and Ellen (1984).

A number of key informants were identified that were integrally related to the respective schools. They had either studied or taught at the schools, or lived on the premises while their parents were teachers. These included former students of the schools and training college, former teachers at both institutions and current residents on the site. Informal interviews were held on the site in order to mnemotechnically trigger latent memories of the respondents. Mnemotechnic devices activate and enhance memory. These could be objects or landscapes (Vansina 1985:44–46). Key to this process was the actual movement of the body through space. Casey (2000) discussed the role of the body in the process of memory 'as psycho-physical in status, the lived-body puts us in touch with the psychical aspects of remembering and the physical features of place' (Casey 2000:189). He described the function of living bodies as giving direction, level and distance to landscapes and places, which, in turn, serve as anchoring points in remembering.

As the various respondents walked through the cultural landscape, they would notice a number of physical objects, but also experience the site. They would be reconciled to the atmosphere of the place and remember more abstract stories and events which would otherwise have been lost to memory. As the elder people carefully traced their steps over a rocky terrain, they would remember the sports they played, the school rituals they were involved in or the thrill of being naughty. Life as part of a larger institution offering education to a few privileged children became a reality to all participants. This experience, its meaning and memory, was documented for posterity and integrally connected to its spatial context.

The specific methodology of the fieldwork was guided by the fact that the sites were divided into specific spatial zones prior to the site visit. During the interview phase, the group steadily progressed from zone to zone. The informants related information about each zone: the original and contemporary function of buildings, the original use of the school grounds, anecdotes and general comments on the heritage of the site. After noting and recording all comments while accompanying the key informants through the zones, the information was documented photographically and spatially on maps.

It should be noted that, even though all participants focused on various aspects of the physical components of the school, the discussions also revolved around the various individual people connected to the school and its history. However, the heritage analysis documents focused on the oral traditions relating to pertinent aspects of the cultural landscape and the history of the site. Additional information gleaned during the fieldwork about previous staff members and related issues, were distributed to the various schools and participating individuals in digital format (recordings and transcriptions).

Conclusion

A landscape of or a landscape as memory can be seen as processes involving individuals or societies, where the past is re-interpreted or re-composed through cognitive processes (Spiegel 2004:3, 7), and where past places are re-implaced and re-experienced through psycho-physical processes (Casey 2000:210). One might therefore understand landscape and the perception thereof as a result of the process of memory, that is, from a cultural process of remembering to a personal and measurable capacity (Kuchler 1993:103). Continuity of intangible cultural values therefore requires a tangible materialisation. Memories are based on referents, which are places, landscapes, structures or other elements of representation (mnemotechnic anchoring points). These may be places where the relationship between the fabric of the place and the intangible associations (meanings and memories) with that place to a specific culture or group, have continued through time.

It is heartening to note that the sphere of influence of landscape architecture is expanding to include a number of other disciplines, especially those within the anthropological and sociological fields. A core principle in landscape architecture is to fully understand context and to be able to assimilate a number of contributing factors and influences in the development of a design intervention. Through applying oral tradition documentation as part of the research phase, a more comprehensive and holistic understanding of the cultural landscape is achieved. Inadvertently, those meanings and memories embedded in the intangible dimension of a place are interpreted, understood and conveyed to future users of the site. It is my hope that the values of integrity and excellence, integral to these significant schools within the context of South Africa, be transferred to the future learners.

Bibliography

1906. A brief account of the Jubilee Celebrations in connection with the Normal Training Institution, Healdtown. Cape Town: Argus Co.

1946. Healdtown Missionary Institution. *The Eagle*. Lovedale: Lovedale Press.

1955. Healdtown 1855–1955. Centenary brochure of Healdtown Missionary Institution. Lovedale: Lovedale Press.

Bakker, K.A. 2003. Preserving intangible heritage resources: examples from South Africa, in ICOMOS International Scientific Symposium entitled 'Place, memory, meaning: preserving intangible values in monuments and sites'. Online: http://www.international.icomos.org/victoriafalls2003/papers.htm (accessed 18 June 2007).

Bernard, H.R. 1988. *Research methods in cultural anthropology*. California: Sage.

Casey, E. 2000. *Remembering: a phenomenological study*. 2nd ed. USA: Indiana University Press.

Cultmatrix cc & Müller, L. 2009a. Site analysis of Lemana High School Campus Elim, Northern Province: Heritage analysis and assessment of the cultural landscape. Unpublished document. HSRP: Cape Town.

Cultmatrix cc & Müller, L. 2009b. Healdtown School Campus Fort Beaufort, Eastern Cape: Heritage analysis and assessment of the cultural landscape. Unpublished document. HSRP: Cape Town.

Ellen, R.F. (ed). 1984. *Ethnographic research: a guide to general conduct*. London: Academic Press.

Historic Schools Restoration Project (HSRP). 2010. About. Online. (Accessed 23 April 2010) http://www.historicschools.org.za/view.asp?pg=About&subm=About

Kotze, L.J. & Jansen van Rensburg, L. 2002. Legislative protection of cultural heritage resources: a South African perspective. Annual Qualitative Methods Conference: Something for nothing. Online: http://criticalmethods.org/p108.mv (Accessed 18 November 2003).

Kuchler, S. 1993. Landscape as memory: the mapping of process and its representation in a Melanesian society, in *Landscape politics and perspectives*, B. Bender (ed). Oxford: Berg.

Mabunda, D.C. 1995. A historico-educational survey and evaluation of Swiss missionary education at Lemana, M.Ed. dissertation. University of South Africa, Pretoria.

Masumbe, B.M.C .& Coetzer, I.A. 2001. The Swiss missionaries' educational endeavour as a means for social transformation in South Africa. *Educare*, vol 30 (1+2):208–228.

Proschan, F. 2008. Basic challenges of sustaining intangible heritage, in sub-regional capacity-building workshop on the implementation of the convention for the safeguarding of the intangible cultural heritage, edited by UNESCO. Online: http://www.unesco.org/culture/ich/index.php?lg=EN&meeting_id=00095#meet_00095 (Accessed 4 January 2009).

Scazzosi, L. 2004. Reading and assessing the landscape as cultural and historical heritage. *Landscape Research* 29(4):335–355.

Spiegel, A.D. 2004. Walking memories and growing amnesia in the land claims process: Lake St Lucia, South Africa, *Anthropology South Africa* 27(1&2):3–10.

Spradley, J.P. 1979. *The ethnographic interview*. New York: Holt, Rinehart & Winston.

Vansina, J. 1985. *Oral tradition as history*. London: James Curry.

---

1   The pilot schools of this project include Adams College and Inanda Seminary in KwaZulu-Natal, Healdtown Comprehensive School and St Matthews High School in the Eastern Cape, Tiger Kloof in the Northern Cape and Lemana in Limpopo Province. The current revival of these schools is indicative of a cultural renaissance brought about by alumni from the various institutions and the democratic Government of South Africa (HSRP 2010).

chapter 8

The Botanical Garden of the University of Pretoria: A Unique Heritage and Valuable Academic Training Facility

Lorraine Middleton
Department of Biology
University of Limpopo
South Africa

Piet Vosloo
Department of Architecture
University of Pretoria
Pretoria
South Africa

Location and features

Website: http://www.up.ac.za/academic/botany/garden

Latitude: 25 45'05.46" S

Longitude: 28 13'45.96" E

Elevation: 1 373 m

Average annual rainfall (1998–2008): 618 mm

Average minimum temperature (1998–2008): 3.3°C

Average maximum temperature (1998–2008): 27°C

Size: approximately 3.5 hectares

Number of living plant accessions: approximately 4 400 records

(Ref: Temperature and rainfall data with the courtesy of the South African Weather Bureau)

Introduction

Botanical gardens are institutions holding documented and adequately labelled collections of living plants for the purpose of scientific research, conservation, display and education (Wyse Jackson & Sutherland 2000). A living plant collection is a group of plants grown for a defined purpose. Such a collection can be displayed either on its own or as part of a more general garden collection (Leadlay & Greene 1998).

Important functions such as an information service and recreation facilities are part of most botanical gardens. Each botanical garden has a character and purpose of its own. Therefore, the type of organisation that owns the garden, its organisational structure, location, research projects and financial needs dictate the mission of the garden.

Out of a total of an estimated 2 178 known botanical gardens in the world (Wyse Jackson & Sutherland 2000; Wyse Jackson *et al.* 2001), only a few are situated in areas with exceptional species diversity and high levels of endemism such as may be found in Africa, South America and Southeast Asia. The majority (60%) of botanical gardens are situated in the temperate regions of the northern hemisphere. There are only 127 (6%) botanical gardens in Africa and the Indian Ocean islands. There are 19 botanical gardens recorded in South Africa. Universities and other research institutions for higher education own more than 30% (± 500) of the world's botanical gardens (Wyse Jackson & Sutherland 2000; Wyse Jackson *et al.*, 2001). In southern Africa, of the 23 institutions for higher education, only five have botanical gardens. The University of Pretoria is one of these privileged few.

Botanical gardens vary greatly in size and most gardens have both landscaped and natural areas. South Africa's Pretoria National Botanical Garden is one of these with 50 hectares of landscaped area out of 76 hectares total area. This garden exhibits the flora of the African Savannah and Afromontane forests best suited to the climate of Pretoria (Botha, Willis & Winter 2000). The Manie van der Schijff Botanical Garden is thus very small in comparison, fragmented in between the buildings with all areas landscaped. Only a few sections have an open vista due to their limited size and it is also densely vegetated in most sections. It is an essentially academic training facility by nature with mixed plantings consisting of about 80% indigenous plants from all over southern Africa.

Historical background

For more than 450 years botanical gardens have been showcasing the world's botanical diversity and have provided many opportunities for people to do research and learn about plants, their uses and value (Wyse Jackson & Sutherland 2000). Not only are plants indispensable to our physical survival on earth, they are also priceless in their role in religion, cultural events, celebrations and our emotional well-being. Gardens matter to people. Cooper (2006) identifies garden appreciation as a special human phenomenon, distinct from both the appreciation of art and the appreciation of nature; and that the garden is an epiphany.

The visibility and physical size of the Manie van der Schijff Botanical Garden provide a contact with nature in a synthetic and ever changing world. This Garden, like many other botanical gardens around the world, has a rich heritage with an endowment of historical trees planted by the founders of the Garden and heritage plants, notably specimens in the cycad collection.

The Garden originated from 1924, when Pavetta species were planted by Prof. C.E.B. Bremekamp, head of the Department of Botany, for research purposes. Prof. Berend Elbrecht who succeeded him as head of the department gave real impetus to the Garden. He was a man with passion and enthusiasm for the southern African flora that live on in the many tree and cycad specimens planted by him during the 1930s. The Botany building was completed in 1940 and was by then already surrounded by plants. After Prof. Elbrecht's retirement in 1944, Prof. M.G. Mes, a plant physiologist, succeeded him and was assisted by Dr H.G.W.J. Schweickerdt who, after his studies at Kew and the National Herbarium, made an important contribution towards taxonomy and the Garden. Prof. Schweickerdt became the head of the department in 1952 and was succeeded by Prof. H.P. van der Schijff in 1963. Under the latter's leadership many changes took place in the department as well as in the Garden. Due to the expansion of the university campus and limited garden personnel, the Garden was limited to the western part of the main campus. The maintenance and planning of the rest of the campus became the responsibility of terrain management in the Department of Facilities and Services. During 1967 the garden around the Botany building was redeveloped and a fishpond and a cycad garden were established. Prof. van der Schijff made many excursions to collect specimens for the Garden. In 1986 the Garden was named after Prof. Manie van der Schijff to honour the contributions he made towards the development of the Garden. Prof. van der Schijff became dean of the faculty of Natural and Agricultural Sciences in 1975 and Prof. N. Grobbelaar head of the Botany Department. During 1975 Prof. Grobbelaar delegated the supervision of the garden to a Garden Committee which was responsible for formulating and implementing the garden policy (Grobbelaar, *et al.* 1986; Coetzer *et al. circa* 1995).

The Commemorative Garden is a part of the Garden where trees are planted by selected people who have made significant contributions to the study of botany during their years of involvement at the Department of Botany. Commemorative plaques have also been erected elsewhere in the Garden to honour other important contributors to science, the Garden and the University.

Utilisation and training

The Manie van der Schijff Botanical Garden is an inter-departmental training facility. Outdoor as well as greenhouse space, fresh plant material and other biological materials are provided for the practical training of students.

The living specimens in the Garden are useful for plant identification courses in plant science, environmental studies, landscape architecture, forestry and horticulture. Systematic indexing of the woody plants and the application of name tags to specimens were started during the 1980s under the leadership of Prof. A.E. van Wyk and is an ongoing project. The majority of the trees in the Garden are indigenous to southern Africa, but exotic species of importance for training are also planted. In one practical session of three hours more indigenous trees can be introduced to a student than the number of tree species in the whole of Europe (Grobbelaar, *et al.* 1986). Several rare woody species with a very limited natural geographical distribution also grow in the Garden including *Eugenia umtamvunensis*, *Eugenia verdoorniae*, *Eugenia woodii*, *Syzygium pondoense* and *Manilkara nicholsonii* (Van Wyk & Van Wyk 1997). These species are probably not represented in any other garden.

The many buildings in and around the Garden, representing a multitude of architectural styles are greatly enhanced by the es-

tablished Garden. As such the Garden provides an ideal site for drawing exercises to students in architecture. Layout projects for landscape architectural students can also be done in the Garden as well as mapping practice for geography students.

The rich bird and insect life, attracted by the many indigenous plants, provide material and on-terrain research opportunities for zoology and entomology students. A culinary herb garden supplies fresh herbs to students in consumer sciences. A substantial number of traditional African medicinal plants can also be found in the Garden. This makes access to material needed in studies in ethnobotany and medicinal plants very easy.

Research projects

The study of indigenous plants with horticultural potential is one of the ongoing projects of the Garden. A comprehensive study of shade-tolerant plants has been done (Middleton 1998) and new projects on succulents with ornamental value have commenced.

The Garden also cultivates certain plants from the Sekhukhuneland centre of endemism (Van Wyk & Smith 2001). These have been rescued from granite mining sites. Some of these plants are still to be described and named.

Special features of the Garden

Plant collections in a garden can be divided into several themes. Thematic collections can be used for educational and scientific purposes or for public display. Thematic collections may be taxonomically based (order, family genus), share a common geographical or ecological origin (forest, desert, alpine), share a specific use (medicinal, crops, fibres) or share a habit or life form (arboretum, succulents, ferns). A garden may also have conservation collections that aim to conserve and maintain populations of rare and endangered species. Conservation collections are usually held *ex situ* and are valuable for species recovery programmes and to provide protected long-term backup collections of wild plants (Leadlay & Greene 1998).

The Garden route

The Garden has an outstanding collection of mature indigenous southern African trees (list available from the authors and Garden Committee) and a garden route was developed to disseminate botanical knowledge to students as well as to the broader community. A formalised plan for a garden route was laid out in the early 1990s. There was a growing need to send students to a garden to do self-study.

The best and most important tree and shrub specimens were identified. A proper walking route had to be worked out that went past specimens close enough to allow viewing, touching and smelling if necessary. A hundred-and-thirty tree species were identified for this purpose. As these 130 trees are properly name-tagged and indicated on a map of the Garden, the locating and study of the trees are quite easy for students. A map and accompanying booklet containing a description of each of the specimens were compiled. Many people were involved in this large and laborious project, which was completed in 1997 (Coetzer *et al.* circa 1995). The brochure and map are available for a small fee from the secretary of the Plant Science Department. These are excellent aids for self-training at leisure. There are also many other labelled plants on the route not described in the booklet.

Cycad collection

Cycads are primitive gymnosperms and are regarded as relics from the past. It is evident from plant fossil studies that coniferous plants existed on earth long before the advent of flowering plants and originated about 230 million years ago. As with the dinosaurs, the cycads reached their peak both in numbers and diversity in the Jurassic Period that lasted 57 million years between 193 million years and 136 million years ago. Of the extant cycad genera, *Cycas* appears to be the oldest and *Cycas thouarsii* may be the most primitive species and appears to have existed in an almost unaltered form for approximately 140 million years (Grobbelaar 2002). Today it is a well-known and widely used garden plant.

In southern Africa all cycad species, except one, are very closely related and are, therefore, grouped into a single genus, *Encephalartos*, which in total has 64 species. The other cycad, which differs considerably, is placed in a separate genus, *Stangeria* with only one species *Stangeria eriopus* and is endemic to South Africa (Grobbelaar 2002).

Most cycads occur in nature as small, scattered populations where their continued existence is in great danger due largely to the activities of humankind. An extreme example is provided by *Encephalartos woodii* of which only one male plant was ever found in the wild (Grobbelaar 2002). The Garden has one specimen of *E. woodii* that was received as a gift in the late 1970s and was grown from a sucker from the parent plant in the Durban Botanical Garden. One of the Garden's oldest cycads is *E. transvenosus* which was collected in the 1930s by Prof. Berend Elbrecht. It is a very large cycad, 5-8 metres tall, and can reach 13 metres. The trees form natural forests on the mountainsides above the village of the rain queen, Modjadji, east of Duiwelskloof in the Mpumalanga province of South Africa (Coetzer *et al. circa* 1995).

Because they are endangered, cycads are strictly protected by special legislation in most countries where they occur naturally. *Ex situ* conservation is recognised as one of the most important

tools available to botanical gardens in biodiversity conservation (Wyse Jackson & Sutherland 2000). The Garden's cycad collection is an important conservation collection and the University of Pretoria is a major custodian of southern African cycads as well as of data and expertise on these plants. The records on the cycad collection were started in 1986 by Dr I.M. Claassen.

The Manie van der Schijff Botanical Garden is world famous for its cycad collection and ranks among the top cycad gardens of the world (list available from the authors and the Garden Committee). The southern African species are contained either in the garden itself or in the greenhouses and on the experimental farm. Rare and endangered species are kept locked up for protection against theft, which unfortunately is a major problem with keeping plants with collector's value in an open garden.

A nursery where cycads are propagated is one of the Garden's projects. The purpose is research and education, selecting material for introduction into the nursery trade, local horticulture and amenity planting. Another role is to release pressure on wild populations for plants that are likely to be the subject of interest by scientists, commercial horticulturists, hobbyists or local gatherers. Above all *ex situ* conservation makes plants available for use in private collections or gardens.

Monocotyledon section

This is the youngest section of the Garden, established in the early 1980s. It was Prof. G.K. Theron, retired lecturer in the Department of Botany, who, among others, saw the potential of this part of the campus as a theme garden. The Garden was planned in conjunction with the then Head of Grounds and Buildings, Mr Paul van Zyl, with inputs from Mr A. Rautenbach and Prof. P.J. Robbertse, a former lecturer in the Department of Botany (Coetzer *et al.* circa 1995).

This entire section is superbly landscaped, and also forms an open-air amphitheatre which is ideal for informal outdoor gatherings, lectures, photo sessions and concerts. It is a particularly attractive and well-known part of the university grounds.

This section houses a systematic or taxonomic collection and the theme of this section of the Garden is monocotyledonous plants as the name implies. Monocotyledons are an extremely important division of the seed plants (Leistner 2000) as they include all the grasses and cereals that form the food basis of most grazers and human beings. Grasses, aloes, bulbous plants and other representatives from this group are planted in this section.

This section is ideal to visually illustrate the very basic difference between dicotyledons and monocotyledons, the two groups of flowering plants (angiosperms) to all levels of students. It is also

indispensable in its function of supplying fresh material to plant identification courses, especially in the important grass families the Poaceae (grasses), Cyperaceae (sedges) Restionaceae (Cape reeds) and geophytic plants such as the Iridaceae, Amaryllidaceae and Liliaceae – which also provide a spectacular spring flowering display.

The monocotyledon garden is also aesthetically unsurpassed in its beauty by most other sections of the campus. This is mainly due to the many accent-plants or form plants found in this group. Tree aloes, palms, cordylines, flaxes and agaves all have architecturally strong lines that lead and please the eye. Landscape architecture students greatly benefit from training in the design with plants from this section.

This part of the Garden, however, is not without its peculiar problems. It is difficult to find enough suitable plants for this section. The plant component is made up of about 70% exotic plants and only 30% or less southern African plants. Another problem is that there are not many groundcovers in this plant group, due to their generally upright growth form. This makes weed control and filling of beds extremely difficult. The use of organic mulch is the best solution for open soil areas between plants.

Except for the larger palms, there are no 'trees' in the normal sense of the word in this group either. Therefore, no substantial shade is really provided for recreational purposes. These plants do not, however, shed leaves in the same manner as deciduous trees, and can be very tidy and easy to maintain.

Monocotyledon Garden Kniphofia species (left)

Stapeilia gigantea in the succulent garden (right)

Seed in the cycad nursery (above)

Succulent garden

A stimulating and educational display composed of succulents has been created in the Garden. One section contains some old collections of euphorbia and aloes. This was constructed like a rocky outcrop and also has some interesting tree specimens to resemble a natural koppie. The old cactus garden was renewed in 2001. Some of the original cacti and agaves were kept and many indigenous plants in the succulent group were introduced, especially in the crassula and mesembryanthemum groups. There are also some interesting succulents from other parts of the world. This allows for a comparative study on the succulents of southern Africa, the Americas and Madagascar. This section of the Garden is currently under construction again due to new buildings on the campus.

Community service

The Garden provides the ideal area for the integration of quality academic support with community service. The Garden is not only an 'open' facility to the university community, but other interested groups can also visit the Garden.

Plant sales held regularly by the Garden staff have become a firm favourite with students, personnel and outside parties. Many botanical gardens rely on plant sales to raise money to support their activities. In addition, it is a long-standing tradition in many botanical gardens to sell or distribute plants and seeds from surplus stock, or stock specifically bred for the purpose of plant sales (Willis & Turner 2001).

The Garden also keeps a seed store with seed collected from the Garden as well as from localities where research is done. The international community benefits from the free seed distributions to botanical gardens in other parts of the world that participate in the seed exchange programme. The *Index seminum* is distributed to more than 200 botanical gardens around the world.

Visitor services, recreation and aesthetic value

An important programme in the objectives of botanical gardens is to provide and manage friendly, efficient services and facilities for visitors to the garden (Botha & Winter 1998). Booklets, maps, brochures, interpretation boards and directional signage are provided. Paved routes are developed and maintained.

The Garden is maintained in an aesthetically pleasing manner to the visitor. Existing landscapes are maintained and improved where necessary. Many unusual and valuable plants fill the Garden. Increasing the number of interesting taxa represented in the Garden is an ongoing project.

All of these activities result in a very pleasing green environment that beautifies the campus, and is a visual manifestation of the success of the University of Pretoria as a world-class tertiary institution.

Concluding remarks

The Manie van der Schijff Botanical Garden is one of the most attractive and highly appreciated assets of the University of Pretoria. It is irreplaceable in its value as a training facility. The Garden simultaneously forms a green and cultural heritage, which should be maintained and managed for future generations. The university has a responsibility to safeguard this heritage and provide and pass on a legacy for future generations.

Acknowledgements

We wish to thank the following members of the Garden Committee for their support and sharing of information: Prof. A.E. van Wyk on trees, Ms J.S.M. Myburgh on cycads and Ms M. Nel on succulents. We also wish to thank Dr L.A. Coetzer and Prof. G. Theron for their valued comments and encouragement.

Bibliography

Botha, D.J., Willis, C.K. & Winter, J.H.S. 2000. Southern African botanical gardens needs assessment. *Southern African Botanical Diversity Network Report* No. 11. SABONET, Pretoria, South Africa.

Botha, D.J. & Winter, J.H.S. (eds). 1998. Business plans 2000. *Gardens and Horticultural Services*. Occasional Publication 10, National Botanical Institute, Cape Town, South Africa.

Coetzer, L.A., De Meillon, S., Hollman J.C., Meyer, J.J.M., Roos, G., Van Greuning, J.V., Van Wyk, A.E., Von Teichman, I.& Zietsman, M., *circa* 1995. Manie van der Schijff Botanical Garden, garden route, description of species. Department of Botany, Faculty of Natural and Agricultural Sciences, University of Pretoria, South Africa.

Cooper, D.E. 2006. *A philosophy of gardens*. Great Clarendon Street, Oxford, UK: Oxford University Press.

Grobbelaar, N. 2002. *Cycads. With special reference to the southern African species*. Published by the author, Pretoria, South Africa.

Grobbelaar, N., Reyneke, W.F., Myburgh, J.S., Kok, P.D.F., Robbertse, P.J., Theron, G.K., Claassen, M.I., Van Rooyen, N., Van Wyk, A.E. & Van Loggerenberg, J.A.D. 1986. *Uit ons Tuin*, no.5:2, Gedenkuitgawe: Manie van der Schijff Botaniese Tuin. Departement Plantkunde, Universiteit van Pretoria, Suid-Afrika.

Leadlay, E. & Greene, J. (eds). 1998. The Darwin technical manual for botanic gardens, *Botanic Gardens Conservation International (BGCI)*. London, U.K.

Leistner, O.A. (ed). 2000. Seed plants of southern Africa: families and genera. *Strelitzia* No. 10. National Botanical Institute, Pretoria, South Africa.

Middleton, L. 1998. Shade-tolerant flowering plants in the southern African flora: Morphology, adaptations and horticultural application. MSc thesis, University of Pretoria, South Africa.

Van Wyk, A.E. & Smith G.F. 2001. *Regions of Floristic Endemism in Southern Africa. A Review with Emphasis on Succulents*. Umdaus Press: Hatfield Pretoria, South Africa.

Van Wyk, A.E. & Van Wyk, P. 1997. *Field guide to the trees of Southern Africa*. Struik Publishers (Pty) Ltd: Cape Town, South Africa.

Willis, C.K. & Turner, S. (eds). 2001. Action plan for southern African botanical gardens. *Southern African Botanical Diversity Network Report* No. 12. SABONET, Pretoria, South Africa.

Wyse Jackson, P., Bridge, B., Dennis, F., Leadly, E., Hobson, C., Holland, F., Traude, P., Skilton, J., Sutherland, L., Willison, J. & Wyse Jackson, D. 2001. An International Review of the *ex situ* plant collections of the botanic gardens of the world. *Botanic Gardens Conservation News, Magazine of Botanic Gardens Conservation International* (BGCI) vol. 3, no. 6:22–33.

Wyse Jackson, P.S. & Sutherland, L.A. (eds). 2000. International Agenda for Botanic Gardens in Conservation. *Botanic Gardens Conservation International* (BGCI), U.K.

part TWO

Science and Strategy

The Science and Strategy section collects the papers closely related to science. These papers illustrate how strategic and quantitative methods, techniques and data are utilised in landscape architectural planning and design decision-making. Although the papers in this section demonstrate the value and necessity for scientific rigour in the work of landscape architects, the section has surprisingly few contributions. In a world of increasing specialisation and dwindling resources and budgets, one would think there should be more emphasis on these aspects. The pattern emerging from the papers in this section is that they all demonstrate an underlying need for scientific rigour and defendable argument. Defendable argument is absolutely necessary to achieve results in a competitive world such as that of the built environment. These papers illustrate the way in which scientifically rigorous research can strengthen argument.

Climate change and energy efficiency have become extremely important factors landscape architects have to respond to in planning and design. The first two papers address aspects arising out of these factors and demonstrate the value of scientific rigour in landscape architectural design. The last two papers focus on the more strategic nature of landscape management and configuration in the context of visual impact assessment and mining.

'Human Comfort and the South African Climate Design Regions in Terms of Small-scale Development Design' captures a range of aspects relating to the planning and design of the landscape for maximising energy efficiency. The emphasis is not on high-tech solutions but on the necessity for understanding the climatic factors specific to a particular region and sets out solid common sense fundamentals in a legible structure, an approach appropriate to a developing country such as South Africa. It is a gentle acknowledgement that one should be cautious of over enthusiasm for high-tech energy efficiency approaches when so much can be achieved with thorough climatic contextual understanding, feeding, planning and design. The paper also attempts to address the climatic aspects related to small-scale development. This is an area where considerable research is required. The extensive reference list also acts as a comprehensive resource for climatically responsive design.

'Estimates of Carbon Storage by Jacaranda Street Trees in the City of Tshwane, South Africa', and 'An International Perspective on Growth Rate and Carbon Sequestration of Trees Used in the Urban Landscape' are the most scientifically rigorous of the papers in the *Reader*. They demonstrate how research can move the motivation for certain facets of landscape architectural interventions from the realm of subjective value addition to the objective quantification of value added. The quantification of the value of landscape architectural interventions is becoming increasingly emphasised in a world of dwindling resources. This is finding expression in the way natural system's ecological functioning is being quantified in the valuation of the ecological services that they provide for the built environment. This paper is a clear demonstration of how this ability to quantify, in this case the carbon storage values in trees, allows the landscape architectural profession to begin to understand ways in which to position themselves in the highly competitive and rapidly growing industry of carbon trading.

Continuing with the need to move intuitive or subjective judgment into the realm of reasoned argument are the two papers 'Sound Landscape Assessment: A Methodology for Visual Impact Assessment in South Africa', and 'Sustainable Tailings Impoundment Landform Design'. The early stages of visual impact assessment were characterised by various methodologies and approaches with widely differing interpretations and judgments on the degree of impact and the mitigation. The first of these two papers proposes a South African specific methodology for visual impact assessment which is intended to act as a consolidation of differing values and methodologies. Developing visual impact assessment procedures and methodologies is becoming increasingly important as South Africa vigorously pursues mega projects aimed at addressing energy shortages, such as the construction of wind turbines and power stations.

'Sustainable Tailings Impoundment Landform Design' is a paper which captures the theoretical application of ecological principles to the deposition and management of mine tailings. An ecological and sustainable approach was adopted as a critical evaluation tool in order to assess, analyse and formulate solutions regarding the environmental and social impacts associated with impoundments throughout the life cycle thereof.

chapter 9

Human Comfort and the South African Climate Design Regions in Terms of Small-scale Development Design

Johan Bothma
Department of Architecture
University of Pretoria
Pretoria
South Africa

Gwen Theron
Department of Architecture
University of Pretoria
Pretoria
South Africa

Introduction

We have worshipped at the altar of growth. Partly, this is the consequence of a need to house continuing migrations of people being drawn from traditional to cosmopolitan settings. Partly, it is the result of a swelling world economy that rewards ever-expanding markets over constancy, development over a steady state, novelty over tradition. Our predilection in favour of growth over maintenance has raised doubts about a sustainable future. Knowles (2003:15)

These days the provision of sustainable energy and efficient energy utilisation methods are topics that are receiving considerable attention worldwide. As one of its Millennium Development Goals the United Nations (UN) aims to ensure environmental sustainability, by integrating the principles of sustainable development into country policies and programmes, reversing the loss of environmental resources and improving the lives of disadvantaged and underdeveloped populations (UN online. Accessed 1 September 2003). The industrial and economic sectors are also spending considerable resources in developing and marketing sustainable and efficient solutions for energy provision.

A scan of publications dealing with energy issues, such as *Refocus* (*Refocus* September 2002 to September 2003), the official magazine of the International Solar Energy Society (ISES), shows that photovoltaic and solar, wind turbine, biomass and even ocean tidal utilisation technologies are being developed and implemented throughout the world at an increasing rate. South Africa has also gotten onto the bandwagon, illustrated by the fact that the World Summit on Sustainable Development 2002 was held in Johannesburg.

More recent events such as the Copenhagen Climate Change Summit held in December 2009, and the eventual signing of the Copenhagen Accord by many world leaders (Copenhagen Climate Council online. Accessed 1 April 2010), underpins the fact that the world understands that humanity is impacting on the environment in detrimental ways and that something needs to be done. The race to develop sustainable energy alternatives has begun.

However, Michels (1979:vii) contends that energy conservation is far more important than solar energy (and by implication other renewable energy resources) utilisation, as design professionals and the societies that they design for and aim to serve, are trapped by the promise of more efficient technologies in the future. To make matters worse, a large obstacle, created by the national utility Eskom, exists in the development and especially implementation of energy efficiency measures in South Africa, according to Van Horen and Simmonds (1998:895–896). The fact that coal and subsequently electricity are inexpensive in this country have meant that the real price of electricity has remained comparatively low, eliminating one of the major potential driving forces in energy efficiency.

Furthermore the South African climate is particularly mild with a relatively short heating season throughout most of the country. Lombard, Mathews and Kleingeld (1999:229) believe that this fact, coupled with the popularity and affordability of small electrical resistance space heaters, means that most homes are built with no regard for climate-responsiveness or thermal response considerations.

Greater efficiency in domestic water usage also warrants serious attention as water demand may soon exceed the available resources in South Africa (Basson 1997:65). Access to safe drinking water, a luxury taken for granted in developed countries, does not exist for many across the world and is particularly severe in this country. According to the State of the Environment of South Africa Report (DEAT online. Accessed 24 August 2003), South Africa has one of the lowest rainfall conversion rates in the world, as only 8.6% of precipitation is available as surface water. Groundwater reserves are also relatively low compared to international averages.

Problem statement

The aim of this article is to identify and describe the climatic factors that influence human comfort and the climatic regions that they form in South Africa; and to conceptually explore the development of climate-responsive design in the local context. Bothma (2004) follows on this and illustrates ways in which residential and small-scale development design can respond to climate to bring about human comfort and increase energy efficiency.

Hypothesis one: The climate factors that influence human comfort can be identified and described

The first hypothesis of this article is that the climate factors that influence human comfort can be identified and described. In Bothma (2004) these factors have been identified as air temperature, humidity, wind, solar radiation and precipitation. These climate factors will be studied from a human comfort perspective. This will be done to determine the relative importance of the factors in different climates and to what degree they can be utilised in climate-responsive design. The different physiological effects of these elements on humans will also be explored.

Hypothesis two: The climatic character of the landscape can be identified and described

The second hypothesis is that the climatic character of the landscape can be identified and described. The description of the basic climate regions is based on weather phenomena, climate-responsive design considerations and human comfort rather than purely geographical considerations. The climatic conditions that define each climate region are defined and parameters for the identification of the different climate regions are set. Lastly this sub-problem must illustrate what influences the specifics of the location of a site will have on its solar access and radiation energy concentrations. This must be done in terms of the site-specific factors of latitude, altitude, slope and topography.

In Bothma (2004) the basic climates have been identified as hot humid, hot arid, temperate and cool. Several other climate regions such as Mediterranean and composite climates have also been encountered, yet from a human comfort perspective these regions seem to fall into the four major types. The descriptions of these must facilitate climate-responsive design that aids human comfort and cannot be purely geographical. Therefore sources with geographical and design perspectives on climate will be considered. To this end climatic classifications of South Africa from a geo-climatic and design perspective are considered. A geo-climatic classification of the country by Schulze (1965) and a more design-orientated classification by Napier (2000) are used to determine the climatic context of South Africa.

Also, the effects of characteristics such as slope, solar aspect and latitude on the amount and concentration of solar radiation that a site receives are investigated. The specific influences of these factors on microclimate are also examined.

Hypothesis three: Climate design devices for the climate regions that enable energy efficiency, can be identified and described

The third hypothesis proposes that climate design devices for the climate regions, that enable energy efficiency, can be identified and described. The third sub-problem assesses strategies for achieving energy efficiency in suburban residential design. Design techniques are investigated that utilise and respond to climate conditions that are comparable to the climate regions of South Africa. The application of the devices in climatic contexts and their potential outcomes or expected effects are also explored.

The climatic factors that influence human comfort

Temperature

Although air temperature is one of the first factors that come to mind when considering human comfort, it is in itself not the most important nor is it an easy element to manipulate or control when considering outdoor environments. Brown and Gillespie (1995:65) illustrate this by showing that an outside air temperature of 20°C can be conceived as being anything from uncomfortably warm if the humidity is high with no wind, to quite cool if it is a cloudy, windy day. According to Hobbs (1980:62) temperature in conjunction with the relative humidity of the air, the amount of air movement, perceived as wind, and radiation quantities determine human comfort and together constitute the most important elements of climate-responsive design. Temperature is nevertheless one of the main climatic characteristics of any geographic region, and must therefore be understood.

Barry (1981:17) explains that as one moves further away from the equator the angle of the incoming rays of the sun becomes sharper relative to the surface of the earth, due to the curvature of its surface. This means that the rays nearer to the poles have to penetrate a larger amount of atmosphere before reaching the earth's surface than at the equator, resulting in a decrease of net and solar radiation and an overall drop in temperature (Figure 1).

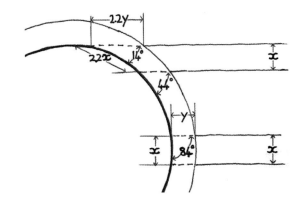

Values are approximate only.

Figure 1: An increase in latitude causes a decrease in the incidence angle and concentration of solar radiation

According to Byers (1974:57) the influences of altitude are rather more complex, but generally a site at a higher altitude is colder than one at the same latitude but a lower altitude. The average environmental lapse rate, described by Barry (1981:40) as the rate at which temperature decreases with an increase in altitude, is roughly 6°C/km in the free atmosphere.

The easiest way of directly affecting perceived temperature is through the control and manipulation of shade and sun. Simply put, this means providing shade when it is too hot and allowing in sunlight when it is too cold. This is true for both outdoor and indoor environments, although it is more effective to manipulate indoor temperatures in this fashion. Nevertheless the human body will radiate heat to any surface or body that is cooler or be heated by anything that is warmer than it. Egan (1975:5) therefore contends that the temperatures of building surfaces are crucial for achieving thermal comfort and that external control of the amount of sunlight that reaches a building is influential in climatically responsive design.

Humidity

The most significant effect of humidity on human comfort is that it changes the perceived temperature of the air. An increase in atmospheric humidity will cause a person to experience a rise in the perceived temperature. Table 1 gives the relationship between actual air temperatures and humidity and the apparent temperature as a function of relative humidity; however, it does not take the influence of wind into consideration.

Table 1: Apparent temperature as a function of relative humidity
(From Henderson-Sellers & Robinson 1986:332)

Air temp (°C)	Apparent air temperature in °C																				
32	28	29	29	30	31	31	32	33	34	35	36	37	38	39	41	43	45	47	50		
29	26	26	27	27	28	28	29	29	30	31	31	32	32	33	34	35	36	37	39	41	42
27	23	23	24	24	25	25	26	26	26	27	27	27	28	28	29	30	31	31	32	32	33
24	21	21	21	22	22	22	23	23	23	23	24	24	24	24	25	25	26	26	26	26	27
21	18	18	18	18	19	19	19	19	20	20	21	21	21	21	21	21	22	22	22	22	22
Relative hum. %	0	5	10	15	20	25	30	35	40	45	50	55	60	65	70	75	80	85	90	95	100

The importance of humidity to human comfort is further illustrated when viewed in terms of the discomfort index used by the Weather Bureau (1987:3–7). Table 2 illustrates this index, used to determine how uncomfortable certain combinations of temperature and humidity are to humans. For example, a combination of 36°C and 10% humidity would have an index of 100, as would 27°C and 80% humidity. In this fashion an index of 80–90 is moderately uncomfortable, 90–100 is very uncomfortable, 100–110 is extremely uncomfortable and above that is hazardous to human health. The index is determined by the equation

$$(2 \times T) + (RH/100 \times T) + 24 = DI$$

where: T = temperature in °C, RH = relative atmospheric humidity and DI = discomfort index.

Table 2: The human discomfort index (From Weather Bureau 1987:10)

	Relative humidity				
Air temp	10%	20%	40%	60%	80%
20°C	66	68	72	76	80
25°C	77	79	84	89	94
30°C	87	90	96	102	108
35°C	98	101	108	115	122

Thus the combination of atmospheric temperature and humidity is the main determining factor with regards to human comfort, both in the outside environment and indoors.

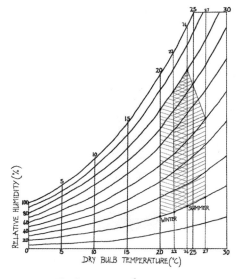

Figure 2: The human comfort zone represented on the psychrometric chart (From Holm 1983:19)

Note: These conditions are relevant for persons doing light work (1 met) and wearing light clothing (0.6 clo) in still air (0,1m/s). The core represents conditions that 80% of the population will find comfortable and the periphery where 70% will be comfortable.

Although all people do not experience the same combinations of temperature and climate to be pleasant there is a certain core range of temperature-humidity relations that is acceptable to most people, as illustrated by Figure 2. This graph is called a psychrometric chart, described by Holm (1996:2) as dealing with the properties of the atmosphere in terms of the behaviour of the mixture of dry air and water vapour and illustrates human comfort response under different conditions.

Wind

Wind is a complex environmental element that is caused and influenced by many factors. Nevertheless it is one of the most useful microclimatic design elements and greatly affects human comfort levels. Brown and Gillespie (1995:123) are of the opinion that wind is of great importance to human comfort as it can be manipulated to a significant extent to promote energy-efficient design.

Wind is a significant factor as it affects human comfort levels in different manners in different climates. Even relatively gentle breezes can make an otherwise uncomfortably hot location seem more bearable. Flach (1981:113) explains that evaporation of perspiration from the skin effectively cools a person as heat is used to change the phase of the moisture from liquid to a vapour gas. According to Sohar (1979:480) one litre of perspiration that completely evaporates dissipates approximately 600 calories, but this becomes increasingly difficult as the humidity of the atmosphere increases. In humid areas wind is especially important for human comfort, as it mixes the more humid air around the body with less humid air to aid in evaporation.

However, the effects of wind become much greater in cool regions. Barry (1981:279) describes the process through which wind augments the convective heat loss through the skin, called the windchill factor. Table 3 illustrates the empirical relationship to calculate perceived temperature due to the effect of wind chill.

Table 3: Wind chill equivalent temperatures (From Weather Bureau 1987:12)

Air temperature (°C)	Wind speed (m/s)		
	2m/s	6m/s	10m/s
5	4	−4	−8
0	−1	−10	−15
−5	−6	−17	−22
−10	−11	−23	−30

From Table 3 it can be seen that temperatures that are still bearable can become dangerous when strong winds blow and that the effect becomes increasingly severe as the temperature drops. Although few locations are likely to experience temperatures below −10°C for long it becomes clear that the wind plays a dominant role in human comfort in cooler climates.

Radiation

The radiation that reaches the earth from the sun provides the energy for all atmospheric systems and processes on earth and is therefore also one of the most important factors to consider when investigating climatic conditions of any area. According to Brown and Gillespie (1995:46) solar radiation is one of the climatic elements that we can most effectively manage and utilise. This is because the path of the sun through the sky and related shading can be accurately predicted, using a variety of tools and methods described by Erley and Jaffe (1979:33–35), Markus and Morris (1980:172–182), Richards (1981), McPherson (1984a:285–286), and Grabovac and Dragovic (1988:638–641) among others. These predictions are done using sun angles and azimuth angles for specific latitudes.

The solar energy that reaches the surface of the earth follows one of three possible paths as described by Mazria (1979:15–16). It is absorbed by the surface of the material, transmitted through the object or reflected back into the atmosphere as long-wave radiation. When sunlight strikes an object it heats up and the object reflects both short-wave light giving it the colour and hue of the surface and long-wave energy, felt as heat, to cooler surfaces, objects or the atmosphere. In this way the amount of radiation that reaches the earth's surface plays an important part in both macro- and micro-climatic conditions. The nature of the reflection can either be specular, as from a polished surface, or diffused as from matt surfaces.

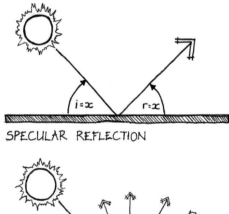

SPECULAR REFLECTION

DIFFUSE REFLECTION

Figure 3: Specular and diffused reflections (From Mazria 1979:16)

Precipitation

The importance of the roles that precipitation and air temperature play in defining the climate of a region can be illustrated by considering popular conceptions of the general climate types of the world. Tropical climates are considered to be places with high temperatures and ample rainfall; deserts have high temperatures with little rainfall; cold regions have low temperatures with snow and rain and temperate regions lie somewhere in the middle. Although this is a deceptively simple way of explaining climate and does not accurately describe the conditions in any of the regions, it does illustrate the fact that precipitation is an integral part of any climate and is thus of great importance when establishing climatic zones for any region.

The relationship between the amounts of precipitation that a given location receives and what happens to it once it has fallen is as important to the climate of a region as the nature of the precipitation. This relationship is called the water balance of that region. Goudie (1984:107) defines it as the relationship between the input of water through precipitation and the losses arising through evaporation, transpiration and changes in its storage, for instance soil moisture and groundwater content. This relationship indicates the relative wetness or dryness of a location and varies drastically for different climates. Very humid climates have a highly positive balance, which means that the input of moisture is far greater than the losses. Conversely arid regions have negative water balances, meaning that the amount of evapo-transpiration in such an area exceeds the average amount of precipitation for that region. Schulze (1997:172) illustrates that South Africa can indeed be considered an arid country as the mean annual evaporation exceeds annual precipitation in almost all regions of the country.

The influences of latitude and the physical character of the site on solar access

Site latitude, sun and azimuth angles

Site latitude refers to the global position of a site in relation to the east to west orientated latitudinal degree lines that circle the earth. The equator is represented by the 0° latitude line and the north and south poles by 90° north and south latitude respectively. The equator is characterised by smaller variations in seasonal weather phenomena, because the incoming solar radiation reaches the earth at angles close to perpendicular throughout the year and thus the amount of atmosphere that it passes through remains relatively constant.

The amount of atmosphere that radiation passes through also influences how much energy is lost in the process. An increase in the depth of atmosphere that radiation passes through results in larger energy losses due to absorption and reflection. This means that the amount of radiation that reaches the surface of the earth at the equator varies comparatively little annually. At higher latitudes the angle of incidence and length of atmosphere that the radiation must pass through varies considerably both daily and annually due to the axial tilt of the planet, resulting in pronounced seasonal weather phenomena and varying day lengths.

When the sunlight impinges on the surface of the earth the slope of the site will also determine the concentration of solar radiation. Smaller incidence angles will result in decreased concentrations of solar energy. The positions of the sun at noon during summer and winter solstices and its equinox are determined by the following formulas provided by Oliver (1973:228–229):

- ◆ Winter solstice: Solar altitude angle = 90° − (latitude + 23½°)
- ◆ Summer solstice: Solar altitude angle = 90° − (latitude − 23½°)
- ◆ Equinox: Solar altitude angle = 90° − latitude

Aspect and the physical location of the site

Aspect refers to the orientation of a slope relative to the sun's path through the sky, in other words whether the slope is on the sunny or shadow side of a topographical landform (Robinette 1983a:12). The influence of the sun changes both daily and seasonally and these influences are different for all slopes. Figure 5 illustrates these considerations.

It is possible for both north and south facing slopes to receive direct sunlight if the slope is gentle enough and the sun climbs high enough in the sky (1). This is typical of lower latitudes throughout the year and during summer in higher latitudes. South-facing slopes can also receive some sunlight during the morning or afternoon when the sun is shining from nearer to the east and west, although the intensity of the rays is reduced due to the low angle of the sun (2).

However, if the sun sinks low enough or if the slope is steep enough only northern slopes receive sunlight. This occurs when the angle of the incoming rays is less than that of the south slope (3). This phenomenon becomes more pronounced with an increase in latitude and is of special importance in cold areas, where the lack of sunlight can cause temperatures to be significantly lower than on the northern slope.

Another consideration of aspect is that shadows are much longer on south-facing slopes than on north facing ones. This occurs because the angle between the shadow line and the ground plane is larger on north slopes and they thus intercept each other over a shorter distance (Figure 6).

Site slope

The slope gradient or gradient of a site further influences the effects that the aspect and latitude have on the length of shadows that are cast on it. If the gradient of the slope is increased shadows are slightly shorter on northern slopes and considerably longer on southern slopes. The gradient of the northern slope also influences the concentration of solar radiation on that slope. In most cases a steeper slope causes the incidence angle of the sunlight to increase, resulting in higher concentrations of radiation. Steeper southern slopes are more likely to be in shadow and for a longer period of the day.

The significance of these elements is that they will determine the specifics of the solar access zone and the solar collectors that will operate within this zone. Zanetto (1984:99) describes solar collectors as any object, surface or space that uses the energy

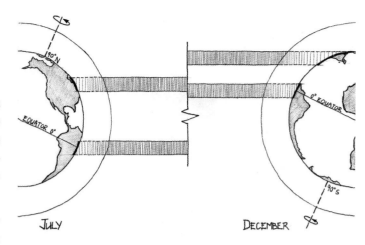

Figure 4: Annual variation of solar radiation with latitude

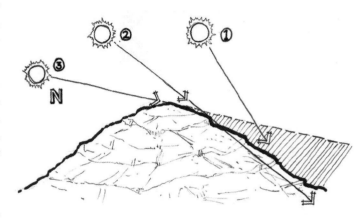

Figure 5: Aspect in relation to sun angles

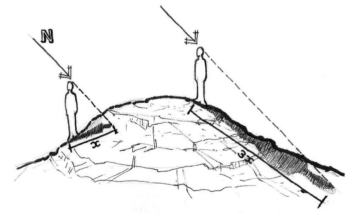

Figure 6: Different shade lengths on north and south slopes

of the sun through direct gain to reduce the amounts of energy that are imported and used in a building. According to Erley and Jaffe (1979:33) the solar access zone or skyspace is the portion of sky north of a collector that must remain unobstructed by objects that block solar radiation, in order for a solar collector to function optimally (Figure 7). When the effects of latitude, aspect and slope gradient are integrated, a complex set of considerations arise that must be considered as a whole in order to effectively design for solar access (Figure 8).

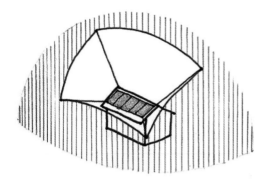

Figure 7: The skyspace of a solar collector (Zanetto 1984:99)

Climatic factors and the influences of site summarised

In terms of human comfort and response, the climate of a region is mostly determined by its air temperature and humidity, wind conditions, radiation levels and amounts and nature of precipitation. Of these, combinations of humidity, wind and radiation levels are of particular importance to human comfort and subsequently climatic design.

Atmospheric humidity can greatly influence the perceived comfort of a given temperature and especially high temperatures can be anything from relatively pleasant under low humidity conditions to intolerable under very high atmospheric humidity. Under such conditions wind plays an important part in improving comfort by removing moisture and increasing evaporation. In cold climates windchill can significantly lower perceived temperatures to the point where they can become detrimental to thermal comfort and even dangerous to human health. The amount of energy that a surface absorbs and subsequently the rate at which it and surrounding temperature heat up, can also be influenced by controlling the amount of solar radiation that it receives.

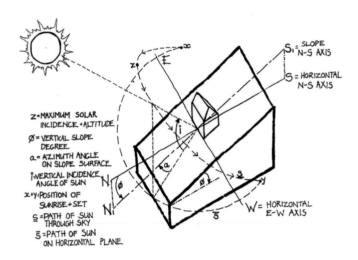

Figure 8: The elements of site slope and aspect that influence passive solar design (Based on Erley & Jaffe 1979:16, Markus & Morris 1980:172)

The specific topography and location of a site can influence the microclimate of an area and will have significant implications for climatic design. There are several site-related characteristics that influence microclimate, mainly due to the influences that these factors have on the concentrations and times of solar radiation exposure. These factors are the vertical incidence angles of the sunlight throughout the day, the horizontal azimuth angles of the sun throughout the day, the positions where the sun rises and sets due to the latitude of the site, the slope gradient of the site, and its aspect or orientation in terms of the cardinal points.

The climatic design regions

The South African climatic context

The climatic classifications of the country, discussed in more detail in Bothma (2004), will serve to better relate internationally developed and used climatic design techniques to local conditions. Three climatic classifications of South Africa are used for this purpose. The first is a widely used geo-climatic classification by Schulze (1965) while the second is a recent re-classification of the country by Kruger (2003) which incorporates more detailed information on plant type distributions. The third is a climatic classification aimed at aiding environmentally sensitive design in small buildings, by Napier (2000).

The detailed geo-climatic classification of Southern Africa by Schulze (1965:313–322) is illustrated by Figure 9. The map creates a good impression of the varying climatic conditions experienced as one moves from east to west.

Kruger's climatic classification (Figure 10) is based on similar criteria as those of Schulze but incorporates more detailed information on plant type distribution, resulting in a complex map of the country. Some zones are almost entirely distinguished from each other by their plant populations, with little variance in actual climatic conditions. However, it does create a detailed picture of the somewhat subtle variance in conditions that exist between certain regions.

Napier's design-orientated climate classification of South Africa is based on rainfall quantities, temperatures, general wind patterns, relative humidity, hours of sunshine and general weather and habitat phenomena to divide the country into nine zones as illustrated by Figure 11. His classification is aimed at aiding environmentally sensitive and climate-responsive design of small buildings, including residential dwellings. Although somewhat simplistic this classification reflects both phyto-geographical and comfort-related climate considerations and the zone descriptions give a good indication of the general conditions that can be expected in each climate region.

Based on these climate classifications and various other literature sources reported in Bothma (2004) the following climate regions, discussed in the four sections below, are established for the purposes of climate responsive design:

♦ Hot humid regions
♦ Hot arid regions
♦ Temperate regions
♦ Cool regions.

Hot humid regions

Hot humid regions are described by Robinette (1983:106) as areas that typically have warm climates with relatively small yearly temperature variations and high average annual humidity levels due to precipitation, the effects of nearby oceans and the effects of

Legend:

M	Mediterranean region
A	Garden Route
K	Little and Great Karoo
W	Desert steppe
SWa	Poor steppe
Ss	Southern steppe
Sn	Northern steppe
SE	South-eastern coastal region
E	Warm to hot and humid subtropical region
D	Drakensberg/Natal Highlands region
L	Transvaal Lowveld
H	Highveld
NT	Northern Transvaal
B	Region B/Namibia

Figure 9: The geo-climatic zones of South Africa according to Schulze (1965:313)

Legend:

1	Northern Arid Bushveld	13	Southeastern Coast Grassland
2	Central Bushveld	14	Eastern Mountain Grassland
3	Lowveld Bushveld	15	Alpine Heathland
4	Southeastern Thornveld	16	Great and Upper Karoo
5	Lowveld Mountain Bushveld	17	Eastern Karoo
6	Eastern Coastal Bushveld	18	Little Karoo
7	KwaZulu-Natal Central Bushveld	19	Western Karoo
8	Kalahari Bushveld	20	West Coast
9	Kalahari Hardveld Bushveld	21	Northwestern Desert
10	Dry Highveld Grassland	22	Southern Cape Forest
11	Moist Highveld Grassland	23	Southwestern Cape
12	Eastern Grassland	24	Southern Cape

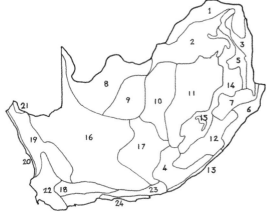

Figure 10: Phyto-geographical climatic analysis of South Africa according to Kruger (13–09–2003)

under-drained lowland evaporation. Temperatures rarely fall outside 18°C to 29°C and rainfall is high and occurs for a large portion of or throughout the year. Holm (1983:15) describes sub-tropical humid climates as having diurnal and annual temperature ranges that are almost equal at around 9°C. The humidity of such places is up to 70% to 80% in the wet season and 40% to 70% in the dry season.

At coastal examples land and sea breezes are predominant while inland fohn (or berg) winds are predominant. Where warm ocean currents exist, usually along eastern shore-lines, orographic rainfall is also high if large topographical features are found there. From these descriptions hot humid conditions can be expected to occur along the northeast coastline of South Africa.

Hot arid regions

Robinette (1983:119) defines hot arid regions as places that have extended periods of overheating, large diurnal temperature ranges, low humidity and precipitation and winds that vary diurnally. The sunlight probability is 0.75 and 0.55 of the possible for the summer and winter respectively. According to Holm (1983:7) hot arid climates have a diurnal temperature range of at least 17°C, which is greater than the annual tempera-ture range of around 14°C. Ground temperature is warmer than air temperature and the annual relative humidity is 10% to 55%. Winds in these regions have local diurnal cycles following the sun's path.

Goudie (1984:109–110) and Slaymaker and Spencer (1998:178) state that hot arid re-gions occur deep in the interior of continental landmasses between 20° and 40° lati-tude, often also in the rain shadow of mountain ranges. Winds blowing over cold sea currents along western shorelines frequently contribute to the aridity of a region. These descriptions describe much of the interior and west of South Africa. Consequently much of the country can be expected to be hot and arid.

Temperate regions

The temperate climatic design zone is perhaps the hardest to define, as its character-istics seem to be the most general of the four. According to Olgyay (1963:161) tem-perate zones are areas that require the maintenance of the seasonal balance of heat production, radiation and convection for human comfort. Robinette (1983b:95) states that summer cooling and winter heating are both important factors and wind patterns may differ seasonally.

McPherson (1984b:163) states that temperate zones experience almost even overheat-ed and under-heated periods, with summers that are relatively humid and warm to hot; and winters that can be cool or sometimes cold. Especially winter conditions are not as severe as in the cool regions. According to Robinette (1983:99) these regions have between 53% and 68% of the possible number of sunny days. These descriptions would suggest that especially the southwest and southern Cape region, as well as less arid parts of the eastern interior, would be temperate in nature.

Cool regions

According to Olgyay (1963:155) in cool regions winter response in design is three times as important as summer response. As the name implies, cool regions are characterised by low temperatures for a significant period of time. Latitude, discussed above, is one of the most determining reasons why certain regions or locations are predominantly

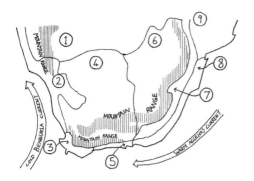

Legend:

1	Sub-tropical plateau
2	Desert
3	Mediterranean
4	Semi-arid plateau
5	Temperate coast
6	Temperate eastern plateau
7	Plateau slopes
8	Sub-tropical coast
9	Sub-tropical Lowveld

Figure 11: The climatic zones of South Africa according to Napier (2000:9.3.1)

cool although other factors such as sea currents and topographical features also have marked influences.

It is important to note that many of the cool regions of the world are closer to the poles, which means that they have long winter periods and that the sun is relatively low in the sky, even during the summer and at noon. Altitude is the second factor which causes a location to be cool, as Byers (1974:57) states, the rate of temperature change with altitude is around 1 000 times greater than that of latitude; so cool regions are often also at high altitudes.

From the above descriptions it can be deduced that South Africa is unlikely to have large cool zones and such areas will probably not be characterised by extremely cold conditions. South Africa, at between 22° and 35° South, lies entirely within the tropical and sub-tropical latitudes; and with the exception mainly of the escarpment most of the country is relatively low above sea level. Nevertheless there are isolated locations that do get very cold during the winter and climate-responsive design can be applied to create more comfortable conditions and reduce energy consumption in these areas.

The climate of South Africa summarised

It was found that most of the South African climate is relatively mild, having neither very high nor very low temperature extremes and only moderate humidity levels. Thus less energy is used for climatic amelioration than in many European and American locations. Due to the high solar radiation levels there is potential for various active and passive solar design techniques and technologies.

The South African climate is predominantly hot, semi-arid or temperate. Most of the western interior is hot arid with the most extreme conditions occurring in the northwest parts of the country. The eastern interior and Highveld is predominantly temperate, with temperatures increasing to the north and decreasing to the south. The only cool region of the country is found in the highlands of the Drakensberg, with a significant portion of the eastern coast being hot humid. A small region of composite climate is found in the northeast-most part of the country that has both hot humid and hot arid characteristics.

Developing a design response to the South African climate

The consensus is that globally and in South Africa there is a need for improved energy efficiency and more sustainable energy production methods. Although the situation is not yet desperate, it is most certainly very urgent and globally efforts to realise these

goals are under way. Climatically responsive urban design is a solution to one of the many facets of the problem and has indeed been implemented for millennia in different parts of the world and in different climatic contexts, to achieve human comfort and optimise the use of scarce natural resources.

South Africa offers good potential for energy-efficient urban design, but many changes are needed if this is to happen. More extensive research is needed in all aspects of this situation, legislative steps have to be taken and greater awareness of the problems must be created in both professional and public sectors.

Policy, legislation and regulation

In the White Paper on the Energy Policy of the Republic of South Africa (1998) it is stated that the theoretical potential for solar water heating in South Africa is 500 GWh per year and although more than 484 000m² of solar water heater panels had at that stage been installed, this constituted less than 1% of the potential market at the time. Current indications are, however, showing that the market for solar water heaters is fast rising, judging by the number of suppliers in business these days.

In addition to this vast potential for utilising the energy of the sun, the climate of South Africa is generally mild compared to that of many other regions of the world. Although harsh conditions do occur in some isolated areas for brief periods, minimum temperatures in particular are not extreme and the need for heating is secondary to that for cooling in almost all areas. Thus the environmental potential for climatic responsive design is substantial in this country, yet so far it has received relatively little attention.

Consideration of climate in large-scale planning frameworks and policies

Ward (2002:57) suggests that an effective means of addressing this situation is through higher density climatically responsive houses. They are less costly to build, they are more land and resource efficient, create a greater communal sense of place and human scale and can support more amenities than the standard one-lot-one-house approach. However, such methods can only be truly effective if they reflect the climatic setting of the region that they are intended for. A common 'design language' for each climatic region must be created that responds to the requirements of each region. Hawkes, McDonald and Steemers (2002:57–47) define this concept as 'typology' in design, or creation of appropriate design solutions through reference to existing successful solutions to similar scenarios.

The strength of this methodology is that it does not copy solutions from one example and apply them verbatim to another design scenario but rather creates a conceptual and functional framework within which specific solutions to each scenario can then be generated. In this fashion 'existing knowledge' forms the basis from which the problem is solved. Thus finding ways to apply international knowledge in the field of climate responsive design to local conditions are needed.

The first step for including the aspects of solar access, daylighting and other climate considerations into integrated planning is to establish planning and safeguard objectives at a municipal level. Pereira, Silva and Turkienikz (2001:217) state that these objectives should be introduced into city codes and land-use planning provision; and should be part of the general planning objectives in terms of urban design. Local planning laws should include zoning and requirements to allow for different levels of solar access in different regions and contexts. Future development of some sites may become severely restricted should climate responsive design not be provided for in municipal ordinances and specifications.

This especially applies to areas which are still undeveloped and where future development is still at the urban planning stage. In this regard a major shortcoming of Spatial Development Frameworks and other macro-scale planning strategies in this country is that they almost never take climate into consideration, much less provide guidance as to how climate should be considered in the growth of cities and settlements. This issue needs to be addressed if climate is ever going to significantly influence urban growth.

Meaningful consideration of site climate in project planning and environmental authorisation

It is vital to apply urban climate and microclimate impact studies in planning practice if this discipline is to contribute to human welfare. However, in many environmental authorisation applications, the section of the consultant's report concerning climate and micro-climate is mainly descriptive and does not indicate specific responses in the development of town plans or at detailed design scale. As a result, projects do not respond to existing micro-climatic variations, nor do they attempt to make beneficial changes to the urban thermal environment.

Currently Environmental Impact Assessment legislation in South Africa requires a description of the climate in which development takes place, but no guidance as to how this information is to be applied. Evans and De Schiller (1996:362, 363) mean that planners need specific guidance on crucial factors such as densities, plot ratios, maximum building heights and desirable building forms at a very early stage in project development and planning proposals; and the EIA process should provide guidance in this regard.

SANS 204

The recent publication of the South African National Standard for Energy Efficiency in buildings, *SANS* 204:2008 (SABS 2008), which is composed of three parts, is a very important step towards ensuring that energy efficiency is inherently integrated into the built fabric of South Africa. This Standard is particularly useful in that it addresses both general issues related to energy efficient building design; and the application of methodologies for both natural environmental (passive) and artificial ventilation and climate (active) control.

In terms of building design the Standard addresses a large range of considerations and parameters, including:

◆ large-scale planning considerations
◆ building orientation and shading
◆ detailed aspects of design such as floor, wall, fenestration, roof and ceiling design
◆ sealing of the building envelope, and air infiltration and leakage
◆ design specification and performance of services
◆ design and operational specifications for air conditioning systems.

Other aspects of building design such as hot water installations, vertical transport and escalators, natural environmental control, renewable energy sources, building operation and maintenance, verification of compliance and inspection and commissioning of the building services systems are also addressed.

While the publication of the *SANS* 204 is considered a large leap in the right direction, the true challenge will lie in ensuring that it is broadly applied in developments of varying size and complexity. However, making sure that designers, developers and contractors alike adhere to the standard may not be straightforward. Manpower and technical experience are likely to be two major challenges that will have to be addressed if effective compliance enforcement is to be achieved. Furthermore, ensuring that the relevant methodologies are applied to low-cost and government-subsidised housing may be difficult, as energy efficiency and thermal performance have in the past frequently, and are likely to continue, taken second seat to cost and fast-tracked delivery requirements.

Development of South African climate responsive design

In recent years there has been a worldwide trend, especially in areas with very long histories, to replace the existing housing stock and architectural heritage with contextually inappropriate, imported designs. Subsequently, large areas of such houses and particularly exquisite examples of them have been destroyed through wrong policies by ill-informed local authorities and badly-advised central governments (Al-Azzawi 1994:1099).

It is therefore vital that design starts learning from and applying the truths that have been discovered over the ages. A number of strategies are suggested to assist in this happening and should be considered together with the various causes identified. Although by no means exhaustive, these measures may see climate-responsive design coming to greater realisation.

Training architects and planners in the field of climate conscious design

The formal curriculums of tertiary architectural design institutions usually include climate-responsive design as a subject. However, the need for greater practical application of learnt theory, in the form of project assignments, exists and could follow the following structure as described by De Schiller and Evans (1996:449). These steps should also be followed in practice:

- Analysis of the climatic characteristics of a study area including monthly maximum and minimum temperatures, corresponding atmospheric humidities, monthly rainfall, average cloud-cover and hours of sunlight, wind speeds and directions
- Evaluation of the direct and indirect influence of these variables on human comfort
- Determining of the relative importance of heating, cooling, reduction of temperature swings, solar protection, wind protection, etc., to achieve comfort indoors and improve outdoor thermal conditions
- Selection of design strategies for the natural conditioning of indoor and outdoor spaces using building design, planning decisions and landscaping; for example, the use of building form, planning layouts, street alignments and landscaping for wind protection in cold climates or the use of cooling breezes in equatorial humid climates
- Development of the design layout incorporating bioclimatic strategies and the adjustments needed to satisfy other planning requirements
- Testing of the results using simulations, model studies, etc. The main concept that must be included in courses is the integration of theoretical knowledge in practical design exercises, to ensure that designers have the ability to create appropriate and realistic design responses to urban climate variations, evaluate the possible benefits against costs and other limiting factors and see the resulting architectural character or town planning patterns.

Development of general relationships and strategies for different areas and regions

Research should be directed towards general hypothesis testing rather than case study description. Oke (1984:8) explains that ideally, relationships should be of a quantitative nature but general 'rules of thumb', guidelines and conceptual frameworks may be equally valuable as these are often more readily understood by the designers that are to use them.

Development of strategies to protect outdoor climatic environments

Spagnolo and De Dear (2003:721) state that thermal comfort in outdoor settings is a topic that globally has received little attention to date with a vast majority of comfort studies being carried out indoors. Yet living outdoors is part of our culture in South Africa and it is therefore important that both planning and detail design take this factor into consideration. Protection of comfort, e.g. by means of solar access and utilisation of breezes should therefore not only be considered in terms of building climatic amelioration needs, but also that of the occupants that prefer to recreate outdoors.

This applies to both low and especially high-density developments, where multiple families or occupants are reliant on a shared outdoor space. Furthermore this way of thinking also applies to restaurants and other commercial venues that wish to utilise the outdoors for recreational purposes; and office blocks, where outdoor rest/recreation areas are a very important and a beneficial amenity for an effective and productive work environment.

Sunshine and pleasant climate are two of the common denominators of many of South Africa's most popular tourist attractions and it is beneficial that these assets be protected by utilising them and integrating them into urban planning considerations. With the emphasis on greater urban density and efficient use of space as our cities grow larger, upfront planning decisions in this regard become more and more important; especially where urban densification takes place in areas with high tourism potential.

Conclusion

It has been established that South Africa offers the potential for various climate-responsive urban design options and that few locations have truly challenging conditions. Nevertheless various climatic contexts exist in this country. Although extensive documentation and classification thereof have been done, little has been from a purely design-orientated perspective, especially from a human comfort point of view. In other words, a lack of adequate, comprehensive descriptions of the South African landscape in terms of energy-efficient urban design and human comfort exists. Therefore it is recommended that further assessments of the various design climates should be carried out and a method of classifying and mapping these should be established.

Bibliography

Al-Azzawi, S. 1994. Indigenous courtyard houses: a comprehensive checklist for identifying, analysing and appraising their passive solar design characteristics: regions of the hot-dry climates. *Renewable Energy*, 5(II):1099–1123.

Barry, R.G. 1981. *Mountain weather and climate*. New York: Methuen & Co.

Basson, M.S. 1997. *Overview of water resources availability and utilization in South Africa*. Pretoria: Department of Water Affairs and Forestry.

Bothma, J. 2004. Landscape and architectural devices for energy-efficient South African suburban residential design. University of Pretoria. Unpublished Masters thesis.

Brown, R.D. & Gillespie, T.J. 1995. *Microclimatic landscape design: creating thermal comfort and energy efficiency*. New York: John Wiley & Sons.

Byers, H.R. 1974. *General meteorology*. Fourth edition. New York: McGraw-Hill.

Copenhage Climate Council. 2010. COP15 Daily Brief: the Copenhagen Accord. [Online] http://www.copenhagenclimatecouncil.com/get-informed/news/cop15-daily-brief-the-copenhagen-accord.html (Accessed 1 April 2010).

De Schiller, S. & Evans, J.M. 1996. Training architects and planners to design with urban microclimates. *Atmospheric Environment*, 30(3):449–454.

Department of Environmental Affairs and Tourism. State of the Environment report of South Africa: Freshwater systems and resources overview. Updated October 1999. [Online] http://www.environment.gov.za/soer/ nsoer/issues/water/index.htm (Accessed 24 August 2003).

Department of Minerals and Energy. *White Paper on the Energy Policy of the Republic of South Africa 1998*. [Online] http://www.gov.za/ whitepaper/1998/energywp98.htm (Accessed 6 August 2003).

Egan, M.D. 1975. *Concepts in thermal comfort*. New Jersey: Prentice-Hall.

Erley, D. & Jaffe, M. 1979. *Site planning for solar access: a guide for residential developers and site planners*. Chicago: American Planning Association.

Evans, J.M. & De Schiller, S. 1996. Application of microclimate studies in town planning: a new capital city, an existing urban district and urban river front development. *Atmospheric Environment*, 30(3):361–364.

Flach, E. 1981. Human bioclimatology, in *World survey of climatology* Vol 3: general climatology, 3. H.E. Landsberg (ed). Amsterdam: Elsevier:1–177.

Goudie, A. 1984. *The nature of the environment: an advanced physical geography*. Oxford: Basil Blackwell.

Grabovac, J. & Dragovic, M. 1988. The influence of planning and architectural design on the efficient exploitation of energy in housing, in Energy and buildings for temperate climates: a Mediterranean approach. Proceedings of the sixth international PLEA conference Porto, Portugal, 27-31 July 1988. E. de O. Fernandes & S. Yannas (eds). Oxford: Pergamon Press:637–644.

Hawkes, D., McDonald, J. & Steemers, K. 2002. *The selective environment: an approach to environmentally responsive architecture*. New York: Spon Press.

Henderson-Sellers, A. & Robinson, P.J. 1986. *Contemporary climatology*. Essex: Longman Scientific and Technical. Co-published in the USA with John Wiley & Sons.

Hobbs, J.E. 1980. *Applied climatology*. Kent, Colorado: Dawson Westview Press.

Holm, D. 1983. *Energy conservation in hot climates*. London: Architectural Press.

Holm, D. 1996. *Manual for energy conscious design*. Department of Minerals and Energy; Directorate Energy for Development.

Knowles, R.L. 2003. The solar envelope: its meaning for energy and buildings. *Energy and Buildings*, 35(1):15–25.

Kruger, A. 2003. (andries@weathersa.co.za). 2003. Reply: Klimaatklassifikasie. E-mail to Bothma, J. (johanbothma@xtracker.co.za) 13 November 2003.

Lombard, C., Mathews, E.H. & Kleingeld, M. 1999. Demand-site management through thermal efficiency in South African houses. *Energy and Buildings*, 29:229–239.

Markus, T.A. & Morris, E.N. 1980. *Buildings, climate and energy*. London: Pitman Publishing.

Mazria, E. 1979. *The passive solar energy book. Expanded professional edition*. Emmaus: Rodale Press.

McPherson, E.G. 1984a. Precision planting for solar control and solar access (Appendix C), in *Energy-conserving site design*. E.G. McPherson (ed). Washington DC: American Society of Landscape Architects (ASLA):281–290.

McPherson, E.G. 1984b. Solar control planting design, in *Energy-conserving site design*. E.G. McPherson (ed). Washington DC: American Society of Landscape Architects (ASLA):141–164.

Michels, T. 1979. Solar energy utilization. New York: Van Nostrand Reinhold.

Napier, A. 2000. *Enviro-friendly methods in small building design for South Africa*. Durban: A. Napier.

Oke, T.R. 1984. Towards a prescription for the greater use of climatic principles in settlement planning. *Energy and Buildings*, 7:1–10.

Olgyay, V. 1963. *Design with climate*. New Jersey: Princeton University Press.

Oliver, J.E. 1973. *Climate and man's environment: an introduction to applied climatology*. New York: John Wiley and Sons.

Pereira, F.O.R., Silva, C.A.N. & Turkienikz, B. 2001. A methodology for sunlight urban planning: a computer-based solar and sky vault obstruction analysis. *Solar Energy*, 70(3):217–226.

Richards, S.J. 1981. Solar charts for the design of sunlight and shade for buildings in South Africa. Pretoria: NBRI, CSIR.

Robinette, G.O. 1983. *Landscape planning for energy conservation*. New York: Van Nostrand Reinhold.

Schulze, B.R. 1965. Climate of South Africa: part 8: general survey, WB28. Pretoria: Government Printer.

Schulze, R.E. 1997. South African atlas of agrohydrology and climatology. Water Research Commission, Pretoria, report tt82/96.

Slaymaker, O. & Spencer, T. 1998. *Physical geography and global environmental change*. New York: Addison Wesley Longman.

Sohar, E. 1979. *Man in the desert, in arid zone settlement planning-the Israeli experience*. G.S. Golany (ed). New York: Pergamon Press:477–518.

South African Bureau of Standards, 2008. South African National Standard 204: *Energy efficiency in buildings*, Vol 1–3. (1st ed). Pretoria: SABS Standards Division.

Spagnolo, J. & De Dear, R. 2003. A field study of thermal comfort in outdoor and semi-outdoor environments in subtropical Sydney, Australia. *Building and Environment*, 38:721–738.

United Nations. Millennium Development Goals. [Online]. http://www.un.org/millenniumgoals/index.html (Accessed 1 September 2003).

Van Horen, C. & Simmonds, G. 1998. Energy efficiency and social equity in South Africa: seeking convergence. *Energy Policy*, 26(11):893–903.

Ward, S. 2002. *The energy book for urban development in South Africa*. Noordhoek: Sustainable Energy Africa (SEA).

Weather Bureau, Department of Environmental Affairs. 1987. *Meteorological observations and instruments*. Pretoria: Government Printer.

Zanetto, J. 1984. *Master planning in energy conserving site design*. E.G. McPherson (ed). Washington DC: American Society of Landscape Architects (ASLA):87–114.

chapter 10

Estimates of Carbon Storage by Jacaranda Street Trees in the City of Tshwane, South Africa

Hennie Stoffberg
Department of Plant Science
University of Pretoria
Pretoria
South Africa

Gretel van Rooyen
Department of Plant Science
University of Pretoria
Pretoria
South Africa

Introduction

Since 1906 the Municipality of Pretoria has planted Jacarandas to such an extent that in 2003 approximately 17% of the City of Tshwane's urban street tree forests were populated with Jacaranda trees (Urban Forestry Department of the City of Tshwane Metropolitan Municipality, personal communication). Due to the fact that the street trees were planted from early in the twentieth century there is a strong association between the Jacaranda trees and the city's history. In spring and early summer Jacarandas create such a display of colour and splendour throughout the city that the City of Tshwane has become known as the Jacaranda City of South Africa. Many of the Jacaranda trees are older than architectural and public infrastructure in the city. These trees have become synonymous with the city and could be viewed as an integral part of the city's cultural, natural and historical heritage (Boje 1984; Botes 1985; Robinson 1985; City Council of Pretoria 1991; Marquart 1998; Record Central 2003).

As is the case with other urban trees, Jacaranda trees hold numerous green infrastructural benefits. Some of the benefits that urban trees hold are, among others, the following (Jim 1987; Huang *et al.* 1987; Rosenfeld *et al* 1998; Simpson 1998; Xiao *et al.* 1998; McPherson 1999; Xiao *et al.* 2000; Akbari *et al.* 2001; Akbari 2002; Nowak *et al.* 2002a; Nowak *et al.* 2002c; Kollin 2003; Maco & McPherson 2003; Stoffberg 2006):

- Energy savings in terms of the heating and cooling of buildings
- Reduction in soil erosion
- Amelioration of the urban heat island effect
- Amelioration of microclimatic conditions
- Air pollution reductions and air quality improvements
- Positive impacts on human health and well-being
- Rainfall interception and reduction in storm water runoff
- Wildlife habitat creation and increase in species diversity
- Reduced noise pollution
- Scenic beauty
- Recreation, environmental awareness and education opportunities
- Contribution to the development of civic pride
- Reduction in the occurrence of crime
- Tourist attraction.

Cognisance should, however, be taken that there are also monetary and environmental costs involved with the propagation, planting and maintenance of urban trees as well as the maintenance of infrastructure (e.g. sidewalks, storm and sewer systems and utility lines) affected by the trees.

Although these cost aspects and many of the benefits mentioned above may be converted to monetary values, they were not within the scope of the study. Instead the present study aims to estimate the monetary value of the Jacaranda street tree population through only accounting for the carbon storage of the street trees. Carbon is stored in plant tissue through the processes of photosynthesis and hence this process ameliorates the climate change by removing carbon dioxide from the atmosphere. The objective of this study is thus to provide additional information on the value of these street trees which would aid in their management. However, this paper does not intend to justify the existence and preservation of the Jacaranda street trees which have been classified as an alien invader in South Africa. Rather it expresses a method of calculation and concluding monetary values that were derived from determining the whole tree carbon storage of Jacaranda street trees which is extrapolated to the city's Jacaranda population. The monetary value is based on market prices of carbon dioxide equivalents traded on current international carbon markets.

Methodology

The Urban Forestry Department of the City of Tshwane Metropolitan Municipality (hereafter referred to as Municipality) provided data containing suburb and street names with the number of *Jacaranda mimosifolia* trees in each street. This database was compiled from a census conducted in the late 1990s as well as from a tree-planting database initiated in 1995 (Table 1 and Figure 1).

Table 1: Suburbs with mean stem circumferences (mm) of trees in descending order of magnitude as well as the standard deviation (mm) in stem circumference for each suburb

No	Suburb	Mean circumference (mm)	Standard deviation (mm)	No	Suburb	Mean circumference (mm)	Standard deviation (mm)
1	Asiatic Bazaar	1687	320	38	Danville	1129	254
2	Laudium	1671	245	39	Lynnwood Glen	1108	187
3	Claremont	1644	316	40	Waterkloof Ridge	1102	176
4	Colbyn	1616	263	41	Eastwood	1098	288
5	Mountain View	1587	298	42	Lukasrand	1089	252
6	Wonderboom South	1552	297	43	Waltloo	1063	215
7	Waterkloof	1538	288	44	Ashlea Gardens	1060	389
8	Sinoville	1532	251	45	Eersterust	1049	257
9	Riviera	1497	206	46	Queenswood	1039	404
10	Pretoria Gardens	1471	297	47	Hillcrest	1027	264
11	Muckleneuk	1467	341	48	Meyers Park	1021	219
12	Brooklyn	1446	187	49	Alphen Park	913	258
13	Rietfontein	1430	196	50	La Montagne	898	310
14	Pretoria Central	1420	342	51	Constantia Park	848	175
15	Villiera	1410	271	52	Maroelana	843	158
16	Eloffsdal	1403	402	53	Waterkloof Park	824	224
17	Rietondale	1400	340	54	Garsfontein	818	191
18	Menlo Park	1400	311	55	Atteridgeville	814	119
19	Lynnwood	1395	486	56	Kilner Park	810	207
20	Salvokop	1392	342	57	Waterkloof Glen	805	170
21	Pretoria North	1389	277	58	Erasmusrand	773	204
22	Sunnyside	1383	227	59	Mamelodi	736	174
23	Pretoria West	1381	205	60	Jan Niemand Park	669	273
24	Nieuw Muckleneuk	1347	250	61	Lynnwood Ridge	626	156
25	Proclamation Hill	1345	170	62	Moreleta Park	624	173
26	Hatfield	1332	171	63	Hazelwood	523	347
27	Lisdogan Park	1331	338	64	Faerie Glen	522	124
28	Trevennai	1312	385	65	Montana	522	200
29	Arcadia	1302	199	66	Philip Nel Park	520	112
30	Kwaggasrand	1286	166	67	Mayville	419	176
31	Samcor Park	1272	361	68	Erasmuskloof	390	162
32	Valhalla	1256	270	69	Saulsville	340	85
33	Silverton	1233	261	70	Elardus Park	323	91
34	Annlin	1218	417	71	Hestea Park	278	85
35	Clydesdale	1216	236	72	Newlands	213	110
36	Pretoria Industrial	1193	193	73	Wingate Park	195	64
37	Westpark	1159	196				

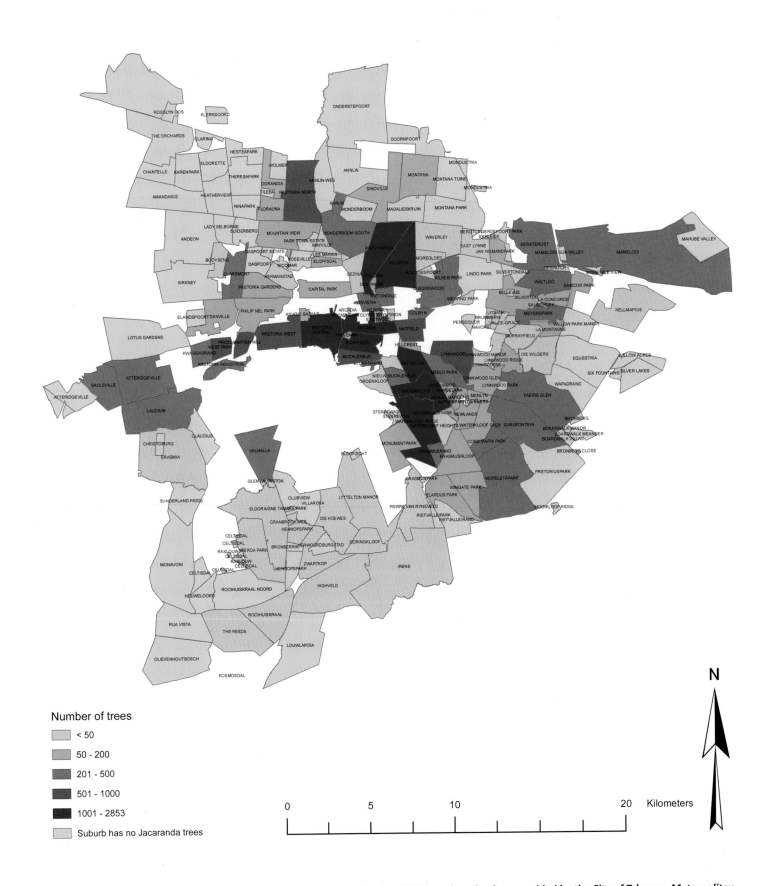

Figure 1: The number of Jacaranda street trees in Tshwane on 27 October 2003 based on the data provided by the City of Tshwane Metropolitan Municipality. The darker colours represent suburbs with larger numbers of trees

Number of trees

- < 50
- 50 - 200
- 201 - 500
- 501 - 1000
- 1001 - 2853
- Suburb has no Jacaranda trees

0   5   10   20   Kilometers

N

During February and March 2004, trees in 73 of the 114 suburbs that have Jacarandas planted as street trees in the Pretoria area of the City of Tshwane were measured for stem circumference at breast height (i.e. 1.37m above ground level). Forty-one suburbs with less than 50 trees were not included in the sample. A total of 1 525 trees were measured in 116 streets. To establish the number of trees to measure, 20 trees per suburb in 13 different suburbs were measured. A low percentage error of 2.17% was calculated showing that 20 trees per suburb provided a statistical representative sample of the mean stem circumference of *Jacaranda mimosifolia* trees per suburb. Not all streets had 20 trees that could be measured and in such instances additional trees in other streets in the same suburb were measured.

The possible effect of local environmental conditions on the variation in stem circumference was determined through two survey transects, of varying length, in the same street. It was assumed (and evident by size) that all the street trees in a suburb were planted within the same year and this planting practice is still strived for by the current Urban Foresters. In this statistical test two sets of 20 trees were measured at opposite ends of Milner Street in the suburb Waterkloof which is an old suburb with well established large trees. The first transect was on the western end of the street where trees were measured consecutively and the second transect where every second tree was measured was at the opposite end of the street. With the first transect, measurements were taken on both sides of the street in a zigzag manner in order to minimise the transect length (approximately 150m long). In the second transect, on the eastern end of the street, every alternate tree only on the northern side of the street was measured, in order to maximise the transect length which was approximately 1 km. Damaged trees were not measured.

Inter-street variation in stem circumference within a suburb was also analysed to determine whether larger stem circumference distributions would be found in different streets of the same suburb rather than in only one street of that suburb. The inter-street analysis was done by measuring 20 trees in each of two streets in the suburbs Brooklyn, Hatfield and Sunnyside and showed that taking measurements in one street per suburb is sufficient for obtaining statistically satisfactory representative measurements.

Longitude and latitude were recorded with a global positioning system (Garmin, eTrex, Venture GPS) at the start and end of each transect in a street. The name of the closest street that crosses the street in which the first tree was measured, as well as that of the closest street crossing it after the last tree measured, were noted for future reference (Stoffberg, 2006).

The data were captured and analysed in Microsoft® Excel. The mean stem circumference and the standard deviation of the stem

circumferences were calculated for each suburb (Table 1) and the circumferences were converted to diameters for application in equation (2). The following equation (Pillsbury *et al.* 1998) was used to estimate the volume of each tree:

$$V(cf) = 0.036147 \, (dbh)^{2.486248} \qquad (1)$$

where $V(cf)$ is the volume of the aboveground woody parts (excluding leaf volume) of the tree in cubic feet, and *dbh* is the stem diameter at breast height in inches. Following from the above, equation (1) was converted to metric units as follows:

$$V(m^3) = 3.29118 \cdot 10^{-7} \, (dbh(mm))^{2.486248} \qquad (2)$$

where $V(m^3)$ is the volume of the aboveground woody parts in cubic metres and $dbh(mm)$ is the stem diameter in millimetres at breast height. After the volume of each tree was calculated its biomass was determined as:

$$Biomass = density \cdot V(m^3) \qquad (3)$$

where *Biomass* is calculated in kilograms and *density* is a given value. A density of 520kg/m³ was used which was determined from three destructively harvested, below *dbh*, stemcore, wood samples derived from a *Jacaranda mimosifolia* tree that grew on the University of Pretoria campus. The wood was oven dried at 60°C to a constant mass.

Fifty percent of the dry biomass per tree was allocated to carbon (McPherson *et al.* 1994; McPherson & Simpson, 1999; Gifford, 2000; McPherson *et al.* 2001; IPCC 2003) and this value was converted to metric tonnes. The mean aboveground carbon quantity per suburb as well as the standard deviation of aboveground carbon per suburb were calculated. The standard error was calculated for the aboveground carbon of each suburb. The mean quantity of aboveground carbon per Jacaranda tree in Tshwane can be calculated as:

$$X = \frac{\Sigma(W_i \cdot X_i)}{\Sigma W_i} \qquad (4)$$

where X is the mean quantity of aboveground carbon per Jacaranda tree in Tshwane, W_i is the total number of trees in each suburb and X_i is the mean aboveground carbon per tree for each suburb. The total quantity of aboveground carbon that has been sequestrated by all the Jacaranda trees in Tshwane (C_{agt}) can be calculated as:

$$C_{agt} = X \cdot N \qquad (5)$$

where N is the total number of Jacaranda trees in Tshwane. The percentage error (%Err) follows as:

$$\%Err = \frac{SE_{total}}{C_{agt}} \cdot 100 \cdot 2 \qquad (6)$$

where SE_{total} is the standard error of the aboveground carbon for the total quantity of trees. To determine the belowground biomass of the Jacarandas a root:shoot ratio of 22:78 was used (McPherson *et al.* 2001) and equations (4) to (6) were repeated to determine the total carbon quantities that include the root carbon. The percentage carbon of the root was also taken as 50% of total biomass (McPherson *et al.* 2001; IPCC 2003).

Results

The total number of trees on which the calculations were based, was 33 630 according to the data provided by the municipality. The data provided by the municipality were that of the number of trees in a particular street based on a census which commenced in 1995. The difference between the number of trees per street as provided by the municipality and that obtained from informal field observations indicated that there were approximately 10% fewer trees in the streets than was indicated by the municipality's data. The carbon calculations have been adjusted accordingly.

A 2.17% error was obtained from the test sample conducted by measuring stem circumferences of 20 trees per suburb for 13 different suburbs to establish the number of trees that had to be measured per suburb (Figure 2). This low percentage error suggested that 20 trees per suburb provided a sufficiently acceptable statistically representative sample of the mean stem circumference of Jacaranda trees in a suburb. The percentage error calculated for all of the Jacaranda trees in Tshwane was 3.59%.

An intra-street variation test conducted in the suburb of Waterkloof showed no significant difference between a long and short transect (ANOVA, Alpha = 0.05, p = 0.362). Inter-street variation showed no significant difference for trees measured in two different streets in the same suburb (ANOVA, Alpha = 0.05, Brooklyn p = 0.164; Hatfield, p = 0.394; Sunnyside p = 0.884).

Suburb names, number of Jacaranda street trees per suburb, mean carbon per tree per suburb, standard deviation and total carbon in each suburb are shown in Table 2 and Figure 3 illustrates total carbon per suburb. The carbon calculations were based on the total number of trees in the suburbs in which trees were measured (73 suburbs) and amounted to 32 302 trees. The highest mean carbon quantities per tree occurred in the Asiatic Bazaar, Laudium and Claremont with an estimated 0.713 tonne carbon (t C), 0.680 t C and 0.670 t C per street tree respective-

ly (Table 2). Approximately 44% (5 425 t C) of the total quantity of carbon that is stored in the Jacaranda street tree population occurs in the suburbs of Pretoria Central, Brooklyn, Waterkloof, Sunnyside, Arcadia and Villieria. These are older suburbs and in relatively close proximity to the city centre. Pretoria Central, Brooklyn, and Waterkloof had the highest total quantity of carbon with an estimated 1 379 t C (11% of the total quantity of carbon), 1 195 t C (9% of the total quantity of carbon), and 801 t C (6% of the total quantity of carbon) respectively.

A per tree mean of 0.378 t C was estimated for all the suburbs in which trees were measured. The total quantity of carbon for all the street trees in all the suburbs of Tshwane (114 suburbs) is estimated at 11 438 t C.

Carbon emission and offsets are often reported as the full molecular mass of CO_2 rather than the atomic mass of carbon. The molecular mass of CO_2 can be obtained by multiplying the atomic mass of carbon by 3.67 (McPherson & Simpson 1999). When applying this conversion factor the abovementioned trees will result in a per tree mean of 1.387 t CO_2 equivalent (CO_2eq) for all the measured suburbs, and an estimated total of 41 978.62 t CO_2eq for all the Jacaranda street trees in Tshwane. Assuming a hypothetical market-related price of US$10 tonne^{-1} CO_2eq, the total value of all the Jacaranda street trees in Tshwane could be estimated at US$ 419 786. The price used is mentioned as 'hypothetical' due to market forces and exchange rate fluctuations that frequent the carbon industry in particular. However, the price does relate to that presented for forestry projects by the Clean Development Mechanism (CDM) of the United Nations Framework Convention on Climate Change (UNFCCC) and in general to carbon markets as presented by www.pointcarbon.com.

Mean carbon per tree in a suburb, mean CO_2 per tree and the associated monetary values of the carbon dioxide equivalent in US dollars are shown in Table 3. The estimated mean value of a Jacaranda tree in the City of Tshwane was US$13.87. This value represents that of the mean amount of carbon sequestrated by the total number of trees at the time of study and it is derived as above from the commodity prices of carbon as it is traded on markets. The estimated carbon dioxide equivalent (CO_2eq) stored in the above and belowground biomass of a mean tree in the Asiatic Bazaar, Laudium, Claremont and Colbyn were 2.618 t CO_2eq, 2.497 t CO_2eq, 2.461 t CO_2eq, 2.317 t CO_2eq respectively.

The largest estimated total quantities of carbon dioxide equivalent that have been sequestrated at the time of measurements of all the Jacaranda street trees per suburb were 5 061 t CO_2eq, 4 386 t CO_2eq, 2 940 t CO_2eq and 2 894 t CO_2eq and were in the suburbs of Pretoria Central, Brooklyn, Waterkloof and Sunnyside respectively (Table 3).

Table 2: Suburb names, number of Jacaranda trees per suburb (n), mean carbon (tonne) per tree per suburb in descending order, standard deviation (t C) and total carbon (tonne) in each suburb as well as the percentage of total carbon per suburb

No	Suburb	n	Mean t C per tree	Standard deviation t C	Total t C	%
1	Asiatic Bazaar	67	0.713	0.286	47.791	0.391
2	Laudium	281	0.680	0.237	191.184	1.566
3	Claremont	344	0.670	0.304	230.642	1.889
4	Colbyn	308	0.631	0.243	194.436	1.593
5	Mountain View	153	0.612	0.250	93.645	0.767
6	Wonderboom South	227	0.582	0.279	132.014	1.081
7	Waterkloof	1412	0.568	0.265	801.359	6.565
8	Sinoville	82	0.553	0.211	45.358	0.372
9	Muckleneuk	559	0.520	0.301	290.647	2.381
10	Riviera	465	0.516	0.170	239.763	1.964
11	Pretoria Gardens	132	0.511	0.226	67.445	0.552
12	Lynnwood	514	0.508	0.406	261.110	2.139
13	Eloffsdal	159	0.487	0.336	77.396	0.634
14	Pretoria Central	2853	0.483	0.277	1379.037	11.297
15	Brooklyn	2535	0.472	0.150	1195.351	9.792
16	Rietondale	454	0.467	0.273	211.941	1.736
17	Salvokop	87	0.462	0.287	40.159	0.329
18	Rietfontein	1028	0.460	0.156	473.021	3.875
19	Menlo Park	378	0.458	0.235	173.310	1.420
20	Villiera	1207	0.458	0.225	552.806	4.528
21	Pretoria North	840	0.443	0.227	372.497	3.051
22	Sunnyside	1836	0.430	0.177	788.651	6.460
23	Pretoria West	702	0.424	0.148	297.842	2.440
24	Lisdogan Park	531	0.415	0.255	220.387	1.805
25	Trevennai	128	0.415	0.324	53.111	0.435
26	Nieuw Muckleneuk	284	0.407	0.196	115.723	0.948
27	Proclamation Hill	896	0.393	0.118	352.157	2.885
28	Hatfield	977	0.385	0.129	375.986	3.080
29	Samcor Park	95	0.381	0.278	36.223	0.297
30	Arcadia	1929	0.367	0.139	708.776	5.806
31	Annlin	492	0.359	0.251	176.627	1.447
32	Kwaggasrand	310	0.352	0.105	109.051	0.893
33	Valhalla	447	0.348	0.171	155.683	1.275
34	Silverton	166	0.332	0.157	55.080	0.451
35	Clydesdale	67	0.317	0.148	21.265	0.174
36	Pretoria Industrial	396	0.297	0.119	117.623	0.964
37	Westpark	622	0.277	0.116	172.483	1.413
38	Danville	67	0.269	0.148	18.051	0.148
39	Ashlea Gardens	409	0.263	0.224	107.491	0.881
40	Eastwood	499	0.259	0.154	129.201	1.058
41	Queenswood	215	0.253	0.183	54.314	0.445
42	Lynnwood Glen	102	0.248	0.096	25.311	0.207
43	Lukasrand	323	0.248	0.150	80.042	0.656
44	Waterkloof Ridge	1509	0.243	0.095	367.287	3.009

No	Suburb	n	Mean t C per tree	Standard deviation t C	Total t C	%
45	Waltloo	248	0.229	0.119	56.683	0.464
46	Eersterust	442	0.228	0.126	100.602	0.824
47	Hillcrest	155	0.218	0.134	33.859	0.277
48	Meyers Park	235	0.208	0.103	48.855	0.400
49	La Montagne	59	0.170	0.148	10.047	0.082
50	Alphen Park	96	0.165	0.085	15.823	0.130
51	Constantia Park	393	0.131	0.068	51.386	0.421
52	Waterkloof Park	189	0.127	0.082	24.096	0.197
53	Maroelana	60	0.127	0.059	7.619	0.062
54	Garsfontein	449	0.122	0.072	54.670	0.448
55	Kilner Park	235	0.121	0.073	28.406	0.233
56	Waterkloof Glen	155	0.115	0.057	17.824	0.146
57	Atteridgeville	268	0.114	0.041	30.545	0.250
58	Erasmusrand	227	0.109	0.078	24.692	0.202
59	Mamelodi	304	0.094	0.056	28.549	0.234
60	Jan Niemand Park	61	0.088	0.093	5.375	0.044
61	Hazelwood	77	0.067	0.109	5.197	0.043
62	Moreleta Park	348	0.065	0.049	22.452	0.184
63	Lynnwood Ridge	108	0.063	0.038	6.856	0.056
64	Montana	93	0.045	0.031	4.195	0.034
65	Faerie Glen	223	0.040	0.022	8.889	0.073
66	Philip Nel Park	56	0.039	0.021	2.182	0.018
67	Mayville	42	0.028	0.023	1.156	0.009
68	Erasmuskloof	70	0.023	0.025	1.625	0.013
69	Saulsville	208	0.014	0.009	2.900	0.024
70	Elardus Park	159	0.013	0.009	2.007	0.016
71	Hestea Park	103	0.009	0.007	0.913	0.007
72	Newlands	60	0.006	0.007	0.346	0.003
73	Wingate Park	92	0.004	0.003	0.344	0.003

Table 3: Names of suburbs, total carbon (tonne) per suburb in descending order, total CO$_2$ equivalent (tonne) per suburb and the associated monetary values of the total t CO$_2$ equivalent for each suburb in US$, based on a value of US$10.00 per tonne CO$_2$ equivalent, as well as the percentages of the total amount

No	Suburb	Total t C	Total CO$_2$eq	US$	% of total
1	Pretoria Central	1379.037	5061.067	50610.67	11.297
2	Brooklyn	1195.351	4386.939	43869.39	9.792
3	Waterkloof	801.359	2940.988	29409.88	6.565
4	Sunnyside	788.651	2894.349	28943.49	6.460
5	Arcadia	708.776	2601.208	26012.08	5.806
6	Villiera	552.806	2028.797	20287.97	4.528
7	Rietfontein	473.021	1735.988	17359.88	3.875
8	Hatfield	375.986	1379.870	13798.70	3.080
9	Pretoria North	372.497	1367.064	13670.64	3.051
10	Waterkloof Ridge	367.287	1347.944	13479.44	3.009
11	Proclamation Hill	352.157	1292.418	12924.18	2.885
12	Pretoria West	297.842	1093.082	10930.82	2.440
13	Muckleneuk	290.647	1066.675	10666.75	2.381
14	Lynnwood	261.110	958.273	9582.73	2.139
15	Riviera	239.763	879.928	8799.28	1.964
16	Claremont	230.642	846.457	8464.57	1.889
17	Lisdogan Park	220.387	808.820	8088.20	1.805
18	Rietondale	211.941	777.822	7778.22	1.736
19	Colbyn	194.436	713.580	7135.80	1.593
20	Laudium	191.184	701.647	7016.47	1.566
21	Annlin	176.627	648.222	6482.22	1.447
22	Menlo Park	173.310	636.049	6360.49	1.420
23	Westpark	172.483	633.014	6330.14	1.413
24	Valhalla	155.683	571.358	5713.58	1.275
25	Wonderboom South	132.014	484.493	4844.93	1.081
26	Eastwood	129.201	474.168	4741.68	1.058
27	Pretoria Industrial	117.623	431.676	4316.76	0.964
28	Nieuw Muckleneuk	115.723	424.703	4247.03	0.948
29	Kwaggasrand	109.051	400.217	4002.17	0.893
30	Ashlea Gardens	107.491	394.492	3944.92	0.881
31	Eersterust	100.602	369.211	3692.11	0.824
32	Mountain View	93.645	343.676	3436.76	0.767
33	Lukasrand	80.042	293.753	2937.53	0.656
34	Eloffsdal	77.396	284.044	2840.44	0.634
35	Pretoria Gardens	67.445	247.524	2475.24	0.552
36	Watloo	56.683	208.027	2080.27	0.464
37	Silverton	55.080	202.144	2021.44	0.451
38	Garsfontein	54.670	200.639	2006.39	0.448
39	Queenswood	54.314	199.331	1993.31	0.445
40	Trevennai	53.111	194.918	1949.18	0.435
41	Constantia Park	51.386	188.588	1885.88	0.421
42	Meyers Park	48.855	179.296	1792.96	0.400
43	Asiatic Bazaar	47.791	175.392	1753.92	0.391
44	Sinoville	45.358	166.463	1664.63	0.372
45	Salvokop	40.159	147.384	1473.84	0.329
46	Samcor Park	36.223	132.938	1329.38	0.297

No	Suburb	Total t C	Total CO$_2$eq	US$	% of total
47	Hillcrest	33.859	124.261	1242.61	0.277
48	Atteridgeville	30.545	112.098	1120.98	0.250
49	Mamelodi	28.549	104.775	1047.75	0.234
50	Kilner Park	28.406	104.251	1042.51	0.233
51	Lynnwood Glen	25.311	92.893	928.93	0.207
52	Erasmusrand	24.692	90.618	906.18	0.202
53	Waterkloof Park	24.096	88.432	884.32	0.197
54	Moreleta Park	22.452	82.399	823.99	0.184
55	Clydesdale	21.265	78.044	780.44	0.174
56	Danville	18.051	66.247	662.47	0.148
57	Waterkloof Glen	17.824	65.415	654.15	0.146
58	Alphen Park	15.823	58.070	580.70	0.130
59	La Montagne	10.047	36.874	368.74	0.082
60	Faerie Glen	8.889	32.623	326.23	0.073
61	Maroelana	7.619	27.963	279.63	0.062
62	Lynnwood Ridge	6.856	25.161	251.61	0.056
63	Jan Niemand Park	5.375	19.728	197.28	0.044
64	Hazelwood	5.197	19.072	190.72	0.043
65	Montana	4.195	15.395	153.95	0.034
66	Saulsville	2.900	10.645	106.45	0.024
67	Philip Nel Park	2.182	8.007	80.07	0.018
68	Elardus Park	2.007	7.364	73.64	0.016
69	Erasmuskloof	1.625	5.963	59.63	0.013
70	Mayville	1.156	4.241	42.41	0.009
71	Hestea Park	0.913	3.352	33.52	0.007
72	Newlands	0.346	1.271	12.71	0.003
73	Wingate Park	0.344	1.261	12.61	0.003

Discussion

Methodological issues

A literature search revealed no biomass or allometric equations for *Jacaranda mimosifolia* locally or internationally, either in urban or natural settings. It is important to note that the volumetric equation used in this report provides only an *estimated* volume. Therefore all calculations derived from this equation are also estimates and thus all the resulting carbon calculations and the derived monetary values may only be quoted as *estimates*. The development of local biomass and allometric equations through destructive sampling could provide more accurate biomass estimates than those derived from equation (1) (Pillsbury *et al.* 1998). However, destructive sampling was not allowed by the municipality.

It is important to note that the Californian *Jacaranda mimosifolia* trees from which equation (1) (Pillsbury *et al.* 1998) was derived, were all urban trees and were therefore exposed to similar harsh street and urban growth conditions that Tshwane's trees are exposed to. The Pillsbury *et al* (1998) equation is thus more applicable to an urban environment than the standard volumetric equation which could also have been used. In some instances an adjustment of −10% to the total carbon storage by street trees is made when allometric equations are used from natural forest systems (McPherson *et al.* 1994); however, this was not deemed necessary in the light of the aforementioned origin of the Jacaranda equation. Furthermore, due to the limited availability of biomass equations for urban tree species, it is general practice to use those few equations that do exist for the urban and indeed natural environment in a generic manner (Goodman 1990; McPherson *et al.* 1994; Nowak & Crane 2002; Nowak *et al.* 2002b). Equation (1) was also used by McPherson *et al.* (2001) for carbon sequestration calculations in an urban setting. This further supports its applicability and appropriateness for such derivations.

Root to shoot ratio

Aboveground to belowground conversions (root : shoot ratios) are commonly used (Scholes & Walker 1993; McPherson *et al.* 1994, 2001; Nowak & Crane 2002; IPCC 2003; Scholes 2004), because it is difficult and therefore also expensive to determine below-

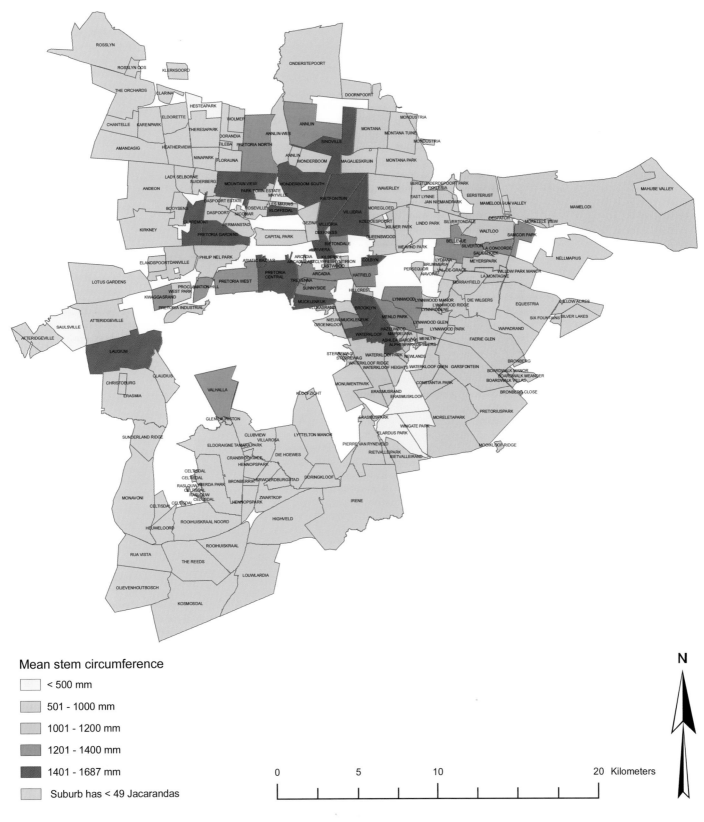

Mean stem circumference

☐ < 500 mm

☐ 501 - 1000 mm

☐ 1001 - 1200 mm

☐ 1201 - 1400 mm

☐ 1401 - 1687 mm

☐ Suburb has < 49 Jacarandas

N

0   5   10   20 Kilometers

Figure 2: The mean stem circumference of Jacaranda street trees in the City of Tshwane as measured in February and March 2004 based on tree number data provided by the City of Tshwane Metropolitan Municipality on 27 October 2003. The darker colours represent suburbs with larger trees

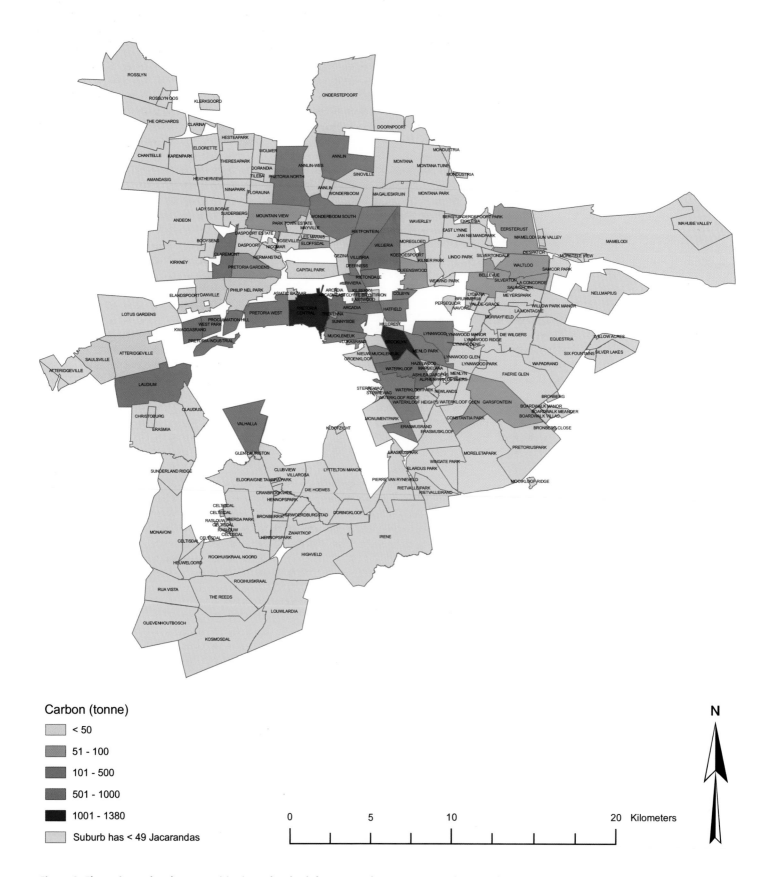

Carbon (tonne)

- < 50
- 51 - 100
- 101 - 500
- 501 - 1000
- 1001 - 1380
- Suburb has < 49 Jacarandas

N

0   5   10   20   Kilometers

Figure 3: The estimated carbon quantities in each suburb for Jacaranda street trees in the City of Tshwane as determined in 2004. The darker colours represent suburbs with larger quantities of carbon

ground biomass. This is especially true of belowground biomass in urban environments. In the light of the above it was decided to use the root : shoot ratio (see Methodology) which was also used by McPherson *et al.* (2001) to determine urban carbon sequestration quantities for *Jacaranda mimosifolia* trees for Inland Empire Communities in California U.S.A.

Wood density

Carbon quantities of the trees measured are relatively low. This can largely be ascribed to the low wood density of *Jacaranda mimosifolia*. However, the density of 520kg/m³ measured for *Jacaranda mimosifolia* in Tshwane corresponds well with the density of 550kg/m³ suggested by the Intergovernmental Panel for Climate Change (IPCC) for *Jacaranda* species in general (IPCC 2003).

Intra-street and inter-street comparisons

The analysis of variance conducted for the *intra*-street and *inter*-street stem circumference variation showed no significant differences. This supports the fieldwork observations that the socio-economic, cultural and environmental conditions within a suburb are relatively homogeneous. It furthermore concurs that the trees in a street and suburb were planted at more or less the same time. The suburbs are homogeneous due to planning practices of past apartheid regimes which planned South African cities according to the socio-economic, cultural and race attributes of the occupants of the particular suburbs.

Calculated carbon quantities

The mean carbon per tree of some suburbs was among the highest calculated, yet some of these suburbs had lower total carbon quantities than suburbs with a relatively low mean carbon quantity per tree, the reason being that not only is a high mean carbon quantity per tree necessary to obtain a large total suburb carbon mass but a large number of trees is also necessary. For example, the Asiatic Bazaar has the highest mean carbon per tree (0.713 t C) but has only 67 trees and as a result has only the 43rd largest total quantity of carbon for all the suburbs (47 t C) (Table 2). On the other hand, Pretoria Central is ranked 14th with regards to mean carbon per tree (0.483 t C), yet it is the suburb with the largest quantity of carbon stored in its street trees (1 379 t C). This can be attributed to the large number (2 853) of Jacaranda street trees present in the suburb. The mean carbon quantity per tree is positively correlated to the mean stem circumference per tree.

The mean carbon per tree for the city's Jacaranda population was calculated as an estimated 0.378 t C while the highest mean carbon per tree for a single suburb was almost double this value (0.713 t C for the Asiatic Bazaar). This suggests that the urban Jacaranda forest in Tshwane still has a large carbon sequestration

potential. Therefore when street trees are removed (especially young trees) it should be appreciated that such a tree had a long life expectancy (more than 100 years) and therefore a relatively high carbon sequestration potential which is then lost. This loss should be considered when these removed trees are not replaced and these losses can be translated into monetary terms. However, when large trees are removed monetary compensation may be required due to the destruction of green infrastructure but especially in the context of these results, due to the release of carbon dioxide.

Carbon trading

It should be noted that the carbon that has been captured by the trees cannot be traded because among other reasons the trees were not part of a registered carbon sequestration project and most were planted before 1990, which is the United Nations Framework Convention on Climate Change (UNFCCC) Kyoto Protocol baseline year. It could furthermore be argued that the municipality would have planted the trees as a part of the normal day-to-day practice. This would indicate that there are no additionalities and that there is thus no extra carbon sequestrated over and above that which would have been sequestrated as part of the normal tree planting. Proof of additionality is a prerequisite for carbon sequestration trading. Although the CO_2 price given is market-related (Booth 2003; McHale 2003), it still is hypothetical because as with other stock exchange commodities the value fluctuates and is exchange-rate related.

Conclusion

It should be stated that *all* trees sequestrate carbon albeit at different rates. The Jacaranda population is therefore not unique in this regard. The carbon sequestration value of Jacarandas is but a portion of the total possible value of a large tree. The authors do believe that this attempt to value the carbon storage of the Jacaranda street trees can be used to motivate for continued preservation of all street trees but more so the motivation for increased planting of street trees in general. This is the first such study of estimating the carbon storage of street trees in South Africa and therefore is important locally as well as for international comparisons.

Acknowledgements

The authors gratefully acknowledge Bertie Dry and Juan Mostert as well as Tshwane Metropolitan Municipality, Afrox, the Bradlows Foundation and the National Research Foundation (Grant no. 2053522) for financial support. Professor F. Steffans of UNISA assisted with statistical analysis and Ina Venter with fieldwork and data capturing and analysis. This paper is dedicated to Linda for her continued support.

Bibliography

Akbari, H. 2002. Shade trees reduce building energy use and CO_2 emissions from power plants. *Environmental Pollution* 116:119–126.

Akbari, H., Pomerantz, M., Taha, H. 2001. Cool surfaces and shade trees to reduce energy use and improve air quality in urban areas. *Solar Energy* 70:295–310.

Boje, V. 1984. Jacaranda mauve woven in thread of city's history. *Pretoria News*. Pretoria, South Africa. 10 October 1984.

Booth, T.H. 2003. International responses to threats of climate change. In: Booth, T.H. (ed.). Carbon accounting in forests. Proceedings of an international workshop on 'Facilitating international carbon accounting in forests'. *CSIRO, Forestry and Forestry Products*, Canberra, Australia, 24 February 2003:1–5. Australian Academy of Technological Sciences and Engineering.

Botes, H. 1985. Pretoria weer in sy koningsgewaad. *Die Transvaler*. Pretoria, South Africa. 31 October 1985.

City Council of Pretoria. 1991. History of Pretoria's Jacarandas. City Council of Pretoria Yearbook 1991.

Gifford, R.M. 2000. Carbon contents of above-ground tissues of forest and woodland trees. *National Carbon Accounting System Technical Report* No. 22, Australian Greenhouse Office.

Goodman, P.S. 1990. Soil, vegetation and large herbivore relations in Mkuzi Game Reserve, Natal. PhD Thesis. University of the Witwatersrand, Johannesburg.

Huang, Y.J., Akbari, H., Taha, H., Rosenfeld, A.H. 1987. The potential of vegetation in reducing summer cooling loads in residential buildings. *Journal of Climate and Applied Meteorology* 26, 1103–1116.

Intergovernmental Panel on Climate Change (IPCC). 2003. Good practice guidance for land use, land-use change and forestry. J. Penman, M. Gytarsky, T. Hiraishi, T. Krug, D. Kruger, R. Pipatti, L. Buendia, K. Miwa,T., Ngara, K. Tanabe, F. Wagner (eds). Institute for Global Environmental Strategies (IGES), Japan.

Jim, C.Y.B, 1987. Urban trees in Hong Kong – benefits and constraints. *Arboricultural Journal* 11, 145–164.

Kollin, C. (ed). 2003. Proceedings 2003 National Urban Forest Conference: Engineering Green, September 17–20, 2003, San Antonio, Texas. American Forests, Washington.

Maco, S.E., McPherson, E.G. 2003. A practical approach to assessing structure, function, and value of street tree populations in small communities. *Journal of Arboriculture* 29, 84–97.

Marquart, G. 1998. First Jacaranda trees planted 110 years ago. *Record East*. Pretoria, South Africa. 25 September 1998.

McHale, M. 2003. Carbon credit markets: Is there a role for community forestry? In: C. Kollin (ed). Proceedings 2003 National Urban Forest Conference: Engineering Green, September 17–20, 2003, San Antonio, Texas. pp. 74-77. American Forests, Washington.

McPherson, E.G., 1999. Street tree growth rates and benefit-cost quantification. Proceedings from the 1999 National Urban Forest Conference, U.S.A. pp.139–142.

McPherson, E.G., Nowak, D.J., Rowntree, R.A. 1994.Chicago's urban forest ecosystem: Results of the Chicago Urban Forest Climate Project. General Technical Report NE-186. Radnor, P.A., United States of America. United States Department of Agriculture Forest Service, Northeastern Forest Experiment Station.

McPherson, E.G., Simpson, J.R. 1999.Carbon dioxide reduction through urban forestry: Guidelines for professional and volunteer tree planters. General Technical Report PSW-GTR-171, Albany, CA: Pacific Southwest Research Station, Forest Service, United States Department of Agriculture. 237 pp.

McPherson, E.G., Simpson, J.R., Peper, P.J., Xiao, Q., Pittenger, D.R., Hodel, D.R. 2001. Tree guidelines for inland Empire communities. Western Center for Urban Forest Research and Education, USDA Forest Service, Pacific Southwest Research Station. Local Government Commission. 116 pp.

Nowak, D.J., Crane, D.E. 2002. Carbon storage and sequestration by urban trees in the USA. *Environmental Pollution* 116, 381–389.

Nowak, D.J., Crane, D.E., Dwyer, J.F. 2002a. Compensatory value of urban trees in the United States. *Journal of Arboriculture* 28, 194–199.

Nowak, D.J., Crane, D.E., Stevens, J.C., Ibarra, M. 2002b. Brooklyn's Urban Forest. General Technical Report NE-290. Delaware, OH, USA, US. Department of Agriculture, Forest Service.

Nowak, D.J., Stevens, J.C., Sisinni, S.M., Luley, C.J. 2002c. Effects of urban tree management and species selection on atmospheric carbon dioxide. *Journal of Arboriculture* 28, 113–122.

Pillsbury, N.H., Reimer, J.L., Thompson, R.P. 1998. Tree volume equations for fifteen urban species in California. Technical Report No. 7, Urban Forest Ecosystem Institute, California Polytechnic State University, San Luis Obispo and California Department of Forestry and Fire Protection, Riverside, California. 57pp.

Record Central. 2003. Minister fights for jacarandas. *Record Central*. City of Tshwane, South Africa. 27 July 2003.

Robinson, M., 1985. Pretoria se perslieflikheid. *Beeld*. Pretoria, South Africa. 22 October 1985.

Rosenfeld, A.H., Akbari, H., Romm, J.J., Pomerantz, M. 1998. Cool communities: strategies for heat island mitigation and smog reduction. *Energy and Buildings* 28, 51–62.

Scholes, R.J. 2004. Carbon storage in southern African woodlands. Lawes, M.J., Eeley, H.A.C., Shackleton, C.M., Geach, B.G.S. (eds). *Indigenous forests and woodlands in South Africa. Policy, people and practice*. pp. 797–813. University of KwaZulu-Natal, Pietermaritzburg.

Scholes, R.J., Walker, B.H. (eds). 1993. An African Savanna. Synthesis of the Nylsvley study. Cambridge University Press, Cambridge. 306 pp.

Simpson, J.R. 1998. Urban forest impacts on regional cooling and heating energy use: Sacramento County case study. *Journal of Arboriculture* 24, 201–214.

Stoffberg, G.H. 2006. Growth and carbon sequestration by street trees in the City of Tshwane, South Africa. PhD. Thesis, University of Pretoria, Pretoria, South Africa.

Xiao, Q., McPherson, E.G., Simpson, J.R., Ustin, S.L. 1998. Rainfall interception by Sacramento's urban forest. *Journal of Arboriculture* 24, 235–244.

Xiao, Q., McPherson, E.G., Ustin, S.L., Grismer, M.E. & Simpson, J.R. 2000. Winter rainfall interception by two mature open-grown trees in Davis, California. *Hydrological Processes*, 14:763–784.

chapter 11

An International Perspective on Growth Rate and Carbon Sequestration of Trees Used in the Urban Landscape

Hennie Stoffberg
Department of Plant Sciences
University of Pretoria
Pretoria
South Africa

Gretel van Rooyen
Department of Plant Sciences
University of Pretoria
Pretoria
South Africa

Introduction

In this chapter comparisons are made between the growth rates of sixteen non-indigenous street tree species growing in the coastal area of southern California, USA and those of the three street tree species *Combretum erythrophyllum*, *Searsia lancea* and *Searsia pendulina* investigated in a South African study by Stoffberg (2006). Comparisons are also made of the sequestration rate and capacity of the three species investigated by Stoffberg (2006) to those of the urban tree species on other continents.

Growth rate discussion

Peper *et al.* (2001) compared the growth of sixteen street tree species growing in southern California. These species were compared in terms of stem diameter at breast height (DBH), tree height and crown diameter growth. Their study was similar to that presented in Stoffberg (2006) in that predictive equations were derived and the comparisons made in Tables 1, 2 and 3 are based on predicted or modelled dimensions for both the local and the Californian species.

Table 1: *Predicted stem diameter at breast height sizes for coastal southern California street tree species investigated by Peper et al. (2001) as well as for those investigated by Stoffberg (2006). The stem diameter of* Combretum erythrophyllum, Searsia lancea *and* Searsia pendulina *street tree species investigated was measured at ground level or just above the basal swelling*

	DBH (cm) 15 years		DBH (cm) 30 years
*Combretum erythrophyllum**	40.42	*Combretum erythrophyllum**	68.13
Pinus canariensis	36.92	*Cedrus deodora*	57.85
Ficus macrocarpa	32.74	*Pinus canariensis*	53.43
Cedrus deodora	32.69	*Ficus macrocarpa*	47.33
*Searsia pendulina**	29.13	*Melaleuca quinquenervia*	46.30
*Searsia lancea**	26.83	*Cinnamomum camphora*	44.93
Schinus terebinthifolius	26.50	*Eucalyptus ficifolia*	42.48
Cinnamomum camphora	24.00	*Saersia lancea**	39.00
Cupaniopsis anacardioides	22.70	*Schinus terebinthifolius*	38.52
Metrosideros excelsus	22.58	*Metrosideros excelsus*	36.99
Jacaranda mimosifolia	19.72	*Ceratonia siliqua*	36.39
Liquidambar styracifolia	18.93	*Magnolia grandiflora*	32.78
Melaleuca quinquenervia	18.65	*Cupaniopsis anacardioides*	32.61
Tristania conferta	18.45	*Liquidambar styracifolia*	27.55
Podocarpus macrophyllus	15.76	*Jacaranda mimosifolia*	26.35
Magnolia grandiflora	15.72	*Tristania conferta*	24.96
Ceratonia siliqua	15.32	*Podocarpus macrophyllus*	21.45
Callistemon citrinus	13.29	*Callistemon citrinus*	20.56
Eucalyptus ficifolia	12.05	*Searsia pendulina**	#
Mean	23.28	Mean	38.76

* Diameter was taken at ground level

No data

Table 2: *Predicted tree height (m) for coastal southern California street tree species investigated by Peper et al. (2001) as well as for* Combretum erythrophyllum, Searsia lancea *and* Searsia pendulina *indigenous street trees investigated (Stoffberg 2006)*

	Height (m) 15 years		Height (m) 30 years
Pinus canariensis	16.21	*Pinus canariensis*	19.24
Cedrus deodora	11.77	*Cedrus deodora*	16.09
Liquidambar styracifolia	9.57	*Combretum erythrophyllum*	11.47
Combretum erythrophyllum	8.47	*Liquidambar styracifolia*	11.37
Searsia pendulina	8.39	*Melaleuca quinquenervia*	10.43
Cinnamomum camphora	7.74	*Cinnamomum camphora*	10.02
Cupaniopsis anacardioides	7.36	*Metrosideros excelsus*	10.00
Tristania conferta	7.22	*Magnolia grandiflora*	9.04
Melaleuca quinquenervia	6.90	*Ficus macrocarpa*	8.95

	Height (m) 15 years		Height (m) 30 years
Ficus macrocarpa	6.86	*Eucalyptus ficifolia*	8.54
Magnolia grandiflora	6.59	*Cupaniopsis anacardioides*	8.24
Metrosideros excelsus	6.26	*Tristania conferta*	7.92
Schinus terebinthifolius	6.23	*Schinus terebinthifolius*	7.59
Jacaranda mimosifolia	5.95	*Ceratonia siliqua*	7.55
Podocarpus macrophyllus	5.73	*Jacaranda mimosifolia*	7.23
Searsia lancea	5.43	*Podocarpus macrophyllus*	6.75
Ceratonia siliqua	4.79	*Searsia lancea*	6.36
Callistemon citrinus	4.48	*Callistemon citrinus*	5.78
Eucalyptus ficifolia	4.11	*Searsia pendulina*	#
Mean	7.37	Mean	9.59

No data

Table 3: *Predicted crown diameter (m) for coastal southern California street tree species investigated by Peper et al. (2001) as well as for* Combretum erythrophyllum, Searsia lancea *and* Searsia pendulina *indigenous street trees investigated (Stoffberg 2006)*

	Crown diameter (m) 15 years		Crown diameter (m) 30 years
Combretum erythrophyllum	10.37	*Combretum erythrophyllum*	17.56
Cedrus deodora	8.04	*Cedrus deodora*	11.70
Searsia pendulina	7.80	*Cinnamomum camphora*	10.44
Pinus canariensis	6.90	*Metrosideros excelsus*	10.01
Cinnamomum camphora	6.79	*Searsia lancea*	8.79
Cupaniopsis anacardioides	6.63	*Ficus macrocarpa*	8.73
Podocarpus macrophyllus	6.58	*Magnolia grandiflora*	8.56
Schinus terebinthifolius	6.53	*Pinus canariensis*	8.25
Searsia lancea	6.35	*Cupaniopsis anacardioides*	8.12
Ficus macrocarpa	5.97	*Schinus terebinthifolius*	8.08
Jacaranda mimosifolia	5.49	*Jacaranda mimosifolia*	8.04
Magnolia grandiflora	5.41	*Ceratonia siliqua*	7.98
Liquidambar styracifolia	5.33	*Podocarpus macrophyllus*	7.90
Tristania conferta	5.10	*Eucalyptus ficifolia*	7.66
Metrosideros excelsus	4.70	*Liquidambar styracifolia*	6.48
Ceratonia siliqua	4.47	*Tristania conferta*	6.22
Melaleuca quinquenervia	4.27	*Melaleuca quinquenervia*	6.16
Callistemon citrinus	3.74	*Callistemon citrinus*	4.85
Eucalyptus ficifolia	2.73	*Searsia pendulina*	#
Mean	5.96	Mean	8.64

No data

In Table 1 it is shown that *Combretum erythrophyllum* has the largest stem diameter at an age of 15 years and 30 years. It is also shown that *Searsia pendulina* and *Searsia lancea* have the fifth and sixth largest stem diameters at age 15 years respectively. These stem diameters are inflated due to it being taken at ground level (see Stoffberg 2006) and are therefore not a true comparison. However, it may be conjectured that the diameter at breast height of these three species will be within the range of the diameter at breast height of the other sixteen species.

Combretum erythrophyllum, *Searsia lancea* and *Searsia pendulina* are positioned fourth, fifth and sixteenth respectively, when considering tree height at an age of 15 years (Table 2). However, both *Combretum erythrophyllum* and *Searsia pendulina* have a tree height of approximately half that of *Pinus canariensis* at an age of 15 years. At age 30 years *Combretum erythrophyllum*'s tree height is approximately 7m less than that of the tallest tree measured namely *Pinus canariensis*.

Regarding crown diameter one observes that *Combretum erythrophyllum* has the largest crown diameter at both 15 years and 30 years. This may be attributable to the cultural practices such as pruning.

When comparing the species at an age of 15 years, then both *Combretum erythrophyllum* and *Searsia lancea* show relatively high growth rates compared to the southern Californian street trees. A comparison at age 30 years indicates that *Combretum erythrophyllum* has a competitive growth rate also at this age, which suggests that this species could be considered a fast growing tree when compared to those investigated by Peper *et al.* (2001).

Carbon sequestration discussion

The carbon sequestration rates of *Combretum erythrophyllum*, *Searsia lancea* and *Searsia pendulina* street tree species investigated in this chapter are compared with those of other studies in Italy, the United States of America and China. Even though comparisons are made they should be interpreted with caution due to a number of variables differing in each study. *Combretum erythrophyllum* does, however, sequestrate carbon at a similar rate to *Quercus ilex* and *Quercus pubescens* growing in Rome, Italy.

Table 4: Comparison of carbon sequestration rate (kg C yr) for various cities and species

Author	City/state and country	Species	Tree size or age	kg C/year
Stoffberg (2006)	City of Tshwane, South Africa	*Combretum erythrophyllum*	Mean over 46 years	29
Stoffberg (2006)	City of Tshwane, South Africa	*Searsia lancea*	Mean over 32 years	8
Stoffberg (2006)	City of Tshwane, South Africa	*Searsia pendulina*	Mean over 15 years	8
Gratani *et al.* (2006)	Rome, Italy	*Quercus ilex*	Tree height 12 m	22
Gratani *et al.* (2006)	Rome, Italy	*Quercus pubescens*	Tree height 12 m	30
McPherson *et al.* (1999)	California, USA	*Populus 'Robusta'*	Mean over 30 years	82
McPherson *et al.* (1999)	Twin Cities, St Paul, USA	*Acer saccharum*	Mean over 60 years	53
McPherson *et al.* (1994)	Chicago, USA	Mean for study	< 80 mm DBH	1
McPherson *et al.* (1994)	Chicago, USA	Mean for study	>760 mm DBH	93
Yang *et al.* (2005)	Beijing, China	11 main species	Mean for estimated 2.3 million trees	5

Methodologies used to calculate carbon sequestration rates varied and differed in the studies presented in Table 4. Further to the application of the different methodologies, variation in carbon sequestration rates are due to, among others, different species, tree ages and sizes along with some of the factors mentioned below. The comparisons in Table 4 are therefore done with some degree of circumspection. Yet limited information exists and therefore these incongruent comparisons are inevitable.

Factors that need consideration for growth and carbon sequestration comparisons

Caution needs to be applied when considering Tables 1 to 4 for comparative purposes. This is due to the numerous different growth conditions of trees in urban areas. The growth of trees in natural environments is the result of mainly species, genotypes, climate (including rainfall), available water, geographic region, soil conditions and type as well as growth inhibitors such as herbivory, pests and diseases. It should also be appreciated that trees in natural environments differ in some instances largely between species and geographic regions along with the other factors mentioned above. Urban trees share the same variables as trees in natural environments. There are, however, numerous additional factors influencing urban tree growth. Some of these factors will be discussed here to illustrate that care needs to be applied when making inter-geographic species as well as inter-species, inter-city and even intra-city growth and carbon sequestration comparisons.

The following are some factors that influence tree growth and carbon sequestration rates in urban areas, which, in turn, influence growth prediction modelling:

- Pruning practices differ depending on city ordinances, utilities and urban foresters' training. Pruning training also differs between training facilities.

- Tree curb distances, tree-curb-paving distances and underground utility composition, structure and layout influence the rooting space available to trees and vary even in the same city between land uses within such a city.

- Tree grids are often found in high density commercial areas. Often the sizes of these grids are limited. If there is no alternative direct source of water, then the size of the tree grid as well as its position as a catchment basin is crucial to tree growth. These grids and water catchment issues vary across land-use, manufacturer specifications, cities and countries.

- Irrigation varies greatly between land-use, for example, inner city and residential as well as between climatic zones such as arid versus Mediterranean within a country. It may also differ according to income status of landowners in different land-uses or suburbs.

- Method of tree planting differs regarding, for example, the size and geometry of the planting hole, as well as the added supplements such as compost or fertilisers during planting.

- Soil compaction practices during road, pavement and lawn construction influence root penetration in these zones.

- Soil type, texture, structure and acidity or alkalinity vary greatly even in the same city, as well as country. Tree growth may differ markedly, for instance, due to differing soil pH, all other factors being equal.

- Soil texture, structure and soil acidity or alkalinity alteration due to building, road and pavement rubble dumped in tree planting zones are problematic in South Africa and conditions will differ in other countries and cities.

- Municipal street tree fertilisation practices as well as those in adjacent land-use, for example, lawn fertilisation practices influence tree growth. Fertilisation may also be influenced by cultural practices derived from, for example, education and income of landowners.

- Street microclimate differs between land-uses as well as within each land-use and influences tree growth.

- Macro and local climate differ in each city and country.

- Annual rainfall is an important factor regarding tree growth and may cause large variations in growth rates within the same and other species.

- Number of frost free days influences the growth season of trees.

- The number of photosynthetic sunny days and the length of photosynthetic time in those days varies.

- There may be growth rate differences between cultivars within species.

Conclusion

The above growth influencing factors vary in most cities across the world and also vary with time in each city. It is noteworthy that the species compared above mostly do comply within reasonable growth bounds. Large variation is, however, apparent regarding carbon sequestration rates which lead to the question as to the appropriateness of such inter-geographic and inter-city comparisons.

There are limited urban growth and carbon sequestration data and equations available. It is thus suggested that those equations and data that do exist be used in a generic manner, yet with the proviso that their original context be noted and taken into consideration during their application. These factors also need to be communicated in literature and commercial publications in which they are applied in order to remain transparent and provide results that may be judged objectively.

Bibliography

Gratani, L. & Varone, L. 2006. Carbon sequestration by *Quercus ilex* L. and *Quercus pubescens* Willd. and their contribution to decreasing air temperature in Rome. *Urban Ecosystems* 9:27–37.

McPherson, E.G. 1998. Atmospheric carbon dioxide reduction by Sacramento's urban forest. *Journal of Arboriculture* 24(4):215–223.

McPherson, E.G., Nowak, D.J. & Rowntree, R.A. 1994. Chicago's urban forest ecosystem: Results of the Chicago Urban Forest Climate Project. General Technical Report NE-186. Radnor, PA, United States of America. United States Department of Agriculture Forest Service, Northeastern Forest Experiment Station.

Peper, P.J., McPherson, E.G. & Mori, S.M. 2001. Predictive equations for dimensions and leaf area of coastal Southern California street trees. *Journal of Arboriculture* 27:169–181.

Stoffberg, G.H. 2006. Growth and carbon sequestration rates of three street trees in the City of Tshwane, South Africa. PhD Thesis, University of Pretoria, Pretoria, South Africa.

Yang, J., McBride, J., Zhou, J. & Sun, Z. 2005. The urban forest of Beijing and its role in air pollution reduction. *Urban Forestry & Urban Greening* 3 2005:65–78.

chapter 12

Sound Landscape Assessment: A Methodology for Visual Impact Assessment in South Africa

Graham Young

Department of Architecture

University of Pretoria

Pretoria

South Africa

Wherever we are, whenever we are awake, we are experiencing the landscape, from the city street to the remote wilderness. We perceive our surroundings using all our senses. We orientate ourselves by the pattern of the landscape. [The] landscape is an amalgam of patterns, our perceptions and the processes that change both patterns and perception[1].

The landscape is a vital part of our natural and man-made environment and in its most healthy state is considered by many to be one of the most important components of an enjoyable life. During the latter part of the last century and into the new millennium, we have witnessed its vulnerability in the face of economic growth and social change. Often, we have failed adequately to predict, recognise or deal with the visual impact of new development on the landscape. The result has been serious erosion of the aesthetic character and scenic quality of many of our rural and urban landscapes.

In planning for future prosperity, more effort must be put into safeguarding the quality of the environment, not only for our own health and well-being, but also for the sake of future generations. The growing emphasis on 'sustainable development' – the balance between social concerns, economic development, cultural concerns and the environment – implies a strong need to integrate issues of landscape conservation and enhancement into the development process.[2] Often this sentiment excludes aesthetic aspects of the landscape.

In South Africa visual impact assessment often, but not always, forms part of the Environmental Impact Assessment (EIA) process, and there is no universally accepted method that guides the visual impact process[3]. Hence the assessment can vary dramatically both in quality and content. This situation is not acceptable and is fraught with difficulties. Given poor quality assessments or in the worst-case scenario, no assessment, the authorities will find it difficult to take meaningful decisions related to the potential visual impact of a development. The most likely result is that the quality and character of the landscape will be compromised if inappropriate development takes place or mitigation measures are not effectively implemented.

It is therefore fitting that a locally accepted methodology and guidelines for visual impact assessment be established for universal application throughout South Africa. The intent of the guidelines and method would be to assist practitioners in predicting and judging the significance of the effects that a new development would have upon landscape character and visual amenity. More importantly, [the guideline and method should] require a commitment to prevent and reduce adverse impacts and to look for positive opportunities for environmental enhancement. In this way, economic well-being and environmental quality can go hand-in-hand.[4]

The author has developed an approach and method[5] that he believes establishes explicit values and principles for the establishment of a universally acceptable assessment method that can be applied to development projects in South Africa. The diagram below graphically illustrates the assessment process.

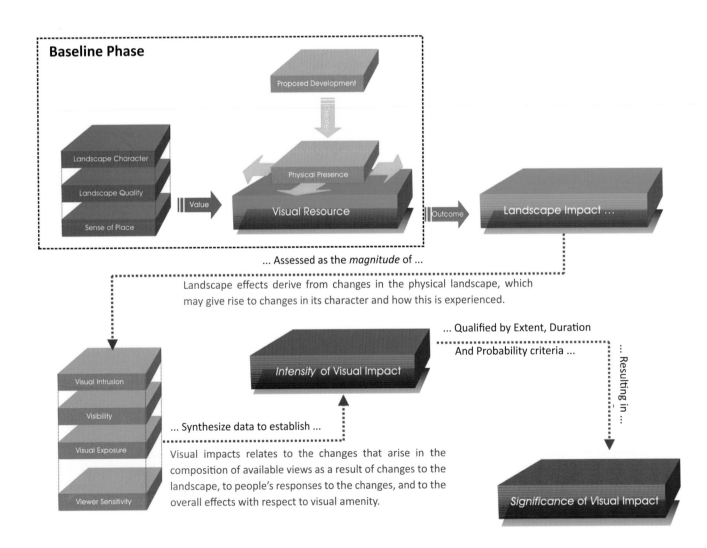

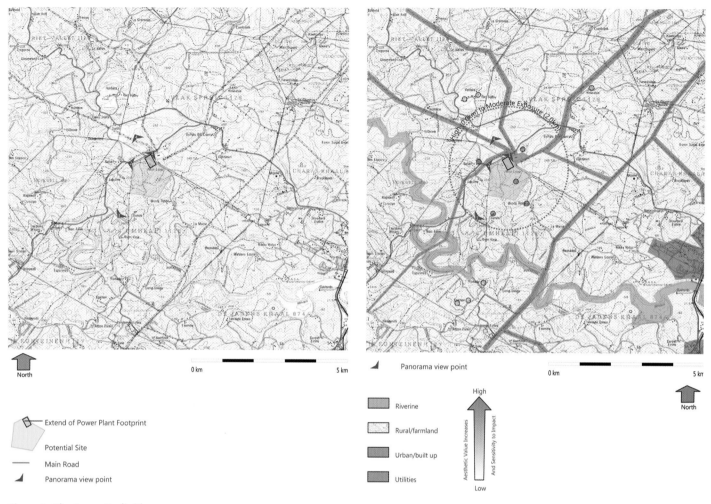

North

0 km   5 km

◢ Panorama view point

0 km   5 km

North

◻ Extend of Power Plant Footprint

Potential Site

— Main Road

◢ Panorama view point

▦ Riverine

▦ Rural/farmland

▦ Urban/built up

▦ Utilities

High

Aesthetic Value Increases
And Sensitivity to Impact

Low

Figure 1: The Avon site (left)

Figure 2: Peaking Plant Avon – land types (right)

Case study: Peaking Power Plant, Avon, KwaZulu-Natal, Newtown Landscape Architects

In line with Government policy regarding the introduction of independent power producers (IPPs) into South Africa's electricity industry, Government nominated the Department of Minerals and Energy (DME) to embark on a process to procure additional new IPP generation capacity. The initial focus of the process was in the Eastern Cape (Coega) and KwaZulu-Natal where the need was most pressing. As part of the EIA process specialist visual impact assessments were commissioned. Through an extensive screening process undertaken by the DME, two sites were identified for the KwaZulu-Natal region at Avon and Georgedale. This case study describes the VIA[6] commissioned for the Avon site as indicated in Figure 1.

In determining visual impact it is understood that the receiving environment has value and that the assessment of likely effects on a landscape resource and on visual amenity is complex, since it is determined through a combination of quantitative and qualitative evaluations[7]. Landscape character, landscape quality[8] and 'sense of place'[9] were used to

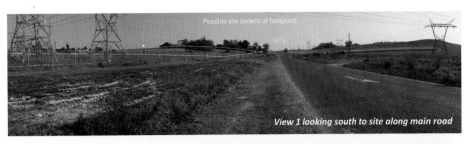
Possible site (extent of footprint)

View 1 looking south to site along main road

Possible site (extent of footprint)

Refer to Figure 1 for location of viewing point

View 2 looking north east to site from main road

Figure 3: Landscape character –
Viewpoints 1 and 2

Possible site (extent of footprint)

View 3 looking north to site from nearby farm road

Possible site (extent of footprint)

Refer to Figure 1 for location of viewing point

View 4 looking south east to site from adjacent farmland

Figure 4: Landscape character –
Viewpoints 3 and 4

Before

After

Figure 5: Photographic simulation – Viewpoint
2 from the main road south west of the site

*Figure 6: Photographic simulation –
Viewpoint 3 from a private farm road
immediately south of the site*

*Figure 7: Photographic simulation –
Viewpoint 1 clearly showing the intrusive
nature of the plant in foreground views
from the adjacent main road*

*Figure 8: Photographic simulation showing
effect of mitigation measures, Viewpoint 1*

North

Panorama view point

0 km   5 km

Visual Exposure Curve

Gradient of curve is proportional to size of object i.e. steeper curve signifies larger object, this equals greater exposure and visual impact

HIGH   MEDIUM   LOW   INSIGNIFICANT

○ Farmstead with High Exposure
○ Farmstead with Moderate Exposure

—— Public Road with High Exposure
—— Public Road with Moderate Exposure

Extent of viewshed i.e. Area from within which the power plant is potentially visible

Figure 9: Viewshed analysis

evaluate the visual resource. The general area in the vicinity of the Avon site is characterised by rolling hills, covered with sugar cane and which afford open panoramic views. The hills fall away to valleys, which drain to the Umhlali River south of the site. Figure 2 demarcates the four main land-types and their relative scenic value. The panoramas in Figures 3 and 4 are views towards and illustrate the nature and character of the landscape. By far the most dominant land type is rural farmland, which gives the area its strong sense of place. The scenic beauty of the study area was rated[10] *moderate* to *high* i.e. it is a landscape that exhibits a positive character with valued features that combine to give the experience of unity, richness and harmony and which are potentially sensitive to change in general.

Figure 10: Photographic simulation showing effect of mitigation measures, Viewpoint 2

Figure 11: Photographic simulation showing effect of mitigation measures, Viewpoint 3

Using the worst case scenario, the change to the landscape (visual resource) caused by the physical presence of the plant was assessed, i.e. the degree to which the change compromises, enhances or maintains the visual quality of the area. To assess the magnitude of impact four main factors were considered.

- ◆ Visual intrusion: the nature of intrusion or contrast of the plant with the surrounding environment and its compatibility/discord with the landscape and surrounding land use
- ◆ Visibility: the land area from which the plant is potentially visible
- ◆ Visual exposure: visibility and visual intrusion qualified with a distance rating to indicate the scale of intrusion
- ◆ Sensitivity: sensitivity of visual receptors to the proposed development.

Photographic simulations were used to illustrate the power plant superimposed over the existing landscape. Views from the road and farms south of the plant would be partially screened by trees located along the southern edge of the proposed development site as illustrated in Figures 5 and 6. The image in Figure 7 clearly indicates that the plant would, however, be highly visible from northern perspectives, particularly from the adjacent road.

The viewshed[11] in Figure 9 indicates that the power plant is visible from two dominant 'strips' north and south of the site. The analysis also indicates that the power plant would be visible from less than a quarter of the zone of potential influence[12] and would be visible from relatively few residential properties. The most prominent public views to the site would occur from the main road, which runs west and then north of the site. The road, however, is not heavily used and caters mainly to the local farming community. The plant would also be visible for a small section of the Shakaskraal Road, immediately north-west of the site. Within the context of the study region, the visibility of the proposed plant was rated *low* primarily due its 'remoteness' (i.e. it occurs in a rural area away from routes to and from nearby residential and tourist areas), and the fact that relatively few people would therefore be affected by it.

Visual exposure was a contributing negative factor, influencing specifically foreground views from the adjacent road, nearby labour housing, a residence west of the site and the Gessla Farmstead south of the site.

Views from residences and tourist facilities are typically the most sensitive, as views from these areas are often frequent and of long duration. The nearest affected residence is the property 750m to the west of the site along with the farmsteads, to the north and south-east of the site.

Synthesising visual intrusion, visibility, visual exposure and viewer sensitivity criteria results in a *magnitude* of impact rating. In determining this rating a weighting system was avoided as attempting to attach a precise numerical value to qualitative resources is rarely successful, and should not be used as a substitute for reasoned professional judgment[13]. It was predicted that the impact would be *moderate* to *high* negative because the plant:

♦ would have a local high negative effect on the visual quality of the landscape
♦ would contrast dramatically with the patterns or elements that define the structure of the landscape
♦ would contrast dramatically with land use, settlement or enclosure patterns
♦ without mitigation would not be able to be 'absorbed' into the landscape
♦ would cause moderate change in landscape characteristics over a localised area resulting in a moderate to high change to key views.

There was a vociferous appeal made against the Avon site, specifically from a visual impact point of view. The VIA was therefore again scrutinised during the Appeals process. The approach and method followed in the VIA gave the Authorities and the public a comprehensible understanding of what the visual impact could be and that it could be mitigated, assuming the effective implementation of the management measures illustrated in Figures 8 and 10.

Ultimately, judgment was based on the training and experience of the author (a qualified and experienced professional landscape architect), supported by clear evidence and reasoned argument. It is this approach that provided the Authorities with a clear 'picture' of what the potential visual impact could be and that mitigation measures could successfully reduce the impact. This enabled the Authorities to take a rational judgment in their proclamation in the Record of Decision and at the Appeals hearing, the end result being that the project was given the go ahead.

1   Bell, Simon, (1999). *Landscape Pattern, Perception and Process*. New York: E. and F.N. Spon. Introduction
2   The Institute of Environmental Assessment and the Landscape Institute. (1996). *Guidelines for landscape and visual impact assessment*, E. and F.N. Spon, London (vii).
3   There is, however, a provincial guideline for which the author was a member of the panel that contributed research for the document: Oberholzer, B. *Guideline for involving visual & aesthetic specialists in EIA processes: Edition 1*. CSIR Report No ENV-S-C 2005 053 F. Republic of South Africa, Provincial Government of the Western Cape, Department of Environmental Affairs & Development Planning, Cape Town. (2005).
4   The Institute of Environmental Assessment and the Landscape Institute. (1996). *Guidelines for landscape and visual impact assessment*, E. and F.N. Spon, London. vii–viii.
5   The approach has developed over the last 25 years in which time the author has worked on over 250 VIA reports in Canada, South Africa and other parts of Africa.
6   Newtown Landscape Architects cc. (November 2006). Specialist Study Environmental Impact Report, Visual Environment for the Proposed Peaking Power Plant at Avon, KwaZulu-Natal, Unpublished Report, Johannesburg.
7   The Institute of Environmental Assessment and the Landscape Institute. (1996). *Guidelines for landscape and visual impact assessment*, E. and F.N.

Spon, London.
8   Warnock, S. & Brown, N., Putting Landscape First. *Landscape Design*. No. 268 March 1998. p.44–46.
9   Lynch, K. (1992). *Good City Form*, The MIT Press, London. p.131.
10 The author uses a modified version of The Visual Resource Management System, Department of the Interior of the USA Government, Bureau of Land Management along principles established in studies of perceptual psychology to rate the scenic quality of a landscape.
11 A viewshed is a two dimensional spatial pattern created by an analysis that defines areas, which contain all possible observation sites from which an object would be visible. The basic assumption for preparing a viewshed analysis is that the observer eye height is 1.6m above ground level.
12 The zone of potential visual influence is the maximum extent in radius about an object beyond which the visual impact of its most visible features will become insignificant due primarily to distance and atmospheric interference. The extent of the zone is determined by the scale, bulk and nature of the proposed development i.e. a cellphone tower would have a smaller zone than say a cement processing plant.
13 The Institute of Environmental Assessment and the Landscape Institute. (1996). *Guidelines for landscape and visual impact assessment*, E. and F.N. Spon, London.

chapter 13

Sustainable Tailings Impoundment Landform Design: Rational Decision-making for the Sustainable Configuration of Tailings Impoundments

Brian Rademeyer
Department of Civil and Biosystems
Engineering
University of Pretoria
Pretoria
South Africa

Mader van den Berg
Department of Architecture
University of Pretoria
Pretoria
South Africa

This project involved the theoretical application of ecological principles to the deposition and management of mine tailings, the result of which is a hypothetical design for a real project presently being undertaken in the Rustenburg region, North West Province. A theoretical ecological and sustainable approach was adopted as a critical evaluation tool in order to assess, analyse and formulate solutions regarding the environmental and social impacts associated with impoundments throughout the life cycle of the latter.

An understanding of engineering constraints and environmental issues provided the knowledge base for the implementation of natural landform design principles. Guidelines for the design, management and rehabilitation of tailings disposal facilities (TDF) were compiled in order to reach the project goal.

This project is innovative, both because it envisages tailings dam design from the aspect of landscape architecture and also because it introduces the concept of visual impacts in a novel way. The overall purpose of this research project undertaken by the Department of Civil and Biosystems Engineering at the University of Pretoria is to develop generic models for the engineering costs and environmental impacts throughout the life cycle of a tailings dam such that the designs can be optimised *ab initio* with respect to the costs and the impacts.

Introduction

Tailings disposal facilities (TDFs) are arguably one of the most significant mining environmental liabilities. Increasingly stringent legislation coupled with more responsible attitudes have in recent years radically changed the situation in such a manner that current practice results in tailings impoundments are left in a relatively safe state with minimum immediate physical environmental impact, provided wind and water erosion are controlled.

While this state would have been considered acceptable a few years ago, it is now internationally recognised that concepts of sustainable development necessitate even more positive outcomes. Figure 1 illustrates the general perception that for tailings impoundments the cost of environmental protection works has, over the years, become a much larger proportion of the total development costs and it suggests that this is ever increasing due to:

◆ a growing expectation for sustainable mine development
◆ more stringent environmental legislation
◆ stakeholders and the general public becoming increasingly aware of the potential short as well as long term environmental hazards.

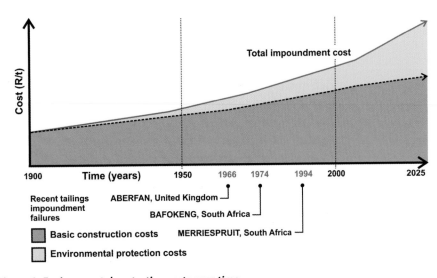

Figure 1: Environmental protection costs over time

The increasing need for energy and minerals results in the alteration of the earth's surface. The environmentally conscious society of today demands that the areas disturbed must be returned to an acceptable predetermined and sustainable land use. In principle it is no longer allowable to leave drastically disturbed land to heal by itself. However, the consideration of mine residue closure liabilities leaves much to be desired – the law is unambiguous and yet the perceptive implementation and enforcement thereof pertaining to mine residue is far from satisfactory. So does the planning and construction of sustainable tailings dams in South Africa require new laws? Probably not! There must instead be a continuation of environmental protection through the existing environmental impact assessment laws, regulations and tools. In particular, there is a need to acquire more skills in the art of environmental improvement that will in turn result in sustainable landscapes.

South Africa's mining industry has since the mid to late nineteenth century developed into a well-established global industry responsible for approximately 7.5% of South Africa's annual gross income (CoM, 2001) and produces almost 15% of the world's gold and 50% of the platinum-group metals (PGMs).

More than a hundred and fifty years ago, Pieter Jacob Marais panned for and found gold in the Jukskei and Crocodile Rivers, north of Johannesburg (Mendelsohn, 1986:1). It was not long after the first discovery that initial prospecting gave way to mining with the subsequent establishment of a great industry along the line of the Witwatersrand. PGM resources of the Bushveld Complex (Figure 2) were discovered by Hans Merensky and Andries Lombaard in 1924 (Matthey 2005).

The Bushveld Complex is composed of four sheets of crystallised magma. These are the Far Western Limb, the Western Limb, the Eastern Limb and the Northern Limb. What makes the Bushveld Complex unique is its extraordinary size, the magnificent exposures of structural details and the importance of the economic minerals. Within the complex, three horizons, the Merensky Reef, UG2 Chromitite and the Platreef are mined for PGMs and make this the largest PGM resource in the world. The Merensky Reef has been the principal source of platinum-group metals (PGMs) since it was first worked in 1925. Although the primary focus of mining is platinum (Pt), other PGMs – palladium (Pd), rhodium (Rh), iridium (Ir), ruthenium (Ru) and osmium (Os) – are recovered as well.

Figure 3: Views of typical ring-dyke impoundment [1] (Use of photograph with permission. Bird's eye view of the AngloGold Ashanti ERGO Daggafontein tailings dam)

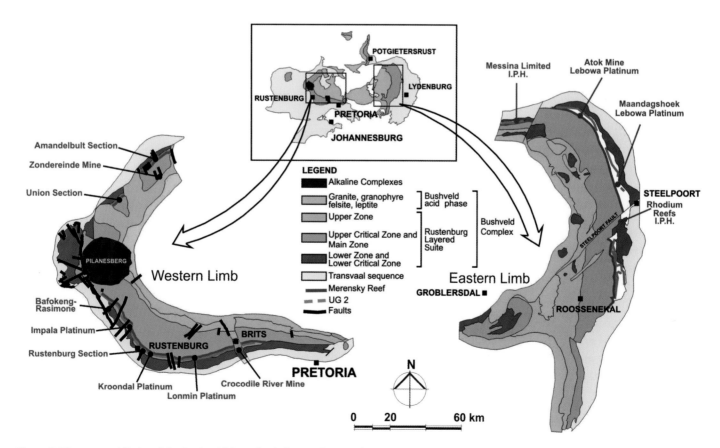

Figure 2: The exposed limbs of the Bushveld Complex (After Eagles 2001)

Figure 4: Panoramic view of impoundment profile [2]

South Africa produced approximately 370 000kg of gold and 266 000kg of PGMs for 2003 (DME, 2004:41, 46).

Table 1: South Africa's precious metals production, 1994–2003 (DME 2004:43, 49)

		Production (kg)	
		Gold	PGM
	1994	580 200	183 900
	1995	523 800	183 000
	1996	498 300	188 600
	1997	490 600	196 000
Time (years)	1998	465 100	199 900
	1999	451 200	216 400
	2000	430 800	206400
	2001	394 800	228 700
	2002	389 300	236 600
	2003	372 800	266 200
	TOTAL	4 596 900	1 929 300

Large quantities of resource are crushed, milled and processed by precious metals underground mines to recover the metals and minerals required for industrial and consumer products. A fine grind ranging from sand-sized to as low as a few microns is often required to liberate the minerals contained in the parent rock. With a product to residue ratio varying between 1:60 000 and 1:200 000, the mining industry has a substantial amount of fine-grained waste, i.e. tailings, to dispose.

Tailings disposal is therefore a significant part of the mining and milling operation at most precious metals mining projects. There are several methods of tailings disposal such as the disposal of tailings slurry in impoundments, dry or thickened tailings in impoundments or free-standing piles, backfilling underground mine workings and open-pits as well as sub-aqueous disposal. The most common method within the South African landscape is slurry impoundments – more specifically the upstream method ring-dyke type raised embankment impoundment. The ring-dyke is best suited to flat terrain in the absence of topographic depressions. Also, these impoundments are usually laid out with a regular geometry, resulting in a uniform configuration (refer to Figures 3 and 4).

In South Africa, the areas around Johannesburg, Carletonville, Klerksdorp, Welkom, Evander, Mokopane (Potgietersrus), Polokwane (Pietersburg), Rustenburg and more recently, Lydenburg, host some of the most striking manmade landforms within the

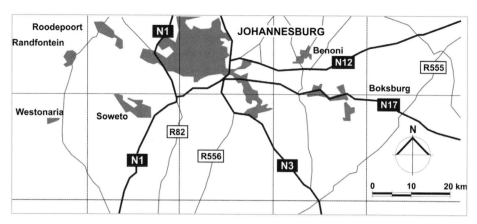

Figure 5: Surface area covered by mining waste within the Gauteng Province

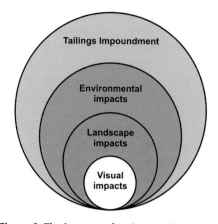

Figure 6: The impacts of an impoundment on the environment

natural landscape demonstrating mankind's ability to modify natural landscapes in so intrusive a manner that it can no longer be considered as acceptable to the majority of stakeholders.

It is also estimated that between 11 500 and 12 000ha land is sterilised by approximately 150 impoundments within the Gauteng Province alone (refer to Figure 5). This covers an area of almost 14 500 football fields if it is assumed that the standard recommended size for an international football field is 110m by 75m (Tutt & Adler, 1994:219). Wilson (1998:15) provides a figure of 40 000ha for the Witwatersrand basin. To sustain the present rate of precious metals recovery which is in excess of 640 000kg per annum, between 3 000 and 9 000ha of land is required for the purpose of residue impoundment. Of this, between 1 000ha and 3 500ha will be required to sustain PGM production within the Bushveld Complex. Figure 5 provides a 'figure-ground' snapshot of gold impoundment footprints after 150 years – will the Bushveld Complex, especially the Eastern Limb, follow suit?

Problem statement

Rational tailings dam planning decisions with regard to engineering and environmental costs and impacts are constrained by the fragmented nature of specialist knowledge and the difficulty in understanding the relative importance of the different impacts in context with an overall design philosophy. Related to this is the uncertainty whether to address certain impacts through mitigation during the initial construction phase, or much later as a function of impoundment closure. It is also problematic that the end use and landform of impoundments are not defined before the onset of the design and assessment of the potential adverse impacts of such a facility. It would therefore appear that impoundment closure plans and post-closure land uses are not informed by following a rational systematic approach.

This paper focuses on not only the management of predictable environmental impacts associated with such impoundments but also the configuration of the latter as a sustainable landform. The following typical issues define the basis of the problem statement:

◆ Impoundment surface instability
◆ Visual intrusiveness and unsightliness of the impoundment
◆ Permanent or temporary take and sterilisation of land.

Impoundment environmental impacts

When a tailings impoundment (external effect) influences the environment, this is referred to as environmental impacts. Historically economic rather than environmental factors have informed the positioning and configuration of impoundments. At present the location and impacts are governed by legislation and guidelines. The main aspects traditionally have been water and dust pollution; however, with the rapid take of land in general and the increase in population density, greater emphasis has been placed on visual impact and change of land use. The impacts disperse into the social and economic spheres and are responsible for impacts on health and the loss and sterilisation of land. Resolving these issues provides a heavy burden for the responsible stakeholder. It requires either an indefinite maintenance liability or a rehabilitation commitment until regulatory authorities relieve the proponent from blame or obligation by issuing an exoneration or closure certificate.

A report on the environmental consequences of the scheme is known as the environmental impact assessment (EIA) report or in some countries also referred to as the environmental impact statement. Turner (2003:32) makes a distinction between two sub-categories of environmental impact, namely landscape impacts and visual impacts (refer to Figure 6). Landscape impacts refer to changes to the fabric, character and the quality of the landscape as a result of the scheme. Visual impacts, a subset of landscape impacts, relate to the changes in available views of the landscape and the experiences of stakeholders.

Integrated environmental planning

South Africa's integrated environmental management procedures are based on international experience in environmental policy and the application of environmental assessment and management tools. It is also generally recognised that the globally applied term 'environmental assessment and management' is comparable with the South African term 'integrated environmental management' (IEM). DEAT (2004:2) defines IEM as the way of thinking that provides a holistic framework that can be embraced by all sectors of society for the assessment and management of environmental impacts and aspects associated with each stage of the activity life cycle, taking into consideration a broad definition of environment and with the overall aim of promoting sustainable development. IEM provides a set of underpinning principles and a suite of environmental assessment and management tools aimed at promoting sustainable development. Achieving the goal of sustainable development requires co-operation between all spheres of government, community-based organisations, non-governmental organisations, researchers and academics, industry and environmental practitioners.

The IEM philosophy (and principles) is interpreted as applying to the planning, assessment, implementation and management of any proposal (project, plan, programme or policy) or activity – at the local, national and international level – that has a potentially significant effect on the environment. Implementation of this philosophy relies on the selection and application of appropriate tools to a particular proposal or activity. These may include environmental assessment tools (such as Strategic Environmental Assessment and Risk Assessment), environmental management tools (such as monitoring, auditing and reporting) and decision-making tools (such as multi-criteria decision-support systems or advisory councils).

Integrated Environmental Management is the direction for environmental management in South Africa. All stages of the project must be evaluated in terms of sustainability, alternatives for development must be identified, and development benefits viewed in the light of environmental impacts.

IEM is designed to ensure that the environmental consequences of schemes are understood and adequately considered in the planning, implementation and management phases. The purpose of IEM is to resolve or lessen any negative environmental impacts and to enhance positive aspects of schemes. Some of the relevant IEM principles are listed below (DEAT 2004 S0:9):

◆ Accountability and responsibility
◆ Alternative options
◆ Environmental justice
◆ Informed decision-making
◆ Integrated approach
◆ Polluter pays
◆ Precautionary approach
◆ Sustainability.

Planning for sustainability

With the economic benefit, this industry is also responsible for great environmental degradation resulting from large quantities of mining waste deposited and inadequate waste management practices. Increasing environmental awareness and the movement towards sustainable development place strict demands on the mining industry to delineate potential environmental and social impacts and alter current mining practices accordingly. The promulgation of the *Constitution of the Republic of South Africa* (Act No. 108 of 1996) and the *National Environmental Management Act* (No. 107 of 1998) (NEMA) are seen as progressive steps towards practicable legislation to the benefit of the social and natural spheres.

Although there are numerous and varied definitions of the term 'sustainable development', the common elements include the need to integrate social, economic and environmental features as well as to address intra- and inter-generational equity. Bruntland (1987) defines sustainable development as development that meets the needs of the present without compromising the ability of future generations to meet their needs and aspirations. NEMA defines such as meaning the integration of social, economic and environmental factors into planning, implementation and decision-making so as to ensure that development serves future and present generations.

The overall objective of achieving sustainable development of tailings impoundments is controlled by legislation. The term 'sustainable' has become laden with so many meanings that it has almost no readily defined meaning. In this context, however, it could be taken to mean that the tailings impoundment should comply with all the legal environmental requirements. Whether these requirements in themselves result in sustainability may well be a different issue. In this context 'sustainable' is understood to mean: 'for ensuring compliance with the relevant legal criteria and good practice'.

Mining legislation requirements

The Mineral and Petroleum Resources Development Act (No. 28, 2002) (MPRDA 2002) and its regulations (MPRDA 2004) set out the process whereby a mine owner is required to decommission and apply for closure at cessation of operations (refer to Figure 7). The closure objectives which form part of the required environmental management plan must *inter alia* identify key objectives, define future land use objectives and provide financially for the remediation of environmental damage.

Section 38(1)(d) of the Act obligates the holder to rehabilitate the environment to:

◆ a natural state
◆ a predetermined state
◆ a land use which conforms to the generally accepted principle of sustainable development.

Section 38(1)(e) states that the holder is responsible for any environmental damage, pollution or ecological degradation inside and outside its boundaries.

Further, the Act:

◆ reiterates that the State has an obligation to protect the environment for present and future generations – i.e. support sustainable development
◆ gives effect to Section 24 of the Constitution of the Republic of South Africa – mineral and petroleum resources developed in ecologically sustainable manner
◆ obligates the holder to rehabilitate the environment
◆ states that the holder is responsible for any environmental damage, pollution or ecological degradation inside or outside boundaries
◆ gives effect to the principles in terms of section 2 of NEMA
◆ applies the IEM regulations as contemplated in Chapter 5 of NEMA which contains inter alia the following:
    ◆ a cradle-to-grave approach being followed
    ◆ the consideration of alternatives which include the consideration of alternatives to the project (the no go option) and alternative means of carrying out the proposed project
◆ requires stakeholder involvement and public participation
◆ requires the adoption of the polluter-pays principle

- requires the adoption of the pre-cautionary principle
- requires a consultation decision-making process.

The *Mineral and Petroleum Resources Development Act Regulations* (MPRDA, 2004):

- provides principles of mine closure (Section 56, MPRDA 2004)
- requires that the incorporation of the closure process begins at commencement of the operation and continues throughout its lifecycle
- obligates the holder of the right to quantify the environmental risks and liabilities.

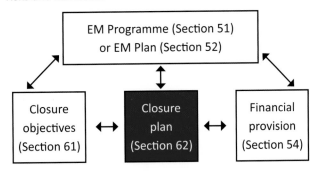

Figure 7: Closure planning process (After MPRDA 2004)

Section 51 and 52 state that the EMProgramme or EMPlan must include the following:

- Environmental objectives and goals for mine closure
- Closure plan (refer to regulation 62 for obligation)
- Management of identified environmental risks and liabilities
- Financial provision, i.e. both methods and quantum thereof.

Section 61 states that the closure objectives EMProgramme or EMPlan must:

- Identify key objectives for mine closure to guide planning and implementation
- Provide broad future land use objective(s) for the site
- Provide proposed closure costs.

Section 62 GN requires that the closure plan must include:

- Closure objectives
- A plan [regulation 2(2)] indicating area for closure
- Summary of conditions of closure as contained in EMProgramme or EMPlan
- Summary of results of progressive rehabilitation
- Identification of long-term management
- Sketch plan indicating final and future land use – i.e. final land use plan
- Summary of environmental risks and liabilities.

Section 54 necessitates that the quantum of financial closure must include costs required for:

- Premature closure [old approach of contributing towards future objective no longer suffices]
- Decommissioning and final closure
- Post-closure management for residual and latent environmental impacts.

To achieve the desired objectives most efficiently and comply with the relevant legislation it is contended that a paradigm shift is required so that the total life of tailings disposal from planning through to construction, operation, decommissioning, rehabilitation, closure, and post-closure maintenance for a designed end land use, is seen as an integrated system.

The concept of closure

The objectives for successful closure of a mining facility as stipulated in the November 1998 edition of Mining Environmental Management, are as follows:

Minimising long-term environmental liability, attaining regulatory compliance and maintaining geo-technical stability, while closing as quickly and cost-effectively as possible. All this should materialise within the general goal of returning the land to a safe and stable condition for the purpose of post-mining alternative functions. A successful closure procedure is a combination of innovative concepts, long-term commitment and multiparty cooperation. (Mudder & Harvey 1998:1).

The TDF should be stabilised to ensure public safety and restrict adverse environmental impacts to an acceptable level before the Department of Mineral and Energy will exonerate the proponent. Once this level of closure is achieved is it possible to transfer ownership of the site, whereafter liability will rest upon a new owner. When entering the closure phase, the mining company is faced with a series of options. All the options relate to the management of waste and the exercising of the company's environmental liability and moral obligation. Stakeholders apply constant pressure on mining companies to comply with increasingly stringent environmental standards and policies. An approach of environmentally sensitive mining and engagement on a socially responsible level is (at least) appropriate from a sustainable development point of view.

Energy flow and sustainability

Sustainability in the mining industry is greatly focused on energy efficiency. The bulk of energy utilised during the life-of-mine is concentrated during the ore extraction and processing phases. The disposal of tailings requires relatively little energy whereas the rehabilitation require more depending on the final landform envisaged. Large-scale earth moving and soil preparation is required to transform the barren and lifeless tailings impoundment into a stable and sustainable landform.

The energy that 'shapes' a natural landform is caused by geomorphologic processes. The material responds to the impact of dynamic energy flows and creates a unique landform over time. This combination of material with specific characteristics and energy of particular intensity and time results in landforms that progress to a state of equilibrium, not in terms of geological timescale, but in terms of human timescale.

An example of such an attained equilibrium is the effect of erosion on most inclined terrains. A rounded crest, steep rocky faces and concave foot slopes are the result of continuous climatic forces impacting on the surface of a landform. Soft material is easily displaced from the higher areas down into the valleys due to its poor resistance to erosion forces. The steep rock faces are more resistant and can therefore withstand the impact of energy and maintain vertical postures.

Energy usage ties in closely with money expenditure and a reduction in energy usage will inevitably result in a reduction in expenses. The energy that is used to deposit the tailings should be utilised in such a way that the final desirable landform can be achieved with minor or no additional energy application.

Integrated environmental planning and design

Integrated environmental planning and design (IEPD), however similar to IEM, necessitates planning across traditional specialist fields with the aim of achieving a sustainable project outcome. The project outcome should be informed by a broad and inclusive knowledge base of every influencing aspect in order to reach a desired goal. Landscape architecture is one such specialist field that is novel in the planning, operation and rehabilitation phases of the mining and quarrying industries and it can provide valuable insight to formulating a sustainable approach for the waste disposal of industries.

The American Society of Landscape Architects (ASLA 2001) defines landscape architecture as the art and science of analysis, planning, design, management, preservation and rehabilitation of the landscape. 'Landscape' is an encompassing term including all natural and human introduced elements of the living and perceivable environment. Mutually beneficial interaction and co-existence between humans and the natural environment are known since the earliest eras and can be seen as a crude origin of the profession.

The term 'landscape' is described as a tract of land with its distinguishing characteristics and features, especially considered as a product of shaping processes and agents (usually natural) (Burchfield 1976). Dictionary Unit (2002) describes landscape as all of the visible features of an area of land.

The term 'landform' refers to an element of and within the landscape with specific shape characteristics. This term also refers to an artificial element, e.g. a tailings impoundment, which can be compared to a natural landform and is subject to the same dynamic geomorphologic impacts.

This paper deals with the challenge of managing mining waste in a sustainable fashion through implementing an IEPD approach. It combines the various specialists' knowledge to satisfy not only engineering but also environmental, social and economic criteria. The creation of a tailings impoundment is considered as a landform planning and design exercise, informed by guidelines originating from natural systems and technical considerations.

The ultimate goal and overall aim is to configure a TDF which will be acceptable in terms of its short term as well as long term impacts on the environment and to create a landform which will be usable and sustainable. In order to formulate an integrated environmental planning and design (IEPD) approach regarding mineral waste management, an understanding of the current mining procedures is required.

A simplified procedure is outlined in Figure 8 and illustrates the differences between the *status quo* processes and the IEPD approach.

When the endeavour of mining is entered into by a mining company, an approximate volume of waste is pre-determined, the appropriate methods for waste deposition are decided and life of deposition is estimated. An expectation regarding rate-of-deposition exists to achieve the goal of viable economic return.

Once the projections are finalised an appropriate site is allocated to accommodate the volume of waste. The selected site is either in a pristine condition or it supports a developed land use which requires a passive or active maintenance strategy. Subsequently, active mineral extraction and waste deposition occur and the deposition site is under continuous active maintenance and care for an extended period of time upon entering the closure phase, the mining company is faced with a series of options (Figure 8). In a few cases impoundments are vegetated in order to provide surface stability, but this approach has proven ineffective and unsustainable. Total reclamation and restoration can be achieved when the impoundment is removed for reclamation and is an option which is not discussed in this paper. In most cases the only suitable option is to rehabilitate in accordance with a pre-defined closure plan.

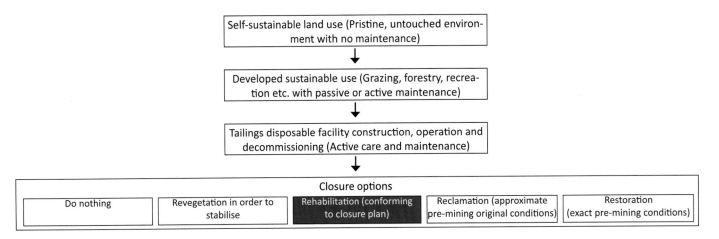

Figure 8: Closure options

Integrated impoundment planning requires the compilation of a closure plan, along with the impoundment scheme plan and with a long-term land use as an ultimate vision (Figure 9). It is an interaction between the present need and the future goal and requires an iterative process in the design phase and continuous revision during operation of the mine.

Integrated impoundment planning incorporates an IEPD approach and will determine the success of the desired long-term land use. The decision for long-term land use is based on the following issues:

◆ Anticipated life of deposition
◆ Municipal or local authority development programmes
◆ Existing local natural and social environments.

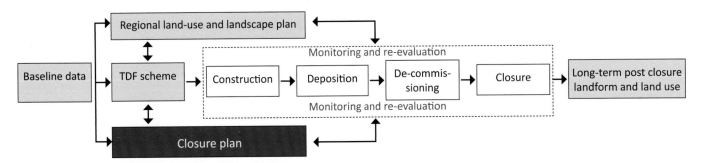

Figure 9: Integrated impoundment planning and design

The IEPD approach is based on the following argument:

The main function of a TDF is to contain tailings/waste within the parameters of safety and stability standards as well as economic feasibility. However, this can be defined as a short-term function concluding when the mine enters the closure phase. Following decommissioning the TDF undergoes an alteration in function. It is no longer a tailings storage facility but a permanent man-made landform located within a specific natural landscape.

The hypothesis therefore states that if the TDF is designed with the short- and long-term land use of storing tailings and functioning as an acceptable natural landform in its context, it will potentially increase the rehabilitation success, support a future alternative land-use and shorten the closure application period. The implementation of the integrated environmental planning and design approach will result in environmental, social and economic benefits in the long-term. This requires the design to respond in changing the geometry and/or cover of the impoundment (refer to Figure 10).

Figure 11: Proposed site in Rustenburg Mining belt

Approach to impoundment landform design

Decision-making involved with impoundment landscape planning and design requires the involvement of many stakeholders such as planners, designers, landscape architects, engineers, scientists and other experts integrating the aesthetic, functional, economic, political and philosophical dimensions. The detailed nature of environmental planning and design requires joint cooperation between the public, landowners and land users as well as planning professionals.

Application of impoundment landform design

The IEPD approach is best demonstrated through an example. The example illustrates the design of a tailings impoundment based on landform design principles and guidelines. The result envisages a sustainable, long term landform function that is defined as the preferred land use subsequent to an iterating planning process and design strategy. These principles and guidelines are hypothetically applied to a typical site in the Rustenburg region that is suitable for depositing tailings from a platinum mine and strives to achieve the following goal: 'To design a landform (TDF) that will provide a diversity of habitats in order to support a suitable surface cover, with the aim of establishing a sustainable and regenerative landscape for the long-term benefit of the natural and social environment.'

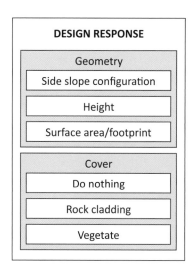

Figure 10: Design response

Geometric alterations to the TDF must occur within the parameters of safety and geo-technical stability along the guidance of the ultimate goal of a regenerative sustainable landform. This research indicates that it is technically possible to construct a TDF with varying slope gradients, slope lengths, bench widths, which in itself will not only imitate natural landforms but may result in something which is truly sustainable. Final rehabilitation may result in a profile similar to adjacent natural landforms with diverse slope configurations and varying microclimates necessary to sustain a diversity of floral and faunal species.

To achieve the preferred land use, several ecological principles and guidelines are derived from natural landforms and systems that feature similarities with tailings impoundments. These principles and guidelines inform the technical design response which is a function of geometric configuration and surface cover. Innovative design responses are required to fulfil the goal of a sustainable and regenerative landform design.

Three main aspects are considered to form the basis of the design brief in order to establish a sustainable and regenerative landform:

♦ Surface stability
♦ Habitat creation
♦ Aesthetics.

Surface stability

Surface stability refers to the erosive potential of the material on the surface that is exposed to the environmental conditions.

The Universal Soil Loss Equation (USLE) provides a method to estimate erosion and provides the following main factors that affect surface stability:

- Surface cover
- Slope configuration
- Climate
- Surface management.

Surface cover

Surface cover refers to the material layer on the surface of a tailings impoundment as well as the vegetation cover that may be established in the rehabilitation phase. The outer slopes of a tailings impoundment mostly consist of the coarser sand fraction of the tailings in the case of cyclone deposition. The outer slopes are exposed to the climate and are most prone to erosion. Studies have shown that unprotected slopes of gold tailings in South Africa can erode at a rate of 500 000 kg/ha/annum (CoM, 1996:69). This is mainly due to the low cohesion forces that exist between the tailings particles and the impacts of wind and water erosion. According to Figure 12 sand has the lowest water velocity threshold and is dislodged at velocities of 0.5 m/s and higher.

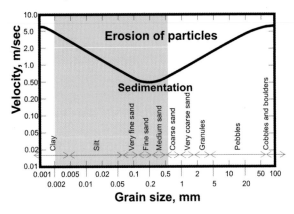

Figure 12: Water erosion thresholds for natural soils

During rehabilitation the material layer may consist of the following or be a combination of:

- *In-situ* tailings
- Topsoil
- Waste rock/stone mulch.

The vegetation cover on tailings impoundmentS may typically consist of:

- No cover
- Grass cover
- Diversity of vegetation species.

The envisaged post-closure surface cover should visually comply with the surrounding vegetation patterns and strive to establish endemic vegetation on the tailings impoundment (refer to previous section on habitat creation and vegetation establishment).

Slope configuration

The USLE distinguishes between slope lengths and gradients as factors that affect surface erosion. Studies have indicated that a steeper slope gradient and long slope lengths increase water erosion considerably (Dorren & Blight 1986). The introduction of benches in the slope configuration of tailings impoundments partly impedes high erosion rates, but a reduction in slope gradient and the application of appropriate surface covers will further increase erosion control.

Marsh (1991) describes slope configuration in its most basic forms; straight, concave, convex and S-profile (refer to Figure 13). Smooth S-profile slopes usually indicate long-term stability and a state of equilibrium among slope forces, i.e. erosion and deposition. Hannan (1984:22) states that: 'Over geological time the forces of erosion and deposition have acted upon natural slopes until an angle is reached which, for a given soil type, is in equilibrium with the effects of catchment area, runoff volume and vegetation cover. This results in a slope which becomes progressively flatter towards the bottom so that flow velocity is maintained at a roughly constant, non-erosive value.'

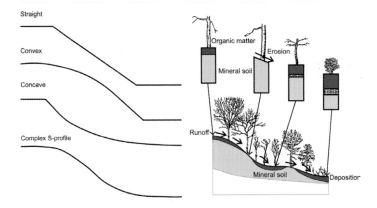

Figure 13: Basic slope profiles (left)

Figure 14: Effects of erosion and deposition (right)

Figure 14 illustrates the dynamics between erosion and deposition of natural mineral soils. This is a geomorphological principle responsible for the shaping of a landform. Clear contrasts exist between natural landforms and tailings impoundments regarding the slope configuration and the vegetation cover (Figure 15). The design and operation of tailings impoundments need to take cognisance of these land forming principles to convert to a sustainable landform once rehabilitation is implemented.

Figure 15: Landform comparison

In order to implement these land forming principles successfully, geometric alterations are necessary to the conventional tailings impoundments design. Geometric alterations to tailings impoundments should occur within the parameters of geo-technical stability which is greatly dependent on the character of the tailings material. In order to propose viable geometric alterations one has to do a thorough assessment of the opportunities and constraints of the possible surface cover (refer to previous section on surface covers). The following factors are taken into consideration to interpret the character of the surface covers:

♦ Particle size
♦ Material texture (refer to Figure 16)
♦ Material composition
♦ Chemical properties.

The combination of physical and chemical properties provides the surface cover with a specific character with unique attributes that respond to environmental conditions in a predictable fashion. Environmental conditions are a function of the climate and the dynamics of energy in the region where the tailings impoundment is situated (see below). The character influences the following factors:

♦ Angle of repose
♦ Erosive potential
♦ Geo-technical stability
♦ Water infiltration rate
♦ Water absorption capacity
♦ Potential to sustain vegetation.

The character of platinum tailings can be described according to the soil texture triangle that is used to classify soil (Figure 16). On the soil texture triangle, platinum tailings particle size will fall in the sandy-loam soil section. When analysed, the tailings consist of 10%–40% silt fraction, 60%–90% sand fraction and a negligible clay fraction (CoM, 1996:19). Natural soils with similar characteristics are colluvium deposits found at the toe of slopes formed by slides and runoff. These soils generally drain very well and have a gentle slope angle due to the relatively high erosion potential.

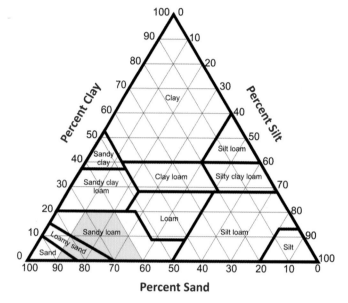

Figure 16: Soil texture triangle for natural soils

By comparing the characteristics of the tailings with similar soils one can get some sort of understanding of what the tailings' response to environmental conditions might be. It is evident that the current deposition angle of 33° will continue to erode until a stable angle is reached which is in equilibrium with the relevant region's eroding conditions. The current approach to this problem is the continuous upkeeping of the side slopes or ineffective attempts to vegetate the surface in order to stabilise. Both these practices have proven unsustainable.

Climate

The term climate describes the environmental conditions of the site where the tailings impoundment is proposed. The climate has an effect on the surface stability of the tailings impoundment in that it weathers/erodes the surface material to a state of equilibrium. The climate in the Rustenburg region is briefly described.

♦ Ambient temperature
 Summer: 16°C–31°C
 Winter: 3°C–24°C
♦ Annual precipitation: 630mm–740mm

- Prevailing wind direction

  Summer mornings: East to north-east

  Summer afternoons: North to north-east

  Winter mornings: South-east to north-east

  Winter afternoons: North-west

Surface management

Surface management refers to the management of human practices that alter the surface conditions. Such practices are needed to maintain surface stability of a tailings impoundment during operation and rehabilitation. The surface management that is required to achieve a sustainable and regenerative landform would typically include; shaping of the side slopes, amelioration of the surface with alternative surface coverings and vegetating of the tailings impoundment. These rehabilitation practices can cause excessive costs and therefore emphasise the fact that IEPD principles should be included in the early design phases of a tailings impoundment to achieve the end land use without major shaping and amelioration expenses.

Habitat creation

Habitat creation can only be successfully accomplished after a comprehensive analysis of the surrounding landscape and its landforms. This includes the specialist field of ecology in the IEPD approach to resolve the multi-faceted problems.

To create habitat for fauna it is necessary to provide appropriate food sources and suitable environments for reproduction. Faunal habitat is often dependent on floral distribution and therefore the focus is on creating suitable habitats for vegetation. Figure 17 provides a simplified analysis of the western slope of an adjacent landform. It indicates the vegetation communities that occur on different sections of the slope and an in-depth study will also disclose knowledge of the growth medium, nutrients, water availability and microclimate.

The growth medium is again a function of the surface covering, featuring characteristics of moisture retention and nutrient availability. Tailings is generally a poor growth medium and requires extensive amelioration to sustain a healthy vegetation cover. Isabel Weiersbye from the School of Animal, Plant and Enviroscience at the University of the Witwatersrand, South Africa, is the programme leader of an initiative to test the performance of woody and semi-woody plant species in the containment of pollution from gold slimes dams. Weiersbye comments that grasses alone produce too little organic litter, nitrogen and potassium which are necessary to keep the whole ecosystem functioning and to ensure a healthy vegetation cover. It can, however, be achieved

with woody species and experiments on the Harmony's Freegold tailings impoundment in Welkom are currently underway (Knoll 2004:25).

Micro climate refers to the surface climate resulting from a combination of macro climatic and surface conditions and is influenced by factors such as:

- slope aspect
- depth of suitable growing medium
- slope gradient.

Northern and western slope aspects in the Rustenburg region feature similar vegetation distributions and densities. The southern and eastern slopes are considered cooler and wetter due to the smaller inclination angle of the sun's rays, thus there is less evaporation and energy absorption. Slope aspect will greatly influence the design response when one has to select between the different surface covers.

The current approach to providing a suitable growth medium is to cap a tailings impoundment with a consistent depth of topsoil over the whole impoundment. This approach is insensitive to the demands of different vegetation species and to the slope aspect. The capping of a tailings impoundment with a suitable growth medium is very expensive but strategic placement of thicker layers of topsoil will considerably increase the spectrum of species that can be established on the tailings impoundment and aid subsequent rehabilitation success.

Slope gradient plays a role in water infiltration and retention in the surface layer. A porous surface layer with a high organic material content will be able to effectively absorb available water on steeper slopes, thus reducing surface water run-off and possible erosion. It is important to coordinate the placement of different surface covers and depths of covers on varying slope gradients in order to maximise rehabilitation success. Figure 14 again illustrates the dynamics in nature and the principles that need to be included in tailings impoundment design.

Slope gradient is usually a determining factor when considering human 'habitats'. Slope gradient places certain restrictions on development and should be understood during the design of the tailings impoundment in order to increase the range of future land uses on the impoundment. Figure 18 provides information regarding the maximum slope gradient for various land uses. The conclusion that can be drawn from Figure 18 is that lower slope gradients have the capacity to facilitate a wider range of land uses.

Figure 17: Types of vegetation communities

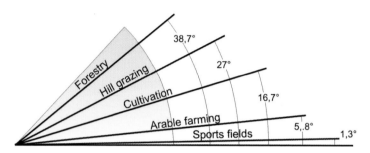

Figure 18: Typical land uses as a function of slope steepness

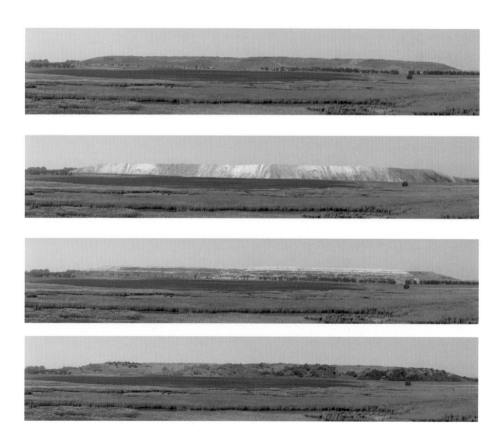

Figure 19: Visual simulations of different surface covers

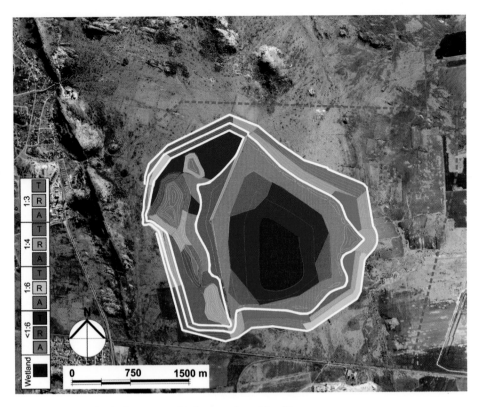

Figure 20: Hypothetical regenerative impoundment landform

Aesthetics

The authors are currently involved in a study to gain knowledge regarding the visual perception of tailings impoundments (Rademeyer *et al.* 2005). This study aims to determine critical threshold distances of detection and recognition of a tailings impoundment with different geometric alterations and surface covers. The effectiveness of mitigation is measured against the capability to 'camouflage' the tailings impoundment with its environment and to reduce visual impacts.

Five factors influencing camouflage are:

◆ silhouette
◆ shape
◆ surface
◆ shadow
◆ size.

Three surface covers are photo realistically simulated in Figure 19 and indicate the difference in visual perception with regards to altering the surface cover. The scenario with the diversity of vegetation species can easily be mistaken for a natural landform and it is assumed that alterations to the overall geometry of the tailings impoundment will further contribute to the camouflaging effect.

Conclusion

The result of following the integrated environmental planning and design (IEPD) approach is best illustrated in a schematic tailings impoundment rehabilitation plan aimed at creating a sustainable and regenerative landform (Figure 20) and also by comparing its profile with that of a typical impoundment (Figures 21 and 22). Four slope configurations (1:3, 1:4, 1:6 and <1:6) in combination with three surface covers (T – In-situ tailings, R – Rock cladding,

Figure 21: Typical tailings impoundment profile

Figure 22: Tailings impoundment profile that is sensitive towards the natural landscape

A – Armouring, i.e. topsoil and rock mix) are applied to the tailings impoundment and indicated in the legend of Figure 20. The combination of different slope geometries and surface cover follows a rational and analytic process considering factors such as slope aspect, flora and fauna specie distribution as well as macro- and microclimatic conditions, specific to the site location.

The hypothetical outcome satisfies the design brief through applying surface stabilising practices in combination with landform design principles. Habitat creation is a function of the context in that it is guided by local ecological systems and vegetation distributions. It is believed that these two aspects will result in an aesthetically pleasing landform, unlike the unsightly slimes dams that are so common in our South African mining landscape.

Configuration of tailing impoundments includes rehabilitation with the aim of eliminating or reducing adverse environmental impacts and creating a new landform that conforms to the principles of sustainable development that will be acceptable in the long-term. The process is driven primarily by legislation which ensures that the mine owner must comply with the intention of achieving those end conditions, which are defined in broad terms by guidelines, hence the need to rationally define the end conditions.

Two measures can encourage rational decision-making and efficient and effective planning:

♦ development of regional landscape plans requiring injection of ideals into the planning process
♦ modification of single-objective impoundment schemes to improve the contextual relationship with the landscape. This can be seen as impact mitigation in environmental assessment terms.

Tailings impoundment schemes should be modified in order to produce multi-objective project designs. Design modifications can prevent negative environmental impacts and promote positive environmental impacts. Although it is a legal requirement to assess the impacts of a scheme on the biophysical, socio-cultural and economic environment, insufficient attention is paid to the impacts on the surrounding land use.

Envisaging the final tailings impoundment during the initial planning phase may result in a differently designed facility. This could result in lower final rehabilitation costs, possibly at the expense of higher initial costs. High decommissioning and closure costs can easily negate short-term benefits of disposal strategies which do not facilitate easy rehabilitation (DME (QLD), 1995:2)). Important to note is that it is perfectly feasible to undertake the afore-mentioned.

Acknowledgements

This paper has been reproduced with the kind permission of the Chamber of Mines of South Africa's Mining and Sustainable Development Conference of 2005. The research presented in this paper is drawn from a collaborative research programme on the optimisation of sustainable post-closure land uses of tailings impoundments through the rational evaluation of engineering and environmental costs for tailings impoundments. The Department of Civil and Biosystems Engineering would like to acknowledge Anglo Platinum, Strategic Environmental Focus (SEF), Steffen Robertson and Kirsten (SRK) and the National Research Foundation (NRF) for their financial support. The NRF provides funds through its Technology and Human Resources for Industry Programme (THRIP).

GLOSSARY OF TERMS

CoM	Chamber of Mines of South Africa
DME	Department of Minerals and Energy
EIA	Environmental impact assessment
EMF	Environmental management framework
EPA	Environmental Protection Agency
I&AP	Interested and affected parties
IEM	Integrated environmental management
IEPD	Integrated environmental planning and design
MPRDA	Mineral and Petroleum Resources Development Act (No. 28 of 2002)
NRF	National Research Foundation
PGMs	Platinum-group metals
RPM	Rustenburg Platinum Mines
SEF	Strategic Environmental Focus (Pty) Ltd
SRK	Steffen Robertson and Kirsten (Pty) Ltd
TDF	Tailings disposal facility
THRIP	Technology and Human Resources for Industry Programme

Bibliography

ASLA. 2001. Definition for Landscape Architecture. http://www.stlouisasla.org/defnla.html. (Accessed September 2005).

Bruntland, G. 1987. *Our common future: The World Commission on Environment and Development*. United Kingdom, Oxford: Oxford University Press.

Burchfield, R.W. (ed). 1976. *A supplement to the Oxford English Dictionary*. United Kingdom, Oxford: Oxford University Press.

Chamber of Mines of South Africa. 1981. The rehabilitation of land disturbed by surface coal mining in South Africa. *Handbook of guidelines for environmental protection*. Vol. 3/1981. Republic of South Africa, Johannesburg: Chamber of Mines of South Africa.

Chamber of Mines of South Africa. 1996. The engineering design, operation and closure of metalliferous, diamond and coal residue deposits. *Handbook of guidelines for environmental protection*. Vol. 1/1979 (Revised 1983 and 1995). Republic of South Africa, Johannesburg: Chamber of Mines of South Africa.

Chamber of Mines of South Africa. 2001. The South African Mining Industry Fact Sheet, 2001. http://www.bullion.org.za/MiningEconomics&Stats/Eco%20Pdf's/FactSheet2001.pdf (Accessed September 2005).

Coppin, N.J. & Bradshaw A.D. 1982. Quarry Reclamation. The establishment of vegetation in quarries and open pit non-metal mines. *Mining Journal Books.* England: Chandlers Printers.

DEAT. 2004. Overview of Integrated Environmental Management. *Integrated Environmental Management, Information Series 0.* Republic of South Africa, Pretoria: Department of Environmental Affairs and Tourism (DEAT).

DEAT. 2005. Proposed regulations under section 24(5) of the National Environmental Management Act (No. 107 of 1998) as amended. Government Notice 12 of 2005. *Government Gazette*. No. 27163. Republic of South Africa, Pretoria: Government Printer.

Dictionary Unit for South African English. 2002. Entry for 'Landscape'. In *The South African Concise Oxford English Dictionary*. Republic of South Africa, Cape Town: Oxford University Press South Africa.

DME. 2000. *Report on the Mining Industry*. Republic of South Africa. Department of Minerals and Energy.

DME. 2002. *EMPR procedural guidance*. Department of Minerals and Energy. Republic of South Africa. http://www.dme.gov.za/minerals/default.htm

DME. 2004. *South Africa's Mineral Industry 2003/2004*. South Africa, Pretoria: Director: Mineral Economics. http://www.dme.gov.za/publications/pdf/annual_reports/SAMI2003-4e.pdf (Accessed September 2005).

Dorren, D. I. & G. E. Blight. 1986. Erosion of the Slopes of Gold-Residue Dams on the Transvaal Highveld – Preliminary Results. *Journal of the South African Institute of Mining and Metallurgy*, vol. 86, no. 12, pp. 475–480.

Eagles, H.V. 2001. T*he Bushveld Complex and the aspects of South African geology that relate to it*. Republic of South Africa, Pretoria: The Council for Geoscience.

Environment Protection Agency (EPA). 1995. *Rehabilitation and revegetation – best practice environmental management in mining*. Australian Federal Environment Department, Commonwealth of Australia.

Gillespie, M. & Mulligan, D. 2003: Increasing species diversity on landscapes impacted by coal mining in NSW, Australia. Paper presented at the Sudbury 2003 Mining and Environment Conference, Sudbury, Ontario, Canada, 25–28 May 2003.

Hannan, J.C. 1984. *Mine Rehabilitation: A Handbook for the Coal Mining Industry*. Sydney, Australia: New South Wales Coal Association.

Johnson Matthey. 2005. http://www.platinum.matthey.com/production/1043941177.html (Accessed September 2005).

Knoll, C. 2004. Woodlands to contain pollution in Goldfields. *Urban Green File*. May/June 2004 Vol. 9. No. 2, pp.24–29.

Krogg, S. 1985. The language of modern landscape architecture. *Landscape Architecture*. March/April 1985, Vol. 75 no.2, pp.56–59.

Marsh, W.M. 1991. *Landscape Planning: Environmental Applications (2nd edition)*. New York, USA: John Wiley & Sons.

Mendelsohn, F. & Potgieter, C.T. 1986. *Guidebook to sites of geological and mining interest on the central rand*. Republic of South Africa, Johannesburg: The Geological Society of South Africa.

MPRDA. 2002(a). Mineral and Petroleum Resources Development Act (No. 28 of 2002). *Government Gazette*. No. 23922. Republic of South Africa, Pretoria: Government Printer.

MPRDA. 2002(b). Mineral and Petroleum Resources Development Act (No. 28 of 2002): Draft Mineral and Petroleum Resources Development Regulations. *Government Gazette*. No.24134. Republic of South Africa, Pretoria: Government Printer.

MPRDA. 2004. Mineral and Petroleum Resources Development Act (No. 28 of 2002): Mineral and Petroleum Resources Development Regulations. *Government Gazette*. No. 26275. Republic of South Africa, Pretoria: Government Printer.

NEMA. 1998. National Environmental Management Act (No. 107 of 1998). *Government Gazette*. No. 19519. Republic of South Africa, Pretoria: Government Printer.

Quebec Government. 1997. *Guidelines for preparing a mining site rehabilitation plan and general mining site rehabilitation requirements*; National Library of Quebec.

Rademeyer, B. 2000. A generic environmental management programme for the quarrying of aggregate resources. Unpublished MSc thesis. Republic of South Africa, Johannesburg: Rand Afrikaans University.

Rademeyer, B., Rust, E. & Jones, G.A. 2003. A system for costing environmental mine closure liabilities. Mining and Sustainable Development Conference. Chamber of Mines conference proceedings. 3-5 Nov. 2003. Republic of South Africa, Sandton: Chamber of Mines.

Rademeyer, B., Van den Berg, M., Rust, E. & Jones, G.A. 2005: Managing the visual impact of tailings impoundments. Publication in preparation. Republic of South Africa, Pretoria: University of Pretoria.

Smith, M. 2004. Rock cladding of tailings dams. *Civil Engineering*. August 2004. Vol. 12, No. 8.

Turner, T. 2003. *Landscape planning and environmental impact design*. United Kingdom, London: Routledge.

Tutt, P. & Adler, D. 1994. *New Metric Handbook. Planning and Design Data*. Oxford, UK: Butterworth Architecture.

Vick, S.G. 1983. *Planning, design and analysis of tailings dams*. Canada: John Wiley & Sons, Inc.

Wilson, M.G.C. & Anhaeusser, C.R. (eds). 1998. *The Mineral Resources of South Africa: Handbook*. Republic of South Africa, Pretoria: Council for Geoscience.

---

1   Quickbird satellite imagery made available by the National Department of Housing.

2   Panoramic photograph of the AngloGold Ashanti ERGO Daggafontein tailings dam (Rademeyer 2005).

part THREE

Design

The papers in this section differ from the previous two sections in that they more directly discuss the nature of design in landscape architecture and/or highlight aspects arising from the analysis of specific design projects. The first paper focuses on the way landscape architects think about design, how design decisions are made and what factors influence these decisions and what their implications could be. The content focuses on the value systems, epistemologies and paradigms that colour the way we 'view' the landscape and approach the design thereof. The second paper pivots the section from design theory and thinking to the application thereof to specific projects (the next seven papers). The section concludes with a paper addressing contractual aspects affecting the implementation of landscape architectural design.

'Structuring Thinking: Plotting a Way for More Active Engagement with Theory in Landscape Architecture' addresses one of the primary concerns raised at the turn of the millennium regarding the state of landscape architecture, namely the discipline's problematic body of theory. The paper does not add to the body of theory guiding design, it rather attempts to develop a mechanism for understanding how to engage with theory in landscape architectural design. It reveals how decision making in design can be demystified to strengthen informed decision making. The paper is first in this section as it covers decision making in planning and design very broadly. Additional meaning can thus be derived from many of the subsequent papers by reflecting them against the tables set out in this paper.

'Landscape as Narrative, Expressed through the Landscape Design at Freedom Park, Tshwane, South Africa', continues with the metaphysical aspects associated with landscape design, addressed by a number of papers in Part 1, however in a more focused explanation of landscape narrative as form generator (ordering and referencing device). The author uses Freedom Park in Pretoria as a vehicle through which to elaborate on using landscape design as a medium to express a nation's political history. This intention has been a tangible theme particularly in post-1994 monument and memorial design in South Africa. The theme of meaning is discussed in relation to how it is catalysed through establishing and reflecting narrative. The paper also illustrates the use of landscape architectural theory (in this case the theory of narrative practices) in the analysis of design. This paper pivots the content shift in this section from broad design discussion, to the analysis and interpretation of specific design projects in the papers that follow.

The next two papers directly address the recently emerged discourse of landscape urbanism and its application in two South African cities, Johannesburg and Cape Town. Landscape urbanism is a controversial discourse; it has fervent proponents and critics. What is undeniable is that it has been one of the most prominent threads in contemporary landscape architectural (and city planning and design) theory. It is encouraging to see South African landscape architects embracing the discourse and attempting to mine it for its significance to local conditions.

The first of these two papers, 'Finding the Void: Park Development in Johannesburg's Inner City', uses a project entered into a competition for the design of a large inner city public urban park to illustrate how the city's 'voids' can be utilised to reclaim, remediate and incrementally stitch a newly created landscape into the existing and proposed infrastructural urban landscape. The predominant landscape urbanist principles employed in the project are the acknowledgement that the void has primacy over the built (landscape as the 'foundation' of cities, and not collections of buildings), and that the restorative and productive cycles of natural systems (and their resultant ecosystem services) are maximised within the city.

The second paper of the two focusing on landscape urbanism, 'Priming for Added Value: How the Application of the Principles of Landscape Urbanism to the Redevelopment of Culemborg "Adds Value" to the Designed Landscape', illustrates various aspects regarding landscape urbanism as explored in a post-graduate project. The paper focuses on the strategic nature of landscape urbanism and illustrates how principles such as programming the surface flexibly can be utilised for the creation of additional value in landscape architectural projects. Operational methodologies which maximise the performance of the 'working landscape' are also emphasised. A further aspect addressed is the way in which landscape architectural representation and communication have changed to address the need for more aggressive motivation and explanation of the value of landscape architectural projects.

'Mine Infrastructure Planning and Design for Closure: Integrating Sustainable Post-closure Land Use from the Outset into Designing Mine Infrastructure' emphasises the value of longer term planning across phases in the life cycle of an intervention in the landscape. The paper illustrates how infrastructure related to a particular mining activity could be planned and designed in a particular way from the outset so as to more easily accommodate a new set of uses after the mine has been closed. This is fast becoming an arena where landscape architects are increasingly involved. The essential principle advocated is that of open programming, a principle brought to the forefront of many contemporary landscape architectural projects in the last few decades, especially through the discourse of landscape urbanism. The project's strength, from a landscape architectural point of view, is the application of fundamental urban design principles (of relation to exterior space/place making) to order a series of buildings so as to create a complex of the nature of a well ordered settlement. This then creates the necessary preconditions for the success of most complexes comprising a series of buildings regardless of their programmatic differences. The project successfully illustrates the role of longer term strategic planning in landscape architecture.

'Not Lost in Translation: Grappling with Meaning in Mauritius' is an extremely practical application of many of the ideas captured in 'De-picturing the Landscape: Notes on the Value of Text for the Conception and Experience of Landscape' in Part 2. It is an informative example of how the landscape embodies (and can embody through the act of design) so much more than the physical alone – a theme very prominent in this section. This aspect of landscape architecture has been sidelined during the modern age, the pursuit thereof often being labeled as frivolous or unnecessary. The concerns of utility, ecology and sustainability have become dominant in design, at the expense of meaning. The domain of meaning in the landscape has become unfamiliar to landscape architects who often find embracing this aspect challenging. This paper is inspirational in that it illustrates the 'writing' of stories into the 'book' of the landscape in an extremely accessible manner.

'Anti-contextual Design: Walled Gardens for Power Plants' carries an important lesson for all designers; namely, always defaulting to standard notions of practice could be limiting. The emphasis on contextual sensitivity too narrowly defined, so prominent since the McHarg era in landscape architecture, can become a pursuit limiting certain aspects of landscape architectural design. Over-zealous contextual responsiveness on the part of designers could result in jettisoning possibilities such as one of the most significant landscape typologies throughout the history of landscape architecture, the walled garden. This paper refreshingly reinvigorates the possibility of utilising the walled garden typology in contemporary settings where an 'anti-contextual' approach may be the appropriate one.

'Green Inklings: The Paper Landscapes of GREENinc' reveals the forgotten world of unrealised projects, of which many exist in the draws of offices. This collection and brief description of 'paper' landscapes captures a rich array of landscape architectural ideas. Many paper landscapes are competition entries which traditionally embody progressive ideas untamed by constraints usually associated with project implementation. This is a very necessary world for any design-oriented discipline. Hopefully this article will inspire landscape architects to revisit their unrealised projects, publish them and allow them to further invigorate discourse associated with the discipline.

The last paper in the section, 'Why a Building Contract Should not be Used for Landscape Work', very necessarily turns our attention to the intricacies of project implementation. All good design and planning intentions could easily fall prey to glitches and difficulties experienced in the implementation process. Due to landscape architecture's relative infancy in relation to other built environment professions (such as architecture), many methods and processes from these disciplines become the default, the reason being that landscape architecturally specific versions often do not exist. Defaulting to other disciplines' processes, due to the uniqueness of the discipline and profession of landscape architecture, often does not result in expediency, but frustration. This paper thoroughly describes how the use of building contracts for landscape architectural work is a process which should not be followed.

chapter 14

Structuring Thinking: Plotting a Way for More Active Engagement with Theory in Landscape Architecture

Clinton Hindes

School of Architecture, Planning and

Geomatics

University of Cape Town

Cape Town

South Africa

Introduction

Theory in landscape architecture is a contested terrain of the discipline. Frustrations have been voiced with regard to a variety of aspects relating to theory:

Relatively young, it lacks the rich theoretical and critical traditions of architecture. (Beardsley 2000:1)

It (landscape architecture in the 1940s) lacked theory and did not engage in criticism. It was pusillanimous.(McHarg 1996:83)

In my opinion, landscape architecture needs a substantive body of theory on the process of land planning, design, and implementation, as well as on the results of that process.'(LaGro 1999:181)

There has been a recent plea by practitioners and academics alike for the creation of a vibrant, all-encompassing body of landscape architectural theory. (Corner 1991:61)

We do not invest an adequate amount of resources studying our design/planning successes and failures from an aesthetic, ecological and functional perspective. (Miller 1997:68)

I, for one, am pleased that a critic of philosophy has addressed himself to the problematic of the garden's marginalised territory and landscape architecture's struggling discourse.' (Hilderbrand 1999:3)

The second most frequently cited concern raised by Fellows (of the ASLA) is that landscape architects need 'better knowledge' in order to be effective. It is a broad concern and was defined in three ways; as a need for a better theoretical and/or technical expertise; as a need for research and testing; and as a need for greater academic rigour. (Miller 1997:68)

This article does not attempt to add to the existing body of theory on landscape architecture as tremendous volumes have recently emerged. What is deemed to be of greater importance is the need to improve the discipline's active engagement with theory. A framework is developed which facilitates active engagement with theory by exposing the internal logic of argument in design. The first part of the paper is dedicated to understanding the nature of theory within the discipline. Emphasis is placed on the relationship between design thinking and broader cultural and artistic paradigms (tides). The concerns expressed with theory in landscape architecture are discussed as symptoms of a disconnection between the discipline and cultural paradigms. The second part combines two systems of inquiry to form a framework which facilitates a reconnection with cultural and artistic tides which is believed will result in the discipline's improved engagement with theory.

Landscape architectural theoretical discourse and its relation to broad cultural and artistic tides

The state of the theoretical discourse

We need a context for genuine criticism. We need to be able to separate garden appreciation from hints on slug control. We need to find a way to break out of the "gardener's ghetto", where gardens are only seen to be of interest to gardeners. (Wareham 2005:181)

The transition from the 20th to the 21st century was a period of tremendous introspection in landscape architecture. The nature of the profession, its methods and domain were dissected, analysed and subsequently criticised or defended. A variety of articles emerged with topics such as 'A profession in peril?' (Miller 1997:66) and 'An apocalyptic manifesto' (as cited in Thompson 2005). These titles bear testimony to the depth of the introspection. A variety of strengths and weaknesses of the profession were identified such as: the public's lack of understanding of what landscape architecture is (the image of the profession), the loss of its intellectual roots together with the subsequent need for a better knowledge base, as well as the breadth of the profession (simultaneously viewed as a strength and weakness). However, one recurring theme concerns the discipline's intellectual grounding, or alternatively stated, the lack of a robust theoretical basis for the discipline. Thompson (1993) and Girot (1999) express their frustration with this shortcoming; 'The paucity of good theoretical writing in landscape architecture is one reason why the subject is likely to remain the poor half-brother of architecture and the impoverished cousin of town and country planning' (Thompson

1993:122), and 'It is precisely this void, this absence of a clear and demonstrable theory of landscape architecture, that explains why most French practitioners have chosen a rather intuitive and experiential approach to design' (Girot 1999:58). The concern is that the body of distinct landscape architectural theory is too limited (in quantity and the degree to which existing theory is engaged with), resulting in a lack of intellectual rigour in design conceptualisation, implementation, motivation and critique.

Although the marginalisation of landscape architecture in the discourse of built environment design during the majority of the 20th century seems to have changed (and possibly even reversed) with the onset of the 21st century, one of the most tangible legacies of the marginalisation is a lack of written landscape architectural theory. 'Writings on architecture have very great antiquity, those specifically devoted to landscape are fairly recent' (Leatherbarrow 2004:3).

Disconnecting: Landscape architecture separated from major cultural and artistic tides

The lack of theory can be seen as symptomatic of a deeper problem, namely that landscape architecture has essentially stood aside from the major cultural and artistic tides of the 20th century. Howett (1987) acknowledges as much in calling for a new generation of American landscape architects who will pursue the highest values and aspirations of their country's contemporary culture, 'Our profession's historic isolation, since Olmsted, from the central philosophical, ideological, literary and artistic debates of our time must finally be overcome...' (Howett 1987:1). Throughout the 20th century landscape architecture has experienced this cultural sidelining with regard to the primary ideational drivers of the built environment, such as philosophy, art and architecture. This sidelining was (and is) expressed and experienced by landscape architects in a number of ways.

In an essay on theory in landscape architecture, Ian Thompson (1993:122) bemoans the difficulty he experienced in assembling written material from which to construct a theory course for his landscape architecture students at the University of Newcastle. Contemplating the reason for this, he suggests that the real problem is that landscape architecture stands apart from the tides of cultural theory in a way that architecture does not, stating that 'it probably has something to do with the 'naturalness' of much landscape design, as apposed to the artificiality of building' (Thompson 1993:128). In a review of the book *Unnatural horizon's: Paradox and contradiction in Landscape Architecture*, Hilderbrand (1999:1) acknowledges the author's struggle to elevate the garden's place in cultural narrative.

The book is a clever and nervy – and at times preposterous – attempt to unpack the reasons why the garden has remained at the margins – not the centre – of art historical discourse. This book claims that the constructed landscape's vagaries, it's contradictions and anachronisms, it's confounding dialectical properties, have all but guaranteed resistance to the garden attaining an essential place in art history. (Hilderbrand 1999:1)

These symptoms are a reflection of broader paradigmatic shifts:

as a discipline, it [landscape architecture] has become increasingly estranged from a sense of traditional and poetic value. In particular, this refers to what might be perceived as the current inability of landscape architecture to simultaneously engage the current and thematic workings of history with the circumstances particular to our own time. (Corner 1991:115)

Cooper acknowledges in a noteworthy attempt to explore the garden philosophically, that very little attention has been paid to gardens in the discipline of philosophy; 'in the absence of a substantial literature, there simply does not exist, within the philosophical community, a shared perception of a "discipline" – the philosophy of gardens – replete with well defined "problems", "methods", and "research programmes"' (Cooper 2006:1).

Four possible reasons can be cited as to why landscape architecture has stood aside from major cultural and artistic tides through much of the 20th century, namely; its uneasy relation to modernism, society's lack of understanding of landscape architecture as a design discipline, the discipline's own over-emphasis of the goal of the stewardship of the natural world, and a limiting sentimental view of what the designed landscape should look like (the aesthetic qualities of the designed landscape). These four reasons are briefly discussed.

Sidelining during modernism

The struggle the Harvard Trio (landscape architects Dan Kiley, Garrett Eckbo and James Rose – studying at Harvard under architect Walter Gropius) had in accommodating plant material in the application of the ideals of modernism is testimony to the difficulty in completely absorbing landscape architectural design into modernism. James Rose wrote in a 1939 article:

It is perfectly possible to use plants with the same knowledge and efficiency with which we use lumber, brick, steel or concrete in building. And when we apply the science of growth to our landscape design standards, so that we can determine accurately the form characteristics and definitely establish the growth rates for individual plants under given conditions, we will be able to use plants with the same expediency as the factory made, modular unit in building. (Treib & Imbert 1997:28)

Architect Robert-Mallet Stevens' rather bizarre abstraction of trees (consisting entirely of articulated concrete planes) in a design at the Exposition des Artes Décoratifs et Industriels Modernes in Paris in 1925, is a vivid reminder of this limited ability of landscape architecture (resulting from it's 'naturalness') to comprehensively absorb the ideologies of modernism.

When the garden was built it was not possible to plant four trees identical in shape and size, as the layout demanded. The designers resolved the problem with reinforced cement. Very simply and without attempting a puerile copy of nature, they expressed the materials' characteristics with the implied silhouette and volume of a tree. (Forestier 1925:24)

The public image of landscape architecture

Landscape architecture's sidelining from major cultural and artistic tides can also be attributed to popular society's (mis-) understanding of the nature of landscape and garden design:

If someone sits down in front of an easel with a brush in their hand, all their thoughts and cultural notions about art hover over their shoulder, but anyone can happily garden without thinking for a moment about art or aesthetics. (Wareham 2005:187)

Not many people naturally consider landscape architecture to fall within the suite of disciplines known as the design professions. Society's over-association of landscape architecture with garden design does not bode well for the appeal of landscape architecture to school-leavers contemplating a 'serious' career. This results in landscape architecture departments (worldwide) struggling with low student numbers, as the activity of landscape architecture is seen by many as hardly being worthy of inclusion as a degree at tertiary institutions.

And so far it (landscape architecture) has failed to attain the public profile of architecture or the fine arts: built works of landscape architecture are not as readily identified and evaluated as paintings, sculptures or buildings. (Beardsley 2000:1)

Stewardship of the natural world at the expense of the poetic (the artistic realm of design)

There is no doubt that ecological concerns have rightfully been paramount in the world over the last number of decades. The concerns regarding the prevention of further environmental damage to the environment have been vigorously voiced through various interest groups. In landscape architecture, ecological concerns and environmental degradation have primarily been addressed through the science of ecology. Landscape architecture has embraced ecological processes and methodologies to the extent that some consider this to have been to the detriment of design (poetic aspects).

In many ways, the next major ideological and highly polemical tract was Ian McHarg's *Design with nature*, published in 1969. Focussed on the evolving study of natural ecology, and rooted in landscape management, McHarg cited the natural world as the only viable source of landscape design. His text provided landscape architects with sufficient moral grounds for almost completely avoiding decisions of design – if design be taken as the conscious shaping of landscape rather than its stewardship. (Treib 2005:111–112)

The adage 'touch the earth lightly' seems to have been taken too literally.

The environmental movement in broad society has also resulted in the popular belief that the solutions to the environmental crises we face are to be found in a return to 'wilderness'. The all too often image associated with visual campaigns on environmental destruction is that of the polar bear on a pristine, virgin-like white landscape. This belief fuels the populist idea that all forms of engagement with the landscape should adopt the approaches and purposes of preservation, conservation and a return to the way things were before civilisation began exerting a negative effect on the environment. Design process in landscape architecture began to avidly adopt scientific and quantifiable methodologies. Landscape architecture as a discipline became so synonymous with ecological planning and the goal of environmental rescue that the cultural and artistic aspects of the discipline were treated with suspicion and labelled as whimsical, thus assisting landscape architecture's sidelining from cultural and artistic tides.

The difficulty of advancing landscape is not only an issue of sentimentality and conservatism; it is further hindered by a growing contingent that believes landscape concerns ought to be directed solely toward the stewardship of the natural world. (Corner 1999:3)

Sentimental aestheticisation of the landscape

A further aspect hindering the uninhibited application of a wide spectrum of cultural and artistic ideas to the landscape is society's extremely narrow view of what the designed landscape should look like. This view is supported by the belief that the improvement of the landscape (through the act of design), should result in something in the order of a Picturesque or Olmstedian landscape.

Consequently, as an image that evokes a virtuous and benevolent nature, landscape is typically viewed as the soothing antithesis to the placeless frenzy of technological urban life; few would share the view that the contemporary metropolis can be construed as a landscape – as some in this book argue – or find it easy to imagine landscapes other than the pastoral and the gardenesque. (Corner 1999:2)

A similar sentiment is expressed by Howett regarding the Olmstedian aesthetic and the continued separation from contemporary culture:

And so it is even today. However much we want to perceive ourselves as contemporary designers who are inventors of original forms that express our time and place and culture, we are, I would like to suggest, still haunted by Olmsted's vision of an idyllic pastoral park. (Howett 1987:3)

Landscape is thus not easily imagined to be a material for the expression of the full spectrum of a society's cultural views and ambitions. This is traditionally considered to be the domain of the disciplines usually considered to be the arts, namely; literature, theatre, architecture, sculpture and painting.

Reconnecting: Landscape architecture's re-emergence as a culturally active discipline (and its growing theoretical discourse)

The sidelining referred to above continued for the majority of the 20th century, but is now showing evidence of a dramatic turnaround as we enter the 21st century, 'There has been a remarkable resurgence of interest in landscape topics during the past ten or so years' (Corner 1999:ix). The entire premise of Corner's book (James Corner being one of the most prominent theorists in landscape architecture over the past 25 years), *Recovering Landscape: Essays on Contemporary Landscape Architecture*, is a recognition that in the latter part of the 20th century there is an increased awareness of 'landscape' as an active component of the culturally loaded emerging body of knowledge on the built environment. He lists three aspects which characterise the recovery of landscape: the specificity of site (mnemonic, temporal and biological aspects); a concern for ecology and environment (on the scale of regional and global ecosystems); and the deindustrialisation of the landscape.

One of the most clearly articulated expressions of this recovery of landscape has been the advent of landscape urbanism. 'Landscape urbanism describes a disciplinary realignment currently underway in which landscape replaces architecture as the basic building block of contemporary urbanism' (Waldheim 2006:11). 'Landscape' (in the broadest sense – its full etymology) has become one of the primary aspects around which theory relating to cities has been developed. One of the ideational drivers for the recovery of landscape has been the growing awareness of the difference between land and landscape. Land representing the view of the landscape through the objective pragmatic (utilitarian) or scientific, and landscape representing the subjective image of landscape held by the viewer. A significant body of theory from the sub-disciplines of cultural geography and the cultural landscape have emerged from this new understanding. Cooper

(2006) in his book on gardens and philosophy sheds light on the culturally loaded nature of landscape; 'one could write an illuminating... history of a nation's cultural development by examining it's changing conception of the garden's scope, design and function' (Cooper 2006:3).

This renewed interest in landscape has resulted in a plethora of publications on aspects of landscape and landscape architecture over the last quarter of a century. The first were predominantly coffee-table books with very little critical discussion. However, a number of books published in the last decade critically discuss landscape architecture, an activity which requires the engagement of theory from which to formulate opinion, thus encouraging the development of theory. A number of landscape architects and landscape architectural practices have also recently published books on their work. Often included in these books are sections dedicated to the identification and explanation of the designer or firm's particular position on landscape architecture. This is an activity requiring knowledge of contemporary landscape architectural theory. It is the increasing number of publications of this nature that are revealing an increasing understanding of the value of critical reflection.

Currently, there is broad interest in site, landscape, ecology, process, and sustainability within the design and planning fields, ... I am invigorated by the proliferation of theories about the practices related to landscape. (Thompson 2005)

Theory itself is not enough: Engaging with it is necessary

It is clear that landscape architecture is reconnecting with major cultural tides and that its body of theory is rapidly growing. However, the techniques and methodologies associated with the conscious engagement with theory need to be better developed in order to make use of the opportunity this emerging theory provides. A statement in a review of the book *Unnatural Horizons* articulates this need:

The need for a literature that addresses the paralysing gaps in landscape architecture's intellectual history – or rather, the gaps in our critical engagement with it – will not be met by Allen Weiss's new book, although it offers some promise. (Hilderbrand 1999:1)

A number of authors have recently proposed various theoretical approaches to landscape architecture. Francis (1990) advocates what he has termed 'Expressivist' landscape architecture, and Corner (1991) proposes a hermeneutic approach. These proposals are instrumental in nature, advocating a particular theoretical approach to landscape architectural planning and design and thus prescribe a particular orientation. This paper, however, seeks to establish a framework for engaging with theory and not to propose a particular theory.

In order to arrive at a framework for engaging with various theoretical positions and types, a mechanism needs to be developed which is more heuristic in its working than prescriptive. A mechanism for managing information (for the facilitation of informed decision making) and applying critical thinking to landscape architectural projects is required.

Reconciling design thinking with theory: Structuring an approach for engaging with theory

The second section of this paper proposes a way to actively engage with theoretical discourse in landscape architecture. The opportunity afforded by the growth in the quantity of theoretical writing can only be fully realised when the mechanisms for engagement with theory have been developed. Two structures of inquiry and their associated theoretical aspects are identified as particularly relevant to the formulation of a framework for facilitating the active engagement with theory in landscape architecture. The structures are Swaffield's (2006:25) presuppositional hierarchy developed for the mediation between theory and critique in landscape architecture (Table 1), and Rowe's (1995:115) elaboration on the structure of normative thinking in architecture (Table 2).

These two structures of inquiry will be discussed and then combined to create a framework for active engagement with theory in landscape architecture. Both attempt to reveal aspects behind the nature of inquiry in the design process without actually proposing a particular theoretical orientation. They encourage an understanding of the role of theory in the design process and thereby demystify the action of tangibly and consciously embracing theoretical positions in design, which often results in a lack of continuity between the theory and the practice. The two structures also create the way for enriching the limiting problem-solving design process by connecting design process to cultural and artistic ideas (ontological and epistemological) as captured in the emerging body of landscape architectural theory. Swaffield explains this connection in elaborating on the assumptions behind the development of his structure of inquiry: 'the basic premise of the framework is that every theoretical expression and every critical act has underlying pre-suppositions about the nature of the world (ontology), the nature of knowledge (epistemology), the purpose of knowledge, and about how valid knowledge can be created (methodology)' (Swaffield 2006:23). These structures are now discussed with regard to the way in which they each encourage engagement with theory, followed by an elaboration on their combination and finally their application to landscape architecture.

Table 1: Structure of inquiry no. 1 – Swaffield's presuppositional hierarchy for mediating between theory and critique in landscape architecture (Swaffield 2006:25)

Assumptions about knowledge and the world	The purpose of knowledge	Examples of theoretical perspective	Examples within Landscape Architecture	Typical research methodology (ie, strategies)	Research methods (examples)	Predominant modes of representation
Objectivism[a]	Instrumental/ **Predictive**[b] *What and how?*	[Post] Positivist **Natural sciences**[c]	Psycho-physical and cognitive models of l/s perception **Landscape ecology**[d]	Experimentation Quasi-experiments **Survey**[e]	**Measurement**[f] Questionnaires Spatial analysis Post-occupancy evaluation	**Mathematical symbols**[g], with written interpretation
[Social] Construction	Interpretive *Who, when, why and through what social process?*	Pragmatism Structuration Practical reason Hermeneutics Critical theory Symbolic interaction Phenomenology	Design process Ecological aesthetics Pattern language Sense(s) of place	Action research Discourse analysis Historiography Ethnography	Observation Interviews Documentary analysis Case studies Design charettes	Written narrative, with illustrative diagrams and photographs
Subjectivism	Critical *Who gains and who loses? What if we do it this way?*	Critical inquiry Post-structural Feminist	'Expressivist' theory 'Critical visual studies'	Rhetoric and argumentation	Literary deconstruction Graphical experimentation Critical reflection Creative intervention	Diverse media: - written - graphic - aural - performance

Note: Superscripts a-g in this table are further discussed in the following text.

Table 2: Structure of inquiry no. 2 – Rowe's elaboration on the structure of normative thinking in architecture (Rowe 1995:123)

Position and orientation (Why?): The critical stance and the larger purpose of the position	Devices (How?): The less tangible (than 'production') leitmotifs that operationally describe the positions production	Production (What?): Visible works that result from the application of a particular position
Functionalist: The orientation of the functionalist position may be described in the following way: architecture is a matter of accommodating the functions that are prescribed for it and of functioning in a manner that is consistent with its material composition and construction. "Form follows function" is its guiding doctrine on both matters of use and building technology.	Explicit expression of a building's essential structure and process of fabrication are hallmarks. Spatial organisation invariably grows out of the programme of uses, in a straightforward manner (Herdeg 1983). Frequently there is an underlying concern with standardisation and systematic organisation on a number of counts.	Functionalist production is perhaps epitomised by the so-called International Style, with its ubiquitous array of steel, concrete and glass commercial buildings, each consistent in basic format, regardless of location and resulting differences in cultural setting. The position can also be seen at work in the spatial organisation of many post-war urban and suburban areas, with their adherence to concepts of transportation efficiency and an economically determined distribution of land uses.

Table continued on the next page

Position and orientation (Why?): The critical stance and the larger purpose of the position	Devices (How?): The less tangible (than 'production') leitmotifs that operationally describe the positions production	Production (What?): Visible works that result from the application of a particular position
Populist: Characterised as such: architecture has drifted too far from popular conceptions, needs and aspirations with regard to building. Therefore an inclusive interpretation of the prevailing socio-cultural climate, and especially its commonplace physical and symbolic qualities, is required as a source for architectural expression.	The architectural devices of this position can be seen to range widely in the use and rearticulating of commonplace elements of the contemporary built landscape.	The work of Venturi and Rauch is probably most directly associated with the appropriation of popular signs and symbols (Scott Brown 1977). In a recent residential development in the Houston area, a skilful layout of housing units was adorned with 'classical elements' in the form of a direct appliqué to the building façades. The message was clear. These are the residences of people with substance and status.
Formalist: Summed up in the following way: architecture is largely an autonomous realm of expression. Here we find an overriding concern with autonomous 'languages' of architecture, their compositional qualities and their inherent and possible meanings.	The architectural devices of formalism, as one might imagine, are apt to be quite diverse. They include exploitation of the formal qualities of regular solids, as seen in Eisenman's 'Houses', with their linguistic, syntactic meta-references.	The important distinction here is the insistence on exploring new formal and figural possibilities, and on reinterpreting traditional architectural conventions, which goes well beyond borrowing. For this reason production is apt to incorporate much more from the private languages of architectural expression.

An elaboration on the workings of Swaffield's presuppositional hierarchy and Rowe's structure of normative positions

In 2002 Swaffield published a reader on landscape architectural theory. It is a collection of seminal texts on landscape architectural design from the second half of the 20th century. Although the book does not address the engagement with theory, Swaffield nevertheless identifies this as a specific need: 'one of the problems we seem to face in landscape architecture is that the knowledge base is fragmented, the conceptual and graphic language is inconsistent, and the presumptions and conditions within which knowledge has been constructed seldom explicit' (Swaffield 2006:26). In 2006 Swaffield published an article which addresses a specific aspect regarding the engagement with theory, namely, a discussion on the relationship between theory and critique in land-scape architecture. He developed a presuppositional hierarchy for mediating between theory and critique (Table 1). It is this presuppositional hierarchy that facilitates the workings of the analytical framework for articulating between theory and critique (and vice versa) that is utilised as a base from which this paper develops a framework for engaging with theory.

Swaffield, however, progresses from the development of the analytical framework to the proposal for the adoption of a 'meta-theory' in the discipline of landscape archi-tecture which is based on what he has termed the 'social constructionist' epistemology (middle row in Table 1), social constructionism being the epistemological position be-tween objectivism and subjectivism. Swaffield explains this adoption of a metatheory:

This analysis is a call for an orientation from which a theoretical foundation might be rebuilt, rather than a bid for a particular theory. However, it is possible to speculate upon the type of meta-theory that might emerge from a sustained application of a con-structionist framework within the discipline. (Swaffield 2006:26)

Although social construction represents a broad spectrum of theoretical approaches (and although Swaffield states that his intention is to not prescribe a particular theoretical orientation), this does still begin to prescribe a particular spectrum of theoretical orientations for the discipline (as proposing social construction as a meta-theory implies not subjectivist and not objectivist), something this paper attempts to avoid. In developing a framework for engaging with theory, the proposal offered in this paper jettisons the notion of adopting a specific direction for the development of theory, or even a spectrum or 'spirit' within which the development should happen. It is this paper's intention to encourage the engagement with theory regardless of its orientation; objectivist, subjectivist or social constructionist.

The second structure of inquiry used to build the framework for the active engagement with theory in landscape architecture is the structure of normative positions as described by Rowe in his book *Design Thinking*. Rowe states that his intention with the book is to 'fashion a generalised portrait of design thinking. A principle aim will be to account for the underlying structure and focus of inquiry.' (Rowe 1995:1). This structure of inquiry he further describes as the 'interior situational logic and the decision making processes of designers in action, as well as the theoretical dimensions that account for and inform this kind of undertaking' (Rowe 1995:2). This provides the thinking methodology/process need for the understanding of informed decision making in design which facilitates the engagement with theory.

The workings of Swaffield's presuppositional hierarchy are combined with those of the structure of Rowe's normative positions to create a comprehensive framework for engaging with theory that this paper seeks to develop (Table 3), and not to propose another specific theoretical orientation. What follows is an elaboration on the nature of Swaffield's heuristic framework and that of Rowe's normative positions which identifies the aspects (methodologies and processes) of each to be combined to create a facilitation framework for engaging with theory in landscape architecture.

Table 3: The combination of the above two structures of inquiry into one framework for engaging with theory in landscape architecture

Ontology and epistemology Assumptions about knowledge and the world	Position and orientation (Why?)	Theoretical perspective (How? – Theory)	Design/planning methodology/device/ principle/approach/ technique (How? – Method)	Design or planning action/ production (What? - Result)
This represents the broader cultural and philosophical aspects within which assumptions are located about the way knowledge is created, for example through science, cultural beliefs or the individual's experience.	Various positions and their associated orientations exist within ontological and epistemological tides.	The theoretical perspective describes the overall intentions of the particular theory in relation to its application to the landscape.	In order to achieve the goals of the theoretical perspective particular methods and principles need to be identified.	This describes the result of the application of the principles and methods in the execution of the design. In practical terms, what happens 'on-site'.

Swaffield's presuppositional hierarchy for mediating between theory and critique (Table 1)

As opposed to the broad concern of this paper for developing a framework for engaging with theory, Swaffield (2006:26) proposed a structure for addressing the more narrow concern of establishing better connections between theory and critique in landscape architecture. This study proposes that the presuppositional hierarchy within the epistemological framework of Swaffield's proposal forms the foundation for a framework for engaging with theory in landscape architecture. 'Engaging with theory' includes the broader goals of setting the preconditions for establishing the links to broader cultural and artistic tides, as well as improving the relationship between theory and critique.

Swaffield's concern primarily centres on what he terms the 'conceptual interdependence between theory and critique'. He proposes a heuristic framework as a structure for exploring the relationship between theory and critique. The framework is based on the assumption that theoretical expressions are located within a set of presuppositions. These address aspects such as ontology, epistemology and methodology. The framework creates the ability to map the relationships (presuppositions) between paradigms (schools of thought), as well as the associated methods and techniques (primarily of a research nature).

The value of this framework exposing and clarifying a presuppositional hierarchy is that it allows designers to locate their applied design approaches (methods and techniques) within the cultural tides from which the discipline of landscape architecture has slipped away. The particular advantage for landscape architecture is that any theoretical expression, be it on the broad philosophical side of the spectrum or practical action, can be 'located' and understood in terms of its origins (moving to the left of the table, Table 3), and its practical techniques (moving to the right of the table, Table 3). It is this mechanism ('locating' design action) that is adopted for the departure point for engaging with theory that this paper proposes.

Rowe describes the theoretical discourse as a major source for the principles that guide designers with regard to the choices they need to make in design decision making. The theoretical position is viewed as the degree to which a corpus of principles has a community of subscribers. This community of designers agrees that this corpus of principles is worthy of emulation in their work (Rowe 1995:115).

The two aspects of normative positions of particular relevance to this paper are their content and structure. Rowe identifies normative positions to have the following elements; the location and identification of a problem or issue under contention, an unfa-

vourable assessment of prevailing practice (its ability to address the problem) together with the identification of untapped opportunities, and a counter proposal with its rationale. There is an inherent critical nature to the content of normative positions which encourages engagement with theory, as a set of criteria need to be identified in order to be able to engage in critique (the formulation of the 'unfavourable assessment').

Regarding the structure of normative positions in architecture, Rowe identifies a simple taxonomic structure that allows aspects of various positions to be commonly portrayed. The three aspects/components are production, architectural devices and orientation (Table 2). Production refers to visible works that result from the application of a particular position. These are aspects (visible in the design expression) that could be used to identify a group of designers advocating a particular position. The architectural devices are the less tangible leitmotifs that operationally describe the position's production. In the 'orientation' of the position lies the links to the wider cultural context, which Rowe describes as 'the critical stance and the larger (social) purpose of the position,' (Rowe 1995:123). Krogg acknowledges the importance for a designer to have an 'orientation' in an essay on certain shortcomings of landscape architectural design process: 'The recognition of one's own orientation is crucial, since it establishes and regulates the actual physical forms and therefore, impact, of the resulting landscapes, available to the artist/designer' (1985:72). These three components of normative positions (production, device and orientation) in relation to each other create a line of argument. The highlighted text in Table 2 describes the orientation of 'populist architecture' and the resultant physical design expression. This line of argument functions in the same manner as the presuppositional hierarchy described by Swaffield.

The highlighted text in Table 1 (superscripts a–g) reads as a sequence either from left to right or right to left and illustrates the application of this same structure to expose the presuppositional hierarchy characterising its internal logic in Swaffield's structure of inquiry. In this case it refers to research in landscape architecture. Reading from right to left in this case; the mathematical symbols[g] are a mode of representation of the research method of measurement[f], which is in turn nested within the survey[e] methodology of landscape ecology[d]. Landscape ecology is a theoretical perspective of the positivist discipline of the natural sciences[c] which predicts[b] the impacts of various actions. Engaging natural sciences in this predictive way ultimately resides in the objectivist[a] epistemology which assumes objective truth residing in the object waiting to be discovered through empirical observation (the superscript numerals emphasise the linearity/sequential nature of the presuppositional hierarchy.

Combining the structures of inquiry into one framework (Table 3)

It is seen from the above elaboration on these two systems that they both achieve two important desired aspects when developing a framework for improved engagement with theory. By both employing the presuppositional hierarchy they create the links between practical design techniques and methods, and the overarching theoretical paradigms and orientations from which they originate, and secondly, these paradigms/theoretical aspects are easily located in broader cultural tides when understood as having epistemological and ontological roots/origins. 'All positions, of course, can be seen as ideological [situated in cultural tides] or biased to some degree. They clearly favour one set of circumstances over others. If they are to be coherent, all must contain some line of argument [presuppositional hierarchy – links between techniques/methods and paradigms/epistemologies]' (Rowe 1995:123). Although Rowe's structure does not extend leftwards of the table (Table 2) into the epistemological and ontological aspects, it is possible to envision this extension by referring to the left half of the Swaffield structure (Table 1).

These two structures of inquiry are very similar regarding the overall intention of acknowledging the workings of the line of argument (presuppositional hierarchy) as part of their internal logic; however, it is their difference in categorising the various facets of the line of argument (moving horizontally across the table) that makes the combination meaningful for this paper's intention. The essential difference between the two is that Swaffield's terminology (the semantic with which he elaborates on the details of the framework) is research orientated, while Rowe's system is design orientated. Both of these orientations are necessary.

The examples given by Swaffield, particularly on the right hand side of the structure (Table 1), are more of a research nature than of a design nature. Concepts such as questionnaires, interviews, discourse analysis and experimentation are typical of research-orientated activity. This is the intention of the structure, to elaborate on the research methodologies. This however limits its applicability to the realm of design. Rowe's structure of normative positions on the other hand uses the language of architectural design, such as methodology and technique, and is intended to be used as a tool to expose the logic of design intention and expression. This is more appropriate to a framework intended for engaging with theory in practice and design (as opposed to research).

For the purposes of this paper, namely to engage theory in landscape architectural design, Swaffield's left half of the table (the epistemological/ontological and theoretical perspective) is utilised, and the right hand side is discarded and replaced by the orientation/device/production aspects of Rowe's structure of inquiry (Table 3). 'Representation' is replaced by 'production', the two columns of 'method' and 'methodology' are combined with 'devices'. The purpose in doing this for the development of the framework in this paper is that it is Swaffield's elaboration on the epistemological and ontological aspects that stretches the framework into the major cultural tides (more so than Rowe), and Rowe's orientation to production is firmly entrenched in the design field. The line of argument (presuppositional hierarchy) is maintained for the relational aspects. This author has further added certain terms which add to the understanding of the framework in the design disciplines, such as design 'principle' and 'action'.

Application of the framework to landscape architectural practice (design) and theory

The application of the framework to landscape architectural theory is illustrated in Tables 4–7. These tables illustrate the way in which the framework illuminates relationships between the techniques/principles applied in design or planning, the methodologies from which these arise, the theoretical orientations/positions giving rise to these methodologies, and finally the epistemological and ontological roots of these positions. The left hand side of the tables tends to be less disciplinary specific (associated with broader cultural tides), and the right hand is more disciplinary specific (associated with the principles of the discipline of landscape architecture). This allows the framework to function in a manner which reconnects landscape architectural principles to cultural and artistic tides. It is important to note that it is not assumed that design action prior to this kind of framework took place in a vacuum (i.e. not related to cultural and artistic tides). All design action is ultimately a reflection of a society's cultural paradigms; however, these links are not always clear. The purpose of this framework is to expose the relationships between cultural paradigms and design action.

A variety of theoretical and epistemological perspectives have recently emerged in landscape architectural theory. Landscape architectural practitioners and theorists have described their approaches to design with reference to various theoretical orientations and in some cases even explicitly to ontological (Girot 1999:59) aspects, and some have proposed specific theoretical orientations for the discipline, such as Corner's (1991) hermeneutics, and Francis's (1990) expressivist approach. The nature of these positions, relation to each other and their resultant methodologies and techniques are often not understood in themselves or in relation to each other.

The following questions are the kinds of questions that arise from this lack of understanding and are addressed by sifting them through the framework for engaging with theory illustrated in

Tables 4–7. This illustrates the heuristic nature of the table in that it facilitates the understanding of these aspects, and does not prescribe any type of action.

Phenomenology is extensively referred to by Meyer (2000) in her discussion of (among others) the work of landscape architects George Hargreaves and Lawrence Halprin with regard to the manner in which they make ecology tacit. What is phenomenology, what are its philosophical roots and what does design expression look like resulting from a phenomenological approach (Table 6)? The theoretical orientation of hermeneutics was advocated by Corner (1991) as an overriding theoretical orientation for the discipline. What is hermeneutics and how does it differ from phe-

nomenology, are their respective epistemologies (assumptions about the way we see the world) different or the same (Table 5)? Why does Corner cite Luis Barragan as an example of a hermeneutic approach to landscape architectural design (Table 5)? What are the epistemological and theoretical roots of the approach of environmental planner Ian McHarg (Table 4)? Why is his method considered to be so scientific? Regarding design decision making in Freedom Park (Table 7), how do the decisions using indigenous knowledge systems differ from design decisions in conventional/traditional landscape architectural decision-making? Plotting these aspects onto the framework relates them to each other and begins to assist in understanding similarities and differences.

Table 4: Application of the combined framework to expose the presuppositional hierarchy of the work of environmental planner Ian McHarg

Assumptions about knowledge and the world	Position and orientation (Why?)	Theoretical perspective (How? – Theory)	Design/planning methodology/device/ principle/approach/technique (How? – Method)	Design or planning action/ production (What? - Result)
Objectivism: (Purpose of knowledge = instrumental and predictive) 'Objectivism is the epistemological view that things exist as *meaningful* entities independently of consciousness and experience, that they have truth and meaning residing in them as objects ("objective" truth and meaning, therefore), and that careful ("scientific") research can attain that objective truth and meaning' (Crotty 1998:6). '– the notion that truth and meaning reside in their objects independently of any consciousness – has its roots in ancient Greek philosophy, was carried along in Scholastic realism in the Middle Ages, and rose to its zenith in the age of the so-called Enlightenment' (Crotty 1998: 42).	[Post] Positivist: Natural sciences 'The positivist perspective encapsulates the spirit of the Enlightenment, the self-proclaimed age of reason that began in England in the seventeenth century and flourished in France in the century that followed. Like the Enlightenment that gave it birth, positivism offers assurance of unambiguous and accurate knowledge of the world' (Crotty 1998: 18). 'Positive statements are reassertions about reality as tested by scientific method, and can withstand detailed and objective scrutiny' (Corner 1991:117). 'One of the positions taken by positivism in landscape architecture and planning is that no action may be taken, or any change initiated, until all factual data have been collected. Teams of experts are assembled to work together in gathering the most complete and accurate data-set' (Corner 1991:117).	Ecological planning: Landscape suitability approach no.1 (The Ian McHarg, or University of Pennsylvania, suitability method) 'LSA [landscape suitability approach] emphasises the natural characteristics of the landscape in determining the fitness of a given tract of land for particular use' (Ndubisi 2002:37). 'McHarg was deeply disturbed by patterns of population growth that resulted in degradation of the landscape. McHarg believed firmly that the dialogue between humans and nature should be one of mutual interdependence. Humans are dependent on nature for air, water, food, and fibre, and nature also provides order, meaning and dignity' (Ndubisi 2002:45). 'The natural sciences in general and the field of ecology in particular offer the most useful insights into applying the ecological view to mediate the dialogue between humans and nature' (Ndubisi 2002:45).	Overlays ('layer cake') 'The first, environmental or ecological design had emerged out of the writings and teachings of educators such as Ian McHarg. Its primary contribution to the design process was to structure the preconceptual design phase according to a more defensible, scientific method' (Meyer 2000:189). 'The McHarg method seeks to understand nature's processes, interactions, and values as the basis for allocating human uses in the landscape. "In essence," he wrote, "the method consists of identifying the area of concern as consisting of certain processes, in land, water, and air – which represent certain values. These can be ranked – the most valuable land and the least, the most valuable water resources and the least, the most and least productive agricultural land, the richest wildlife habitats and those that have no value, the areas of great or little scenic value, historic buildings and their absence, and so on"' (Ndubisi 2002:45).	'Applications of the McHarg method usually include the following steps: 1. The goals, objectives and land use needs are defined, and study boundaries are established. 2. An ecological inventory of the relevant physical & biological processes is conducted. 3. The resultant inventory is mapped. 4. Each factor map is examined to determine which areas are suitable for each proposed land use. 5. All factor maps pertinent to determining the landscape suitability for a particular land use are overlayed. 6. The suitability maps for the individual land uses are combined into a composite map using transparent overlays' (Ndubisi 2002:47).
[Social] Construction (Purpose of knowledge = interpretive)				
Subjectivism (Purpose of knowledge = critical)				

Table 5: Application of the combined framework to expose the presuppositional hierarchy of Corner's (1991) proposal for landscape architecture theory to adopt the position of hermeneutics

Assumptions about knowledge and the world	Position and orientation (Why?)	Theoretical perspective (How? – Theory)	Design/planning methodology/device/ principle/approach/ technique (How? – Method)	Design or planning action/production (What? - Result)
Objectivism	N/A	N/A	N/A	N/A
[Social] Construction (Purpose of knowledge = interpretive) 'A hermeneutic approach to landscape architectural theory might better provide an ontology grounded in the continuity of culture, as opposed to an ideology of blinkered reconstruction on the one hand, or of abstract destructive freedom on the other. What is sought is "a dialogue between culture in its present form and those possibilities forgotten or dormant in the depths of its tradition, alive in memories, in literature, in philosophy" Veseley 1984:12). Such dialogue demands that one view the history of human endeavour as a deep repository of meaning, wherein certain profoundly human situations continually recur and are embodied in an infinitely rich variety of ways. This quarry of human consciousness might thereby provide the very source of our [landscape architects'] work, recalling the past while also disclosing new possibilities for a future that transcends the given present' (Corner 1991:139). 'Truth, or meaning, comes into existence in and out of our engagement with the realities in our world. There is no meaning without a mind. Meaning is not discovered, but constructed. In this understanding of knowledge, it is clear that different people may construct meaning in different ways, even in relation to the same phenomenon. Isn't this precisely what we find when we move from one era to another or from one culture to another? In this view of things, subject and object emerge as partners in the generation of meaning' (Crotty 2003:9).	Hermeneutics: 'Hermeneutics was, and is, the science of biblical interpretation. The actual explanation of what a biblical text means is known as exegesis. Behind all exegetical activity, governing how it is carried out, lies a complexis of theories, principles, rules and methods. That complexis came to be known as hermeneutics' (Crotty 2003:87). 'Hermeneutics is a theory of understanding and interpretation' (Corner 1991:132). The following is a synopsis of Corner 1991:125-127: 'These three working assumptions (see below) form the basis of hermeneutics: a theory of understanding and interpretation. 'Situational interpretation: The world is not all-knowable, as modern technology might have us believe. Luminous and opaque, the life-world does not fit neatly into any one viewpoint. By extension, therefore, "truths" are only relative concepts, subject to shift and change. Hence, the world known in one way is always interpretable in another. 'The primacy of perception: Primary knowledge is that which comes from direct experience. The medium of ideation – and subsequent embodiment – in landscape architecture is the landscape itself. This not only encompasses the physical materials and natural processes that constitute landscape, but also includes the codes and languages through which landscape is culturally understood. It is only through the actual undertaking of perception-based work – imaginary drawings, models, artifacts, and the actual building of landscapes – that the landscape architect can best find access to the enigmatic richness of landscape space and time. 'The "happening" of tradition: An active engagement with tradition. With the phenomenon of tradition so defined, it becomes possible to imagine an approach toward theory that critically engages the archaeology of previous engagements while also projecting into the future... attempting to find new joints of meaning between our ancestry and our future' (Corner 1991:125–127).	The landscape as palimpsest: 'The landscape itself is a text open to interpretation and transformation. It is also a highly situated phenomenon in terms of space, time, and tradition and exists as both the ground and geography of our heritage and change. 'Landscape is not only a physical phenomenon, but is also a cultural schema, a conceptual filter through which our relationships to wilderness and nature can be understood' (Corner 1991:129). 'Residua in this topographic palimpsest provide loci for remembrance, renewal, and transfiguration of a culture's relationship to the land. 'As a human-made projection, landscape is both text and site, partly clarifying the world and our place within it. The textual landscape is thus a hermeneutic medium' (Corner 1991:129).	Plot, map, dig, set: 'The textual landscape is thus a hermeneutic medium. Landscape architecture might therefore be thought of as the practice of e-scaping and re-scaping our relationship to nature and the 'other' through the construction of built worlds. 'In the desire to reflect both on our modern context and on our inheritance, landscape architecture might practise a hermeneutical plotting of the landscape – a plotting that is as much political and strategic as it is relational and physical. 'The landscape architect as plotter is simultaneously critic, geographer, communicator, and maker, digging to uncover mute and latent possibilities in the lived landscape. 'With every "projection" there might follow a rebirth: the artefact of culture and the enigma of nature rendered fuller with every pass. To plot, to map, to dig, to set: are these not the fundamental traditions of landscape architecture?' (Corner 1991:129).	'As a partial attempt to exemplify such an approach [hermeneutics], one might consider the work of Luis Barragan' (Corner 1991:129). 'The built order is truly original and abstract, derived from the tenets of early Modernism, but the spaces are still rooted in the continuity of Barragan's culture, becoming meaningful to a larger culture through their appeal to primordial experiences we as human beings all share. The cultural archetypes are inexhaustibly formulated with a religious passion – walls, steps, gates, paths, seats, and so on, are the elements of both memory and prophecy, providing "places" for collective orientation and perpetuation of culture. 'The serenity of enclosure and setting; the poetic accommodation of ritual and cultural situation; the sensual control of body placement and motion so as to arouse expectation and intrigue; the surrealistic quality of composition and arrangement; the hierarchical control of space, light and tactile experience: all embody the possibility of a lived continuity within a forward-probing culture recalling its heritage' (Corner 1991:130).
Subjectivism	N/A	N/A	N/A	N/A

Table 6: Lawrence Halprin's Sea Ranch (1962) and George Hargreave's Candlestick Point Cultural Park 1985–93 as examples of a phenomenological approach to landscape architecture

Assumptions about knowledge and the world (Epistemology and ontology)	Position and orientation (Why?)	Theoretical perspective Design/planning methodology/device/ principle/approach/technique (How? – Theory and method)	Design or planning action/production/ representation (What? - Result)
Objectivism	N/A	N/A	N/A
Social construction 'Truth, or meaning, comes into existence in and out of our engagement with the realities in our world. There is no meaning without a mind. Meaning is not discovered, but constructed. In this understanding of knowledge, it is clear that different people may construct meaning in different ways, even in relation to the same phenomenon. Isn't this precisely what we find when we move from one era to another or from one culture to another? In this view of things, subject and object emerge as partners in the generation of meaning.' (Crotty 2003:9). 'Constructionism (often with the prefix "social") assumes that there may be a "real" material and social world, but that knowledge of that world is inevitably shaped by the social setting' (Swaffield 2006:22).	Phenomenology (Generic): '**Phenomenology**, however, treats culture with a good measure of caution and suspicion. Our culture may be enabling, but paradoxically it is also crippling. While it offers us entrée to a comprehensive set of meanings, it shuts us off from an abundant font of untapped significance' (Crotty 1996a:71). 'The "things themselves", as phenomenologists understand the phrase, are phenomena that present themselves immediately to us as conscious human beings. Phenomenology suggests that, if we lay aside, as best we can, the prevailing understandings of those **phenomena** and revisit our immediate **experience** of them, possibilities of new meaning emerge for us or we witness at least an authentication and enhancement of former meaning' (Crotty 1996a:78). Phenomenology (Application to landscape architecture): 'Though theories of place making, **phenomenology**, and site art provided bridges for landscape architects experimenting with ways to make environmentalism manifest in their work, they also posed new challenges' (Meyer 2000:204). '...contemporary environmental and site artists, such as Robert Smithson, Michael Heizer, Mary Miss, and Robert Irwin, who were making site-specific works outside the gallery; and contemporary critics and artists who were translating the ideas of **phenomenologists** about bodily experience, duration, immersion, and place making into design and art theories' (Meyer 2000:191). 'To some it may seem odd that landscape architects looked toward art and design theory and practice when seeking direction about folding ecological principles and environmental values into their creative processes. But this simultaneous look to art as well as science and to theories of site specificity and **phenomenology** as well as ecology was critical to the successful integration of environmentalism into landscape architectural design' (Meyer 2000:191). 'These theoretical trends [**phenomenology**] found mature landscape architectural expression in Catherine Howett's and Anne Whinston Spirn's writings in the late 1980's' (Meyer 2000:194).	The experience of the specificity of site: 'One of the most widely read essays, Kenneth Frampton's "Towards a Critical Regionalism" (1983), alluded to the particular environmental factors that informed design responses – topography, light, climate, and context – emphasizing their tactile and phenomenal influence on the body. This inflection would, in Frampton's view, lead to works that were more place specific, more resistant to globalization, universal solutions, and a "cleared site", or tabula rasa, mentality' (Meyer 2000:194). 'Given the influence that Smithson had as artist in the professional studios of landscape architecture, most landscape architects who have heard of phenomenology have probably learned about it through them. What specific lessons have designers gleaned from him? In their working **method**, landscape architects found alternatives to the abstraction of ecological analysis, especially the large-scale mapping of individual ecological systems such as hydrology, soils, and vegetation. Instead of mapping large parcels and attempting to gain a comprehensive conceptual understanding of the whole, artists like Smithson concentrated on observing specific **phenomena** and processes at a particular place. They began with that which was knowable through human **experience** at the scale of the **body**' (Meyer 2000:197). 'In fact, Halprin might be considered to have developed a **phenomenologically** based language of landscape architecture, as he reconceptualized landscape space as bounded flow, a fluid medium experienced in a multisensory way by the **moving body**' (Meyer 2000:199). 'Designers and artists who employ a phenomenological method frequently speak of a "return to things" that can be known through direct **experience** and immersion in a place.' '...they made the environment legible to a culture distant from the natural world by employing the materials and processes of nature (an 'aesthetics of **experience**' rather than an 'aesthetics of the object').	Sea Ranch: 'The **phenomenal experience** of these varied ecosystems was one of strong contrasts. By working with the site's structure, and character, Halprin created a memorable place, characterized by a vivid staccato like experience, from wet to dry, shady to sunny, calm to windy and quiet to noisy. Halprin's conceptual quarrying of the site for its **experiential** qualities, ...' (Meyer 2000:201). '...Halprin's conception of the landscape as a temporal medium, the body's role in the experience of place, and space as a qualitative, fluid presence contribute to a type of landscape architectural practice that is an art of environmental engagement' (Meyer 2000:201). 'He [Halprin] also developed new drawing tools for depicting landscape space and created an expanded morphology of landscape forms based on the direct observation of surfaces shaped by natural process, such as erosion and deposition' (Meyer 2000:199). Candlestick Point Cultural Park: 'If phenomenal art or the phenomenology of design requires an awareness of both the **fleeting phenomena and tactile character of a place as well as the nature of its construction**, Candlestick Point Cultural Park falls well within this genre' (Meyer 2000:215). 'This sensibility to natural process and phenomena builds on the work of Smithson. These natural processes and **phenomena** are the genesis of form and aesthetic experience. No exhibits or interpretive signs intrude on the visitors' **experience** of the environment' (Meyer 2000:213). 'The park is a theatre of environmental spectacle; the site's wind processes channel and deflect the wind's flow to create a rhythmic **experience** of calm and force, sound and silence, stillness and movement' (Meyer 2000:214).
Subjectivism	N/A	N/A	N/A

Table 7: The application of the framework to reveal the presuppositional hierarchy in certain decision-making in Freedom Park

Assumptions about knowledge and the world (Epistemology and ontology)	Position and orientation (Why?)	Theoretical perspective (How? – Theory) Design/planning methodology/device/ principle/approach/technique (How? – Method)	Design or planning action/production (What? – Result)
Objectivism	[Post] Positivist Natural sciences 'If landscape architects worked in a rational manner, with **scientific understandings of natural systems**, and in collaboration with other scientists, McHarg argued, they could enhance human life and develop the landscape in a way that prevented, rather than caused, environmental damage' (Meyer 2000:143).	Environmental Planning (Natural systems/ecological analysis as basis for decision-making) The McHarg Landscape Suitability Approach Natural systems analysis in 'layer-cake' formation. Landscape ecology 'The ecological survey recognized Salvokop as a site of significant ecological value. It is characterized by thickly wooded savanna on its northern and eastern slopes, giving way to Highveld grassland on its southern slopes, where there is also a small forest of *Protea caffra*' (Knoll 2004:18).	Suitability zoning 'From this survey, the landscape architects identified the more or less ecologically sensitive zones of the site, and so defined those areas where development should be excluded or limited. A consequence of this review was that the proposed conference centre, parking area, administrative and information building, were moved from the southeast to the north of the hill' (Knoll 2004:18).
Social constructionism	Hermeneutics 'Even more importantly, to see hermeneutics as a sharing of meaning between communities or individuals is to situate hermeneutics within history and within culture' (Crotty 1998:91). Interpretivism 'A positivist approach would follow the methods of the natural sciences and, by way of allegedly value-free, detached observation, seek to identify universal features of humanhood, society and history that offer explanation and hence control and predictability. The interpretivist approach, to the contrary, *looks for culturally derived and historically situated interpretations of the social life-world.*' (Crotty 1998:67).	Cultural landscape (Cultural ways of seeing – indigenous knowledge systems as basis for decision-making) Symbolic and metaphoric associations with cultural aspects	'After much debate between the design team and the advisory panel (traditional healers, African culture and indigenous knowledge system specialists), it was agreed that the pathway (a spiral pathway with contemplative spaces), originally planned to move up the hill in a westerly direction, would be routed in an easterly direction. East is significant because it is here that the sun rises, marking the beginning of a new day, and metaphorically, a new beginning in the history of South Africa' (Knoll 2004:18).
		Culture metaphorically referenced/ Abstraction **Device** 'So here we finally arrive at the critical fork in the landscape architect's road – whether to try to design a symbol by molding signal - laden forms and materials, and thereby provide a valuable service to society, or to mold those or other forms and materials so that they are assigned new meanings evoking rich, fundamental thoughts and images, and thereby comment constructively upon society's ideas and visions.' (Krogg 1985:72) **Application to Freedom Park** 'During the design process, it was agreed that symbolism should not be translated literally but rather that the imagery should be abstract, simple and devoid of clutter' (Knoll 2004:18).	'The fundamental layout of the *Isivivane* is derived from an African homestead which traditionally encompasses the *lesaka* (burial place) and the *kgotla* (meeting place)' (Knoll 2004:18). 'the *lesaka* is a circular structure, commonly found in African villages, where generation upon generation are buried. At Freedom Park, the *lesaka* is transcribed as a flat circle of stone, edged with brushed concrete' (Knoll 2004: 18).
Subjectivism	N/A	N/A	N/A

Conclusion

The paper first elaborated on the nature of the concerns with theory in landscape architecture. The primary concerns expressed by the landscape architectural fraternity are that there is too little theory, and secondly, that there is not enough engagement with theory. These problems were discussed as symptoms of the broader problem of a disconnection of the discipline from major cultural and artistic tides. The framework developed in this paper utilises the 'mechanics' of a line of argument (presuppositional hierarchy) to form the basis of a method to actively engage with theory in the discipline. Through this process it is believed that the actions of landscape architects can be explained by reflecting against the framework revealing the motivations/assumptions behind them. This technique to 'locate' design action will assist practitioners and students of landscape architecture to better understand decision-making and to relate those decisions to broader cultural and artistic tides.

Bibliography

Beardsley, J. 2000. A word for landscape architecture. *Harvard Design Magazine*, Fall 2000, No. 12 p.1–6.

Cooper, D.E. 2006. *A philosophy of gardens*. New York: Oxford University Press.

Corner, J.A. Discourse on Theory 1: Sounding the Depths – Origins, Theory and Representation. *Landscape Journal*, 1990. Vol. 9 No. 2 p.61–78.

Corner, J.A. Discourse on Theory 2: Three Tyrannies of Contemporary Theory and the Alternative of Hermaneutics. *Landscape Journal*, 1991. Vol. 10 No.2 p.115–133.

Corner, J. (ed). 1999. *Recovering landscape: Essays in contemporary landscape architecture*. New York: Princeton Architectural Press.

Crotty, M. 1998. *The foundations of social research: Meaning and perspective in the research process*. St Leonards, Australia: Allen and Unwin.

Forestier, J.C.N. 1925. Les jardins de l'exposition des artes décoratifs. *La Gazette Illustrée des Amatuers de Jardins* 1925.

Francis, M. 1990. Expressivist landscape architecture. *Landscape Journal* 1990. Vol. 7 No. 1 p.30–40.

Girot, C. 1999. Four trace concepts in Landscape Architecture. In *Recovering landscape*. J. Corner (ed). New York: Princeton Architectural Press:58–67.

Herdeg, K. 1983. *The Decorated Diagram*. Cambridge, Massachusetts: MIT Press.

Hilderbrand, G. 1999. Book review of Unnatural horizons: Paradox and contradiction in Landscape Architecture. *Harvard Design Magazine*, Summer 1999, No. 8 p.1–4.

Howett, C. Systems, signs and sensibilities. *Landscape Journal*.1987. Vol. 6 No. 1 p.1–12.

Knoll, C. 2004 Freedom Park, a landscape narrative of South Africa's history and heritage. *Urban Greenfile*. Vol. 9 No. 2 p.18–23.

Krogg, S. 1985. *The Language of Modern Landscape Architecture*. March/April 1985. Vol. 75 No. 2 p.56–59.

LaGro, J. Research Capacity: A Matter of Semantics? *Landscape Journal*. 1999. Vol. 18 No. 2 p.179–186.

Leatherbarrow, D. 2004. *Topographical stories*. Philadelphia: University of Pennsylvania Press.

McHarg, I. 1996. *A quest for life*. New York: John Wiley & Sons.

Meyer, E. 2000. The Post-Earth Day Conundrum: Translating Environmental Values into Landscape Design. In *Environmentalism in landscape architecture*. M. Conan (ed). Washington, DC: Dumbarton Oaks:187.

Miller, P. 1997. A profession in peril? *Landscape Architecture*, August 1997, p.66–88.

Ndubisi, F. 2002. *Ecological Planning: A historical and comparative synthesis.* Baltimore: Johns Hopkins University Press.

Rowe, P.G. 1995. *Design thinking*. Cambridge: MIT Press.

Scott Brown, D. 1977. Suburban Space, Scale and Symbols. *Via*, 1977 no.3. p. 41–47.

Swaffield, S.R. 2006. Theory and Critique in Landscape Architecture: Making Connections. *Journal of Landscape Architecture*, 2006, Vol. 1, p.22–29.

Swaffield, S. 2002. *Theory in Landscape Architecture: A reader*. Philadelphia: University of Pennsylvania Press.

Thompson, B. 2005. Landscape architecture: A terminal case? *Landscape Architecture*, April 2005, p.26–45.

Thompson, I. 1993. Landscape Design: signposts to a post-modern future? *Landscape Research*, 1993, Vol. 18 No. 3 p.122–129.

Treib, M. & Imbert, D. 1997. *Garrett Eckbo: Modern Landscapes for Living*. Berkley: University of California Press.

Treib, M. 2005. *Settings and stray paths: Writings on landscapes and gardens*. New York: Routledge.

Veseley, D. 1984. Architecture and the Conflict of Representation. *AA Files* no. 8. London: Architectural Association.

Waldheim, C. 2006. *The landscape urbanism reader*. New York: Princeton Architectural Press.

Wareham, A. 2005. Where have all the critics gone? In *Vista: The Culture and Politics of Gardens*. N. Kingsbury & T. Richardson (eds). Francis Lincoln Limited:181–188.

chapter 15

Landscape as Narrative, Expressed through the Landscape Design at the Freedom Park, Tshwane, South Africa

Graham Young

Department of Architecture

University of Pretoria

Pretoria

South Africa

Introduction

It takes time to know a place and its stories.[1]

We Africans are people of stories! In the past, it was through traditional tales that history and cultural meaning were passed down orally from one generation to the next.

South Africa has a story to tell! An incredibly meaningful story about how the country took its 'long walk to freedom'[2]. While the 20th century appeared to be closing much in the same way that it began – characterised by hostility and disruption – a new era was beginning at the tip of Africa away from the public glare. Unfolding were the delicate and surreptitious beginnings of negotiation. Challenged by a need for peace, South Africa's former enemies exchanged war and violence for truth and reconciliation, in a process that is an inspiration for the resolutions of conflicts across the world. Humanity had finally prevailed. With this triumph, new challenges have emerged and new heroes and heroines raised to inspire South Africans to achieve even greater heights.[3]

To tell this story of emancipation, the National Government mandated through an act of parliament that a place, a monument, be built[4]. Freedom Park Trust (FPT) was tasked with managing the process and a design team[5] was appointed to conceive of and guide the implementation of the project that would be built on a hill in Tshwane.

To begin with, the place (the site) already had a story; its geology, ecology and cultural histories all had their own narratives, waiting to be told[6]. Understanding the site from these perspectives is easy. But, the story that Freedom Park would tell had to come from the nation and this would be more difficult because of South Africa's diverse and multifaceted society.

Figure 1: Freedom Park seen from the Union Buildings across the valley from it

In its attempt to solicit the story, the FPT started the process of accessing the public's notion of what Freedom Park should become. Research took place, public focus group workshops were held and extensive consultation with artists, historians, academics and a variety of rural and urban communities was carried out. Through this process the framework for the story began to materialise in 2002. This was a multifaceted and tedious process[7] fraught with many political, cultural and religious issues but FPT 'stayed the course' and the outline for the narrative began to come to light.

'Freedom Park is about you and me – it is about the South African tale in the voice of the South African people. Using our unique culture, heritage, history and spirituality, Freedom Park tells the nation's stories. It honours the efforts of our heroes and heroines who died in the struggles for humanity and freedom'.[8] Freedom Park is to tell this story through the lens of 'South Africa's pre-colonial, colonial, apartheid and post-apartheid history dating back 3.6 billion years.'[9] An ambitious undertaking indeed.

The concept has acquired different meanings for different peoples and has a myriad of connotations, not the least freedom from political oppression that stemmed from the colonial and apartheid eras. Former President Thabo Mbeki cautioned against people regarding Freedom Park in this narrow sense. 'History,' he said, 'is full of epochs and endeavours to free humanity from the constraints of nature, from socio-economic backwardness and political oppression. Many technological advances have been made over thousands of years so that humanity can be freed from poverty, under-development and illness. It is in this context that we see Freedom Park. In the narrow sense of the word Freedom Park would refer only to political freedom and therefore, be only a symbol of acknowledgement of the heroes and heroines of our struggle for freedom. In the broad sense of the word, we are dealing with freedom from the adverse impact of the forces of nature, freedom that comes with technological revolution, freedom occasioned by socio-economic factors, and freedom from political oppression, ensuring that the body, the mind and the soul have been freed to fulfill themselves.'[10]

It is, however, in the retelling of the South African story that originated with a mandate by President Nelson Mandela[11] and which was also the natural outcome of the Truth and Reconciliation Commission process that the focus of the narrative for Freedom Park came about. It was necessary to retell the story because, 'for centuries, many myths and injustices have hidden [it's] true history.'[12]

Background

This essay proceeds from the premise that 'narrative[13] is a fundamental way people shape and make sense of experience and landscapes. Stories link the sense of time, event, experience, memory and other intangibles to the more tangible aspects of place. Because stories sequence and configure experience of place into meaningful relationships, narrative offers ways of knowing and shaping landscapes not typically acknowledged in conventional documentation mapping, surveys, or even the formal concerns of design.'[14]

In recent years, the ongoing debate among many landscape architects in understanding narrative practices and imbuing meaning

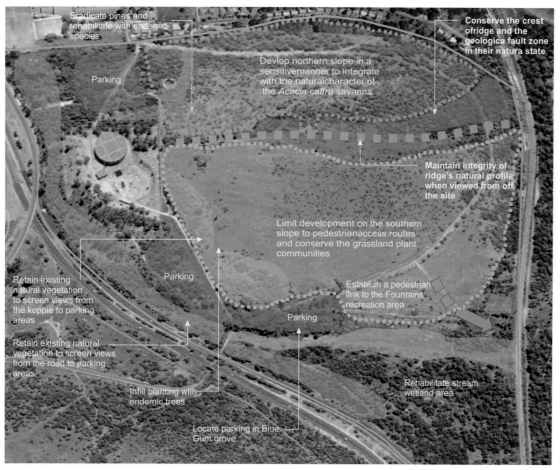

Figure labels (within image):

Eradicate pines and rehabilitate with endemic species

Parking

Devlop northern slope in a sensitivemanner to integrate with the naturalcharacter of the *Acacia caffra* savanna

Conserve the crest ofridge and the geologica fault zone in their natura state

Maintain integrity of ridge's natural profile when viewed from off the site

Retain existing natural vegetation to screen views from the koppie to parking areas

Parking

Limit development on the southern slope to pedestrianaccess routes and conserve the grassland plant communities

Establish a pedestrian link to the Fountains recreation area

Retain existing natural vegetation to screen views from the road to parking areas

Parking

Infill planting with endemic trees

Rehabilitate stream wetland area

Locate parking in Blue Gum grove

Figure 2: Landscape development concept

Salvokop's natural system

♦ The quartzite ridges of Gauteng are regarded as one of the most omportant natural assets in the entire region of the northern provinces of South Africa

♦ They are characterized by a unique plant species composition that is found nowhere else in South Africa or the world

♦ Salvokop is one of these most valuable natural systems and is a biodiversity treasure

♦ The general ecological sensitivity of Salvokop is very high

♦ It is important to conserve as much of the koppie in its natural state and that any development that takes place should be of low impact

by design has emphasised and focused attention on the uniqueness of the landscape as a medium to effectively express narrative. 'Landscape as a subject, a medium, and an inquiry [is] no longer marginal, but central to contemporary cultural debates and concerns.'[15]

Given this opinion it seems proper that this uniquely South African story, or at least aspects of it, could effectively be told through the medium of landscape. And that landscape architects, whose language, subject and canvas is the landscape, along with architects and artists could design a place that operates as a 'focusing lens' for discovering and knowing the meaning behind the place. And if this could successfully be done, would the experience of visiting Freedom Park ultimately lead to reducing perceptual and emotional barriers so that it could act as a catalyst for 'healing, reconciliation and nation building'? As a 'cultural' story the narrative expressed at Freedom Park is a critical component of the contemporary South African discourse concerning the issues of nationhood, national values, truth and reconciliation, equality and development and the beginnings of a collective vision for the future.

Narrative and attempts to instill designs with significance or meaning are an increasingly common intention in contemporary landscape design. This essay will examine this and the issues raised in this discussion through the description of a variety of landscape narrative types as expressed in The Garden of Remembrance, *Vhuwaelo, Isivivane,* and

Figure 3: Salvokop before the development of Freedom Park within its Pretoria context

S'kumbuto[16] and will present the strategies used to express the narrative through the medium of landscape. But first it will briefly discuss meaning, narrative theory and practices that formed the framework within which the landscape design took place.

Meaning

We live within the world of stories, and we use stories to shape those worlds. In history, fiction, lived experience, myth or anecdote, stories tell of origins, explain causes, mark the boundaries of what is knowable and explore the territories beyond. As we remember, interpret, plan and dream through stories they give form to the transience of experience.[17]

Whether they come as the sound of dogs at night or a human voice at the threshold of sleep, recollected from memory or read from the marks on a page, a picture, or a landscape, stories are only knowable through some form of communication.[18]

Communications theory tells us that the two parties in conversation must share a common semantic channel or there will not be communication; no meaning. Can the [place] operate as such a channel and does the designer possess the power to create significant landscape, especially given the multitude of communications channels in today's pluralistic world?[19]

But how can the South African story be told in a society so diverse and fraught with so many different and conflicting political agendas? Is it not easier to tell a story

when a society is relatively homogenised, because the designer shares the values and belief system of the people? Folk cultures produce places that are almost immediately communicative and

communicative over long periods. Because their connections between form and intention are understood within the culture and evolve slowly over time, it is possible for the makers, the people, and the meaning of place to remain in contact.[20]

Given our fractured past, the disjointed nature of South African society and the fading of the Rainbow Nation[21], the unity or homogeneity necessary for instant meaning is deficient, to say the least.

But even if it is possible to tell the story and tell it through the medium of landscape, is it possible to instill a place with meaning from the outset? Treib asks 'Can a [landscape] designer help make a significant place?' 'Yes ,' he replies. Then he asks 'Can a [landscape] designer design significance into a place at the time of its realisation?' He answers 'No, or let's say no longer'. He goes on to say 'If the society was homogeneous and shared a common system of belief, when the symbolic system was endemic, when the makers of places operated unselfconsciously fully within the culture, it was possible. But even then, meaning was enriched through habit and the passage of time.'[22]

With these issues in mind, Treib[23] again challenges:

Since the commissioning body might include meaningfulness as part of the brief, why commission a [landscape] designer? Of course, there are pragmatic aspects of design that can best be addressed by those with an education, technical knowledge, and experience. One also hopes that the landscape architect possesses equal skill in understanding people and culture, as well as horticulture and form. Creating significant landscapes remains a quest of the profession, as well it should. Providing [only] symbols is not

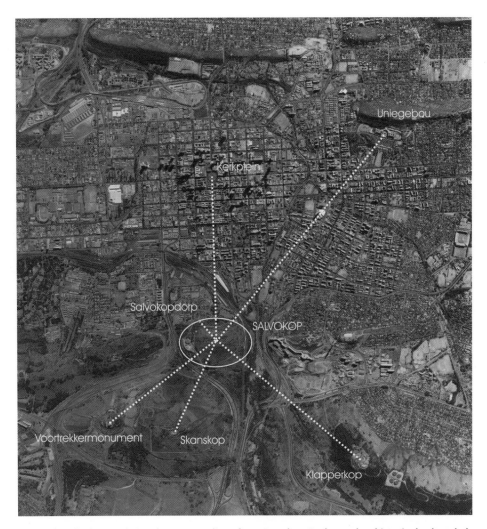

Figure 4: Salvokop and visual connector lines from Freedom Park to other historical cultural elements in the city

the same as creating meaningful places, although it may be one point along the path. To my mind, significance lies with the beholder and not alone in place. Meaning accrues over time; like respect, it is earned, not granted. Meaning condenses at the intersection of people and place, and not alone in the form the designer's idea takes.[24]

The design, however, is the filter through which the visitor experiences the place and 'while this transaction between people and place is never completely symmetrical', Treib believes that we can 'circumscribe the range of possible reactions to a designed place'.[25] The implication is that the landscape designer cannot make a place mean, but he can, perhaps, stimulate reactions (emotions) to that place, which fall within the desired limits of the intended (or wished for) reaction to the place. Feelings of happiness, sadness, joy, contemplation or delight!

Treib concludes:

Significance, I believe, is not a designer's construct that benignly accompanies the completion of construction. It is not the product of the maker, but is, instead, created by the receivers. Like a patina, significance is acquired only with time. And like a patina, it emerges only if the conditions are right.[26]

So, is it really possible to build into landscape architecture a semantic dimension that communicates the maker's intention to the inhabitant? In attempting to answer this and to define meaning Treib suggests two categories he had once proposed in discussing the idea of formalism in the landscape.[27] The first, trace, is the unintentional marking or making of space through use. The second, intent, concerns the conscious spatial definition and/or construction that considers dimensions beyond that of functions; that is, the semantic as well as the syntactic aspects of landscape design.

What is narrative?

Narrative refers to the story, what is told, and the means of telling it, implying both product and process. Narrative is thus a more comprehensive and inclusive term than story. 'While every story is a narrative, not every narrative necessarily meets the conventional notions of a story as a well-wrought tale plotted with a sense of clear beginning, middle, and end.'[28] 'A narrative may be as simple as a sentence, "I went down to the crossroads," or as extensive and complex as the notion of progress. Beyond conscious awareness or inherent in daily actions, it may be as mundane, varied, scripted, or open-ended as our own lives.'[29]

Coming from the Latin *gnarus* and Indo-European root *gna,* 'to know', narrative implies knowledge acquired through actions and contingencies of lived experience.[30]

Narratives are there in landscapes.

Narratives intersect with site, accumulate as layers of history, organise sequences, and inhere in the materials and processes of the landscape. In various ways, stories "take place". The term landscape narrative designates the interplay and mutual relationship that develops between landscape and narrative. To begin with, places configure narratives. Landscape not only locates or serves as background setting for stories, but is itself a changing, eventful figure that engenders stories. In turn, every narrative, even the most abstract, allegorical or personal, plays a critical role in making places. It is through narrative that we interpret the processes and events of a place. We come to know a place because we know its stories.[31]

Landscape narrative

To conceive of landscape narratives means linking what is often treated as a material or visual scene with the less tangible, but not less real, network of narratives. Working within this narrative realm provides access to experience, knowledge, contingencies of time and other aspects of landscapes not available through other means. In turn, working with landscapes offers the potential for unique narrative forms: spatial stories, continuous narratives, or the anchoring of memories and history to sites. Landscape joins with a very human capacity and penchant for telling stories. For the designer then, it is a matter of not only learning how to tell stories in landscapes but developing a critical awareness of the processes and implications of narrative: whose story is told and what values and beliefs inhere in the telling?[32]

Strategies for designing place and story

Potteiger and Purington (1998) put forward five strategies for interpreting landscapes and for telling stories through the medium of landscape design.

Naming is the way that stories are anchored to place. Names are abbreviated stories of discovery, biography, and identity. Sequencing the ordering of names, trees, paths, and other elements, events and characters, structures meaning, for every part is understood in terms of what comes before and what follows. Concealing and revealing information, whether in a decipherable sequence or all at once, creates drama, suspense or surprise that engages the reader with a story. Narratives are also a way of gathering or drawing together broader experience into a tangible and cohesive place. Finally, opening involves ways of creating places responsive to cultural and natural process.[33]

Narrative practices

Unlike verbal narratives, spatial narratives are silent but persistent. With few protocols for reading a landscape from left to right or front to back, the viewer enters at different points, is free to pause to take in the whole image, inspect its parts, or review. This changes the traditional relationship between author, text, and reader where the author exerts control of the telling. Instead, the spatial narrative is more about showing, relinquishing control to the viewer who must put together the sequences, fill the gaps, and decipher the meaning.[34] And since most landscapes are shaped by environmental and cultural processes, they do not have an author or a narrator. This means that the viewer must find the stories and become the narrator.

Potteiger and Purington[35] suggest that there are nine main forms of landscape narratives. The essay will discuss four of these with reference to elements at Freedom Park:

◆ Associations and references – elements in the landscape that become connected with experience, event, history, religious allegory or other forms of narrative
◆ Narrative as form generator – using stories as a means of giving order (selecting, sequencing, etc.) or developing images in the design process. It is not necessary that the story be explicitly legible in the final design form
◆ Storytelling landscapes – places designed to tell specific stories with explicit references to plot, scenes, events, character, etc. The stories may be either existing literary or cultural narratives or produced by the designer
◆ And memory landscapes – places that serve as the tangible locus of memory, both public and personal. This may develop through implicit association or by international acts of remembering: e.g. monuments, museums, preserved buildings, districts and regions.[36]

Garden of Remembrance: Association and reference narrative

It is in the narrative, the story (content) and it's telling (expression), that the 52ha Freedom Park (Figure 1) retells the cultural tale of South Africa's various and diverse communities by

rediscovering their history, retelling their stories, healing the wounds of the past and looking toward a progressive, united future. The objective of the Freedom Park Trust is to unite all cultural groups, realising that all cultures have a meaningful and important role to play in nation building. Thus Freedom Park will stand as a monument with which all South Africans can identify.[37]

The plot of the cultural narrative (in this case reference is made to the narrative form of associations and references) starts by making reference to the natural processes and restoring the semblance of an original natural order to the site. Although the site was relatively healthy it had been impacted with pine and blue gum plantations and the aggressive invasion of weeds. Parts of the ridge line and aspects of the northern and southern slopes, however, remained in relatively good condition.

In fact, quartzite ridges, of which the Freedom Park site is one, are regarded as being of the most important natural assets in the entire region. And according to Prof. George Bredenkamp[38] at the University of Pretoria (Botany Department), these ridges are characterised by a unique plant species composition that is found nowhere else in South Africa or the world. Since these ridges are considered to be transitional between the grassland and the savanna biomes, floristic elements from both these biomes contribute to the floristic richness of the quartzite ridges. Its conservation would therefore promote ecological processes and benefit regional and local biodiversity. The general ecological sensitivity of Salvokop, the site of Freedom Park, is high and it was important to conserve, restore and regenerate as much of the koppie in its natural state as is possible, specifically the quartzite ridge line, and locate development away from sensitive areas.

Healing, then, is one of the key metaphors which structure the plot of Freedom Park at many levels. Because the broad thematic narrative for the site is also derived from Indigenous Knowledge Systems (IKS)[39] and *Ubuntu*[40] points of view, it was imperative for the designers to understand the entire site as, 'the garden', or as it is named The Garden of Remembrance. It is within this garden, the greater garden, the collective[41], that other gardens or elements occur but always with reference back to 'the garden', (the collective that is Freedom Park) their importance confirmed because of their relationship to the garden; the healthy garden, the whole garden. Thus The Garden of Remembrance is symbolic and makes associations and references to *Ubuntu* and the aspirations

Figure 5: Concept sketch of Vhuwaelo (spiral path) (NBGM Landscape Architecture Joint Venture)

of Freedom Park, that it be a place for 'healing the wounds of the past and looking toward a progressive, united future for the country'. The landscape (the garden) is then the medium through which the stories of Freedom Park are told and which provides clues to the selection of materials (plants, minerals, water and rocks). It also provides cues and guides design interventions about the site.

The Freedom Park story therefore begins with the reading of the existing ecological narrative and 'letting the site reveal itself'. An ecological analysis was commissioned which led to the mapping of the site into sensitivity zones. Architectural and landscape interventions were then planned to avoid the sensitive areas (Figure 2). And the most disturbed areas were to be the sites where major interventions took place. S'kumbuto[42] (the memorial) was located along the ridge in a previously disturbed area and to avoid the remains of an old stone fort, while //hapo[43] was located at the bottom of the hill immediately adjacent to Salvokop Village where the impact of alien vegetation was taking hold.

Figure 6: Design team and IKS and tradition healer advisors discussing the location of Isivivane

The landscape design retells the site's ecology by re-establishing the structural combination and health of the various plant communities. In disturbed areas and sites damaged by new construction, activities indigenous grass species and other pioneer species were planted, to 'kick-start' the succession process that would ultimately lead to a naturally functioning and healthy ecosystem. The various plant communities and their relative state of 'wholeness' also become a metaphor of different times in South Africa's history and progress to freedom; some reflecting scars of the past, others in the early stages of recuperation and yet others where healing has taken place and are strong, fit and vigorous in their growth. These are the communities that can withstand the 'fires of adversity' that from time to time will try to overwhelm them. Only indigenous species are used on the site because they are most suited to long term survival and ecological

Figure 7: Entrance to Isivivane *with is material choice and stone walls making reference to Great Zimbabwe and* Thulamela

health – again a metaphor that 'Africa's problems need African (local) solutions'. The pathway system or spiral path that winds its way up the hill will pass through most of these plant communities and discrete design devices will structure ways of reading the landscape through strategically placed signs that elaborate on the ecological and/or cultural significance of the plants. Meanwhile, the landscape is in the process, (like the Nation), of becoming an integrated, complex, and diverse evolving narrative of ecological time signifying health and long term sustainability.

The hill itself also has cultural meaning. The location of Freedom Park on a hill has symbolic importance as well as historical and cultural significance (Figure 3). For instance, the Voortrekker Monument is located opposite Freedom Park to juxtapose the past with the processes of moving forward.[44] The crest of the hill also offers open views to Church Square, the Union Buildings, Klapperkop, Skanskop and locally, to Salvokop Village which lies at the northern base of the hill. These view lines serve as important 'connectors' to the past and future (i.e. Union Buildings now signifying the hope of our new democracy) and have been emphasised in the development framework for the site (Figure 4).

In African culture high ground on a rock symbolises many things.

Essentially, the rock is our home – African people used to live in mountains where they constantly listened to the voice of silence. Mountains and hills served as a seat of governance for many of the royal kraals. Mountains were considered sacred by some groups who used to go to the mountains to pray for rain, or to bury kings on rocks or in caves in the mountains, thus believing that ancestors resided there – a step to the heavens and to our humanity.[45]

The choice of a hill for Freedom Park can therefore also be seen as having symbolic meaning.

Constituted by boulders, plants, soil and water, the garden will represent a home founded on solid rock and its spirit flows and cleanses like water.[46]

Vhuwaelo: Narrative as form generator

Narrative as form generator can be illustrated through *Vhuwaelo*.[47] It is a wooded decked pathway system (or spiral path) that winds its way up the hill to allow for universal access.[48] It traces the land's natural and cultural histories to develop a connection between the viewer and both the constructed places and natural spaces through which he passes.

The spiral pathway is therefore seen as a connector of ideas along which a symbolic narrative is to be expressed and played out. The spiral pathway forms the basic infrastructure required to achieve the interpretative objectives as stated in the landscape development framework.[49] Interpretation is the 'communication path' that connects visitors with the natural and cultural resources (e.g. ecology, geology, myths, belief systems and the use of plants for medicinal purposes) of the site. Good interpretation is a bridge leading people into new and fascinating worlds. It brings new understanding, new insights, new enthusiasms and new interests.

Figure 8: Isivivane *during a cultural celebration in the early morning*

Anchoring The Garden of Remembrance is this pathway system with 'contemplative spaces' attached to it. These are small natural spaces placed discreetly into the landscape where the visitor can sit and become 'immersed' in the landscape away from the general activities of the park. These spaces along with the spiral pathway system are referred to as *Vhuwaelo*, which is the connector of ideas along which the narrative is to be expressed and played out. It also forms the basic infrastructure required to achieve the interpretative objectives stated above. The belief is

Figure 9: **Isivivane** *boulders enveloped in mist,* *symbolic of* impepho

that by encouraging an awareness of Salvokop's natural and cultural environment, values are taught.

The gently sloping pathway winds its way up the hill from a position near //hapo on the north side of the hill, where it intersects with the extension of Paul Kruger Street – designated as a 'high street' in the Salvokop Urban Design Framework. This entrance, through //hapo will become the main access point to the site and will ultimately connect, via pedestrian walkways, to Pretoria Station and the proposed Gautrain Station north of the site.

After much debate and consultation between the design team and the advisory panel it was agreed that the spiral pathway (Figure 5) originally designed to move up the hill in a westerly direction, would be routed in an easterly direction. East is significant because it is here the sun rises, marking the beginning of a new day – and metaphorically, new beginnings in the history of South Africa. The pathway winds its way up the eastern slope through thick wooded savannah. The experience of walking through dense bush will evoke a sense of mystery and be a reminder of the difficult combative times during previous eras.

Upon leaving the 'forest', the visitor enters a small opening defined by two parallel quartzite ridge lines. Here the landscape is characterised by natural rock outcrops, stunted vegetation and fascinating endemic plants. An intimate space naturally occurs here in this sensitive environment. In early discussions about the significance of this place[50] (Figure 6) it was suggested that a small 'shrine' would be incorporated as a place for burning *impepho* (incense)[51] and in the African tradition and on special occasions, *umqombothi* (traditional beer) would also be drunk here. On leaving this place, the pathway descends gently to reach the first of a series of memorial spaces, *Isivivane*.

Figure 10: *Paying her respects at* Lesaka *the spiritual centre and burial place at* Isivivane *(left)*

Figure 11: *One of the two waterfalls at* Isivivane *symbolising cleansing and healing (right)*

Isivivane: Storytelling landscape

Isivivane is essentially a storytelling place. It is a refuge, with a narrative that expresses the 'final resting place for all the people who fell in the fight for freedom in the eight conflict events, which eventually shaped South Africa.'[52] *Isivivane* roughly means 'cairn of stones' but its deeper meaning is 'monument', 'memorial', 'testimonial', as well as 'fervour, concentration of energy and commitment to solidarity and oneness of purpose'[53].

The place has been designed primarily with deference to African symbolism and belief systems but also, intentionally contains universally recognisable symbols. During the design process, it was agreed that symbolism was not to be translated literally but rather that it remained abstract, simple and devoid of clutter. By doing this it was felt the ensuing aesthetic would be powerful and evoke strong emotions. When entering the contemplative place (Figure 7), visitors should experience a sense of the reverence for the place. Stone, water and the prudent use of plant materials formed the basic design elements. The location of *Isivivane* at the far south-eastern section of the hill is also significant as it is here (the place designated by the traditional healers) that it will 're- ceive the rising sun throughout all seasons of the year'.

Stones and boulders have special significance in African cosmol- ogy. They represent mountains and caves, which served as the people's shelter and places of safety, as well as shrines for ances- tral devotion. In ancient times, mighty people were buried on the rocks in the mountains. In modern practice, a tombstone, *letlapa*, is used to create protection believed to serve as a home for the deceased.[54] Rocks are considered sacred as, according to Credo Mutwa, they are the stones and bones of the earth and some of the mountains are identified as places where the gods reside. Because they are timeless and ancient, because they have been here long before us, they carry sacred networks of information.[55] For these reasons *Isivivane* is considered a symbolic 'resting' or 'burial' place.

The fundamental concept for the layout of *Isivivane* is that of an African 'homestead' encompassing the *Lesaka* (burial place) and the *Kgotla* (meeting place).

The *Lesaka* in African culture, 'is a circular structure commonly found in southern African villages where generation upon genera- tion are buried',[56] it is a place where the spirits of those who have fallen in the struggle for freedom over time, can come home to rest. It is built out of stone and comprises nine boulders, one from each province,[57] placed near the edge of a circle. Balancing these, are two larger boulders completing the circle. One boulder rep- resents the national government and the other the international community. Contained within the boulders circle are the stones that have come from countries outside South Africa – symbolic of combatants and exiles that fell while they sought refuge in inter- national countries. The circular pattern is all-important. It is sym- bolic of unity and equality and being placed in a circle at the same level, the boulders engage in a 'dialogue' (Figure 8).

Figure 12: S'kumbuto *built into the ridge of the hill is Freedom Park's main memorial place (top)*

Figure 13: Wall of Names, one of the main elements of S'kumbuto, *which commemorates those who died in the struggle for freedom (bottom)*

A fine water spray has been designed into *Lesaka*. A mist will raise up from the stone floor to eventually envelop the boulders (Figure 9). The significance of this smoke or *im-pepho* is to emphasise the sanctity of the place and to be representative of the cleansing and healing process central to helping the South African nation heal from its past. The spiritual (Figure 10) and ancestral significance of the *Lesaka* is captured in the words of a Venda elder, which will be installed at the entrance to *Isivivane*.[58]

Figure 14: Amphitheatre and Sanctuary at S'kumbuto

Near *Lesaka*, also on the terrace, a lone tree was planted in the middle of a circular bench. It is an *Acacia galpinii* (*Mologa* or monkey thorn) symbolic of *'lekgotla'.* [59] It will provide dense shade in the summer months and cover for visitors who wish to rest and reflect on the place and the meaning of the *Isivivane*. The bench is orientated with a beautiful view across *Lesaka* to the natural valley and hills south of the site.

A symbolic reference to African culture and the spiritual bond that formed between the Nguni people and the *Ziziphus mucronata* inspired the choice of nine buffalo thorn trees that form a green backdrop to *Isivivane*. In earlier times when a person died far away from home (often in battle) the elders of the family would send a party to 'fetch the spirit'. Branches from the *hlahlankosi* or buffalo thorn tree were used for this ceremony. The party would carry a branch from the tree and at the spot where the person had died would call out the name of the dead person and announce that they had come to take his spirit home.[60]

Another of the interpretations of *Isivivane* is that of 'paying homage to the hospitality of place'. This is represented by a cairn of stones often found in the countryside near a village and adjacent to a footpath. When African people passed a village but could not go into it, they indicated that they had passed the place by picking up a stone, bringing it to their mouth and breathing on it, then placing it on the heap of stones. This accumulated mound of stones, called *Isivivane,* was believed to bring good luck by travellers paying homage to the landscape and all that it contained.[61] An abstraction of this idea is captured in the sloping packed-stone wall, which has been formed between the main terrace and the spiral pathway.

To further capture the essence of the Garden of Remembrance being 'a home founded on solid rock' and where 'its spirit flows and cleanses like water' two waterfalls have been designed into the stone-packed walls near *Lesaka*, beneath some buffalo thorn trees and above the spiral path. Water flows over troughs and down stone pitched walls and into shallow pools, to create an ambience that would, perhaps subconsciously, remind the visitor that in this place 'the spirit flows and cleanses like water' (Figure 11).

Finally, to complete the experience of visiting the *Isivivane*, a small 'spring' of water emanating from a bowl carved into the top of a large boulder placed near the exit to the space, acts as a basin in which visitors can wash their hands in respect after paying homage to the spirits of those people who have fought and died for the freedom of South Africa.

S'kumbuto: Memory landscape

S'kumbuto[62] is located at the top of the hill comprising a number of elements that together form the main memorial space of Freedom Park (Figure 12). It contains the Wall of Names, an amphitheatre, the Sanctuary and the Gallery of Leaders.

The Wall of Names is divided into eight sections (Figure 13), each representing a different conflicting event and epoch in the history of South Africa. These are the Pre-colonial Wars, Genocide, Slavery, Wars of Resistance, South African, World War 1, World War 2 and the Liberation Struggle. These walls are arranged on the southern side as one enters the *S'khumbuto* from the spiral path. Walls start at a height of approximately 1m. As one gets closer to the turning point to enter *S'khumbuto*, the walls rise significantly and 'push in' on the visitor. The narrowing of this space creates

Figure 15: The Reeds designed as a rising line that emphasises and is symbolic of the intensity of the fight for freedom

a sense of acceleration, symbolising a growth in tension and conflict before the visitor reaches the 'apex' or turning point, which relates to the 1994 inauguaration of President Nelson Mandela and the dawning of a new democracy. At this point the visitor move out of the tight space into the light with a focus on vast views over the city and some of its significant landmarks, such as the Union Buildings. On the northern side of *S'khumbuto* the Sanctuary emerges out of the landscape with the amphitheatre flowing onto its roof.

Water plays an important figurative role as both cleanser and source of life. The sanctuary thus 'sits' in a reflective pond, with an eternal flame burning inside (Figure 14). From the Sanctuary space a narrow passage, flanked with high stone walls not unlike those found in Great Zimbabwe, leads into a beautiful indoor space behind and underneath the amphitheatre forming the western flank of *S'khumbuto*. This space is reserved for the commemoration of significant leaders or heroes of the struggle.

S'khumbuto appears to grow out of the hilltop and a concerted effort was made to keep the profile of the hilltop intact. High brushed stainless steel poles, the Reeds, with white lights on top are an integral component of *S'kumbuto* and provide a strong rising sculptural arc (Figure 15) that emphasises a rising line representative of the intensity of the fight for freedom. Inspiration for the concept of the Reeds to demarcate *S'khumbuto* was obtained from the traditional use of reeds or sticks originally used to define a place and provide enclosures to Zulu homesteads. Reeds are also widely used during traditional African rituals. These strong vertical elements symbolise the connection between earth and heaven; between the nation and spirits of people that have sacrificed their lives. The rising line of reeds finally terminates high on the hill to signify the triumphant struggle for freedom. And when the reeds are at their tallest, they open up and 'move to the future' with enthusiasm and energy.[63] They also point to the north, to the rest of Africa, with reference to the African Renaissance as articulated by former President Thabo Mbeki in a speech to the nation and the world[64].

Conclusion

A walk through Freedom Park weaves the story of where we come from and the historical and cultural events that shaped South Africa. Ultimately, all South Africans have suffered the consequences and have been victims of an unjust past. The deep wounds uncovered by the Truth and Reconciliation Commission remain, unfortunately, as the scar tissue that forms the fibre of South African society today. Former president, Thabo Mbeki, hailed Freedom Park as 'an island of peace that invites one to reflect and contemplate'. A visit to the park is a liberating, spiritually enriching and inspirational experience: a pilgrimage to dispel the myths and prejudices that have concealed and distorted the image and achievements of South Africans throughout the ages. Freedom Park integrates history, culture and spirituality, making it a must see heritage attraction for South Africans and international visitors alike.[65]

In telling this South African story at Freedom Park and by applying landscape narrative as the main ordering and referencing device, the landscape design straddles the line between conception and reception, controlling and initiating. The design process has anticipated the audience's reactions, perceptions and experiences of place such that the landscape with its natural and cultural references become more visible, tangible and palpable, giving form to an experience that aesthetically engages visitors. A landscape which tells stories within stories and through its spatial narrative 'offers distinct opportunities for different forms of narratives such as the gathering of past and present into a synoptic view, parallel or intersecting story lines, collages that create non-linear associations, multiple layers of stories and narratives open to participants.'[66]

1   Potteiger, Matthew and Purington, Jamie. 1998. *Landscape narrative, design practices for telling stories*. New York: John Wiley and Sons Inc:vii.

2   Reference to President Nelson Mandela's autobiography: Mandela, N. *A Long Walk to Freedom*, Macdonald Prunell, Cape Town, 1995.

3   This is derived from a pamphlet distributed by Freedom Park to explain the purpose of the project, location and the principles of its design. The piece describes the first, tentative negotiations between the ANC and the National Party, which first took place outside South Africa in Angola. Some discussions had even begun with Nelson Mandela while he was in jail.

4   Soon after the democratic elections of 1994, the office of the President was being inundated with requests from diverse sources for official approval for the development of monuments and museums and for the commemoration of historic events and important leaders. Almost all the requests came from communities, leaders and individuals whose heritage was neglected during the previous political dispensation in the country. Notably, the requests came from women, sections of the black community and non-racial progressive organisations in South Africa. Clearly, the diversity of requests received, with their overlaps, different representations and multiple perspectives of our heritage, called for a coherent set of principles and criteria to harmonise these initiatives. Cabinet therefore approved the establishment of the Legacy Project as a mechanism to establish commemorative structures that will be based upon a coherent set of principles and criteria. The Legacy Project principles were developed taking into consideration the need for redress, consultation with affected parties, environmental sensitivity and linking heritage with economic development. In essence the Legacy Project sought to maintain coherence in aligning the resources and expertise of government to establish a system to acknowledge and honour a largely neglected part of South Africa's inheritance. At the same time it sought to change the nature of commemoration by making spaces that are people friendly, functional and accessible. As a Legacy Project the Freedom Park development process was initiated by the Department of Arts and Culture and the Freedom Park Trust was established to be the implementing agent. Freedom Park was legislated by the *National Heritage Act,* No 25 of 1999 Section 7.1 (a). Freedom Park should be classified as a 'Grade 1 Project because it is a heritage resource with qualities so exceptional that they are of special national significance'. From an article by G.A. Young translated by S. le Roux, which first appeared in *Beeld Newspaper* – April 2004.

5   The team comprised landscape architects (NBGM Landscape Architects), architects (OCA Architects) and artists who worked in conjunction with traditional healers, academics, historians and poets to conceptualise the project.

6   Narratives are already *implicit* to landscapes, inscribed by natural processes and cultural practices. Rakatansky, M. 1992. 'Spatial narratives'. In J. Whiteman, J. Kipnis and R. Burdett [eds]. *Strategies in architectural thinking*. Chicago Institute for Architecture and Urbanism and MIT Press, Chicago and Cambridge. pp.201–221 in Potteiger, Matthew and Purington, Jamie, 1998. *Landscape narrative, design practices for telling stories*, John Wiley and Sons Inc, New York:19.

7   The process has in fact not stopped. It was and is ongoing in its refinement for the various elements that make up Freedom park and //hapo (the museum) which will be completed in 2011.

8   The Freedom Park Trust, undated promotional pamphlet that explains Freedom Park.

9   The Freedom Park Trust. *A Heritage Site for Reconciliation, Humanity and Freedom in South Africa,* The Freedom Park Trust, Tshwane, undated:2

10 Statement by the President of South Africa at the launch of Freedom Park in 2002 in The Freedom Park Trust, *A Heritage Site for Reconciliation, Humanity and Freedom in South Africa,* The Freedom Park Trust, Tshwane, undated:3.

11 It originated in President Nelson Mandela's speech at the Freedom Day Celebrations, Umtata, 27 April 1999 when he stated 'the day should not be far off, when we shall have a people's shrine, a Freedom Park, where we shall honour with all the dignity they deserve, those who endured pain so we should experience the joy of Freedom.'

12 The Freedom Park Trust. *A Heritage Site for Reconciliation, Humanity and Freedom in South Africa,* The Freedom Park Trust, Tshwane, undated:2.

13 *Narrative* refers to both the 'story', what is told, (i.e. the content – events, characters, setting) and the means of 'telling the story' (i.e. the expression – structure/manifestation in this chase, the landscape). from Potteiger, Matthew and Purington, Jamie; *Landscape narrative, design practices for telling stories*, John Wiley and Sons Inc, New York, c. 1998:3.

14 Potteiger, Matthew and Purington, Jamie. 1998. *Landscape narrative, design practices for telling stories*, John Wiley and Sons Inc, New York:ix.

15 Meyer, E. 2000. *The post earth day conundrum: translating environmental values into landscape design,* in Conan, M. [ed]. 2000. *Environmentalism in Landscape Architecture*, Dumbarton Oaks, Washington, DC:191.

16 These are not all the main elements: in totality Freedom Park comprises The Garden of Remembrance, *Isivivane, S'kumbuto* (comprising the Wall of Names, Amphitheatre, Sanctuary, Eternal Flame, Gallery of Leaders and the Reeds), *Tiva* (a large body of water), *//hapo, Moshate* (a hospitality suite for high level delegates), The Pan African Archives and Uitspanplek.

17 Potteiger, Matthew and Purington, Jamie. 1998. *Landscape narrative, design practices for telling stories*, John Wiley and Sons Inc, New York:3.

18 Ibid.:3

19 Treib, M. 1995. Must landscape mean?' in Swaffield, S. [ed]. *Theory in Landscape Architecture – A reader*, University of Pennsylvania Press, Philadelphia, 2002:98.

20 Treib, M. 1995. Must landscape mean?' in Swaffield, S. [ed]. *Theory in Landscape Architecture – A reader*, University of Pennsylvania Press, Philadelphia, 2002:99.

21 Archibishop Desmond Tutu coined the phrase soon after the emergence of the 'new' South Africa in 1994 with the inauguration of President Nelson Mandela. He said we are the people of a 'Rainbow Nation'. During the 'honeymoon' period of the country's newfound democracy there was a heady jubilation and the people of South Africa wholeheartedly embraced this notion. Today, 16 years on, many are cynical about it.

22 Treib, M. 1995, 'Must landscape mean?' in Swaffield, S. [ed]. *Theory in Landscape Architecture – A reader*, University of Pennsylvania Press, Philadelphia, 2002:99

23 Ibid.:99.

24 Treib, M. 1995, 'Must landscape mean?' in Swaffield, S. [ed]. *Theory in Landscape Architecture – A reader*, University of Pennsylvania Press, Philadelphia, 2002:p.100.

25 Ibid.:100.

26 Ibid.:101.

27 Marc Treib, 'Traces upon the land: The formalistic landscape.' *Architectural Association Quarterly 1,* no 4 (1979):28–39.

28 Prince, G. 1987. *A dictionary of narratology.* University of Nebraska Press, Lincoln. p.91.

29 Potteiger, Matthew and Purington, Jamie. 1998. *Landscape narrative, design practices for telling stories*, John Wiley and Sons Inc, New York:3.

30 Turner, V. 1981. 'Social dramas and stories about them.' In one narrative, W.J.T. Mitchell (ed). University of Chicago, Chicago:163.

31 Potteiger, Matthew and Purington, Jamie. 1998. *Landscape narrative, design practices for telling stories*, John Wiley and Sons Inc, New York:6–7.

32 Ibid 1998:24 and 25.

33 Ibid 1998:73.

34 Chatman, S. 1978. *Story and discourse: narrative structure in fiction and film.* Cornell University Press, Ithaca:124.

35 Potteiger, Matthew and Purington, Jamie. 1998. *Landscape narrative, design practices for telling stories*, John Wiley and Sons Inc, New York:11.

36 Potteiger and Purington. Such five other landscape narrative forms are: Narrative Experience; Narrative Setting and Topos; Genres of Landscape Narratives; Proccess and Interpretive Landscapes.

37 The Freedom Park Trust. *Towards diversity, unity, reconciliation and nation building,* Freedom Park, undated.

38 In Young. G. (2002). Freedom Park national legacy project, landscape architecture report, for Freedom Park Trust, Newtown Landscape Architects cc. Unpublished report, Tshwane.

39 The conceptual design for the Garden evolved as an iterative process between the design team (landscape architects and architects) and an advisory panel established by the Freedom Park Trust. The panel, comprising traditional healers, artists and academics specialising in African culture and Indigenous Knowledge Systems (IKS), provided guidance and assistance on cultural matters. Traditional healers from different backgrounds also conducted a comprehensive reading of the site's plants to determine those which have medicinal and cultural value and should be preserved and protected.
    IKS and *Ubuntu* therefore underpin the philosophy and general approach to the design of Freedom Park and the selection of materials. The design team are constantly referring to reports and research material being produced by the IKS panel and other Freedom Park personnel and researchers for conceptual ideas. The team then interpret and integrate these ideas into the design narrative. The concepts are then tested by the Phase 2 Committee, a combination of Freedom Park senior personnel, technical advisors and the design team, before they are developed into final design. During this process Dr Wally Serote, CEO of Freedom Park, introduced the idea coming from *Ubuntu* as it would be practised by the elders of a community when seeking consensus on important issues. When matters of importance are being discussed in 'council' the individual places his/her idea on the table for debate and discussion by the group. This person is not to defend their idea because it now becomes the 'property' of the group. The individual can add to the discussion but not to the determent of keeping the discussion going or to dogmatically defend their idea. Once the discussion comes to its natural conclusion, a decision is taken that is binding. Often in these situations when I had to make a presentation I would find myself trying to defend my idea because my 'western' ego had been taught to do this. It wasn't until many attempts at presenting work that I became comfortable with the *Ubuntu* way of doing things, and relaxed and let the discussion take its natural course.

40 *Ubuntu*, a traditional African philosophy, recognises how we are inextricably bound in each other's humanity. Translates as 'I am because we are'. Dorah Lebole, Greenhouse Project director says 'there is a bigger world, …within your own experience, there is a bigger experience where it is possible for you to get beyond your immediate experience and seek out that [which] is human and unites us as human beings. In Africa we have this concept of *Ubuntu* which is humanness which means I'm not human without you being present and my allowing you to be present. I am human because you are human. So out of that concept we therefore then see that we have a shared experience but also we can find one another and create a peaceful coexistence. I say it's a concept here in Africa but I also believe it's present in all human beings if it allowed to thrive and to prosper. This is a spirit of sharing. If I have something and I can see you are suffering and there's something that I can give to you, which maybe is something I need but I find that by giving this to you I create a relationship with you, I create a better understanding between us.' Ubuntu operates from the fact that 'I am because you are', meaning I cannot be myself if you are not yourself, 'you've got to be ok for me to be ok'. It's not only about 'me', but rather that together we can be able to make it. So if you recognise that I am who I am because *you* are, then everything else will be taken care of. Credo Mutwa explains it this way 'This is *Ubuntu*, that I must do to other people what I want other people to do to me. But I am a *muntu*, a human being, because of the other human beings around me.' Globaloneness Project, *Ubuntu interview Ubuntu* http://www.globalonessproject,org/interviewee/credo-mutwa.

41 Again reference is made *to Ubuntu*, to be a human (an individual) you need to have other humans around you (the group).

42 *S'kumbuto* is Freedom Park's major memorial, which stands testimony to the

various conflicts that have shaped South Africa today. *S'kumbuto* comprises of a number of elements including, the Wall of Names, Amphitheatre, Sanctuary, Eternal Flame, Gallery of Leaders and the Reeds.

43   *//hapo,* a Koisan name meaning that 'a dream is not a dream until it is dreamt by the community', is an interactive exhibition space where Southern Africa's history, dating back 3.6 billion years, unfolds in narrative and visual form.

44   It is interesting to note that recently the ANC government mandated that the Voortrekker Monumant and Freedom Park are to be 'linked' – another act of reconciliation.

45   Freedom Park Trust (2004), *Freedom Park, Garden of Remembrance*, Freedom Park Trust, Pretoria.

46   Motsei, M, (2003), *Sacred rocks, ancient voices, spiritual significance of a rock and water in African healing,* paper produced for Freedom Park Trust. This thought also ties back to the notion of the garden as healing place discussed earlier in the essay.

47   A Venda word meaning a place of tranquillity and reflection Universal access refers to access for all those with physical or other disabilities as well as those caused by age.

48   Access for the handicapped, including those in wheelchairs, the elderly and the blind.

49   Newtown Landscape Architects. Freedom Park National Legacy Project, Landscape Architecture Report. Unpublished Report, Tshwane, March 2002.

50   It incidentally is also the place where the important discussion took place between the designers, artists and traditional healers, to decide on the location for *Isivivane.*

51   *Impepho* or incense that is often burned in traditional or religious ceremonies to signify a holy place and/or represent spiritual cleansing.

52   The events of conflict are: Pre-Colonial Wars; Colonial Wars and Genocide; Slavery; Wars of Resistance; South Africa War, First World War and its impact on South Africa; Second World War and its impact on South Africa; Struggle for Liberation.

53   Ngubane, Prof. H. (2003). *The role of research in the indigenous knowledge sector of Freedom Park,* Youth Workshop, Pretoria, 26 May 2003.

54   Motsei, M. 2003. *Sacred rocks, ancient voices, spiritual significance of a rock and water in African healing,* paper produced for Freedom Park Trust.

55   Credo Mutwa in Freedom Park Trust. (2004). *Freedom Park, Garden of Remembrance*, Freedom Park Trust, Pretoria.

56   The Freedom Park Trust. (2004), *Freedom Park, Garden of Remembrance,* Freedom Park Trust, Pretoria.

57   To construct *Isivivane,* the nine provinces of South Africa were asked to provide a boulder from a place within the province with historical and cultural significance.

58   By an elder to Archbishop Dandala, The Freedom Park Trust. The original version is:
Ndi Mu-Afrika
Arali na nga gwa mavu a heli dnaga ni do nngwana
Naho na nga lima na gwa nit shi isa phanda
Ni do di wana ndi henefho
Naho wa nga gwa wa lima
Wa shumisa mitshini mihulu
Yo sikwaho nga vhathu vha nama
U lima na u gwa lifhasi
U swika fhasi hu sina mugumo
Henefho
Kha lifhasi lenelo ndi do wanala…
Nga Muhulwane, Vhafuwi vho Davhana

59   *Lekgotla* is the place where elders would gather to discuss important matters. Often this place would be beneath an old and large shade tree.

60   Manqele M. and O'Donoghue, R. (1994). *Trees, Goats and Spirits,* Indigenous Knowledge Series, KwaZulu-Natal Nature Conservation Service, Pietermaritzburg.

61   The Freedom Park Trust. (2004), Freedom *Park, Garden of Remembrance*, The Freedom Park Trust, Pretoria.

62   siSwati word meaning 'memorial/place of remembrance'.

63   The words in this section are derived from an interview with the author and other design team members, which was first published as an article 'Freedom Park A Spiritual Journey' in *The Urban Green File,* Vol. 11, No. 2 June 2006.

64   The then South African Deputy President, Thabo Mbeki's speech to South Africa and the world at the United Nations University on 9 April 1998.

65   Freedom Park. *A tribute to democracy in South Africa*, undated brochure, Tshwane.

66   Potteiger, Matthew and Purington, Jamie. 1998. *Landscape narrative, design practices for telling stories*, John Wiley and Sons Inc, New York, 1998:11.

chapter 16

Finding the Void: Park Development in Johannesburg's Inner City

Graham Young

Department of Architecture

University of Pretoria

Pretoria

South Africa

Introduction

The problems of postmodern organisation in the landscape became obvious with the proliferation of sprawling cities, gated enclaves, residential communities and mega-malls. Schumacher and Rogner write that the extension of this dispersed system 'fueled the rapid decompression of urban industrial cities and the decentralisation of both mass production and mass consumption'[1].

Given this 'decompression', the question facing Johannesburg in particular is what to do about abandoned inner city sites caused by the flight of business and other commercial interests to Randburg, Midrand and Sandton, along with the acres of railway land that slice through the centre of the city, cutting it in two. Johannesburg, however, is unlike many other 'new world' cities where 'decompression' is a major issue. In fact, the reverse is also true! People are instead flocking to the inner city to find work and a place to live. The city has changed dramatically because of these two opposing trends. Old office buildings are being converted into residential units to accommodate the demand and new residential units are being constructed, specifically in Newtown on the western edge of the CBD. Johannesburg's CBD is instead 'compressed' and available land for open space is extremely elusive, over-utilised and mostly derelict.

In September 2009 Johannesburg Development Agency (JDA) in collaboration with Johannesburg City Parks and the Department of Planning and Urban Management initiated a design competition 'to conceptualise and design a large inner city public urban park. The growing residential densities within the inner city of Johannesburg coupled with the lack of adequate green public open space suggests the need for a large scale inner city public park.

The vision for this park should be of the nature of Central Park in New York'. The competition document also alludes to the 'Inner City Regeneration Charter', a strategic document which outlines how the City will address issues of urban regeneration and economic development in the inner city. The strategy cites as one of its six main principles, 'Public spaces, art, culture and heritage'. These references imply that a public park intervention is necessary and could be a catalyst for development, but where in Johannesburg's dense, 'compressed' CBD, does one find this scale and form of space?

A relatively recent theory, landscape urbanism and the approach it advocates to understanding the challenges facing the regeneration of decaying urban environments specifically through the use of brownfield sites, perhaps provides a way to understand the problem.

In the *Landscape Urbanism Reader* Charles Waldheim states that 'landscape urbanism describes a disciplinary realignment currently underway in which landscape replaces architecture as the basic building block of contemporary urbanism. For many, across a range of disciplines, landscape has become both the lens through which the contemporary city is represented and the medium through which it is constructed.'[2] Waldheim sees landscape urbanism, like landscape architecture, as an interstitial design discipline,

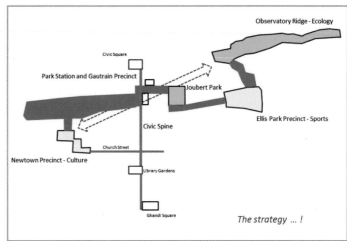

Figure 1: Long-term vision for THE SEAM inner city park connecting Observatory Ridge, a natural ridge (bottom of image) to Newtown, a cultural precinct (top of image)

Figure 2: Observatory Park looking west to Ponte Tower residential block (top)

Figure 3: Observatory Park looking east to the historic water tower, a landmark on Observatory Ridge (centre)

Figure 4: Observatory Park looking west along the SEAM Centre towards Johannesburg's CBD (bottom)

Figure 5: Ellis Park Precinct

Figure 6: Ellis Park Precinct, water feature celebrating the source of the Jukskei River (Photo MMA)

operating in the spaces between buildings, infrastructural systems, and natural ecologies. He advocates patience and slow growth in cultivating a new urban form in these residual spaces, with the full participation of all assembled on the commons (including major, institutional landholders as well as the dispossessed).[3]

The idea of landscape urbanism reorders the values and priorities of urban design, emphasising the primacy of void over built form, and celebrating indeterminacy and change over the static certainty of architecture. Its most powerful contribution, however, may be that it recalls nature's restorative cycles and tries to put them back to work in the city'.[4]

Large-scale urban parks are increasingly integral to the sustainable development of cities. They offer the city the opportunity 'to stake out new and unique identities, promoting the peculiarities of local geography, ecology, history and cultural quality of life. These large open spaces are seen by many city officials as fundamental to assuring the competitive attractiveness of their cities, retaining and attracting new talent, new residents and businesses, and promoting economic development'.[5]

Given this argument, the competition originators must be applauded for advocating the essential, catalytic importance of a major inner city park but reference to Central Park as main indicator for the nature and form of the intervention, needs to be challenged!

The planning and design of large urban parks must confront a number of significant challenges, such as multiple competing stakeholders, phased financing, segmentation, inaccessibility and difficult implementation, especially on brownfield or contaminated sites. Consequently, the design of large parks today must inevitably be strategic and time-based. Design initiatives cannot simply be wilful, subjective or formal approaches, but need instead to be intelligent and flexible with regard to what is inevitably a complex field of dynamic variables.[6]

Case Study: THE SEAM

THE SEAM[7] employs an approach that makes reference to landscape urbanism theory. It requires identifying a series of voids at CBD wide scale and proposes that once the voids have been created they should incrementally be reclaimed, remediated and creatively stitched back into the dense urban fabric, to be utilised by the citizens of the city as places to recreate, socialise and safely move between districts.

THE SEAM (Figure 1) manifests itself as a linear system of parks that begins as a natural ecosystem (Observatory Ridge), and then penetrates the urban fabric to the west along a series of existing and created voids, to culminate at Newtown – a heritage and cultural precinct. At the western end of Observatory Ridge, on a site with spectacular views across the city and which has spiritual and cultural significance (many religious groups gather and congregate on the ridge and gold was first sought in these quartzite ridges), a new park, Observatory Hill Park, is proposed (Figures

2, 3 and 4). The park would also serve as a catalyst for high density mixed-use development proposed along its northern edge. The site would be the starting point for the development of the project and is significant as the ridge line is the watershed between river systems that originate on the ridge and flow either to the north, and ultimately the Indian Ocean or to the south, and the Atlantic Ocean.

THE SEAM then steps down Observatory Ridge in an exciting series of exaggerated steps to meet with Ellis Park Precinct and Stadium Square[8], which consolidates public space between the two main stadiums and other sports and recreation facilities (Figures 5 and 6). Using Observatory Ridge as natural void, a series of new parks (voids) are also proposed to stretch east down Bezuidenhout Valley and would be central to new high density housing schemes. Already some new neighbourhood parks have been developed by the JDA in this general area as is illustrated by Bertrams Road Park[9] in Figure 7.

Ellis Park Precinct is linked to a proposed new major park intervention at Doornfontein Station through the westward extension of the precinct. The park space is integral to a proposed high density residential and a mixed use development located south of the railway line (on reclaimed industrial land) and a mixed use development proposed adjacent to the park along its eastern edge. The development would include the recently completed End Street Park[10] along its western edge, a once dilapidated space which has been transformed into a robust, colourful and somewhat enigmatic play park (Figures 8 and 9).

Figure 7: Bertrams Road School Park (top left)
Figure 8: End Street Park in context (top right)
Figure 9: End Street Park, playground detail (bottom right)

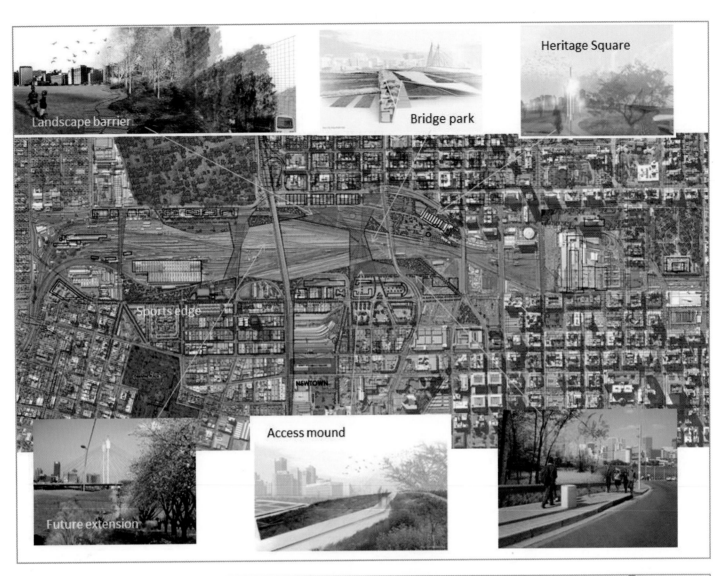

Landscape barrier

Bridge park

Heritage Square

Sports edge

Access mound

Future extension

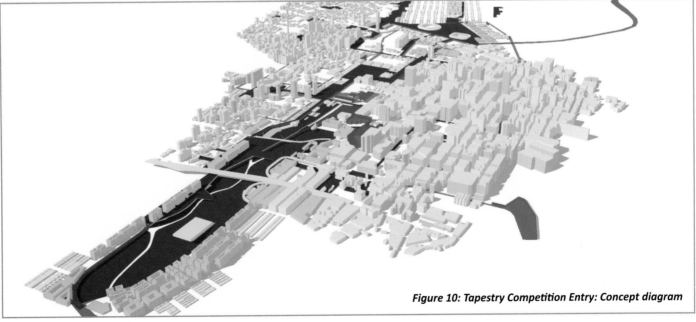

Figure 10: Tapestry Competition Entry: Concept diagram

Figure 11: Tapestry competition entry: Using the park as the integrated bridging device to connect Braamfontein with the CBD

Going further west, the void, making use of the existing railway line, is reclaimed using a landscaped deck structure that would connect Doornfontein Park to the Johannesburg Art Museum and Joubert Park. Joubert Park is then linked to the new Gautrain Station and Park Station precincts along Leyds Street. These are celebrated as the 'Gateway to Johannesburg'.

Again an infrastructural void, west of Park Station and above the existing railway lines, is reclaimed and designed as a multi-functional urban park precinct, which would provide panoramic views to the west and south-west of the CBD. This new precinct is 'stitched back' into the old and new urban fabric as a 'tapestry'[11] and becomes the catalyst for mixed use developments on adjacent reclaimed brownfield sites (programmed primarily as housing units) and sites along the southern edge of Braamfontein (Figures 10, 11 and 12).

From this elevated position, THE SEAM steps down in a series of smaller, greener parks designed on brownfields sites, to culminate in a series of squares and open spaces that already exist in Newtown Cultural Precinct.

The project would offer extraordinary opportunities for city residents to have access to open space and networks of paths, squares and parks that could take hours to navigate in their own time. It also offers distinct opportunities that would otherwise be impossible in the compressed urban fabric of Johannesburg, allowing instead significant space for extensive leisure, social and recreational amenities.

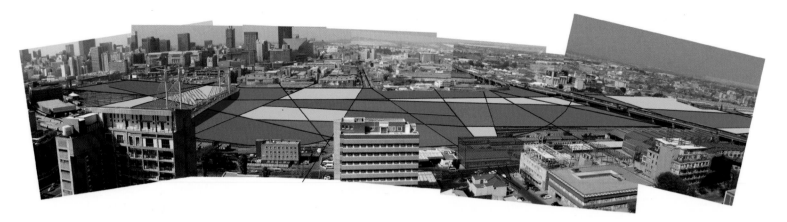

THE SEAM employs an approach that entails defining and utilising void to reclaim, remediate and incrementally stitch back a newly created landscape into the existing and proposed urban fabric. It builds upon existing energy, connecting heritage, cultural and sports nodes with natural features to provide a generous and beautiful large-scale public landscape for a broad constituency of public users. It would become a place to recreate, socialise and safely move between areas. As such, the park would become a leading-edge model for the design and sustainable management of an inner city park system.

Figure 12: Tapestry Competition Entry: Access route through centre of the park

1   Shane, G. 2003. The Emergence of 'Landscape Urbanism' – Reflections on Stalking Detroit, Harvard Design Magazine, Fall 2003/Winter 2004, No. 19.
2   Waldheim, C. [ed]. The Landscape Urbanism Reader, Princeton Architectural Press, New York. 2006 p.11.
3   Guy Debord, The Society of the Spectacle, trans. D. Nicholson-Smith (New York: Zone Books 1995) in G. Shane. The emergence of 'Landscape Urbanism' Reflections on stalking Detroit, Harvard Design Magazine, Fall 2003/Winter 2004.
4   Ruth Durack, Director, Urban Design Centre of Northeast Ohio, 'Shrinking smart the promise of landscape urbanism' in Cleveland Urban Design Collaborative Quarterly, 3:3/4 – Winter 2004: http//www.cudc.kent.edu/e-cudc-Quarterly/viewpoint/durack4.html
5   Corner, J. Shelby farms park, one park, one million trees, twelve landscapes, topos. 2009, Vol. 66 Landscape Strategies, 2009.
6   Corner, J. Shelby farms park, one park, one million trees, twelve landscapes, topos. 2009, Vol. 66 Landscape Strategies, 2009.
7   Competition entry by NLA + GreenInc + MRA a joint venture between Newtown Landscape Architects cc and GreenInc landscape architects and Mashabane Rose Architects.
8   The precinct was designed by a joint venture comprising Albonico, Sack Mzumara Architects and Urban Designers + MMA Architects + Newtown Landscape Architects.
9   Designed by Newtown Landscape Architects.
10 The park was designed by Newtown Landscape Architects.
11 After the first round of the competition four projects were short listed and the consortium asked to submit refined proposals after comment. THE SEAM did not advance past the first stage as (the author believes) the organisers were still looking for a 'Central Park' type solution. Newtown Landscape Architects was then asked to join the MMA architects + Fiona Garson Architect + Cohen & Judin team as the lead landscape architect. The images for this section of park are from the 'Urban tapestry' proposal put forward by this new consortium. A competition winner was not announced but this consortium's entry was judged as being 'the strongest and having the most chance of becoming feasible'.

chapter 17

Priming for Added Value: How the Application of the Principles of Landscape Urbanism to the Redevelopment of Culemborg 'Adds Value' to the Designed Landscape

Clinton Hindes
School of Architecture, Planning and
Geomatics
University of Cape Town
Cape Town
South Africa

Gideon Roos
Master of Landscape Architecture
Programme
University of Cape Town
Cape Town
South Africa

Introduction

This article discusses how the application of certain axioms and approaches of landscape urbanism add value to landscape projects, as well as facilitate the easier assessment and quantification of value. A thesis project undertaken at the University of Cape Town is used as the vehicle to reveal these aspects. The project entitled 'Landscape patch: A primer for post-industrial landscapes' (Roos 2009), concerns the redevelopment of a disused industrial site west of the Cape Town CBD known as Culemborg (Figure 1). The project vigorously applies the principles of landscape urbanism to the site through the development of an operational methodology which maximises the performance of the 'working' landscape (performance meaning the ways in which a landscape improves the built environment of, adjacent to, and in some ways further beyond the site). It is the project's focus on this operational methodology (and not on a static finite product) that specifically lends itself to a discussion of value.

The project is first briefly described, followed by an elaboration on specific aspects of the project in relation to landscape urbanism and their relevance to 'adding value' through landscape design.

Project approach

The project accepts the city's vision (as reflected in existing urban design proposals) for the entire western portion of the CBD and utilises this vision as a signpost to the intended future structure and nature of the area (Figure 2). It is also acknowledged, as is

Figure 1: Culemborg within the western portion of the Cape Town CBD (Roos 2009:105)

Figure 2: A detailed portion of Figure 1 illustrating notional allocation of future land uses (Roos 2009:116)

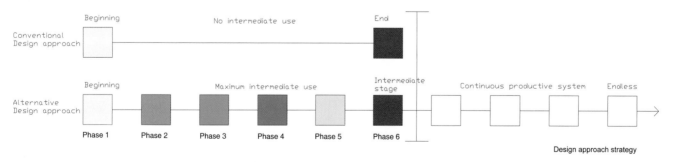

Figure 3: Moving from the binary application of a static solution to a maximised number of intermediate phases (approaching continuous) (Roos 2009:55)

EMBEDDED ENERGY

TRANSPIRATION

EVAPORATION

INFILTRATION

NETWORK FLOW

Figure 4: An illustration of the intention of focusing on the performative aspects of the 'working' landscape of Culemborg (Roos 2009: 48)

usually the case with large post-industrial site developments, that the redevelopment is gradual and essentially never-ending. The traditional phased approach is jettisoned for continual and gradual change (Figure 3). The project then focuses on this 'extended' (re) development period and primarily concerns itself with the operational methodologies for maximising performance over this period, and hence increasing the potential for the creation of value the working landscape could generate. The project is initiated with the intention of releasing latent (inherent) site potential as soon as possible with the least resource input. From these initial actions the resultant processes are nudged toward an ultimate vision, in this case aligned with that which the city has adopted. The design and planning concern thus shifts from what the design and planning intervention/s will ultimately look like, to what they do and how they work (Figure 4).

Project application

Starting with what is there, the existing landscape of Culemborg is divided on plan into a series of homogeneous patches which are areas of uniform nature. Acknowledging the inherent potential of each of these patches as they are (in order to minimise initial intervention), a decision is made on the nature of the possible landscape performance thereof to address particular needs of the immediate and wider context (e.g. urban agriculture on vacant lots or temporary shelter in abandoned buildings). A sequence is then set in motion where over a period of time each patch gradually changes its state or function (Figure 5). The materiality of these patches is approached as if they were

Site construction strategy for maximising intermediate use

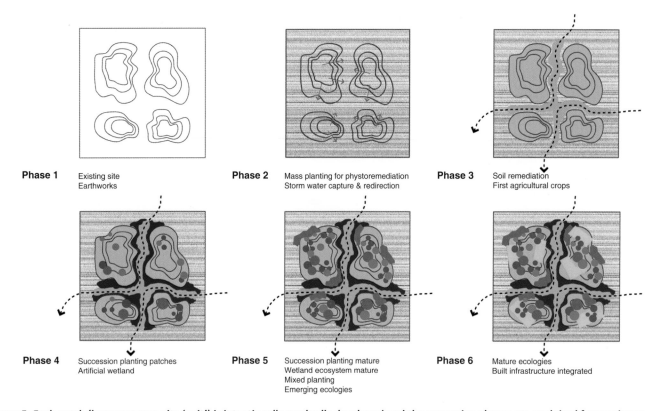

Phase 1 Existing site
Earthworks

Phase 2 Mass planting for phystoremediation
Storm water capture & redirection

Phase 3 Soil remediation
First agricultural crops

Phase 4 Succession planting patches
Artificial wetland

Phase 5 Succession planting mature
Wetland ecosystem mature
Mixed planting
Emerging ecologies

Phase 6 Mature ecologies
Built infrastructure integrated

Figure 5: Each patch (homogeneous site 'unit') is intentionally gradually developed and the successive phases are exploited for maximum performance (Roos 2009:56)

primers for future conditions, some known, in the sense that they are guided to the vision for the precinct, and others not, in that they may be temporarily utilised to perform a particular function unrelated to the ultimate intended use. The 'agricultural crops' referred to in Figure 5 are only productive for a specific period (phase 3) as the site is gradually changed into a constructed wetland (phase 5). Some of the processes set in motion may produce by-products such as biomass for composting. These products are recycled into a patch that may be in a phase where composting is necessary.

These numerous processes are then understood and managed over time through a series of operational matrices and tables such as the one in Figure 6. These are the strategic tools used to manage material and energy flows over time, which are managed for maximum performance. These matrices (with their material versus time relationship) allow the designer to quantify the performance of the landscape over time (Figure 7). These quantities

are relatively easily generated as the landscape is understood as a collection of horizontal surfaces (patches), each managed for particular performance. This is similar to the nature of an agricultural patchwork of fields which are specifically programmed (spatially and in time) for maximum productivity.

In the Culemborg project no particular static end point is reached. However, varying degrees of compliance to the urban design vision are achieved at various points. The redevelopment is thus not seen as a series of sequential development phases between various grand urban design schemes, but a continual process of maximising landscape performance on a smaller scale while nudging toward the (no doubt continually changing) urban design vision. It is precisely this continual state of flux and the management thereof that release the potential for maximising landscape performance. Just like the maximising of productivity in agriculture, the fields are continually changing.

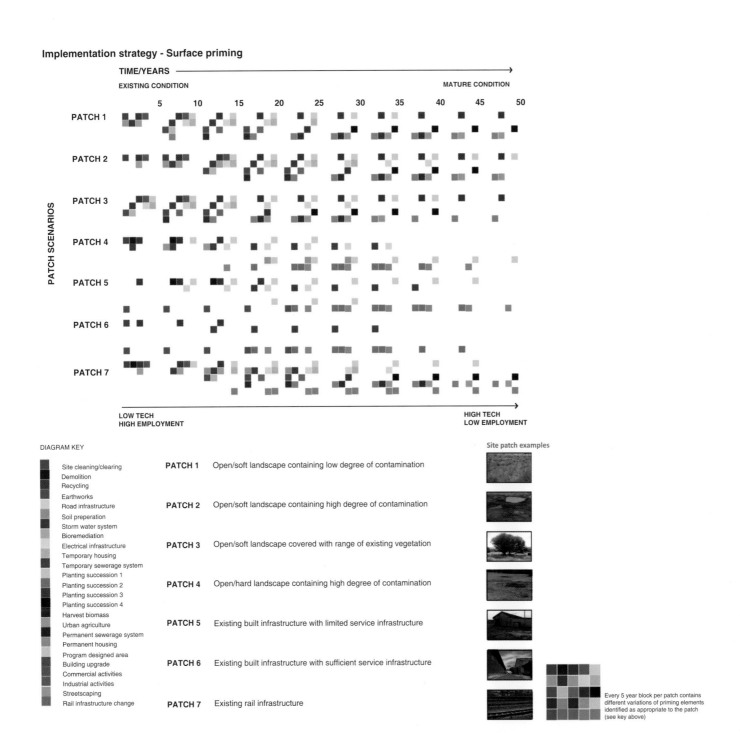

Implementation strategy - Surface priming

TIME/YEARS ⟶

EXISTING CONDITION | MATURE CONDITION

5   10   15   20   25   30   35   40   45   50

PATCH SCENARIOS

PATCH 1
PATCH 2
PATCH 3
PATCH 4
PATCH 5
PATCH 6
PATCH 7

LOW TECH
HIGH EMPLOYMENT ⟶ HIGH TECH
LOW EMPLOYMENT

DIAGRAM KEY

Site cleaning/clearing
Demolition
Recycling
Earthworks
Road infrastructure
Soil preperation
Storm water system
Bioremediation
Electrical infrastructure
Temporary housing
Temporary sewerage system
Planting succession 1
Planting succession 2
Planting succession 3
Planting succession 4
Harvest biomass
Urban agriculture
Permanent sewerage system
Permanent housing
Program designed area
Building upgrade
Commercial activities
Industrial activities
Streetscaping
Rail infrastructure change

PATCH 1   Open/soft landscape containing low degree of contamination

PATCH 2   Open/soft landscape containing high degree of contamination

PATCH 3   Open/soft landscape covered with range of existing vegetation

PATCH 4   Open/hard landscape containing high degree of contamination

PATCH 5   Existing built infrastructure with limited service infrastructure

PATCH 6   Existing built infrastructure with sufficient service infrastructure

PATCH 7   Existing rail infrastructure

Site patch examples

Every 5 year block per patch contains different variations of priming elements identified as appropriate to the patch (see key above)

Figure 6: The various patches undergo a sequence of guided changes maximising the performance/output (Roos 2009:59)

Starting with what you have (latent value) and not what you want (created value)

And like the landscape architect, the landscape urbanist always begins with the given. (Mostafavi 2003:7)

Initial engagement with the landscape of Culemborg is entirely divorced from the urban design vision. The principle followed is that the specificity of the site may reveal potential for the crea-

tion of value in ways not necessarily related to the intended programme of that site. On an ideological level, Richard Weller, when referring to the relationship between the scales of planning and design in an explanation of landscape urbanist approaches, highlights the way programmatic 'openness' and 'closedness' were approached in the Culemborg project: 'Perhaps then here is a clue for how planning's pretences to the whole [Cape Town's vision for Culemborg] and design's preoccupation with the parts can come

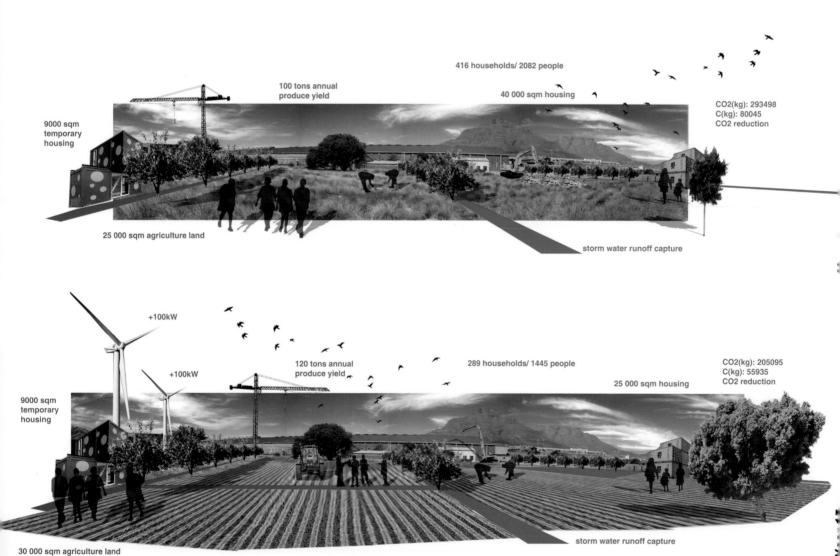

9000 sqm
temporary
housing

100 tons annual
produce yield

416 households/ 2082 people

40 000 sqm housing

CO2(kg): 293498
C(kg): 80045
CO2 reduction

25 000 sqm agriculture land

storm water runoff capture

+100kW

+100kW

120 tons annual
produce yield

289 households/ 1445 people

25 000 sqm housing

CO2(kg): 205095
C(kg): 55935
CO2 reduction

9000 sqm
temporary
housing

30 000 sqm agriculture land

storm water runoff capture

Figure 7: The gradual development of the Culemborg site (5, 15 and 25 year stages). The blue labels on the perspectives illustrate the quantified performance of the landscape over time. These are the products of this 'working' landscape (Roos 2009:139)

together in a more finely tuned and instrumental [use of matrices] landscape architecture' (Waldheim 2006:83). Alan Berger, on a much more practical note in his work with the 'Project for reclamation excellence', acknowledges the necessity for strong site specific responses on brownfield sites such as Culemborg:

Altered landscapes (sites where vast quantities of materials have been added or removed from the landscape, resulting in several chemical, biological and physical changes) require a more humble recognition of their physical limitations and the fiscal resources needed to enact changes upon them. Designing for altered landscapes therefore requires an adjustment of open-ended design objectives toward optimal landscape performance from a minimal energetic input. (Berger 2008:116)

This releases tremendous potential for the creation of value.

In Culemborg various surfaces offer opportunities for immediate use, such as fertile soils not polluted for urban agriculture, structures fit for habitation (but intended to be demolished) for temporary housing, large open fields for public events/gatherings, and ecological functions such as rainwater retention/detention. These temporary functions create value in various forms for the city which are not directly linked to the urban design vision, but with relatively little investment can at least in some way begin to create value.

Another departure point in the Culemborg project was to sow a variety of grasses across as much of the site as possible (which is not immediately put to a specific programmatic use), the creation of what Landscape Architect Michel Desvigne called an 'intermediate nature' (Desvigne 2009). This very simple and inexpensive technique has been used with great success in his work with the reclamation of post-industrial redevelopment projects in France. The value generated by this simple action is twofold, firstly the entire site is given a completely different visual quality improving the overall attractiveness, and secondly, from an ecological point of view (besides the obvious increase in biodiversity), the processes of succession could reveal the adaptability of plants to the specific conditions and contaminants in the soil, subsequently leading to a more informed ecological soil remediation programme (Figure 7 – first two images, and Figure 8). A further starting point could be to simply scarify the top layer of a fallow surface to collect rain water and create conditions necessary for plant succession to be initiated.

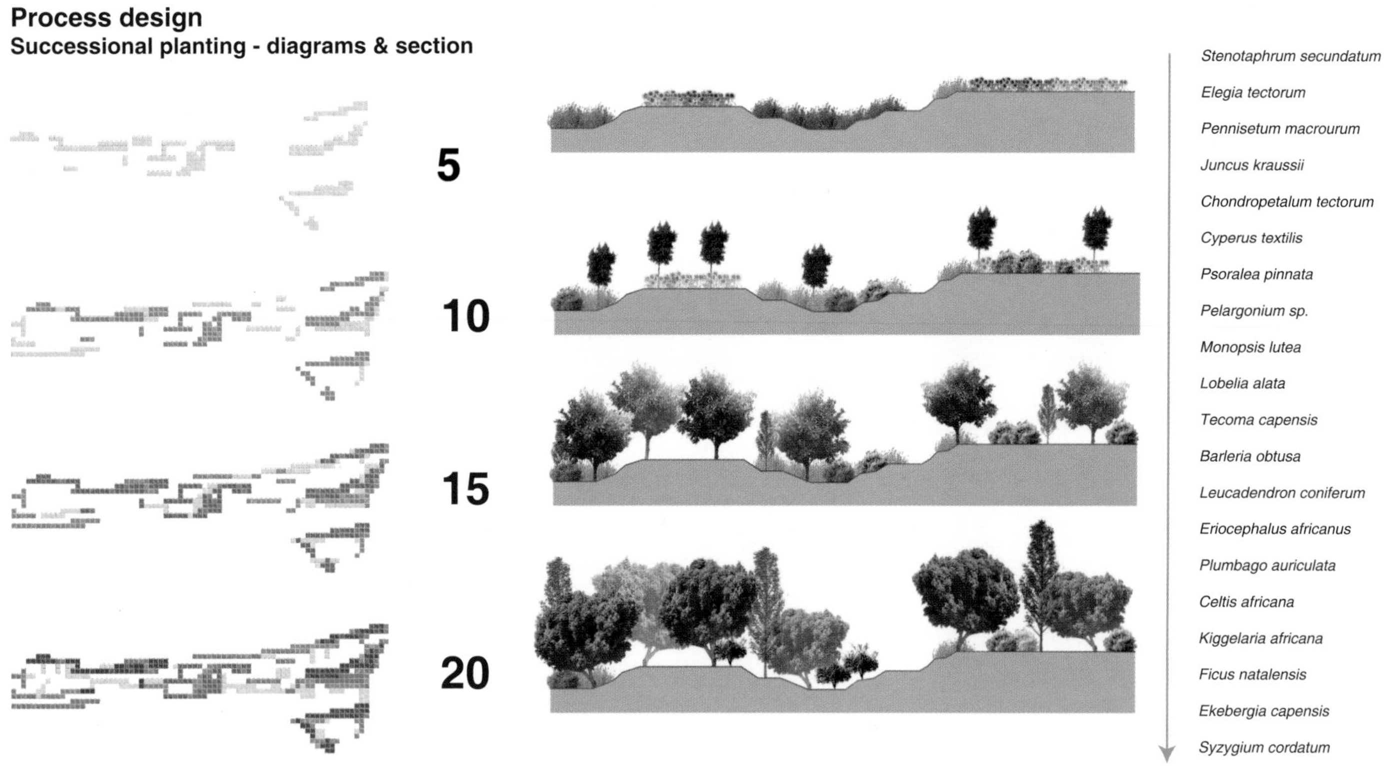

Process design
Successional planting - diagrams & section

5

10

15

20

Stenotaphrum secundatum

Elegia tectorum

Pennisetum macrourum

Juncus kraussii

Chondropetalum tectorum

Cyperus textilis

Psoralea pinnata

Pelargonium sp.

Monopsis lutea

Lobelia alata

Tecoma capensis

Barleria obtusa

Leucadendron coniferum

Eriocephalus africanus

Plumbago auriculata

Celtis africana

Kiggelaria africana

Ficus natalensis

Ekebergia capensis

Syzygium cordatum

Figure 8: A successional planting scheme (Roos 2009:165)

Process design
Design for continual flux & the unexpected:
Surface priming for disaster relief

Modified permeable paving &
tent foundation:

Grass block pavers
600 x 400 x 100mm
Steel anchor bolts
Casted steel ring connectors

Xenephobia refugee camp, South Africa

Standard UN tent sizes

Figure 9: Priming surfaces for various uses, such as temporarily housing people displaced in xenophobic violence (Roos 2009:181)

Successively, this preparation creates the conditions under which plants and animals thrive, thereby performing ameliorative functions through various nutrient-, water-, and material-recycling processes. In essence, the designer attempts to use the altered site's condition adaptively to guide a series of time-based processes of landscape evolution. Rather than imposing a single solution that requires heavy initial investment and perpetual active maintenance. (Berger 2008:120)

The creation of value on brownfield developments such as Culemborg is achieved by initiating as many landscape processes as possible with the intention of increasing landscape performance and productivity with the least material and energy input. For the full potential of the creation of value to be released, it is important to divorce the search for initial potential uses from the ultimate programmatic vision.

Priming the surface

Once these various process sequences have been set in motion a greater degree of control is exercised to create as much value as possible, and to give the processes directionality to reach the intended urban design vision. One of the principles used to achieve the greatest potential for multiple uses is 'priming surfaces' for future known and unknown uses. Richard Weller's view on the landscape urbanist's approach to site development explains the use of priming surfaces in the Culemborg project:

Instead of master plans, which guide the arrow of time to a fixed point, landscape urbanists, while cognisant of the whole, make partial interventions, strategic moves which might incite loops of non-linear change throughout the system. (Weller 2006:69)

The nature of the way surfaces are primed is determined by two factors; the easiest way to 'incite' change which would most easily add value, and secondly, to set in motion changes towards realising the structural qualities of the whole (the city's vision for Culemborg).

This is best described as 'designing the primer and not the paint', or alternatively stated, designing the preconditions for programme and not the programme itself. This allows for intermediate uses to be accommodated while gradually setting in place the conditions necessary for an advanced programmatic stage. Performance of the landscape is maximised.

The agricultural field is ploughed, prepared in anticipation of the crop that will (hopefully) appear at a later date. In this way the appearance of the field is always both incomplete and complete, in as much as at each stage of its development it attains a degree of temporal finitude. (Mostafavi 2003:8)

This is achieved in the Culemborg project in various ways. Firstly, successional planting with 'wild grasses' is initially introduced to enrich soils for urban agriculture and perform a remedial function on low level pollutants (Figure 5 and 8). Secondly (accommodating more unknown uses), portions of the Culemborg site that would possibly become permeable parking lots are surfaced with permeable pavers which could be used for large public gatherings such as music concerts. These blocks were primed with the introduction of stainless steel hooks to which various temporary structures (marques, tents, etc.) could be connected. In the Culemborg project, these surfaces are 'primed' in this way to deal with the ever present threat of xenophobic violence, or any disaster (natural or man-made) where temporary housing for a large number of people is immediately required (Figure 9). These blocks are laid with the correct dimensional modules to suit the erecting of the standard United Nations relief tents.

Construction

Biomass

Social

Hydrology

Recycled

Figure 10: Universally understood imagery (Roos 2009:175)

Into the matrix (operational diagrammes and their potential for value quantification)

What happens in the landscape on various patches, how it occurs, over what time frame, what products are generated, what happens to these products and what are the quantities involved? These are the questions associated with the operative methods developed to manage the 'workings' of the Culemborg landscape. This shift from the visual qualities of landscapes to the procedural (performative and strategic) aspects necessitates different kinds of tools for information management. The two variables around which these tools are shaped are time and performance.

In order to manage the changes that particular patches go through on the Culemborg site, a series of tables, graphs and matrices are developed. It is these performative and productive qualities of landscape urbanist techniques that offer the most potential for adding value to projects. The values portrayed on the images in Figure 7 are derived from a series of matrices that are quantified with various calculations. This is a relatively simple application of the quantification of the performance of a landscape. However, they reflect the contemporary need for landscape architects to quantify the 'value' of their projects (in a performative sense).

Graphic language for the communication of value

Landscape architecture has experienced a shift in representational style over the last decade or so. This is understood by reflecting on one recent change in the content of landscape architectural designs, that being from a preoccupation with a static final product (what the landscape looks like) to the processes or systems inherent in the landscape (what the landscape does and how it works) (Figure 4). This reflects a shift in what is currently valued in designed landscapes, less so aesthetics, and more so the performative and productive aspects.

Landscape architectural communication has changed in two particular ways:

◆ There is a noticeable increase in operational, strategic and procedural representational tools, such as matrices and flow charts. These are characterised by a particular energetic visual quality

◆ There is a shift from attempting to portray the landscape realistically toward the intention to reflect the workings of the landscape and the effects these have and the resultant value it generates.

Underlying these two aspects is the rejection of a discipline-specific visual language (which only landscape architects can decipher) to a visual language which requires no interpretation, or more accurately stated, can be easily interpreted by popular culture. The magazine 'Popular Mechanics' clearly illustrates this tendency within another discipline. Complicated mechanical drawings are reduced to simple, attractive and colourful images immediately understood by an audience far broader than the discipline's boundaries. Proponents of landscape urbanism have in fact stated that their intention with the visual images of their projects is to immediately communicate the value thereof to politicians, the public and clients (potential investors). 'Ultimately, digital simulation provides a platform for the users, designers and altered landscapes to meet on common ground' (Berger 2008:124). This has been described as a branding of the products of landscape architecture.

If landscape architects are intending to sell the 'value' of their products, taking a leaf from marketing, perhaps branding these products in a particular way would prove to be useful.

Image types extensively used today are brightly coloured assemblages and collages, composed of immediately recognisable images of trees, people, plants, earth-moving equipment, mountain bikers etc. (Figure 10). Quantities are often included on the drawings and not left for the pages of dull technical reports. There is even a disregard for attempts at realistic representation to the point that rules of proportion and perspective are ignored. The emphasis is clearly on what the landscape does and not what it looks like. A recent series of cartoon-like storyboards have appeared in the *Landscape Architecture* magazine of late. This is a series in which landscape architect Chip Sullivan addresses various issues of relevance to landscape architecture in a humouristic cartoon-like fashion. Perhaps this form of communication needs more serious investigation as a tool for landscape representation, and more specifically communication.

Conclusion: The increasing emphasis on value

The above strategies employed in Culemborg, starting with what is there, priming surfaces for various uses, and the use of matrices for information management, are strategies at the heart of landscape urbanist methods and techniques and are extremely useful when engaging with value in the landscape. With waning public and private resources dedicated to landscape issues, funding will have to be increasingly sourced from private (corporate) arenas.

Today's language of potential investment is a language of corporate social and environmental responsibility. This is a language of quantities. The principles and approaches of landscape urbanism allow landscape architects to think differently about creating landscapes for increased performance, and to begin to facilitate the quantification of its operations. The focus of landscape planning and design begins to shift to investigations of how landscapes are made. It is in this sphere that the real value of landscape architecture can be maximised.

Bibliography

Berger, A. 2008. *Designing the reclaimed landscape*. New York: Taylor & Francis.

Desvigne, M. 2009. Intermediate natures: The landscapes of Michel Desvigne. Birkhauser: Germany.

Mostafavi, M. 2003. Landscape urbanism: A manual for the machinic landscape. *Architectural Association*. London: AA Publications.

Roos, G. 2009. Landscape Patch: A Primer for Post-Industrial Landscapes. University of Cape Town Masters Thesis, Cape Town, South Africa.

Waldheim, C. (ed). 2006. *The landscape urbanism reader*. New York: Princeton Architectural Press.

Weller, R. 2006. An art of instrumentality: Thinking through Landscape Urbanism. In *The Landscape Urbanism Reader*. C. Waldheim (ed). New York: Princeton Architectural Press, p.69–86.

chapter 18

Mine Infrastructure Planning and Design for Closure: Integrating Sustainable Post-closure Land Use from the Outset into Designing Mine Infrastructure

Brian Rademeyer
Department of Civil and Biosystems
Engineering
University of Pretoria
Pretoria
South Africa

Thania le Roux
Department of Architecture
University of Pretoria
Pretoria
South Africa

Abstract

When warehouse-like facilities such as offices, workshops and change and lamp rooms are planned only to be functional, it can quite easily result in structures that are architecturally mundane and uninspiring, and visually intrusive. Such structures could have a negative aesthetic impact and limit other land uses within the zone of visual influence.

Mining structures are more often than not erected for immediate purposes with little or no consideration for aesthetic value or use, post-closure. Apart from the negative visual impact, other problems arise once mines are decommissioned and the infrastructure is dismantled and removed. What remains are disturbed surfaces and structures which upon abandonment go to ruin.

A paradigm shift is needed whereby the injection of capital into infrastructure development for mining activities can be seen as a catalyst for the introduction of values, spaces and places for people that are not without meaning or aesthetic value after mine closure. This article investigates mining as a temporary intervention, focusing on more sustainable and contextually apt end land-uses after mine closure. In this regard a need exists for a design model that stipulates guidelines for sustainable mine planning with solutions to local social, environmental and infrastructural problems. A new approach is needed to counteract the negative and exploitative impacts of mining on a social and biophysical level.

We describe the application of integrated planning and design principles to a proposed platinum mining operation, the result of which is a hypothetical mine layout and architectural design for a real project formerly known as the Kruidfontein project, North West Province, South Africa. The project area is located on the northern periphery of the Pilanesberg National Park, stretching over several farms and approximately ten thousand hectares.

Although the proposed Kruidfontein project has sufficient economical platinum ore reserves to support mining activities for several decades and has the potential to earn significant foreign exchange, employ people and consume local goods and services, it will negatively impact on ecosystem goods and services, and could negatively impact on several strategic tourism initiatives in the region, one of which includes a proposal to link the Pilanesberg National Park with the Madikwe Game Reserve. A significant portion of the proposed mining project overlaps with a part of the proposed regional Heritage Park Corridor development.

The challenge was therefore to plan and design the mine infrastructure to meet the short-term requirements during mining, resulting in economic prosperity as well as to fulfil the longer-term requirements imposed by the heritage corridor development that could open up an important tourism node and conservation area for the North West Province.

An understanding of mine layout and building materials constraints provided the knowledge base for integrating the mine infrastructure from the outset with a pre-determined post-closure strategic end land use. Case studies, conceptual site plans and layouts, and detailed designs and drawings for achieving this goal are presented in this article.

Introduction

A significant amount of time and effort usually goes into planning mining environments to minimise risks, prevent long-term impacts and degradation, and to reduce wastage of resources and energy. This is done in the context of generally accepted sustainable development practices and in light of the more recent awareness of climate change. The International Council on Mining and Metals (ICMM) requires that mining and metals sector investments should be technically appropriate, environmentally sound, financially profitable and socially responsible (DoIR 2006). With a growing awareness within communities of the potential for conflicts in land use arising from mine developments, it is and has become imperative to plan new mines from the outset with completion and closure in mind. In most countries laws and regulations require the return of the area used for mining to a carefully planned and predetermined post-closure state.

Stakeholder engagement is necessary at various stages of the project-permitting process. In a few countries, some progressive regulations related to mine closure planning have come into operation, such as in the Western Australian Government's 2006 Guidelines for Mining Proposals and the South African Government's requirement for Social and Labour Plans under the mining laws and the Socio-Economic Empowerment Charter for the South African Mining Industry. In addition, regardless of whether or not there are specific laws or regulations relating to integrated mine closure planning, there is a general regulatory and public trend to insist on integrating social aspects at the earliest possible stage of planning the mine.

Figure 1: Photographs of the Duisburg-Nord Landscape Park project, Duisburg, West Germany

Outer rim of the volcanic crater forms the perimeter of the Pilanesberg National Park

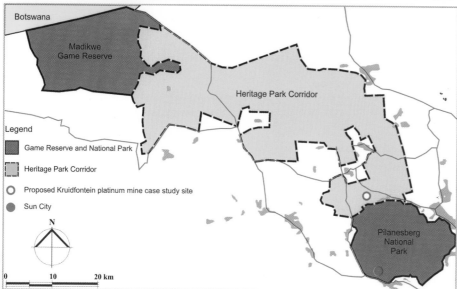

Botswana

Madikwe Game Reserve

Heritage Park Corridor

Legend

▨ Game Reserve and National Park

⬚ Heritage Park Corridor

○ Proposed Kruidfontein platinum mine case study site

● Sun City

N

0   10   20 km

Pilanesberg National Park

Figure 2: Photographs of the Bafokeng Rasomine Platinum Mine (BRPM), a typical modern platinum mine near Rustenburg, South Africa

Figure 3: Panorama photograph of the setting of the proposed Kruidfontein Platinum Mine

Figure 4: Proposed Kruidfontein mining complex within the planned Heritage Park Corridor

Integrated mine infrastructure planning and design

Traditionally, industrial and mining infrastructure has been in conflict with our general concept of what is generally considered as beautiful or aesthetically pleasing. The challenge that planners and designers face today is to transform ruined and derelict sites into places that challenge not only our understanding of what makes a place functional but also what makes it beautiful. This change in attitude focuses on the relationship between industrial-like landscapes and nature; between what is perceived to be ugly and what is perceived as being beautiful. This is best illustrated with a real-life project in West Germany (Figure 1).

The Duisburg-Nord Landscape Park, on the grounds of the former Thyssen Steelworks in Duisburg, Western Germany, does not place nature and the industry in opposition. The site's industrial ruins include towering smokestacks, cavernous ore bunkers, and bermed railroad tracks. These features constitute not only an important part of the region's history, but are also extraordinary structures which are important landmarks within the regional landscape.

Peter Latz, the designer, resisted the desire to abolish the industrial traces, believing that if the realms of nature and industry were combined, the overall experience would

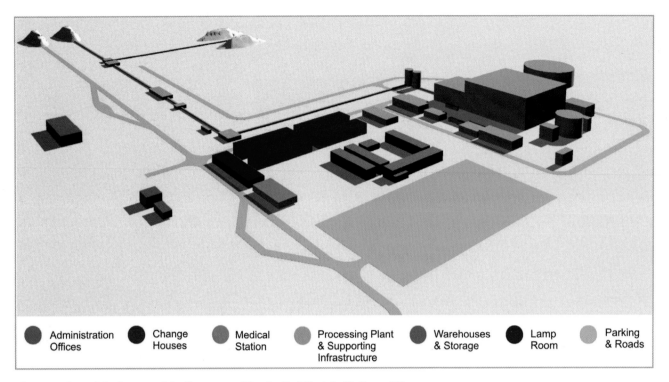

Figure 5: View of the layout originally proposed for the Kruidfontein Platinum Mine

Legend:
- Administration Offices
- Change Houses
- Medical Station
- Processing Plant & Supporting Infrastructure
- Warehouses & Storage
- Lamp Room
- Parking & Roads

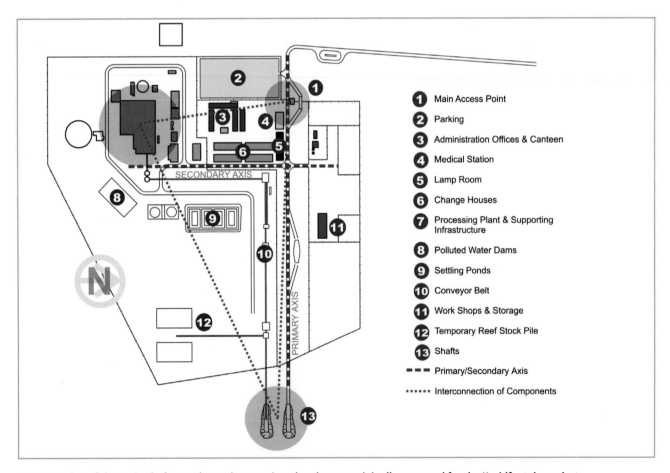

Legend:
1. Main Access Point
2. Parking
3. Administration Offices & Canteen
4. Medical Station
5. Lamp Room
6. Change Houses
7. Processing Plant & Supporting Infrastructure
8. Polluted Water Dams
9. Settling Ponds
10. Conveyor Belt
11. Work Shops & Storage
12. Temporary Reef Stock Pile
13. Shafts
- - - Primary/Secondary Axis
····· Interconnection of Components

Figure 6: Plan of the main shaft complex and processing plant layout, originally proposed for the Kruidfontein project

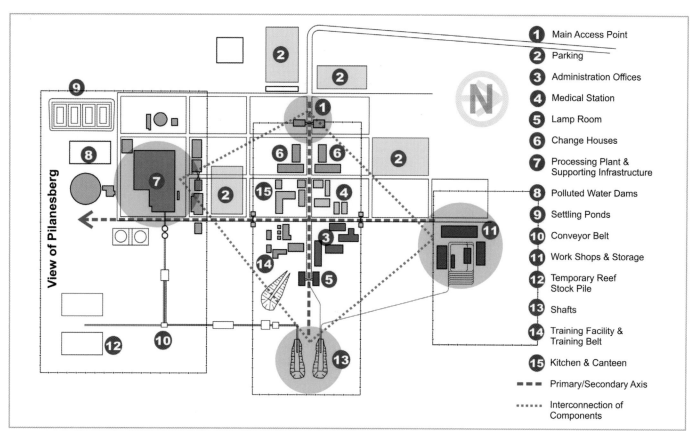

Figure 7: Revised plan of the mine infrastructure incorporating post-closure end use

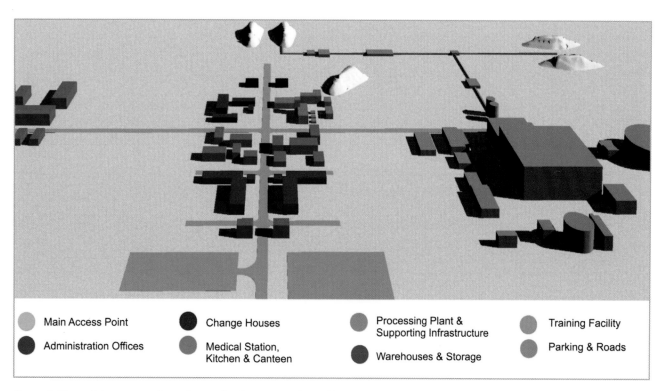

Figure 8: View of the proposed new layout for the proposed Kruidfontein Platinum Mine, integrating the initial interim mine infrastructure use with post-closure end use

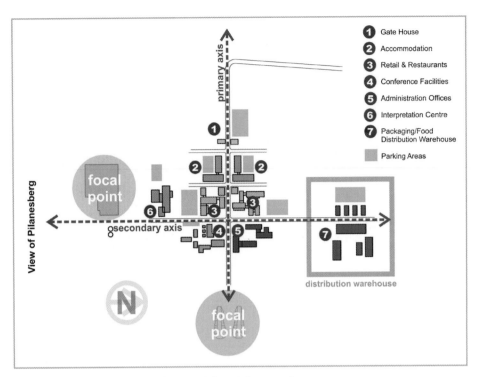

Figure 9: Post-closure land use layout of the mining complex

be richer. The industrial skeletons have surpassed the function they were originally intended for. While some structures were adapted for various leisure activities, the larger, overwhelming structures which evoke associations, emotions and an aura of secrecy, were used to create narratives and stories that allude to a mythical past (Reed 2005).

Whereas the Duisburg-Nord Landscape Park was planned some years after industrial processes ceased, this article deals with a scenario which is philosophically different in that an end land use is established first and prior to the commencement of the activity, i.e. mining. Mining is therefore accommodated as an 'interim' and 'temporary' use of the site with an entirely different longer-term post-closure use in mind for the site once the mining is complete. This is the key to the planning and design of mine infrastructure for closure and requires a paradigm shift from traditional mine planning approaches.

In an industry where time is money, and production is key, architects and engineers are under pressure to develop solutions rapidly for the spatial planning of buildings and supporting infrastructure for mining complexes. This often results in what can be maybe best described as a 'chaotic' or 'seemingly unstructured' conglomeration of buildings and infrastructure in proximity to each other. The Bafokeng Rasimone Platinum Mine (BRPM), near Rustenburg in the North West Province, is a typical example of a modern platinum mine where infrastructure was planned for the life of the mine only (Figure 2).

Mining infrastructure should be planned and designed with the object of integrating post-closure land use from the outset of the project. The proposed Kruidfontein Platinum Mine, which is located immediately North of the Pilanesberg National Park (PNP) in the North West Province of South Africa, is discussed and used as our case study (Figure 3).

Before

After

Approximate scale of typical mining infrastructure as was originally proposed for the Kruidfontein platinum project.

Figure 10: Before photograph and after photomontage of the typical infrastructure as originally envisaged for the Kruidfontein Platinum Mine project (SEF 2003)

The PNP is set in the crater of one of the largest volcanic complexes of its kind in the world covering an area of 55 000ha. Mining in the vicinity of the park could impact on several tourism initiatives; one such initiative includes the possible establishment of a corridor stretching between the PNP and Madikwe Game Reserve (Figure 4). Although conflict in land use is likely to occur within this corridor, it was realised early on in the initial environmental assessment that there are several opportunities in terms of planning and designing infrastructure which could be in support of rather than in direct conflict with the longer-term tourism use in the aforesaid corridor. The opportunity also exists for the reuse of mining infrastructure creating the future 'gateway' to the Heritage Park Corridor.

The layout of the main shaft complex and processing plant, originally proposed for the Kruidfontein project (Figures 5 and 6), represents a fragmented, disconnected industrial-like development, similar in nature and scale to that of BRPM (Figure 2). Buildings are grouped together according to function and placed randomly next to transport routes creating an *ad-hoc* infill-type development linking the shafts with the processing plant.

No designated end use was originally envisaged for Kruidfontein after decommissioning and closure. Even if there was, the lack of order in the complex, weak spatial definition, and the stark treatment of building forms would be some of the biggest challenges to overcome in meeting the demanding requirements of a new and different future use for the complex. A subsequent recommendation and further refinement to the conceptual layout suggests that the change houses, medical station and kitchen and canteens are mirrored with the administration offices, lamp room and training facilities along the main north-east secondary axis

(Figure 7). This will help to channel the major people traffic flows entering the site to go underground or to the plant away from the mine administration complex, preventing possible disruption during shift change.

Design strategy

The solution to the problem is not merely the beautifying of buildings and the spaces around them, but rather a focused and concerted planning and design of the complex during the initial mine planning stages. Two main planning strategies have been identified, namely: pre-construction urban planning and visual impact management.

Pre-construction urban planning

Order and legibility

Order is related to the way in which people perceive and understand the environment. This perceptual order is related to the legibility of the environment or the ease with which its parts can be recognised and organised into a coherent pattern. The main elements for achieving order are paths/movement networks, edges, nodes and landmarks/focal points.

A strong axis for the organising discipline for the grouping of buildings is a common method of layout. With this generic layout tool, buildings and open space are arranged about an axis. Unity is established by presenting the viewer with controlled focal points along an axial vista. The system of setting up axes and subsidiary axes, which determine the location of compositional elements, is developed so that some points on the grid gain an added significance (Moughtin, 2003). The proposed new layout is ordered along two main axes (Figures 8 and 9).

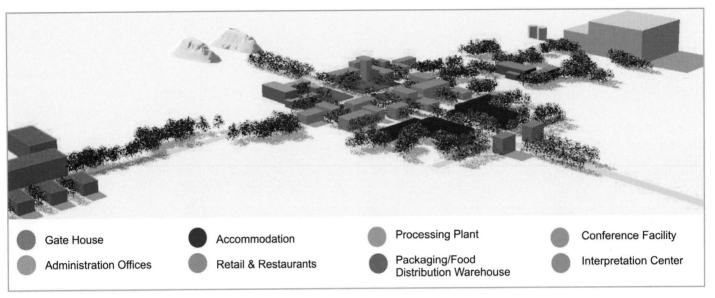

● Gate House	● Accommodation	● Processing Plant	● Conference Facility
● Administration Offices	● Retail & Restaurants	● Packaging/Food Distribution Warehouse	● Interpretation Center

Figure 11: View of the proposed end use layout for the Kruidfontein project

The primary axis stretches from the access point to the shafts, which becomes the main focal point. The secondary axis connects the processing plant and workshops. These axes become the arteries of activity, generating structured pedestrian movement networks to and from the main elements in the complex. A node is formed where these two axes coincide, which becomes the centre of activity and point of orientation in the complex. Buildings, according to their hierarchy, function and inter-relationships are arranged around this activity node and further along the two main axes.

Arranging the building mass

The densification of the building mass around movement networks and transport corridors ensures that roads, streets and public spaces are well-defined, safe and legible.

Orientation of buildings

Buildings should have views, good solar orientation, or ideally, both (Lewis 2005). Vistas and views of the Pilanesberg National Park are impressive and ought to be utilised.

Defining public and private space

Building mass mediates the public, semi-public and private spaces which give the users a choice between activity and privacy. By orientating active 'fronts' to streets and public spaces, and inactive 'backs' to the private realm, activity is encouraged in streets and public spaces, and security and privacy is maintained in private spaces or courts (Lewis, 2005).

Relationship between buildings and spaces

The scale and proportion of buildings affect the quality of urban space. Building height and form must be proportional to the spaces they define. Users feel comfortable in and around human-scaled buildings and spaces as opposed to monumental structures that are overbearing and visually dominating. Apart from the processing plant, the dimensions of the buildings, spaces and streets are compared with the proportions of the human figure (Moughtin 2003). Man becomes the measure used for the built environment. The processing plant, however, benefits from its monumental scale to become an important focal point.

Mixing uses and recycling buildings

Buildings are designed to accommodate different uses in a set context. This means that the complex becomes a flexible vessel for change, adapting at any given point during the life of the mine, and thereafter. Provision is made for adding to or subtracting from the building mass without compromising the inner workings and dynamics of the spatial layout.

Providing green areas and corridors

Green areas are important elements in place-making. They enhance legibility and increase the variety of uses in a space. These areas and corridors tie buildings and spaces together as integral components of a place.

Treating the street as a place

The environmental quality of streets/movement networks needs to be delivered through good landscape design. All elements – paving, lighting, street furniture, signage and vegetation – should work together to create their own character.

Parking

Heavy vehicular routes are relayed around the complex with parking areas located outside the centre. The two main axes will remain pedestrian-orientated. No vehicular movement is envisaged through the complex during the operational phase, although provision should be made for flexibility in the urban fabric to accommodate some vehicular movement and parking areas in the complex when the end land use commences.

Visual impact management

Kruidfontein Mining Complex is situated in a landscape that is characterised by flat, undulating topography with uninterrupted views for several kilometres over the plains (Figure 3). Except for the backdrop of the Pilanesberg from a northern viewpoint, the size and height of the project components, such as the waste rock dumps, processing plant and tailings dam, will be visually dominant in the landscape. The impact is a function of subjective factors, which are based on the cultural and experiential associations of the viewers as well as the value they place on the visual environment over other social considerations (SEF 2003).

General mitigation measures for the visual impact of mining activities are included in the environmental assessment for the Kruidfontein project. These measures focus mainly on minimising the visual intrusion by proposing physical barriers, such as trees and berms to 'screen' structures from receptors and onlookers. A tall order, one might think, taking into account that some structures vary between 15 and 25m in height. Instead of addressing the root of the problem (the physical appearance of the buildings) mining companies will rather take the path of least resistance.

As no end use is normally envisaged for the mining infrastructure, mitigation measures are usually as cost-effective as possible. Utilitarian sheds are erected and waste rock is used to construct the screening berms. If an end use was known, the buildings could be designed with that use in mind while at the same time addressing the visual impact of the mining operations.

Figure 12: Views of the mine training facility which will be refurbished and used as a conference facility after mine closure

Figure 13: Human-scale spaces and walkways are proposed and will be created between buildings

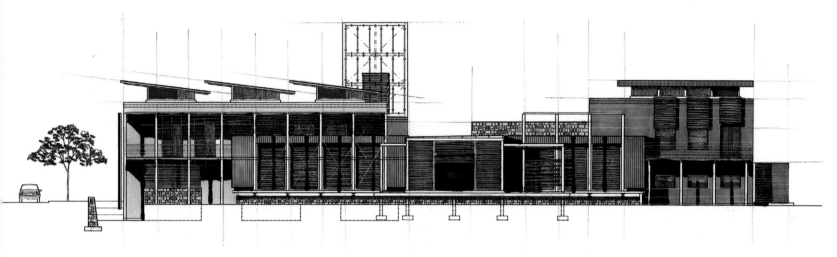

Figure 14: Elevation of the conference and leisure complex

In the case of Kruidfontein an appropriate and potentially feasible end land use does exist. The locality of the project within the planned Heritage Park Corridor allows architects and engineers to formulate context-specific design guidelines and objectives during the pre-construction planning phase of the mining project.

Kruidfontein has a relatively flat topography and low vegetation. This presents the opportunity for a high degree of individuality and creativity in the design process. Designs may be more articulated, more elaborate and with a greater range of scale and more vigorous form: a place which does not condone object buildings disconnected from its urban context. The true character of a space is enhanced through the use of material, texture, architectonics and a degree of transparency. The advantages of planning and designing the mining complex with an end use in mind are that:

◆ the layout is functional during and after the life of the mine
◆ the spaces within the landscape are ordered and clearly defined which enhances circulation and movement
◆ the shafts and processing plant are used as focal points on axes within the layout which assists with orientation
◆ the buildings are placed relatively closer with the objective to create spaces which result in a smaller overall footprint of the complex.

End land use planning and design

The Pilanesberg National Park (PNP) has, as an immediate strategy, identified the phasing out of accommodation facilities and visitor comfort stations from the basin of the crater and is exploring new opportunities on the periphery of the park. Peripheral development could include the facilitation of new developments outside the PNP that can divert the internal pressures and stimulate the creation of new regional products generating new opportunities for local communities (Contour Project Managers 2001).

The proposed Kruidfontein mining complex borders the PNP and is within the tourism demand area of the park and nearby Sun City. It also forms part of a planned Heritage Park Corridor. Therefore, selecting a tourism-based initiative as a possible end land use for the proposed mining development seems to be the feasible alternative to pursue. The designated end land use for the proposed Kruidfontein mining complex is visualised as a local and international tourism-based conference and leisure complex including conference facilities, interpretive centres, restaurants and entertainment areas, and eco-tourism activities (Figure 11).

Post-mining planning and design strategies

Order and legibility

The main entrance to the conference and leisure complex (Figure 12) will be located at the current entrance with reception and information offices close at hand. The retail and commercial development will be located along the primary axis. Self-catering units and lodge rooms will replace the change houses and laundries. The mine administration offices will be used as the new administration building for the complex. The training facility will be refurbished to house the conference centre for up to 160 delegates. Restaurants, bookshops, Internet cafés, and theatres are located along the secondary axis and arranged around the tree-shaded square. A new indoor and outdoor interpretive centre is proposed on the southern side of the complex in front of the old processing plant. The warehouse complex, outside the main complex, will be used to develop a second industry to provide the local community with new job opportunities. A secondary industry could include a packaging warehouse for perishable foods destined for Sun City and the PNP.

Focal points and nodes

The two shafts at the end of the primary axis will serve as the main focal points within the landscape (Figure 9). The processing plant next to the secondary axis will act as the secondary focal point of the complex. The open gathering space at the intersection between the primary and secondary axes will become the generator of activity in the complex.

The shafts and processing plant will remain intact to become symbols of remembrance. The IBR shell of the plant will be removed to expose the infrastructural skeleton against the backdrop of the Pilanesberg: a monumental landform in the otherwise flat landscape.

Scale

The infrastructure of the complex (excluding the processing plant and workshop complex) should retain a human scale as far as possible. Buildings will be limited to two storeys, not exceeding 10m in height. The form and spatial layout of these buildings will allow the easy accommodation of private, semi-private and public spaces in the new complex. The use of locally obtained materials, such as adobe, wattle and waste rock are favoured with an eye on reuse and recycling. The use of shading devices, colours, textures and detailing on the façades will add to the identity and character of the complex.

Activity centres

Buildings will be placed close to the street to ensure pedestrian-orientated, mix-use development close to transit stations. The quality of the pedestrian experience will prevail over the movement and storage of vehicles (Lewis 2005). The visual impact of parking facilities will be mitigated by placing retail, residential or service uses along the main street. Wide sidewalks with shaded seating, pedestrian level lighting, special paving, planters, bicycle racks and waste receptacles will be provided. Pedestrian areas will be shaded by trees, trellises, awnings, porches or building overhangs. Retail display windows will be generous. Landscape features such as public art, fountains, kiosks and identification graphics along walkways will be integrated.

Roads and parking

The complex is designed to accommodate vehicular traffic and parking. The primary and secondary axes will be dedicated pedestrian routes. Roads for heavy vehicular traffic are located outside the complex between the main road from Mabeskraal and the proposed packaging warehouses. The transport interchanges and supporting infrastructure are located near the main entrance to the complex.

Landscape planning and vegetation

Existing trees and vegetation will be retained as far as possible. Indigenous plants and trees will be used in the landscaping of the complex and the parking areas. Tall canopy trees will be used along key streets to give it a comfortable and pleasing sense of visual containment and to create separation between vehicles and pedestrians. Roads and streets will be designed to the minimum width feasible to mini-mise cost and storm water runoff. Walkways and open gather-ing spaces will be paved and shaded by trees, shrubs and plants. Trees will be planted during the initial mine construction stage in order to mature during the life of the mine to create the antici-pated end-use people spaces.

Conclusion

At the heart of the matter is the ability of the mining industry to gain permission for access to land containing new mineral re-serves. It is evident from the case study that post-closure use can be included from the outset of mine planning and design. By do-ing so, it can be demonstrated at a very early stage in the life of the mine that a tangible and real contribution can be made to a sustained development and use of land in the longer term with-out wasting valuable resources and allowing infrastructure to go to ruin. It is therefore proposed that doing it slightly differently could contribute significantly towards building a very convincing case for granting a 'social licence to operate' in an environmen-tally sensitive area which would otherwise be difficult, if not im-possible, to justify.

It is well established that living or working in ugly environments has significant negative psychological influences on humans. These can range from behavioural to health impacts such as slow recovery from illness and manifest on a broader scale in a lack of environmental pride and ownership, and poor land-care prin-ciples – all aspects that increase liabilities in a working mine. In addition to the human aspect, working in an aesthetically pleas-ing and uncrowded environment is known to reduce aggression levels, reduce absenteeism and increase productivity.

Better working places can be created by incorporating the basic principles of architecture into the planning of a new mine. Order, building form and spatial definition forms the basis from which any designer should embark on his quest for good place-making. Once this is achieved, spaces in themselves become beautiful.

Acknowledgements

This article has been reproduced with the kind permission of the Australian Centre for Geomechanics, Third International Seminar on Mine Closure, South Africa, 2008. The research presented in this article is drawn from a collaborative research programme at the University of Pretoria on the planning and design of mine infrastructure for post-closure use from the outset. The authors would like to acknowledge the financial and information contri-butions of Anglo Platinum.

Bibliography

Ching, F., 1996. *Architecture. Form, space & order*. New York: John Wiley & Sons, Inc.

Contour Project Managers. 2001. Heritage Park Concept Plan (Pilanes-berg National Park – Madikwe Game Reserve Corridor). Rustenburg. Unpublished Report.

DoIR. 2006. Mine closure and Completion. Leading practice sustainable development program for the Mining Industry. Department of In-dustry and Resources (DoIR). Commonwealth of Australia, Austral-ian Government, Department of Industry, Tourism and Resources.

Lewis, S. 2005. *Front to back. A design agenda for urban housing*. Oxford: Architectural Press.

Moughtin, C. 2003. *Urban design. Street and square*. Oxford: Architec-tural Press.

Reed, P. 2005. *Groundswell. Constructing the contemporary landscape*. New York: Thames & Hudson.

SEF. 2003. Environmental Management Programme Report for the Kruidfontein Project located on Rooderand Portion 2. Strategic En-vironmental Focus (SEF), CSIR Main Campus, Pretoria. Unpublished Report.

Winters, N.B. 2005. *Architecture is elementary*. Utah: Gibbs Smith, Publisher.

chapter 19

Anti-contextual Design:
Walled Gardens for Power Plants

Johan N. Prinsloo
Department of Architecture
University of Pretoria
Pretoria
South Africa

The sound thunders across the dry dust plain. The animals hide in the shadows of thorn trees; the sun sinks, someone sweats. The dust sticks to this sweat of a face. She sometimes thinks the smoke cloud is bringing rain, but it only brings spit from coughs. The smoke is billowing from towers stacked on a large block powering above the world far below; her eyes cannot help to squint upwards to 'the obelisks of industry vomiting toward the firmament their combinations of smoke'. (Baudelaire, *Salon of 1859*)

Currently, to build any 'obelisk of industry', you need to create a vast level surface; you create dust. A coal-fired power station pollutes the air with smog and noise. A coal-fired power station is a large mass; people look like ants. This then the physical context for a landscape architectural response.

The Johannesburg based firm, GREENinc, was appointed as landscape architects on a coal-fired power plant project in the Savannah district of a developing country. No amount of landscaping can offset such a carbon footprint. The landscape architects were confronted with a fixed site layout and programme, a site clearing plan and an undefined budget. After clearing was completed, the site closely resembled the Namib desert (Figure 1), only here a structure was to be built resembling, well, a power plant. The purpose of this article is not to describe the full project with all its complexities (e.g. site rehabilitation, visions for a decommissioned plant, mitigation of visual impact), but to zoom in on a design response which, on a site plan, might be mistaken for a parking bay.

The landscape architects soon realised that it would be folly to 'landscape' the entire site, given the amount of funds and other resources (especially water in a dry climate) that it would consume; the sheer size of the site would dilute any design interventions and result in an environment which is not 'what it was' [first nature] nor a rich contemporary cultural landscape [third nature]. The vast site, much of it cleared of vegetation as mentioned, called for a massive rehabilitation programme through the hydro seeding of pioneer grasses and planting of pioneer trees and shrubs – the estimated quantities are staggering. A second nature, a rehabilitated functional landscape, was to emerge on the site.

But what about our sweating face, the worker walking great distances in the sun, dust, smog and noise? Talk of staged succession and 'landscape as infrastructure' bothers her little. The landscape architects assumed she yearns for beauty, stillness and delight, as they do. Not forgetting that landscape is by definition a human construct, and not forgetting humans, the landscape architects insisted that pockets of third nature be created within the new veld. But how does one create places of beauty, stillness and delight within a landscape more harsh than the seventh circle of Inferno? The designers' (including architectural consultants Thinus Venter and Werner Lotz) response to the context was thus to excommunicate the context and create isolated spaces. Integration with context was for once deemed inappropriate. Reaction to it was not, and the design was generated as a series of responses to the site conditions: high and thick walls (partly) keep out heat, noise and apocalyptic views, overhead foliage and structures (partly) keep out sun and dirt in the air, plants found in moist ravines keep out ugliness and running water keeps out stress and evaporates to keep out dry heat (Figures 2–7).

These spaces were designed where people would walk every day, i.e. en route to the canteen which forms part of an administrative complex also including an office block, fire station and first aid centre, all serviced by a parking lot and helipad. There is no reason, as Joane Pim reminded us many years ago, that people working in industrial environments such as power plants, mines and Midrand should not have access to beauty outside. On the contrary, it is especially such conditions which ask for moments of respite from all types of ugliness. The power plant walled gardens are attempts at shelter, like a rock outcrop or *kloof* in the Highveld, for habitation.

This, of course, is nothing new and the walled garden was the predominant Western landscape design type until the Renaissance. We find walled enclosures in Ancient Egypt: water, fruit trees…were oases for the rich in the desert, like the island of Ra [Re]

Figure 1: View of site after clearing (Digital photograph, 2008)

Figure 3: Perspective of initial concept for walled garden (2008)

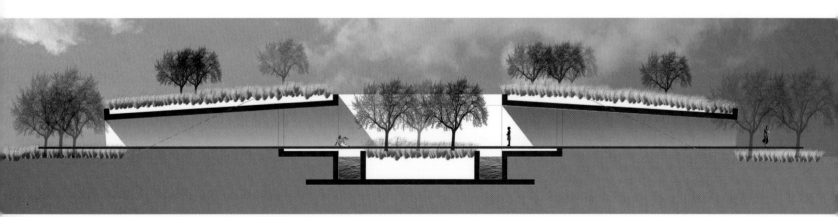

Figure 2: Section of initial concept for walled garden with earth walls (2008)

rising at the beginning from the dark waters, Nun. In Ancient Rome, public parks were enclosed by colonnades, we also find walled villa gardens and courtyards: water, fruit trees … were oases for the rich in the crowded city. We don't find open public parks. In the Middle Ages, we find a distinction: the *hortus delicarium*, a walled space of fruit trees and water as an oasis of pleasure for the rich. But also the *hortus conclusus,* walled spaces signifying the purity of the Virgin Mary that were oases for the devout in a sinful world. We don't find public parks. The fenced-off hunting grounds of the nobility were the closest to our idea of 'park'. Thus, for 1 500 years the walled garden was almost the only form of third nature found as physical and spiritual islands in the cities and countryside. They spake not of 'landscape as infrastructure'. The Renaissance started breaking down the walls and extended the designed landscape to include views of the countryside (now for the first time since Antiquity, to be heralded as beautiful) and to be viewed as a pattern from a building or terrace. The Baroque took this further and grandiose vistas were cut into the landscape. The line between third and first natures was blurring. Landscape was firmly fixed as *view.* The need for enclosure did not vanish and the *giardino segreto* [secret garden] was a walled place of escape (a garden of love) within a garden. We don't find open public parks. The Romantic era brought the outside scenery (untamed nature) closer and made 'informal' gardens that influenced the ideal of landscape design up to the present era. Third nature imitates first nature. We don't find public parks. The Industrial Revolution caused big cities and the need for the countryside inside. The desire to walk and live among trees in smog rendered the ideal of the garden city. We find open public parks. The idea of a walled garden found expression in the private outdoor rooms of the rising wealthy middle class in North America after the Second World War. In South Africa, people can still be found lazing next to swimming pools and mowing the lawn on Saturday mornings. The contemporary walled suburban garden is a private space of pleasure, as it was throughout history, yet it does not stand testimony to our highest achievements in art and culture, as it did. If it does, we are in trouble.

Landscape architects tend to regard the garden as the lowest of projects to work on. The walled garden is everything we don't strive for and contra our visions for future green cities, or rather systems, where everything is interconnected: building as landscape, landscape as infrastructure, man as beast and tree as city. Everything becomes everything else. The idea of a walled island becomes undemocratic, unecological, indulgent and generally frowned upon. They add nothing to the solution of the problem of cities with which landscape architects grapple: inner-city rejuvenation, reusing wasted lands, designing infrastructural systems to function as public spaces, etc.

But what about our sweating face, the worker walking great distances in the sun, dust, smog and noise? Talk of staged succession and 'landscape as infrastructure' bothers her little. Landscape architects should assume she yearns for beauty, stillness and delight, as they do. I am sure they do. Public parks (and other open spaces) are created on limited budgets and, as an attempt to 'landscape' the site of a power plant would, resources are thinly spread over large areas and the polis are left with large lawn surfaces, endless paving and off-the-shelf street furniture, some community artworks at entrances and volume upon volume of ill-defined, monotonous spaces which look impressive on aerial photographs showing 'open green space networks'. Our sweated face walks endlessly without going through a threshold, without entering an intimately scaled space off-set by a large open space, without seeing a well-articulated detail, without being prompted

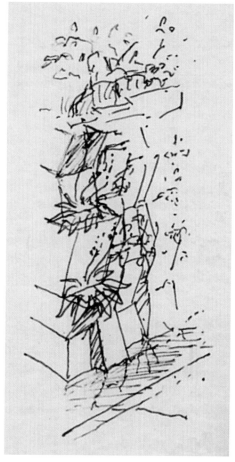

Figure 4: Design development of walled garden, concrete walls (Sketches, 2008)

Figure 5: Design development of a planted wall (Sketches, 2008)

Figure 6: Spatial investigation of movement through walled gardens (Sketches, 2008)

to take an alternative route on which she finds a view of a sculpture which makes her, perhaps on a somber day, question her Being. She walks along a 1.2m wide pathway which serpentines forever, she can barely read the pattern on the floor at the junction where many paths meet, because it is completely flat. She has nowhere to read a book, because the noise of the street and the soccer players never ends.

What about public walled gardens? There is one in the botanic gardens in Maputo. It is in ruin, which makes it even more special. Jean Nouvel's Centre de Poblenou Park in Barcelona is one on a large scale. The themed gardens at Parc de la Villette are also examples of enclosed public outside spaces, places that turn their backs to their contexts and provide solitude, not solutions. Of course landscape architects should grapple with the problems of the city and work towards healthy, sustainable landscape urbanism, but until that day, the day when a mountain will remain blue when you reach it, we must sometimes not forget to create pockets of Utopia. Landscape architecture is more than problem solving. Landscape is more than a machine.

Figure 7: Perspective of one of the walled gardens (Digital collage, 2008)

chapter 20

Not Lost in Translation:
Grappling with Meaning in Mauritius

Johan N. Prinsloo
Department of Architecture
University of Pretoria
Pretoria
South Africa

When we write, we make invisible things visible. When we speak, we make silent things audible. When we draw aimlessly in the sand, we make unknown things tangible. Flowers left on a lover's windowsill do all these things, and they smell nice, like her hair. Landscapes too embody the world of Ideas. Otherwise we would call it Nature. Landscape architects don't design nature. They write stories, and Nature is a character and sometimes a setting. It is difficult you see, because these stories must work. They can fall apart. They can die by the sun. They are temporal, and rather temperamental. They are read spatially, as if walking through Pamuk's Istanbul or stepping on Miss Golightly's toe. They are not read from beginning to end, as if starting on page thirty-two, then jumping to page three, staying on it for two hours then skipping the rest, apart from the quick slip on the wet pavement on page twelve. The reader is, however, less captivated. The reader's breakfast affects his mood, and he stumbles through our books thinking of tomorrow's meeting with fools, or what those flowers were doing on his girlfriend's windowsill. And he sometimes stumbles through our books twice a day; *Catcher in the Rye* was great, but I'm only going to read it once a day. And he speaks Afrikaans, or English, or Xhosa, or German, or Mandarin, or is two years old. And our books are often prescribed, our reader has no choice being in the street, and that park is the closest to his apartment and he cares little who wrote it, or what the plot is. It is difficult, you see. And have you read those outside spaces that are badly written, the tabloid townscapes or the gossip gardens? They don't want you to think too much. They are sensational. They seek cheap thrills. If they want to tell a story of a hundred soldiers that died in a forest, they will give you a full-size tank and a hundred life-like statues. If they want to tell a story of music,

they'll put a loudspeaker to your ear and sing your brains out. If they want to remind you of Tuscany, they'll plant lavender, olive trees and erect a fountain of Cupid.

So landscape architects write stories, but they don't make books. They make landscapes. More accurately, they design outside spaces that form part of landscapes. In Mauritius there are many stories to be told. NLA+GREENinc was appointed as landscape architects on the Corniche Bay integrated resort scheme with architects Foster+Partners from London. This article will not describe the project in its entirety, but focus on the telling of stories. It was difficult, you'll see.

Following the popularity of Lewis Carroll's *Alice in Wonderland* (1865), 'As dead as a dodo' has become a common phrase that denotes something which is unambiguously and unequivocal-

ly dead. Once being the home of the extinct *Raphus cucullatus*, the Republic of Mauritius has become an archetypal landscape of the tension between human intervention and the bio-physical environment. Already known by Arab sailors in the tenth century, Mauritius has been inhabited by Portuguese, Dutch, French, British, Indian, African and Chinese farmers, businessmen, aristocrats, slaves and soldiers of Buddhist, Muslim, Hindu and Christian belief. This rich cultural diversity is reflected in the colourful tapestry of celebrations, shrines, building styles, temples,

Figure 2: The site with Le Morne Brabant in the background. Note the banyan tree on the right (Digital photograph, 2008)

Figure 3: Walking through a banyan tree (Digital collage, 2008)

churches, dress, languages, decorated buses and thematic resorts. Artists and writers such as Malcolm de Chazal breathe life into the landscape with their images and words:

The light would reach us more quickly in the morning and fade more slowly at night if the whole earth were divided into vast flower beds that called forth the light at dawn and clutched it longer at nightfall. Nature instituted summer for flowers long before man took summer over for his own uses.

The island has thus become a collector of the exotic (Figure 1): less than 2% of the island's vegetation cover can be considered indigenous and the concept of a 'first people' is non-existent. The island is a technicolour of peaceful paradoxes: invasive guava plants that line the roads have become the objects of festive fruit picking outings on public holidays, the clear ocean waters are polluted with beautiful Hindu offerings, Catholic shrines are entombed in mystical banyan trees from the east, the biologically competitive casuarina trees littered on the coastlines leave no room for natural forests, but create high canopies that provide shade for the endless picnic-goers ... a highly contested ground.

It is thus impossible to imagine and naïve to long for an untouched Mauritius; an island isolated from the world. Working within this context, the formulated design approach was thus to extract the layers (physical and non-physical) of the site through research and site analysis and conceive a landscape design which, as a new layer, critically responds to this depth of context.

The 176ha site (Figure 2) is situated on the south-western coast of Mauritius with dramatic views to Le Morne Brabant, Ile aux Bénitiers [referring to the coral formations

Figure 4: A clearing in the forest (Digital collage, 2008)

Figure 5: Exploring the nature of the viewing platform

Figure 6: Viewing platform (Digital collage, 2008)

Figure 7: Drainage line collage (Digital collage, 2008) [consists of 5 images]

found in the vicinity of the island, named after Catholic stoups found at church entrances], the village of La Gaulette and the setting sun over the Indian Ocean. The site can topographically be classified into a hillside and a coastal area, separated by National Road B9 running parallel to the coastline. Significant to the vicinity of the site is Le Morne Brabant, a mythical volcanic rock that rises from the sea. Apart from its strong visual presence, it has become a symbol of the resistance against slavery after a tragic event that occurred in the nineteenth century: The almost inaccessible cliffs of the outcrop were frequently occupied by groups of maroons [runaway slaves] in the eighteenth and nineteenth centuries to avoid capture. After slavery had been abolished, a police expedition was sent on 1 February 1835 to inform the hideaways of their

new-found freedom. They saw the policemen, thought they were coming to capture them, and jumped to their deaths. Since then Le Morne has become associated with the abolition of slavery and was inscribed on the UNESCO World Heritage Site list in 2008. The Le Morne Cultural Landscape Management Plan states that 'Le Morne Brabant peninsula is one of the most striking landscapes of Mauritius' and 'Le Morne holds great importance in the history and memory of Mauritius'. The site itself carries a memory of a route used by maroons leading up the hill. The exact location of the route is not known. More recently the site was used as a hunting ground and the platforms from which huntsmen would wait on their prey are still present.

Figures 8 and 9: Plants on display
(Sketches, 2008) (left)

Figure 10: Walled garden
(Digital collage, 2008) (below)

Figure 11: Drainage line crossing (Digital collage, 2008)

Now that we have the background and setting of our story, how is it written? One of the challenges for any landscape architect is to filter through information. What information (invisible things) can and should be translated to material spaces (visible things)? This filtering of design informants must happen on many different levels. From the way in which form is articulated (style if you must) to the embodiment or celebration of history and memory (meaning).

The said cultural diversity of Mauritius and resulting lack of a well-defined architectural vernacular render a thematic response to an existing style problematic. Most hotel developments on Mauritius are, however, stylistically modeled after vague images of sugar plantation mansions or primitive (more Polynesian than Mauritian) 'island huts' – landscape elements such as street furniture often perpetuate these themes. In contrast, the Corniche Bay landscape design does not attempt to stylistically reflect any one of the many cultures (real and imagined), but rather take cues from local patterns (e.g. salt pans), building techniques and materials (e.g. basaltic rock walls), and contemporary landscape architecture design ideas.

In responding to the dense meanings of the landscape, it was decided to design spatial interventions that evoke interest and hint at content, rather than to translate ideas literally into form. Not to erect the loudspeaker or statues of soldiers in the forest. The decision was thus taken not to attempt to translate invisible things into visible things, but rather have visible things point towards

the invisible, like footprints in the sand point to a lion. Footprints aren't creatures, but signs of their existence. If you see a footprint and you don't know what animal left it there, you can consult a guide book for identification. The guide book will also tell you that *Panthera leo* weighs 250kg. Imagine it otherwise and driving in the Kruger National Park and seeing information boards everywhere: in the trees, bolted onto elephants, pointing towards rivers, stuck on your forehead, regularly updated signs next to footprints... the veld would be cluttered with content. For the same reason, it was proposed that a guide book (in digital format loaded on cell phones or GPS devices or other gadgetry) would be linked to these spatial interventions to tell the stories of the island and the site. As in Medieval gardens where the meaning was amplified by texts, so too are the experience of these spaces densified by an external source. Landscapes are stories, but not books.

These spatial interventions are designed at different places on the site, each with a unique character and sense of place: one space is a low wall around a banyan tree with a pathway leading the visitor through the gothic stems of the tree (Figure 3). In another, higher up on the hill, an area is cleared of its exotic plants and replanted with the slow-growing ebony trees. Dark, monolithic elements march through the clearing, hinting at the maroon route (Figure 4). Over the course of many years, people can witness the growth of a forest and realise how long it takes to replace what was once there. Still higher on the hill, a look-out point: a simple surface from where the visitor can gaze over the ocean and

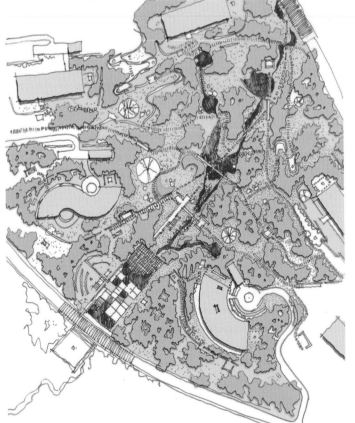

Figure 12: A villa in a garden (Digital collage, 2008)
Figure 13: A network of villas, paths and outside spatial interventions (Digital collage, 2008)

towards Le Morne Brabant (Figures 5 and 6). Lower down, in one of the drainage lines, a space is created in which water is sparsely collected and rare indigenous plants are cultivated (Figure 7) – by placing these plants in areas like this, and not in the mass of the landscaping, they are not lost for the education and appreciation of the visitor (Figures 8 and 9). For the more esoteric of heart, walled spaces provide spaces for individual repose (Figure 10). Where the drainage lines cross the roads, water is also collected and through the roads crossing at low levels (Figure 11) the visitor is immersed into the landscape and, for a short interlude, taken away from the far away views of the mountains and ocean. All these spaces are made accesible to the visitor by a network of pathways that stitch all the elements (including the villas, see Figure 12) together (Figure 13). All of these spaces seek to respond to the layers of landscape in which they are situated and, as pockets of intensified experience, give glimpses of the Mauritius few tourists ever see.

When we write, we make invisible things visible. When we make landscapes, we make bridges between the invisible and visible.

chapter 21

Green Inklings:
The Paper Landscapes of GREENinc

Johan N. Prinsloo
Department of Architecture
University of Pretoria
Pretoria
South Africa

Introduction

In the common tongue, the word 'reality' has a strange association with 'material' and is even more strangely opposed with 'idea' and 'abstract'. (I beg you not to associate 'common' with stupid or 'tongue' with tongue.) It is also used to describe that which is not easy-going, but hard and tough. As nails. The dreams of a rich poet sleeping under a shady tree next to a clear water stream in Switzerland are thus the furthest thing away from 'reality.' When someone in any tiresome meeting proposes an idea which lifts the soul and makes the instant coffee smell good, he is politely asked – after some murmuring and sniggering – to 'get back to reality'. He calmly goes back to doodling on the minutes of the previous meeting. His ideas never make it to the Action column. Reality has come to mean the world of practical action, the 'stop dreaming and mow the lawn' life of hard knocks. Landscape architects get knocked hard all the time. When a project runs over budget, 'landscaping' gets mowed down to lawn and gravel. Landscape is seen as a luxury. Breathing clean air and fresh water will become luxuries if this attitude persists. Beauty is also a luxury, like being saved when drowning. There are other reasons why only a small minority of the work landscape architects do is ever seen by the public. And not only because some of the work is beyond closed gates, but because much of the work is never built. Many days, and many more nights, are spent in solitude in the dreaming and drawing of landscapes that are never to be visited, because they will never exist. *Distinguo!* They will never exist in reality. *Distinguo!* They will never exist materially. In addition to the said phenomenon of budget cuts are the numerous unsuccessful competition entries (even winning a competition does not guarantee construction), the client bankruptcies and even

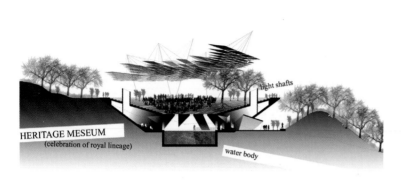

HERITAGE MESEUM
(celebration of royal lineage)

light shafts

water body

The Lebone II school for the Royal Bafokeng

All children are criminals. So one would assume, if you look at our places of learning; schools have a disconcerting resemblance to jails. They are good examples of 'reality'. GREENinc, with architects Mashabane Rose, entered a competition for the design of a combined primary and secondary school of excellence for the Royal Bafokeng near Rustenburg. The aim was not to create a jail. The site for the school is situated in a natural bowl in the bushveld with dramatic cliffs as backdrop. People often want to develop in beautiful places because they are drawn to the beauty of the place. When they develop there, they replace exactly that to which they were drawn, and then complain that there is no beauty left in the world. For this reason the design team decided not to situate the school on the beautiful site, but next to it, in a quarry. Yes, a quarry; a desert-like ditch; a scar in the earth. Development usually harms, but it can also heal. By building all the main facilities of the school in the quarry, existing vegetation is not removed and the scarred ground is rejuvenated. Within the natural bowl, a more sacred space was proposed – a place of gathering and history (Figure 1). A place at the end of a route. Route? Instead of ordering the school around a series of quadrangles, like at most other South African schools and Pretoria Central Jail, the school is ordered along a series of streets (Figure 2), like at most places where people live. All children are people, we assumed. The streets allowed for a fragmented ordering of elements and instead of placing the school in the landscape as a fortified environment isolated from its context, the existing landscape (that beyond the extent of the quarry) is allowed to bleed through the man-made streets, courtyards, assembly spaces (Figure 3), sports fields and food gardens of Lebone II – a microscopic version of a village. Field guides for the different grades were proposed that linked points in the landscape with information and tasks. The landscape thus becomes a middle ground between the formal and the informal, the

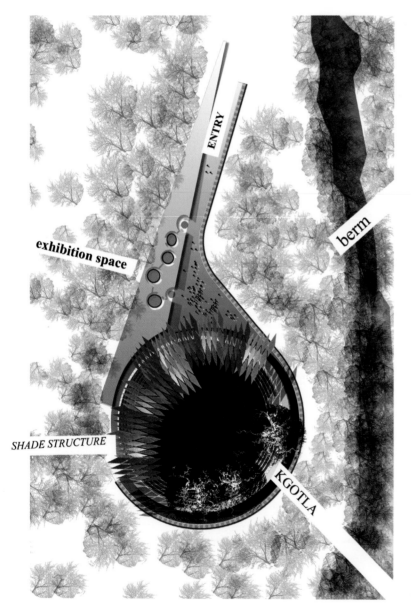

ENTRY

berm

exhibition space

SHADE STRUCTURE

KGOTLA

Figure 1: Gathering and celebration space [Kgotla]. Lebone II school competition entry, Rustenburg (Digital collage, 2007)

self-induced change of plans, literally. This article thus wishes to open the gates to some of the never-to-be-built projects by landscape architects GREENinc. These few words and images will allow you to visit these landscapes, just like you have maybe visited New York and London without ever having gone there, in books and films.

Figure 2: Street. Lebone II school competition entry, Rustenburg (Digital collage, 2007)

Figure 3: Main assembly space. Lebone II school competition entry, Rustenburg (Digital collage, 2007)

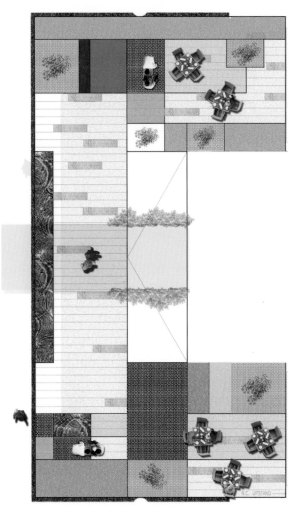

man-made and natural, predictable and unforeseen, the ordered and the chaotic – worlds too often separated in the design of schools leading to the formation of a rigid common mind and will. The result is a rich tapestry of outside spaces (Figure 6) in which students can engage in physical and imaginative activities: students learn from traditional teaching methods, but also by interacting with their environment, man-made and natural. From jail to *schola ludus* [play site].

Figure 4: Layered plan of sky garden. Headquarters business park at Jeddah Corniche, Saudi Arabia (Digitally rendered plan, 2008)

Figure 5: Perspective of sky garden. Headquarters business park at Jeddah Corniche, Saudi Arabia (Digital collage, 2008)

Figure 6: Plan of school proposal on aerial photograph. Lebone II school competition entry, Rustenburg (Digitally rendered plan, 2007)

Jeddah sky garden

Gardens are associated with soil. Soil is associated with the earth. Only sometimes, do gardens fly. As with the sky garden for a skyscraper in Jeddah (in Saudi Arabia) designed by the architects Batley and Partners. Skyscrapers are often unpleasant to be in, especially because you can't get out. That then the brief: to design an inside outside space; a place where people can step outside inside. Or something like that. The design was generated through a process of layering and weaving of elements inspired by the context: the Arabian desert and culture. Water is used sparsely as in the Islamic courtyard gardens; built-in tables are finely carved like the shutter windows and doors of old Jeddah; plants are used sparsely, like an oasis in the desert; shades of light coloured stone from the area are used for the floor. The sky garden is like a Persian carpet (Figures 4 and 5); many Persian carpets represent gardens.

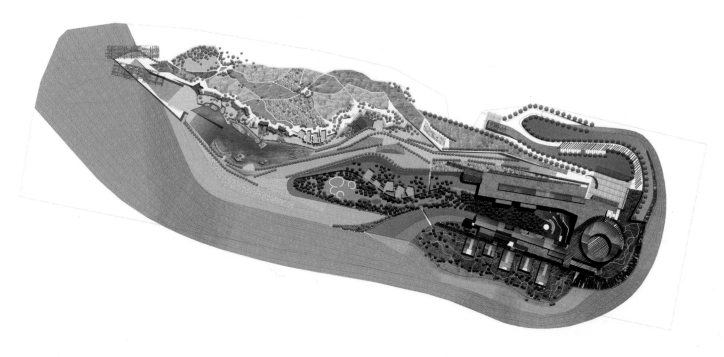

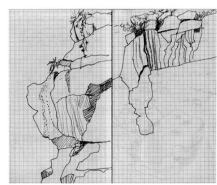

Figure 7: Plan of precinct, coloured area indicates public park. Pan-African Parliament competition entry, Midrand (Digitally rendered plan, 2007)

Figure 8: Investigation of kloof concept. Pan-African Parliament competition entry, Midrand (Digital photographs and ink sketches, 2007)

Figure 9: Cliff face. Pan-African Parliament competition entry, Midrand (Digital collage, 2007)

Figure 10: Welcome. Eastern Cape legislature competition winning entry, Bisho (Digital collage, 2006)

Figure 11: High-tech ecology. Siemens campus proposal, Midrand (Digital collage, 2007) (above, pp. 262–263)

Figure 12: The rabbit and the tortoise. 2010 World Cup public art competition entry, Johannesburg (Digital collage, 2008)

Figure 13: Dorms and park. Aga Khan University winning competition entry, Dar-es-Salaam, Tanzania (Digital collage, 2008)

Pan-African Parliament

The Pan-African Parliament is to be built in Midrand, next to the N1 highway. There was a design competition. GREENinc and Mashabane Rose Architects' proposal didn't win, but made the top five. A parliament complex cannot help but be a paradox: a place built on the foundations of freedom where the chosen voices of the people of the continent gather to debate, is a highly secure zone with public access limited to (according to the proposal) a viewing gallery. Another paradox is Midrand, that in-betwe-

en city built on the seemingly endless openness of the highveld, yet there are no open spaces for the people who live there. They have to jog on the treadmills in the gym overlooking the highway of patient souls. The landscape architects sought to use the parliament complex as an opportunity to rectify this and proposed a public park as part of the precinct (Figure 7). To make a large park on an endless plain, one needs to make spaces that are not plain. People who know the Highveld, will know its *kloofs* [ravines].

They will know that the *kloofs* are the opposite of the endless openness, but vertical spaces full of water, figs struggling through rocks, mosses and ferns, krans aloes and birds' nests, dassies and baboons, fishes and kingfishers, caves and overhangs, sand banks and *ghwarrie* trees... linear lines of diverse life cutting through the (apparent) monotony of the grasslands. The *kloof* thus became an analogy for the design of an un-plain park (Figure 8). The design proposed a linear man-made cliff consisting of a system of modular retaining blocks containing cavities in which plants could be grown (Figure 9). By cutting into the slope of the site and retaining the soil with the 'cliff', a flat area emerged on which a large open water body was proposed as part of a wetland system that would purify grey-water and storm water run-off from the buildings and other hard surfaces. The architectural quality of the landscape is inversely complimented by the landscape quality of the architecture: the building extends away from the highway as a cut into the slope and dissolves into the landscape as a thin green line.

Other

There have been many others. There was a winning entry for the Eastern Cape legislature in Bisho, but it is currently frozen (Figure 10). There was an extensive proposal for the Siemens campus in Midrand, of which only a portion was built – a landscape where high technology is used to create a bio-diverse ecology (Figure 11). There was a competition entry with The Library (an art duo from Johannesburg) for a 2010 World Cup public art installation, *The fable of Aesop of the rabbit and the tortoise* (Figure 12). There is a pending design proposal for an Aga Khan University in Dar-es-Salaam (Figures 13 and 14). All these paper projects thus present GREENinc's struggles, not only with the positivist mindsets of those involved in the built environment bent on development, profit and edifices, but also with their own ideas and suspicions on what good landscape architecture should be. Throughout, design methodologies oscillated between sober problem-solving exercises for highly functional urban environments to irresponsible tomfoolery such as generating master plans by tracing random aerial photographs; experiments to conjure up beautiful forms. Hopefully the only constant – beauty: the search for good lines was always as important as reactions to climate and soil conditions, the sculpting of positive spaces as important as selecting appropriate planting material, the embodiment of content as important as the analysis of context and all mediated through forms that fit, and sometimes even invoke the unfashionable senses of humour and Romance. It therefore comes as no surprise that many of the images included here are collages that somehow communicate more effectively these inklings than any plan or section can; stockpiles of handdrawn sketches, CAD plans, 3-D models and photographs. Although these projects will never be

Figure 14: Weaving into urban fabric. Aga Khan University winning competition entry, Dar-es-Salaam, Tanzania (Digitally rendered plan, 2008)

built, they exist at least here as virtual landscapes and can be visited where all landscapes are experienced to their greatest fulfillment, *ex situ* in memory.

Paper projects often exhibit the landscape architect's best work, yet are never seen by the public or other designers. They are perfected realities and, by being visited in exhibitions and books like this, can hopefully inspire some to allow them to filter through to become material realities and lessen the blows, or at least provide cover, from the life of hard knocks.

chapter 22

Why a Building Contract Should not be Used for Landscape Work

Piet Vosloo

Department of Architecture

University of Pretoria

Pretoria

South Africa

This article is based on a five-part article by the author titled 'Landscape contracting in SA', published in the Sep/Oct 2008, Nov/Dec 2008, Jan/Feb 2009, Mar/Apr 2009 and May/Jun 2009 issues of *Landscape SA*. The survey research referred to in this article was part of the unpublished research undertaken by the author for a PhD thesis at the University of Pretoria. The author hereby acknowledges all references to the said articles and UP thesis.

Abstract

Problematic contractual issues that regularly arise in landscape contracting from the use of standard forms of construction contracts for pre-main contract, in-main contract and post-main contract landscape work are identified and discussed. These forms of contracts have mostly been written for traditional building and engineering works and are shown to be inadequately addressing the unique contractual aspects relating to landscaping works.

The article focuses on the issues to be addressed in the various contractual relationships between an employer, a principal contractor and a subcontractor with regard to landscape works to be done. It addresses the problems surrounding the contractual practical termination of the landscape subcontract, the defects liability period and interim landscape maintenance as well as landscape maintenance work after the landscape installation has reached final completion.

The article proposes an appropriate addendum to the JBCC Nominated/Selected Subcontract Agreement when used for landscape works to provide for the particular requirements of landscape contracting. The requirements for a landscape maintenance contract for use after termination of the landscape installation (sub) contract are discussed.

part THREE | Design

265

building contract, landscaping, landscape architect, landscape architecture, landscape construction, landscape maintenance

Introduction

The intrinsic differences between working with live plant material as opposed to the inanimate components of other building trades render the forms of contract and subcontract typically used in the building industry in South Africa to some extent unsuitable for landscape work and this can lead to financial disadvantage and risk for the employer, contractor or consultant. The forms of construction industry contract include the Joint Building Contracts Committee (JBCC) for building works, the Fédération Internationale des Ingénieurs-Conseils (FIDIC), the New Engineering Contract (NEC) and the General Conditions of Contract (GCC) for civil engineering works; none of which were written with the specific requirements of landscape works in mind. Through expedience and a lack of widely accepted alternative forms of contract, contracts developed for the building trades have been and still are widely used for landscaping work.

Carson (1992:52) finds that in the United Kingdom:

much of the practice of landscape architectural contracts has followed that of architectural and building work, even in areas where the basic materials are of a fundamentally different character. Building contracts deal basically with inert materials such as concrete, steel and timber. Inspection of these items is fairly straightforward and defects which are not detected at the building stage may appear and be rectified during the 'defects liability period'. Applying this type of contract to tree and shrub planting leads to problems which building contracts do not have.

Loots (1995:985), however, emphasises the need for the standardisation of contracts used in the construction industry:

numerous man-hours are wasted by senior people in the industry being required to understand and accommodate the many different ways of expressing the same action in over fifty different forms of contract issued by professionals and major employers in any one country.

The South African Institute of Architects (SAIA, 1999:4.312:1) describes some of the benefits of using pro-forma contract documentation, namely:

The advantage of using model documentation is that there is a fair distribution of risk between the parties to the agreement. A further advantage is that the parties become familiar with their obligations and are in a position to enter into the building agreement with confidence.

The Construction Industry Development Focus Group 6: Procurement (Figure 1), which was the precursor to the Construction Industry Development Board (CIDB), recommended in 2004 that only the following construction industry contracts be used in South Africa:

- JBCC Series 2000
- FIDIC
- GCC 2004 (incorporating the COLTO General Conditions of Contract of 1998)
- NEC (incorporating the Engineering and Construction Contract, ECC).

The CIDB (2004:2) concludes by stating:

There is no doubt that the reduction in the prolific number of forms of contract in use in South Africa to the aforementioned four series of documents will assist in eliminating many of the inefficiencies and losses associated with having to interpret the many varied approaches used to establish the risks, liabilities and obligations of the parties to a contract and the administration procedures associated therewith.

The landscape contractual environment in South Africa

The JBCC Series 2000 publications

Background

Whereas the JBCC is a contract documentation system that originated in South Africa and is being widely used in the private construction industry and more recently also in the public sector, it has up to now not had any representation from an organised landscape professional consultants' or a contractors' body such as the South African Landscapers Institute (SALI) or the Institute of Landscape Architects of South Africa (ILASA).

At the beginning of 2006 the JBCC was constituted from representatives from:

- the Association of South African Project Managers
- the Association of South African Quantity Surveyors
- the Master Builders South Africa
- the South African Association of Consulting Engineers
- the South African Institute of Architects
- the South African Property Owners Association
- the Specialist Engineering Contractors Committee.

The Department of Construction Economics at the University of Pretoria (UP 2000:14) finds that the JBCC has the following advantages:

- All the documents in the JBCC Series 2000 suite have been generated from the Principal Building Agreement (PBA) which ensures consistency of language, definitions, clause numbering and layout; all of which ensures a good measure of standardisation and ease of use
- It has been in use since 1991 and has the support of the major sectors of the building industry in South Africa
- An improved distribution of risk is offered to both contracting parties
- Better and more effective security is offered to the employer
- It does not allow for retention to be kept on the contractor; the construction guarantee replaces retention which will help the contractor to keep a better cash flow
- The final account has to be completed in three months
- Before the agreement can be signed and the site handed to the contractor, the construction and payment guarantees and the agreed bills of quantities must be in place
- There is one subcontract agreement for both the nominated and selected subcontractor situation.

One of the generally perceived disadvantages of the JBCC approach is that of accepting an adversarial paradigm as the real situation and stressing damage control as opposed to the philosophy of the NEC to pro-actively identify and resolve potential disputes. In the NEC's stated objectives concepts occur such as: collaboration, teamwork, partnering, shared standards, common objectives, trust and the sharing of costs, risks and reward (CIDB, 2004).

The UP (2000:14) believes that the following other aspects could be disadvantageous in the use of the JBCC forms of contract:

- It is complex to use for the uninitiated; the JBCC regularly offers workshops on the use of its documents
- Some employers still prefer to have the retention clause in place of the construction guarantee.

The JBCC Series 2000 currently includes the following documents that are relevant to landscape and related works:

- The JBCC PBA
- The JBCC Minor Works Agreement (MWA)
- The JBCC Nominated/Selected (N/S) Subcontract Agreement
- The Standard Preliminaries
- The Contract Price Adjustment Provision
- The Tender Form
- Waiver of Contractor's Lien
- The Construction Guarantee
- The Contract Instruction by the Principal Agent
- The Contractor's Instruction
- The Payment Certificate
- The Payment Certificate Notification

- The Recovery Statement
- The Transfer of Ownership
- The Certificate of Practical Completion
- The Certificate of Works Completion
- The Certificate of Final Completion.

The JBCC also supports the Master Builders South Africa's (MBSA) domestic subcontract agreement insofar as those issues that are common between the JBCC PBA and the MBSA domestic subcontract have been addressed and cross-referenced.

Using the JBCC forms of contract for landscaping work

The JBCC agreements make full provision for subcontracting, whether for the contractor's domestic subcontracts, nominated/selected subcontracts or direct contracts. According to Vosloo & Maritz (2005:50) the contracts within the JBCC family of contracts suited to landscape construction work are:

- the JBCC N/S Subcontract Agreement for use between a main contractor and the subcontractor. The same form of agreement is used for both nominated and selected subcontracts, as the contractual relationship between the contractor and the subcontractor is essentially the same, whether the subcontractor is nominated or selected. The differences are dealt with in the JBCC PBA, as they affect the main contractor's liability to the employer for the consequences of the subcontractor's default or insolvency (Vosloo & Maritz 2005:50)
- the JBCC MWA. This is a form of contract suitable for a direct contract between the employer and landscape contractor for the landscape works. It can be used with the JBCC PBA as a direct contract in terms of Clause 22: Employer's Direct Contractors, or as an independent direct contract on its own.

Landscape contracting in the United Kingdom

In the UK the Joint Council of Landscape Industries (JCLI) have developed forms of contract for landscape related works since 1969 (Clamp 1988:99) at which time the Joint Contracts Tribunal (JCT) 1968 Minor Works Form (developed essentially for smaller building construction works) was used as a point of departure.

The JCLI was established in an effort to co-ordinate and standardise the contract documentation in use by various organisations involved in the larger landscaping industry such as the Arboriculture Association, the Institute of Leisure and Amenity Management, the British Association of Landscape Industries, the Horticultural Trades Association and the Institute of Chartered Foresters.

The primary documents currently in use in the UK for landscape contracting are the JCLI Landscape Works Agreement and JCLI Landscape Maintenance Works Agreement.

The JCLI Landscape Works Agreement

The JCLI agreement makes provision for contracts where the landscape contractor is the principal contractor or where he is a direct contractor in JBCC terminology. In what could be considered the biggest difference between the JCLI contract system and forms of contract used in South Africa for landscape works, under the JCLI Landscape Works Agreement (2002a:8–9) provision is made for the following different contractual situations:

- Plants defects liability and post practical completion care by contractor: This optional clause, if so selected, has two sub-options. The first places the care of plant material and the resultant obligation to replace defective plants during a specified defects liability period with the contractor. Provision is made for varying defects liability periods for grass, shrubs and ordinary nursery stock trees, and semi-mature, advanced or extra large trees. The second sub-option excludes the care of all plant material after practical completion from the agreement.
- Plant defects liability and post practical completion care by employer: This optional clause, if so selected, places the care of trees, shrubs, grass and other plants, after practical completion of the works, with the employer who shall also be responsible for the replacement of any plant subsequently found to be defective. This option could place the employer at the risk of not being able to be ascertained at practical completion, especially in the case of plants that were planted during the dormant season and before they can show acceptable new growth.

It is also worth noting that in the UK's construction industry, specifically when using the JCT contract system, there may be occasions where the traditional 'soft landscaping' work such as top-soiling, grading, soil amelioration, planting and grassing, tree works and the preparation for these works (including site clearance and excavations) and 'soft landscape' maintenance are not considered to fall within the definition of construction work and should therefore only be commenced with as a separate contract after the practical completion of the building/engineering contract (JCLI 2002b:1). The reason for this approach lies primarily in the numerous industry regulations regarding labour, health and safety and site supervision applicable to traditional construction works contracts.

The JCLI Landscape Maintenance Works Agreement

This model form of contract (JCLI 2002c) is intended for use by UK landscape architects and landscape contractors for landscape maintenance projects up to a value of £150 000 per year.

It is appropriate for all types of landscape maintenance projects and has considerable flexibility to accommodate varying circumstances (JCLI 2002d:1), one of which is the use thereof for landscape maintenance during the defects liability period in conjunction with the JCLI Landscape Works Agreement.

The JCLI Landscape Maintenance Works Agreement is also suitable for landscape maintenance work after practical completion of landscape construction works undertaken under the JCT or NEC forms of contract.

It is interesting to note that the JCLI Agreement for Landscape Works (JCLI 2002a) specifically omits the maintenance of plants after practical completion:

If a defects period(s) is required for the plants, a separate agreement between the Contractor and Employer is required to cover the care of plants during the defects period(s) after practical completion (JCLI 2002d:1).

It is proposed that in cases where the Landscape Maintenance Works Agreement is used in conjunction with the Landscape Works Agreement:

◆ The maintenance contract should last for at least the longest soft landscape defects liability period specified in the construction contract
◆ Partial possession under the construction contract will cause phased commencement of the maintenance contract, but the end of the maintenance should be the same for all parts
◆ The construction and maintenance contracts should be separate but tendered together, accepted together and signed at the same time (ibid:1).

Building and landscape contracts – essential differences

The main contract

In this section construction contracts are analysed particularly in terms of their ability to meet landscape contract requirements.

The nature and purpose of a main contract need to be clarified in order to understand the role and function of the subcontract, which is the form of contract under which a large portion of landscaping work is undertaken in South Africa.

Standard forms of contract

Construction projects are always unique, and Collier (2001:57) suggests that standard forms of contract invariably require amendments and supplements. The authors of standard forms of contract such as the JBCC and JCLI, however, recommend to their users to avoid or limit changes or supplements to the standard forms of contract. Collier (2001:52) argues that while it is true that an increase in the number of contractual supplements can decrease the effectiveness of a standard form to the extent that the contracting parties have to read and understand more, and providing that the supplements do not conflict with the original unchanged contents, there is no reason not to make supplements to a standard form of contract.

Contract work stages, works completion and associated maintenance

In the JBCC forms of contract, completion is defined in three stages (refer to Figure 1):

◆ Practical completion is when the works, in the opinion of the principal agent, have reached the stage where it is fit for the intended use and the employer can take beneficial occupation of the works. At this stage the contractor must be provided within seven days with a list of defective or outstanding works items.
◆ Works completion: When the listed works items, in the opinion of the principal agent, have been satisfactorily completed, a works completion certificate must be issued after which the ninety days defects liability period commences
◆ Final completion: At the end of the defects liability period, and provided that all defective works items that may have been noted have been satisfactorily completed, the principal agent issues a certificate of final completion. At this stage the principal contractor's liabilities in terms of his N/S subcontracts end and any remaining N/S subcontractors' obligations to the principal contractor have to be ceded in a direct contract between such subcontractors and the employer.

Practical completion

In most contract formats practical completion refers to that date when the principal agent of the employer certifies that the works have reached a stage where they can be considered fit for the intended use and usually that determines the date of the commencement of the defects liability period or, as is proposed by the author in the case of landscape contracts, determines the commencement of the landscape maintenance contract.

The practical completion definition given by Clamp (1988:105) is when, in the landscape architect's opinion, 'the works can safely be used for the purpose for which they were designed'.

He also finds that the phrase has not yet been defined in courts in the UK and expresses the hope that it never will be, since this may legally confine the way in which the landscape architect arrives at his decision.

In the JCLI Practice Note No. 5 (JCLI 2002b:2) it is recommended that in cases where the project manager or landscape architect is unable to certify practical completion due to factors such as seasonal planting requirements, he may nevertheless certify practical completion upon receiving the contractor's written undertaking to complete the outstanding work within an agreed time. This will of course also affect the defects liability period and where applicable, the commencement and completion dates of any landscape maintenance contract.

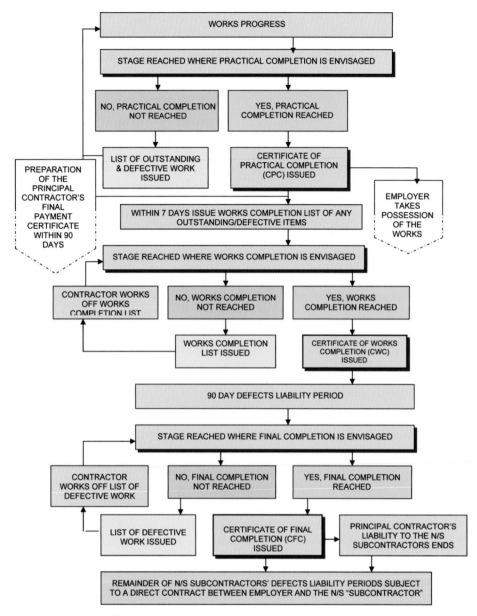

Figure 1: Schematic flow diagram of the works completion process of the JBCC Principal Building Agreement

Partial or sectional completion

Clamp (1988:106) notes that Clause 2.6 of the JCLI form of contract provides for sectional completion of the landscape work and partial possession by the employer. While the landscape contractor remains responsible for the balance of the site, a certificate of practical completion can be issued for those part(s) handed over. The relevant proportion of retention or the construction guarantee may be released and the contractor relieved of responsibility for any liquidated and ascertained damages for the part(s) handed over.

A consequence of partial or sectional completion of the landscape works will be the staggered commencement of the defects liability and maintenance periods; in this regard the JCLI (2002b:2) recommends that the staggered completion of the maintenance works be avoided. This can be achieved by deciding on appropriate dates when the tender documents are prepared.

Defects liability periods and associated landscape maintenance

The risk for the works is usually transferred back to the employer when practical completion has been certified and the employer takes occupancy of the works. Some contract formats such as the GCC make provision for the contractor, or any of his subcontractors, to remain responsible for the care of any part of the work upon which they are performing any outstanding work during the defects liability period until that work is completed (Loots 1995:540).

However, it is the author's belief that such clauses are intended for electro-mechanical building systems that may require a measure of maintenance until such time as those works are completed, and clearly not for landscape works that require daily or very regular maintenance over an extended period.

If it is expected of the landscape subcontractor to maintain the landscape works, specifically the planting and associated irrigation works, during the principal contractor's defects liability period, the subcontract will require a specification for such maintenance work and, where applicable, the corresponding bills of quantities item. The landscape subcontractor will contractually somehow have to receive payment for such maintenance work through the main contractor, even though at that stage the instruction for and certification of new work should have ended and the parties should be in the process of determining the final account and payment certificate.

An extended landscape maintenance contract, not contractually linked to the main construction or subcontracts, could therefore be a practical solution to this contractual dilemma.

Extended landscape maintenance contracts

Clamp (1986:129) finds that

in the UK most landscape contracts...provide for the regular maintenance of planted areas for the first year after practical completion by the contractor who has supplied and installed them. At the same time the firm then also accepts responsibility for the replacement of all trees, shrubs and grassed areas which may have failed during the same period for any reason other than theft or vandalism. Only in the most rare instances is it advisable for an employer to use his own staff or pay another contractor to carry out this work during the first 12 months after practical completion. The risks of dispute arising from such divided responsibility are self evident. If the subsequent maintenance is entrusted to the initial contractor problems arising from lack of communication between the parties and resulting in the second contractor being blamed for the death of the initial contractor's plants, can be avoided.

In the JCLI Practice Note No. 5 (JCLI 2002b:2-3) it is recommended that at the time of preparing tender documents, a decision must be made by the employer and/or the landscape architect as to whether the contractor or employer will be responsible for the care of planting after practical completion in terms of the JCLI landscape construction agreement.

If a defects liability period is required for the planting, a separate landscape maintenance agreement between the employer and the landscape contractor will be needed to cover this responsibility. Even when the contractor is responsible for care after practical completion, the defects liability period should still not exceed the duration of the maintenance contract.

The JCLI (2002b:2) recommends that the landscape construction and maintenance agreements should be separate but tendered together, accepted together and signed at the same time. The landscape maintenance contract should commence immediately after practical completion of the construction works has been reached.

In forms of contracts such as FIDIC that were designed specifically for building or engineering constructions the term 'maintenance' refers to the obligation of the contractor to maintain the works in the same state as at the inception of the 'maintenance period' (or as referred to in the JBCC the defects liability period).

It is, however, suggested in this article that the nature of landscape maintenance work is clearly outside of the intended meaning in FIDIC and GCC since it entails further intentional work (such as plant pruning, feeding and fertilisation, staking and tying, and irrigation) that may be construed to imply long-term operational maintenance.

The subcontract

Few general building contractors have the in-house expertise to undertake all the trades required on a typical construction project. Specialised construction work requiring skills, materials and processes not normally associated with general building work such as concrete and masonry work, are usually undertaken through subcontracts. Landscaping work is one such trade that has evolved to the extent that most landscape and related works on a construction project are carried out by a specialist landscape subcontractor.

The most significant issues that determine a subcontract relationship are those relating to the management of risk to the employer, contractor and subcontractor. SAIA (1999:3.431:1) notes that these risks relate primarily to performance to the requisite quality of the work, timeously and of payment for the work.

This fundamental interpretation of a subcontract is perhaps the reason for the concept of nominated subcontractors diminishing and that all subcontractors are rather seen as 'selected' in the sense that the principal contractor has satisfied himself timeously on the selection and appointment of these subcontractors.

Uher (1991:507) notes that in Australia the subcontracting process is negatively affected by an inequitable relationship between principal contractors and subcontractors with regard to subcontract conditions. He found that the risk for subcontractors is directly related to the proliferation of non-standard subcontract conditions prepared by the principal contractor and in which the risks to the principal contractor are usually minimised to the detriment of the subcontractor.

Collier (2001:151) finds that a principal contractor and a landscape subcontractor may find that they have specific obligations to each other arising from the nature of the work of the subcontract and its division of responsibility may not be specifically addressed in the principal contract, or, at best only implied. With specific reference to landscape subcontracts, these may include:

◆ to provide temporary facilities such as an on-site holding nursery to accommodate plants harvested on the site or to store contract-grown plants

◆ to provide a temporary water supply for the irrigation of plants referred to above

◆ to provide specific construction equipment such as hoists and cranes to get large plants and planter soil and compost to interior courtyards and planters

◆ to make good the damages caused by the principal or other subcontractors to areas already planted and provided with irrigation equipment, bearing in mind that landscaping and irrigation are usually the last trades to be completed on construction projects

◆ to comply with health and safety requirements that the principal contractor is obliged to satisfy under the principal contract

◆ to prepare co-ordination drawings of irrigation pipe layouts with other subsurface site services

◆ to furnish work programmes and progress reports not required by the principal contract

◆ to carry special insurances not specifically required by the principal contract.

Problems in using a building contract for landscape works

During the research conducted by the author the following contractual issues were shown to be problematic when using a build-ing contract for landscape construction and maintenance works. Respondents in the questionnaire survey had to indicate to what extent they were in agreement with the following statements:

If no provision has been made in the landscape subcontract specification for landscape maintenance to be done by the landscape subcontractor during the defects liability period, the landscape subcontractor's construction guarantee to the main contractor should be released in a reasonable time after practical completion for the whole project has been certified and not only after the defects liability period has ended.

Sixty-seven point eight six percent to eighty-three point six one percent (67.86% to 83.61%) of respondents in all three data categories, i.e. developers, contractors and consultants agreed with the given statement. The biggest disagreement with the statement came from the civil engineering works contractors (41.67%) and the architectural (building) contractors (37.5%) in the contractors' category.

A landscape construction guarantee cannot realistically be given and liability for the landscape installation cannot be accepted if there is no further maintenance contract between the employer and the landscape contractor.

The majority of respondents (60.42% to 78.57%) in all three data categories agree with the given statement. In the contractors' category, however, the majority of building and civil engineering works contractors do not agree with the statement. Significantly, 29.41% of the landscape architects also do not agree with the statement. The reason may be that some landscape architects believe the statement may reflect negatively on the quality and thoroughness of their works inspection during the construction phase.

The definition of the term 'practical completion' for building and construction work (typically: 'fit for use') is not really applicable in the case of landscape work.

The majority of respondents per category in all three categories agree with the given statement, except for the majority of private sector developers (61.11%), building contractors (75%), project managers (55.56%) and quantity surveyors (80%) who are in disagreement.

In the author's opinion the following reasons may be given for the disagreements:

◆ The fact that the landscaping on a typical construction project is often not essential for that facility to be utilised for its purpose is perhaps not always appreciated by private sector developers and project managers

◆ Building contractors may fear that a delayed practical completion with regard to landscape subcontract work may negatively affect their performance in terms of the main contract

◆ Quantity surveyors may feel that a delay in or extension of only the landscape subcontract's practical completion is not allowed for in the typical forms of contract currently in use and as such may prefer a single 'fit all' definition of practical completion.

Provision should be made for a non-penalty carrying and cost disbursing extension of a landscape (sub)contract in cases where delays to the completion of a project, for any reason not attributable to the landscape (sub)contractor, extend the completion date into a 'non-growing season' or a season where the specified plant material, e.g. green instant lawn, is not commercially available.

The majority of respondents in all three categories (developers: 57.14%, contractors: 81.25% and consultants: 91.67%) agree with the given statement. For the majority of public sector developers this issue is not relevant, but significantly 72.22% of the private sector developers/owners are in agreement

Delays to the finalisation of the contract's final account could occur in cases where a 3-month landscape maintenance period (to coincide with the 90-day defects liability period of the main contract) is included in the landscape subcontract and which will require additional monthly maintenance payment certificates through the main contractor.

The responses from all three data categories indicate that the majority of respondents in all three categories (developers/owners: 50%, contractors: 72.92% and consultants: 81.67%) agree with the given statement. Significantly 72.22% of the private sector developers/owners are in agreement; 62.5% of building contractors disagree with the statement.

In cases where the landscape sub-contractor has to complete his/her work in areas already in use by the employer, issues such as works risk and public liability insurance become problematic.

The majority of respondents in all three categories agree with the given statement, although for some public sector or parastatal developers/owners the issue is largely irrelevant. Significantly, in the consultants' category the majority of project managers and quantity surveyors disagree with the statement.

It is in both contracting parties' (employer and main contractor) interest to have a mandatory landscape maintenance contract (of say 3 to 12 months duration) as a separate, direct contract between the employer and the landscape (sub)contractor who installed the landscape.

The overwhelming majority of respondents in all three data categories (developers/owners: 78.57%, contractors: 82.98% and consultants: 95%) agree with the given statement. For some public sector and parastatal developers/owners the issue is irrelevant, but very significantly, 94.44% of private sector developers and 92% of landscape contractors are in agreement. The question may well be asked why then is the practice of a mandatory landscape maintenance contract between an employer and the landscape contractor not more widespread or common?

If, for whatever reason, the long-term landscape maintenance contractor is different from the person who installed the landscape, it is often difficult for the landscape maintenance contractor to define/calculate the risks associated with the maintenance contract, such as the responsibility for live plant material and systems (e.g. irrigation installations) inherited from the landscape installation contractor.

The majority of respondents in all three data categories (developers/owner: 53.57%, contractors: 65.96% and consultants: 78.33%) agree with the given statement. The majority of Central and Provincial Government Departments disagree with the statement, whereas the majority of private sector developers (66.67%) are in agreement. It is also significant that 72% of landscape contractors and 82.35% of landscape architects agree with the statement.

Contractual aspects that a landscape contract should address

The results from the survey conducted among the three parties involved in construction contracts (employers, contractors and professional consultants) indicate that the JBCC forms of contract are the most widely used forms of contract in South Africa for landscape and related works and are therefore discussed in more detail hereafter.

Pre-main landscape contracts

Pre-main contracts can be defined as those contracts that are entered into between a landscape contractor and the employer for certain work to be done before and in anticipation of a main contractor appointment for the bulk of the construction works. Pre-main contracts typically include growing contracts to ensure the required number and species of plants will be available for the main contract, including environmental protection and rehabilitation work, and the relocation and protection of existing flora.

It is usually the responsibility of the landscape architect, as the employer's agent, to advise his client well in advance of the construction of the project if there could be benefits or requirements to have plant material grown for the project or to protect and conserve existing flora on the site.

The JBCC MWA is considered to be the most suitable for pre-main contract landscape work, specifically for plant growing and conservation contracts, on condition that the following aspects are addressed:

- Transfer of ownership of the contract-grown or the rescued and relocated plant material at the termination of the pre-main contract to the in-main landscape contractor
- Guarantees and/or defects liabilities for such plant material grown, relocated, conserved or replanted; which guarantees should cease on acceptance of the plant material by the in-main contract landscape (sub)contractor
- Insurance of the plant material
- Payment conditions (for the costs of procurement and plant growing, maintenance and handling costs)
- The exact description of the area (the 'site') over which the contractor is entitled to have freedom of operation, or any limitations on the use of the employer's land
- Responsibility for obtaining any permit that may be required from the relevant authorities for the removal, relocation, transport and possession of specified plant species, usually those that are threatened and have a Red Data classification.

For any of these pre-main contracts, the landscape contractor will be in direct contract with the employer under the direction of the project manager and/or landscape architect on the employer's behalf.

Growing contracts

The objectives of a growing contract could be one or more of the following:

- To procure/collect the specified plant species at a lower cost (due to their smaller size) than that of the same species obtainable in retail nurseries.
- To have the required number of plants available at the specified time.
- To have plants of the required size available at the specified time.
- To have the plants acclimatised to the intended planting conditions.
- To provide replacement stock for landscape maintenance on large contracts.

Conservation contracts

Almost all engineering and construction projects have an impact on the environment to a greater or lesser degree. Loots (1995:663) states that these projects

almost invariably generate noise; land surface disturbance and a variety of other environmental ills [are] associated with the provision of infrastructure services such as impoundments, road-building.

Recent expanded environmental legislation, such as contained in Chapter 5 of the National Environmental Management Act (Act 107 of 1998), imposes an obligation on most land developments to follow an environmental approval process which usually includes the compilation of an Environmental Management Plan that will be enforceable through its inclusion in the relevant construction contracts and subcontracts.

The objectives of a conservation contract could include:

- To conserve existing flora under threat of building/construction activities
- To relocate, maintain and replant existing flora
- To propagate rare endemic species from those that have to be relocated to allow building/civil works activities
- To create site conditions before and during site constructions that would prevent environmental degradation such as:
    - plant cover loss
    - soil erosion
    - sedimentation of water bodies and courses
    - lowering of water quality
    - increase in storm water runoff.

The following conservation contract specification clauses will need to be addressed:

- Responsibility for obtaining any permit that may be required from the relevant authorities for the removal, relocation, transport and possession of specified plant species, usually those that are threatened and have a Red Data classification
- Specific horticultural requirements, e.g. pruning, root development, propagation, and regular replanting to bigger containers
- The exact description of the area (the 'site') over which the contractor is entitled to have freedom of operation, or any limitations on the use of the employer's land.

In-main landscape contracts

The term is used to describe those landscape contracts that are entered into between the landscape contractor and the employer or between the landscape subcontractor and the main contractor during the duration of the project's main construction contract.

Under this heading the following three forms of in-main landscape contracts are discussed:

- Direct contracts between the employer and landscape contractor
- Landscape subcontracts
- Domestic landscape subcontracts.

Direct contracts between the employer and landscape contractor

Direct contracts refer to those entered into between the employer and other contractor(s) to undertake work at the same time and on the same site that was handed to a principal contractor to undertake the bulk of the works.

Collier (2001:143) suggests that for vastly differing work by different contractors on the same project, an employer may be better served by entering into separate contracts. On projects where phased construction of the works can be accommodated, separate contracts may be easier and result in cost saving for an employer.

Loots (1995:613), however, finds that in contractual situations like this

any delays caused by the subcontractor in the direct employment of the employer would be delays for which the employer was responsible and the main contractor would be entitled to claim awards of extension of time and possibly additional cost compensation from the employer.

The advantages of this form of contract are:

- For the employer: no mark-up for attendance and profit on the landscape contractor by the main contractor
- For the employer: this contract can easily be an extension of a pre-main contract
- For the landscape contractor: direct and probably earlier payment of certificates by the employer.

The disadvantages of this form of contract are:

- There is normally no contra-responsibility between the main building or civil works contractor and the landscape contractor. It is, however, possible to make reference in one contract to the other, and define the various parties' responsibilities
- Due to the nature and timing of landscape works it is often difficult to prove liability and/or responsibility for damages to landscape work caused by other contractors working in the same areas at the same time. Because of the absence of co-responsibility brought about through a main and subcontractor relationship, the various contractors often do not display due care and consideration for the landscape work in progress, e.g.

trenching through landscaped areas, trampling newly planted shrub beds, damaging irrigation pipe lines and control cables, etc.

- For the landscape architect who administers the contract on behalf of the employer, it creates an undefined, difficult and time-consuming relationship between himself and other consultants, such as the employer's principal agent.

The JBCC MWA is considered to be the most suitable for direct contracts between the employer and the landscape contractor.

Landscape subcontracts

In these forms of contract the landscape subcontractor is appointed by the principal building or civil works contractor on the instruction of the employer's principal agent in the case of nominated subcontracts, or after consultation with and approval by the principal contractor in the case of selected subcontracts.

In South Africa the bulk of commercial landscaping work is done under subcontracts and the JBCC N/S Subcontract Agreement and the SAFCEC General Conditions of Subcontract are probably most often used for this purpose. Internationally the NEC and FIDIC form of subcontract (for engineering type contracts) and the British JCT form of subcontract for building contracts are commonly used.

All the forms of subcontract referred to above have been developed for the more 'traditional' specialist building trades such as structural steelwork, electrical and mechanical installations, etc. and do not cater for the specific nature of landscape work, specifically planting. The inherent problematic differences between these traditional specialist building trades and landscape work, and the contracts that govern them, can be summarised as follows:

- The use of inanimate components in the 'traditional' specialist building trades as opposed to live matter (plants) used in landscape contracts
- It is difficult to prove any contractual defects liability for landscape work (at least for the planting or 'soft landscaping') if the landscape construction contract is not coupled to a landscape maintenance contract during such defects liability period or even thereafter
- Since retention or a construction guarantee for landscape work, specifically planting and the associated irrigation installation, cannot really be applicable after practical completion without a landscape maintenance contract in effect or without some provision in place for such maintenance work, the principal contractor often holds these against the landscape subcontractor to force him to undertake such maintenance nonetheless

- If a three-month maintenance agreement is included in the subcontract (to coincide with the 90-day defects liability period of the main contract), it will, unless some special provisions have been made, require additional monthly maintenance payment certificates that could conceivably delay the completion of the final account. In this regard Collens (1979:242) finds that 'the final account of the building contract may have to be delayed until the defects liability period of the landscape subcontract has expired which invariably is at a date much later than the end of the building defects liability period'.

The JBCC N/S Subcontract Agreement can be made suitable for use between the main contractor and the landscape subcontractor on condition that the following issues are addressed and agreed to beforehand:

- What constitutes practical and works completion in the case of the landscape subcontract?
- How can sections of the JBCC N/S Subcontract Agreement be terminated at such a stage and in such a manner that the landscape subcontractor can enter into and commence with a direct landscape maintenance contract (at least for the plants and irrigation system) with the employer as soon as works completion in terms of the JBCC PBA has been achieved?

The aspects to be considered in answering the latter question are the reduction or termination of sections of the subcontract construction guarantee, determining and settlement of the subcontract amount and transferring the landscape subcontractor's defects liability for planting and the irrigation system to a new landscape maintenance contract between the employer and landscape subcontractor.

Domestic landscape subcontracts

In these forms of contract the main contractor appoints the landscape subcontractor directly without any approval by or instruction thereto by the employer or any of his agents. No prime cost amounts are allowed in the tender documents and the main contractor must price the landscape work from specified items in the schedule of quantities. The domestic subcontract agreement as prepared by the MBSA (MBSA 2005), and which is compatible with and endorsed by the JBCC, is often used in these instances.

The purpose of the domestic landscape subcontract is usually for the employer to have landscape work done under the main contract and for the following reasons he may elect not to nominate or select the landscape subcontractor:

- The small scale or relative simplicity of the landscape work
- There being too little time to go through selected subcontract tender procedures

- Insufficient pre-planning of contract programming.

The landscape domestic subcontractor provides everything necessary for the landscape subcontract works and executes the landscape subcontract works in terms of the agreement to the reasonable satisfaction of the main contractor. Any comments, approvals or disapprovals of the landscape works by any of the employer's agents must be made via the main contractor.

The disadvantages of this type of contract are:

- The landscape architect has very little input, if any, on the appointment of the landscape subcontractor; often the landscape architect is not involved at all in contract management and works inspections
- In terms of the MBSA domestic subcontract (MBSA 2005:11–12) only the main contractor may issue instructions to the subcontractor. All instructions from others, such as the principal agent and the landscape architect must be given and authorised via the main contractor
- In terms of the MBSA domestic subcontract (MBSA 2005:6) and on reaching interim completion on the subcontract works, the works risk and responsibility for that completed subcontract pass onto the main contractor
- Although the MBSA Subcontract Construction Guarantee makes provision for the return of the subcontract construction guarantee to the subcontractor on reaching interim completion of the subcontract works, this rarely happens in practice unless the subcontractor expressly required this in his tender to the main contractor. More often the domestic subcontractor has to wait until the project as a whole has reached practical completion before his construction guarantee starts reducing in terms of the JBCC PBA conditions (Griessel 2007).

Post-main landscape contracts

The term is used to describe those contracts that are entered into between the employer and the landscape contractor for landscape work (usually landscape maintenance) to be done after the main contractor has completed the main construction contract and it becomes contractually difficult for him to have the landscape subcontractor under his control for an extended period normally not allowed for in the principal construction contract.

For landscape projects the need often exists for a post-main contract after installation of the landscape to maintain the work through its initial critical period. In areas where extreme climatic conditions such as frosts and droughts can occur, the survival of the plant material is largely determined by the maintenance care the landscape receives in this initial period.

The responsible agent of the employer, such as the landscape architect or project manager, should advise his client to allow, in the operational budget of the project, for landscape maintenance that will ensure a sustainable landscape or otherwise risk the chance that the capital spent on the landscape installation could be negated within a short time. There are distinct benefits to having the landscape contractor who installed the landscape also take on the responsibility of maintaining it for a certain critical initial period. Even if the employer has in-house landscape maintenance resources, a transitional phase of, say, six months is recommended during which the landscape contractor will still be on site and can look after systems such as water features and irrigation installations.

Clamp (1986:128) finds that it is clearly inequitable for an employer to expect the landscape contractor (or subcontractor) to include the cost of landscape maintenance after the practical completion of the works in his initial tender for the construction of the landscape, unless it has been specified in detail and identified separately in order that the landscape contractor (or subcontractor) could price for such work. Clamp furthermore finds (ibid:128) that contractual disputes will inevitably arise if another landscape maintenance contractor is employed, or if the employer himself, adequately or inadequately accepts the responsibility for such maintenance:

In the event of plants being found to be dead at the end of the Defects Liability Period as a result of sub-standard stock, inadequate plant handling in transit or negligent planting by the landscape subcontractor, it is always difficult, if not impossible, to provide sufficient evidence to refute the counter-claim that their death arose from some act or lack of care or inadequate watering on the part of those responsible for their subsequent care during the Defects Liability Period.

Post-main landscape contract format

The post-main landscape maintenance contract is entered into by the employer and the landscape contractor and is distinctly separate from the landscape installation contract where the landscape contractor was most likely a subcontractor to a main building or civil works contractor.

Under the JBCC form of contract the main contractor and his selected and/or nominated subcontractors' defects liability period usually ends three months after the certificate of works completion has been issued. In the case of extended defects liability periods, typically for mechanical installations, such remaining defects liability periods are ceded to the employer by the main contractor and are then subject to a direct contract between the employer and the subcontractor(s).

The nature of maintaining a mechanical system, which usually consists of mostly pre-determinable works and material items, is different from that of maintaining landscape work consisting of live plant material and supporting systems such as irrigation. The risk of unforeseen maintenance work and costs, intentional or accidental damages to the landscape by its users and the very fact that plant material grows and thus requires constantly changing maintenance, renders the transfer of a landscape subcontractor's liability to the employer inappropriate. The employer could be forced to enter into a contract with a landscape contractor without knowing what the extent of his obligations to that contractor will be.

The landscape maintenance contract cannot be a construction type contract, as issues such as liability for damages to plants due to vandalism and insufficient maintenance need to be spelled out. This is especially applicable in projects that are accessible to the public and subject to vandalism. An employer enters into a landscape maintenance contract to ensure that the project is and appears well-maintained at all times. Performance is thus also time-related and if, during a specific time period, the landscape appears ill-maintained, that 'loss' to the employer cannot be made up by the contractor in a subsequent period, hence the contract value has to be decreased accordingly.

Landscape maintenance contracts should ideally be for 12 months to ensure that at least one growing and winter season are included. On large landscape maintenance contracts the capital outlay required of the contractor for equipment and manpower will probably make contract costs proportionally exorbitant if the contracts are less than 12 months.

As previously suggested, the landscape maintenance contract should preferably be awarded to the landscape contractor who originally installed the landscape. The main reason for this recommendation is that the responsibility for plant defects can then be carried by the landscape contractor as he will still be on site and cannot disclaim liability for patent, latent or maintenance defects.

In instances where the employer is able, with his own staff and resources, to maintain the landscape, a reduced maintenance contract, typically of six month duration is, however, still recommended. Such a contract can so be worded that there is an overlapping period during which the landscape contractor will work alongside the employer's maintenance staff to point out the working of systems and any specific horticultural requirements.

The JCLI Agreement for landscape maintenance works (2002c:8) makes provision for a schedule of liquidated damages whose rates must be used to price losses suffered by the employer as a result of non-performance of the landscape maintenance contractor.

The JBCC PBA or JBCC MWA can be made suitable for use as a landscape maintenance contract between the employer and the landscape contractor on condition that the following issues are addressed:

- Works risk (damages to the works) and the liability for works insurance; either carried by the employer or the landscape maintenance contractor
- The provision of a performance guarantee by the contractor as opposed to the construction guarantee applicable during the construction phase
- Penalties for unsatisfactory work; since the objective of landscape maintenance is to have a certain specified minimum standard of maintenance resulting in an acceptable or required appearance over a specified period. Maintenance work not achieving this appearance or performance level has to be penalised with a non-refundable deduction in the contract amount
- The contract completion process as described in the JBCC documentation (refer to Figure 1) will need to be modified since the practical, works and final completion stages as well as the 90-day defects liability period for the planting and irrigation system will not be applicable.

Recommendations and conclusion

Since the results from the survey conducted by the author have shown that the JBCC forms of contract are the most widely used for landscape and environment-related works in South Africa, the recommendations are focused thereon.

An addendum to the JBCC N/S Subcontract Agreement titled 'Specific conditions of subcontract for landscape and related works'(SCSLW)

Instead of attempting to write a new contract format specifically aimed at landscaping and related environmental type works, which will be contrary to the recommendation of the CIDB to limit the number of contract formats for the construction industry in South Africa and which will most probably not be supported by the JBCC (Bold 2006), it is rather recommended that an addendum to the JBCC N/S Subcontract Agreement be compiled that could be titled 'Specific conditions of subcontract for landscape and related works'. This approach is in line with the JBCC's policy of compiling addenda to its standard forms of contract, such as the State Addendum to the JBCC PBA, to cover specific contractual aspects not dealt with in the 'standard' contracts.

These aspects include:

Simultaneous landscape construction and maintenance tenders

Any in-main landscape subcontract should recognise in its intent and clauses that the installation of the landscape is the first of a two-part process and should allow for a smooth and practical transition from the landscape installation subcontract to the landscape maintenance of the planting and irrigation system.

It is recommended that the example of the UK's JCLI Standard Form of Agreement for Landscape Works be followed where it requires of the employer and his principal agent to take a decision at the time of preparing the tender documents whether the employer or the landscape subcontractor will be responsible for the maintenance of the landscape works, specifically the planting and associated irrigation system, after works completion or after the employer has taken possession of the works. The two options are:

Option 1: Landscape maintenance by the employer

In the first option the landscape subcontractor's responsibility for the planting and the associated irrigation system is terminated when the main contract reaches works completion and the subsequent landscape maintenance work is then undertaken by the employer.

In this instance the landscape subcontractor's responsibilities and obligations in terms of the subcontract will be limited to the remaining landscape subcontract works excluding planting and the associated irrigation system.

It is recommended that the landscape subcontractor should timeously advise the main contractor that he will be unable to guarantee the planting and associated irrigation system sections of the landscape subcontract works and to be responsible for defects in such sections of the works if no provisions have been made for landscape maintenance after works completion. At most the landscape subcontractor can give a guarantee or warranty on inanimate items such as electrical pumps, electronic irrigation controllers and accept defects liability for the 'hard landscaping' items. Even in these cases there exists the possibility that breakages and failure could be ascribed to insufficient and unqualified maintenance by another party.

In cases where Option 1 is used, the following contractual issues become pertinent and should be addressed during the writing of the landscape subcontract:

- Termination of a section of the landscape subcontract:
  It is recommended that the current JBCC works completion process (refer to Figure 1) be reconsidered in the case of a

landscape subcontract to allow for a logical and practical process by which sections of it can be terminated on reaching works completion of the principal contract in order that the landscape subcontractor can enter into a landscape maintenance contract directly with the employer and which contract could extend past the defects liability period of the main and other subcontracts. Refer in this instance to Figure 2 in which the proposed landscape contracting process is shown schematically.

◆ Cancellation of a part of the subcontract construction guarantee and adjusting the final account:

The cancellation of a part of the landscape subcontract construction guarantee and adjustment of the final account between the main contractor and the landscape

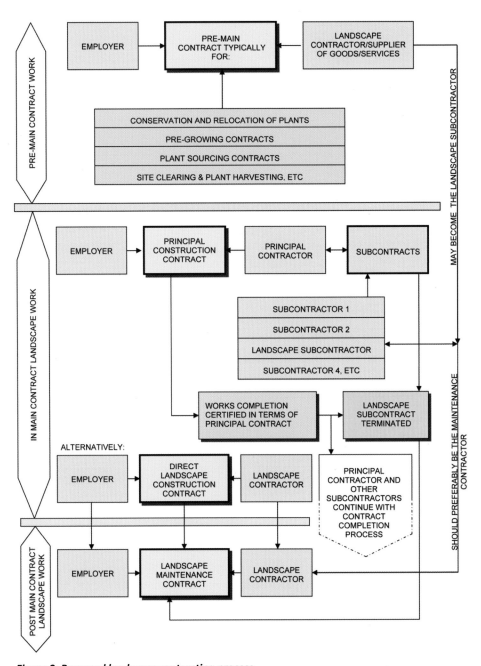

Figure 2: Proposed landscape contracting process

subcontractor once works completion has been certified should be agreed on beforehand and described as such in the SCSLW. It serves little purpose for a main contractor to hold a construction guarantee or any form of retention for planting and the operation of the irrigation system on the landscape subcontractor if the latter has no obligation in terms of the landscape subcontract to maintain the landscape during the main contract's defects liability period.

Option 2: Landscape maintenance by the landscape subcontractor

In this instance a distinction is made between the inanimate (or 'hard landscaping') works items, such as pavings, masonry, timber and concrete structures, street furniture, water features, etc. on the one side and live components such as plant material and their associated irrigation systems on the other side at the works completion stage of the main contract. The maintenance of the latter could then be dealt with in a separate agreement between the employer and the landscape subcontractor (who now becomes a direct contractor), whereas the inanimate work items in the landscape subcontract are dealt with in the normal way in accordance with the JBCC N/S Subcontract Agreement conditions and procedures.

It will also be required of the landscape construction subcontract tenderer, at the time of tender, to provide a separate landscape maintenance tender to come into effect directly after works completion of the construction works for a period of at least twelve months to cover one complete growing and establishment cycle.

The tenderers should be made aware of the fact that although they will be tendering for two separate contracts, in evaluating the tenders the combined tender prices will be considered and that the successful tenderer will be appointed for both contracts.

In cases where Option 2 is used, the following contractual issues become pertinent and should be addressed during the writing of the landscape subcontract:

◆ The defects liability period: The 90-day defects liability period in terms of the subcontract agreement will only be applicable to the landscape works not requiring maintenance, such as the 'hard landscaping' works and should exclude planting and the associated irrigation system
◆ Landscape maintenance during the defects liability period and thereafter: Collens (1979:244) recommends that at the time of practical completion (author's note: or works completion in the case of the JBCC N/S Subcontract Agreement), the site should be offered for inspection to the employer or his representative, so that a clear understanding is reached on the

subcontractor's responsibility for maintaining the landscape works.

If his contract calls for continued maintenance after works completion has been reached, then the start date is to be agreed at such inspection.

A redefinition of the term 'practical completion' for landscaping works

The different forms of contract used in the South African construction industry each have their own definition of and process required for reaching practical, works and final completion. It is not the author's intention to compare these forms of contract in order to find a common definition and process, but rather to identify the stage where the works are handed over to the employer for his beneficial use, when the works risk is transferred back to the employer and when the contractor's and subcontractors' defects liability period commences.

It is therefore recommended that a more exact description of the term 'practical completion' is needed in the case of landscape works. Collier (2001:340) points out that a contract's substantial or practical completion depends on completion to such a degree that the works, in whole or in part, can be occupied or otherwise utilised by the employer, despite the fact that there may remain certain items of work still to be completed. Landscape works, and specifically planting, are in very few instances critical to the use and occupancy of the facility, at most the later completion of the landscape work may result in some inconvenience for users of the facility and this can probably be properly managed by the main contractor.

The generally accepted definitions of practical completion, i.e. 'fit for intended use' or as the JBCC (2005:2) defines it as 'the state of completion where, in the opinion of the principal agent, completion of the works has substantially been reached and can effectively be used for the purposes intended…' may thus not be totally applicable to landscape works and the following criteria and considerations may be applied by those responsible for deciding on practical or works completion:

◆ Does the works under consideration consist of animate (live plants) and inanimate components? If so, consider distinguishing between these; the completion of the inanimate components, i.e. the more traditional building trades such as concrete and masonry work, paving work, plumbing and electrical work may be considered essential for the beneficial occupation and use by the employer, whereas the completion of the planting installation (the animate components) may not be considered essential

- Discretion in these matters should always lie with the principal or other agent (preferably the landscape architect) on condition that they understand the inherent differences between landscape work and the more traditional building trades and are therefore also aware of the resultant implications on the contractual relationships between employer, main contractor and landscape subcontractor.

Conclusion

In conclusion it can be said that if the users of, and contracting parties in, landscape works contracts are made aware of the constraints and potential contractual pitfalls when using building contracts for landscape works, as pointed out in this article, it should lead to more equitable contractual relationships with less risk to all the role players involved.

Bibliography

Bold, P. 2006. Personal communication.

Carson, R. 1992. Planting: paying for results. *Landscape Design,* July/August Issue 1992. pp.52–53.

Clamp, H. 1986. *Spon's landscape contract manual – A guide to good practice and procedures in the management of landscape contracts.* London: E. & F.N. Spon Ltd. 195 pp.

Clamp, H. 1988. *Landscape professional practice.* Aldershot UK: Gower Technical Press Ltd. 201 pp.

Collens, G. 1979. Professional practice. In A.E. Weddle (ed). *Landscape Techniques.* London: William Heinemann Ltd. 265 pp.

Collier, K. 2001. *Construction Contracts. (3rd ed).* New Jersey: Merrill Prentice Hall. 386 pp.

(The) Construction Industry Development Board (CIDB). 2004. Best Practice Guideline C2: Choosing an appropriate form of contract for engineering and construction works. March, 2004: 1st ed of CIDB Document 1010. Pretoria. 19 pp.

Griessel, P. 2007. Personal communication.

Joint Building Contracts Committee (JBCC). 2005. JBCC Series 2000: Minor Works Agreement. (3rd ed). Johannesburg.

Joint Council for Landscape Industries (JCLI). 2002a. JCLI Agreement for Landscape Works. February 2002 revision of the 1998 edition. London: Landscape Institute. 24 pp.

Joint Council for Landscape Industries (JCLI). 2002b. JCLI Practice Note 5: Explanatory notes regarding the JCLI Agreement for Landscape Works. London: Landscape Institute. 4 pp.

Joint Council for Landscape Industries (JCLI). 2002c. JCLI Agreement for Landscape Maintenance Works. February 2002 revision of the 1998 edition. London: Landscape Institute. 20 pp.

Joint Council for Landscape Industries (JCLI). 2002d. JCLI Practice Note 7: Explanatory notes regarding the JCLI Agreement for Landscape Maintenance Works. London: Landscape Institute. 8 pp.

Loots, P.C. 1995. (ed). *Construction law and related issues.* Cape Town: Juta & Co. Ltd. 1213 pp.

Master Builders South Africa (MBSA), 2005. MBSA Domestic Subcontract Agreement. March 2005 edition. Midrand. 36 pp.

(The) South African Institute of Architects (SAIA). 1999. Practice Manual.

Uher, T.E. 1991. Risks in subcontracting: Subcontract conditions. *Construction Management and Economics* Issue 9, 1991. Kensington, New South Wales: pp. 495–508.

University of Pretoria. 2000. Comprehensive Project Management Programme for Built Environment Practitioners 2000: Module 5 Course Notes.

University of Pretoria, Department of Construction Economics. 14 pp.

Vosloo, P.T. & Maritz, M.J. 2005. Landscaping: An analysis of current contracting processes and documentation. *Acta Structilia* Vol. 12 No. 2, 2005. Bloemfontein: University of the Free State: pp. 42–69.

Index